THE
SACRED BOOKS OF THE EAST

Translated by
VARIOUS ORIENTAL SCHOLARS

Edited by
F. MAX MÜLLER

Vol. 13

SACRED BOOKS OF THE EAST

(50 VOLUMES)

Series Editor : *F. Max-Müller*

ISBN: 978-81-208-0101-1 (Set) Rs. 20000 (Each Vol. Rs. 400)

These volumes of the Sacred Books of the East series include translations of all the most important works of the seven non-Christian religions that have exercised a profound influence on the civilisations of the continent of Asia. The Vedic Brahmanic system claims 21 volumes, Buddhism 10, and Jainism 2; 8 volumes comprise Sacred Books of the Parsis; 2 volumes represent Islam; and 6 the two main indigenous systems of China. Translated by twenty leading authorities in their respective fields, the volumes have been edited by the late F. Max Müller. The inception, publication and the compilation of these books cover almost 34 years.

I. BUDDHISM

Vol. 49: Buddhist Mahayana Texts (2 Parts)
Vol. 11: Buddhist Suttas
Vol. 10: The Dhammapada and Sutta Nipata
Vols. 35 & 36: The Questions of King Milinda (2 Parts)
Vol. 21: The Saddharma Pundarika or the Lotus of the True Law
Vols. 13, 17 & 20: Vinaya Texts (3 Parts)

II. CHINESE

Vol. 19: The Fo-Sho-Hing-Tsan-King
Vols. 3, 16, 27, 28, 39 & 40: The Sacred Books of China (6 Parts)

III. A GENERAL INDEX

Vol. 50: A General Index to the Names and Subject-matter of the Sacred Books of the East

IV. ISLAM

Vols. 6 & 9: The Qur'an (2 Parts)

V. JAINISM

Vols. 22 & 45: The Jaina Sutras (2 Parts)

VI. PARSIS

Vols. 5, 18, 24, 37 & 47: Pahlavi Texts (5 Parts)
Vols. 4, 23 & 31: The Zend-Avesta (3 Parts)

VII. VEDIC-BRAHMANIC SYSTEM

Vol. 8: The Bhagavadgita with the Sanatsujatiya and the Anugita
Vols. 29 & 30: The Grihya-Sutras: Rules of Vedic Domestic Ceremonies (2 Parts)
Vol. 42: Hymns of the Atharva Veda together with Extracts from the Ritual Books and the Commentaries
Vol. 7: The Institutes of Vishnu
Vol. 25: The Laws of Manu
Vol. 33: The Minor Law Books
Vols. 2 & 14: The Sacred Laws of the Áryas as Taught in the Schools of Apastamba, Gautama, Vasishtha and Baudhayana (2 Parts)
Vols. 12, 26, 41, 43 & 44: The Satapatha Brahmana According to the Text of the Madhyandina School (5 Parts)
Vols. 1 & 15: The Upanishads (2 Parts)
Vols. 34 & 38: The Vedanta Sutras (2 Parts)
Vol. 48: The Vedanta-Sutras (with the commentary by Ramanuja)
Vols. 32 & 46: Vedic Hymns (2 Parts)

VINAYA TEXTS

Translated from the Pāli by

T.W. RHYS DAVIDS

and

HERMANN OLDENBERG

PART I

THE PÂTIMOKKHA

THE MAHÂVAGGA I-IV

MOTILAL BANARSIDASS PUBLISHERS
PRIVATE LIMITED • DELHI

9th Reprint: Delhi, 2018
First Published in 1885 by Oxford University Press.

ISBN: 978-81-208-0114-8

MOTILAL BANARSIDASS
41 U.A. Bungalow Road, Jawahar Nagar, Delhi 110 007
1 B, Jyoti Studio Compound, Kennedy Bridge, Nana Chowk, Mumbai 400 007
203 Royapettah High Road, Mylapore, Chennai 600 004
236, 9th Main III Block, Jayanagar, Bengaluru 560 011
8 Camac Street, Kolkata 700 017
Ashok Rajpath, Patna 800 004
Chowk, Varanasi 221 001

UNESCO COLLECTION OF REPRESENTATIVE WORKS— Indian Series
This book has been accepted in the Indian Translation Series of the UNESCO Collection of Representative Works, jointly sponsored by the United Nations Educational Scientific and Cultural Organization (UNESCO) and the Government of India

Printed in India

by RP Jain at NAB Printing Unit,
A-44, Naraina Industrial Area, Phase I, New Delhi–110028
and published by JP Jain for Motilal Banarsidass Publishers (P) Ltd,
41 U.A. Bungalow Road, Jawahar Nagar, Delhi-110007

RASHTRAPATI BHAVAN,
NEW DELHI-4
June 10, 1962

I am very glad to know that the Sacred Books of the East, published years ago by the Clarendon Press, Oxford, which have been out-of-print for a number of years, will now be available to all students of religion and philosophy. The enterprise of the publishers is commendable and I hope the books will be widely read.

S. RADHAKRISHNAN

PREFATORY NOTE TO THE NEW EDITION

Since 1948 the United Nations Educational, Scientific and Cultural Organization (UNESCO), upon the recommendation of the General Assembly of the United Nations, has been concerned with facilitating the translation of the works most representative of the culture of certain of its Member States, and, in particular, those of Asia.

One of the major difficulties confronting this programme is the lack of translators having both the qualifications and the time to undertake translations of the many outstanding books meriting publication. To help overcome this difficulty in part, UNESCO's advisers in this field (a panel of experts convened every other year by the International Council for Philosophy and Humanistic Studies), have recommended that many worthwhile translations published during the 19th century, and now impossible to find except in a limited number of libraries, should be brought back into print in low-priced editions, for the use of students and of the general public. The experts also pointed out that in certain cases, even though there might be in existence more recent and more accurate translations endowed with a more modern apparatus of scholarship, a number of pioneer works of the greatest value and interest to students of Eastern religions also merited republication.

This point of view was warmly endorsed by the Indian National Academy of Letters (Sahitya Akademi), and the Indian National Commission for UNESCO.

It is in the spirit of these recommendations that this work from the famous series "Sacred Books of the East" is now once again being made available to the general public as part of the UNESCO Collection of Representative Works.

PUBLISHER'S NOTE

First, the man distinguished between eternal and perishable. Later he discovered within himself the germ of the Eternal. This discovery was an epoch in the history of the human mind and the *East was the first to discover it.*

To watch in the Sacred Books of the East the dawn of this religious consciousness of man, must always remain one of the most inspiring and hallowing sights in the whole history of the world. In order to have a solid foundation for a comparative study of the Religions of the East, we must have before all things, complete and thoroughly faithful translation of their Sacred Books in which some of the ancient sayings were preserved because they were so true and so striking that they could not be forgotten. They contained eternal truths, expressed for the first time in human language.

With profoundest reverence for Dr. S. Radhakrishnan, President of India, who inspired us for the task; our deep sense of gratitude for Dr. C. D. Deshmukh & Dr. D. S. Kothari, for encouraging assistance; esteemed appreciation of UNESCO for the warm endorsement of the cause; and finally with indebtedness to Dr. H. Rau, Director, Max Müller Bhawan, New Delhi, in procuring us the texts of the Series for reprint, we humbly conclude.

CONTENTS.

CONTENTS

INTRODUCTION

TO THE

VINAYA TEXTS FROM THE PÂLI.

IN the present MSS. the Vinaya Pi*t*aka is divided into the following books:

1. Pârâ*g*ika, } called collectively the Sutta-vibhaṅga.
2. Pâ*k*ittiya, }
3. Mahâvagga, } called collectively the Khandhakas.
4. *K*ullavagga, }
5. Parivâra-pâ*th*a.

These books constitute that part of the sacred literature of the Buddhists which contains the regulations for the outward life of the members of the Buddhist Sa*m*gha—nearly the oldest, and probably the most influential, of all Fraternities of monks.

It is impossible to frame any narrower definition of the Vinaya than this, since the gradual change of circumstances in the Fraternity resulted in a gradual change also in the Vinaya itself. To give any more detailed account of what the Vinaya is, it will be necessary to trace what can be at present ascertained of its history; to show—that is, so far as it is yet possible to do so—the causes which led to the establishment of the oldest Rules and Ceremonies of the Order, and to follow step by step the accretions of new literary work around this older nucleus.

For this purpose we propose to consider first the Rules of the work called the Pâtimokkha; for the later texts presuppose its existence. It is one of the oldest, if not the oldest, of all Buddhist text-books; and it has been inserted in its entirety into the first part of the Vinaya, the Vibhaṅga[1].

The Pâtimokkha—the meaning of the name will be discussed later on—seems to have owed its existence to the ancient Indian custom of holding sacred two periods in each month, the times of the Full Moon and of the New Moon.

The Vedic ceremonies of the Darsapûrnamâsa sacrifice, and of the feast or sacred day (Upavasatha) connected with it, are known to have been very old, and the custom of celebrating these days would naturally be handed on from the Brâhmans to the different Samanas, and be modified and simplified (though, as it seems, sometimes increased in number) by them, in accordance with their creeds and their views of religious duty. According to Buddhist tradition[2]—and we see no sufficient reason for doubting the correctness of the account—the monks of other, that is, of non-Buddhistic sects, used to meet together at the middle and at the close of every half-month, and were accustomed then to proclaim their new teaching in public. At such times the people would crowd together; and the different sects found an opportunity of increasing their numbers and their influence.

The Buddhists also adopted the custom of these periodical meetings, but confined themselves to meeting twice in each month[3]. And the peculiarity which gave to these meetings among the Buddhists their distinguishing character seems to have been borrowed by them neither from the Brâhmans nor from other dissenters, but to have been an original invention of the Buddhists themselves. The Brethren and Sisters made use of these half-monthly gatherings to confess to the assembled Order the sins and faults which each of them had committed; and to take upon himself, or herself, the penance which the transgressor had thereby incurred. It would be unnecessary to dwell here upon the details of these penitential meetings, as we can

[1] The opening sentence only is found in the Mahâvagga. See below, p. xv.
[2] Mahâvagga II, 1, 1.
[3] Ibid. II, 4, 2.

refer the reader to the second book of the Mahâvagga, where he will find them fully set out.

It was for use at such penitential gatherings that the text, now known as the Pâtimokkha, was composed. A list was drawn up—which of course it would be necessary from time to time to complete, and rectify—of those offences which ought to be confessed and atoned for; this list was read out in the half-monthly meetings of the Order; and the Brethren and Sisters who were present were asked if they were innocent of each one of the offences therein mentioned.

The use of such a list must have already begun in very early times. Tradition even ascribes the first laying down of each clause to the Buddha himself. This tradition is of course very far from being conclusive; but neither should we hold it impossible that the Pâtimokkha, either in its present shape, or at least in its most essential parts, can reach back to the Buddha's own time, or to that of his personal disciples.

It is no doubt natural, through the influence of the history of early Christianity, or perhaps of the school of Socrates, to imagine that early Buddhism was far removed from all fixed and absolute forms, either of creed or of liturgy; and to represent the intercourse of Gotama and his disciples as purely and simply an interchange of spiritual edification, where the spirit was all in all, and the letter was nothing. But it should be remembered that Gotama continued to live for many years, almost for two generations, after he had formulated the essential points of his system, and after he had founded the brotherhood of his Order. And at that time the stream of scholastic and legal ideas which emanated from the earlier Brâhmanism was flowing in full force through the religious circles of India. A rich phraseology of sacred and ecclesiastical expressions, an armoury of technical terms in philosophy and in theology (still preserved in the Brâhma*n*as and Upanishads), had been developed and made ready for the use of the Buddhists, and *G*ainas, and other reforming schools. And earlier speculation had raised a whole series of problems, and long-continued custom had elaborated a multifarious system of ecclesiastical observances, which the newly risen sects, orthodox or heretical, could grapple with, or could adopt. It seems to us that Gotama's disciples, from the very beginning, were much more than a free and unformal union of men held together merely through their common reverence for their Master, and through a common spiritual aim. They formed rather, and from the first, an organised Brotherhood.

But if we look upon the Sakyaputtiya Sama*n*as—for that is the name which the people in the earliest times gave to the community—as from the first an organised body, it is highly probable that the earliest formularies, both of their creeds and of their liturgies, arose in a time, if not during the life of Gotama, yet at most not long after his decease. Now among the oldest expressions of belief we may with certainty rank the four sentences known as the Four Noble Truths and the summary of the so-called Noble Eightfold Path: and the oldest liturgical formularies preserved to us are, without any doubt, the Pâtimokkha and the various Kammavâ*k*as. It is true that these liturgical formularies, being so much more extensive, may possibly have been modified or added to before they reached the form in which we now possess them; but there is not the slightest trace of any other liturgies having ever been in use in the Buddhist fraternity.

It is of course impossible to attempt to draw a line between the part which Gotama himself may have had in the settlement of the list of offences contained in the Pâtimokkha, and the part that may have been taken by his disciples. Nor indeed, considering the limited character of our knowledge, is that a point of much importance. But it should perhaps be noticed in this connection that Buddhist tradition does ascribe to one among Gotama's disciples—to Upâli—an especial connection with the Vinaya. This tradition reaches back at least as far as the time when the existing recension of the Pâli Pi*t*akas was made, for we find it both in the Sutta- and in the Vinaya-Pi*t*akas.

Thus in the *K*ullavagga (VI, 13, 1) we find the passage—'At that time the Blessed One proclaimed the Vinaya in many a way to the Bhikkhus, exalted the Vinaya, exalted the learning of the Vinaya, exalted again and again the venerable Upâli. Then thought the Bhikkhus, "The Blessed One hath proclaimed the Vinaya in many a way, hath exalted the Vinaya, hath exalted the learning of the Vinaya, hath exalted again and again the venerable Upâli. Come now let us learn the Vinaya from the venerable Upâli." And so many Bhikkhus, old and middle-aged and young, learnt the Vinaya from the venerable Upâli.'

And again in a Sutta of the Aṅguttara Nikâya[1], where those Bhikkhus are enumerated who, in any particular respect, are the first and foremost in the Brotherhood, Upâli is mentioned as the first among the custodians of the Vinaya (the Vinaya-dharâ). And further, as is well known, it is Upâli who, according to the tradition, plays, at the First Council, the same part of propounder with regard to the Vinaya Texts which Ânanda does with regard to the Dhamma Texts[2]. There may well be some truth in this very ancient tradition that Upâli was specially conversant with the Rules of the Order; but it would be hazardous on that account to ascribe to Upâli a share, not only in the handing down of existing Rules, but in the composition of the Pâtimokkha itself[3].

As regards the order in which the various offences are arranged in the Pâtimokkha, the principal division corresponds to the division of the Order into Brethren and Sisters: there is a Bhikkhu-pâtimokkha and a Bhikkhunî-pâtimokkha. In each of these two chief divisions the offences are divided into various classes, beginning with the heaviest—with those, that is, that result in the exclu-

[1] Phayre MS., vol. i. fol. kau.

[2] *K*ullavagga XII.

[3] In the Ceylon Chroniclers (Dîpava*m*sa, Bhâ*n*avâras 4 and 5) Upâli even becomes the first in a series of Vinayapâmokkhâ, or 'Chiefs of the Vinaya;' but no such office is known to the older tradition; and had it existed it would certainly have been mentioned in connection with the dispute about the so-called Ten Points of the Vinaya at the Council of Vesâlî.

sion of the offender from the Order. Inside each class the sequence of the clauses follows no invariable rule. Sometimes offences of a related character are placed together in groups[1], but sometimes those which would naturally come together are found scattered in quite different parts of the same class[2]. It is perhaps worthy of notice that there sometimes seems, as in the two cases first mentioned in the last note, to be an effort to arrange the offences in groups (vagga) of ten: and in three cases we find regulations formulated with the utmost brevity (the offences being merely expressed by a locative case dependent upon pâkittiyam) at the commencement of such a vagga. It seems to us, at least in the present state of our knowledge, quite impossible to draw any conclusions from such peculiarities as to the comparative age of any different parts of the Pâtimokkha. The irregularities in arrangement may very well be due to want of literary clearness in the compilers of the present Form of Confession, and it would be hazardous to attempt to trace in it any historical argument.

The various points in regard to the Pâtimokkha dealt with in the foregoing paragraphs do not of themselves show that it was at all older than the rest of the Vinaya Pitaka; and indeed the work, as a separate work, is not considered among Buddhists to belong to the Pitakas at all, and is therefore not included in the list of works of which the Pitakas consist. But every single Rule or Clause in the Pâtimokkha is in fact found word for word in the Sutta-vibhaṅga, the quotations being so complete that the Pâtimokkha might be entirely put together again by piecing together extracts from the Vinaya Pitaka. And it is not possible that the Pâtimokkha originated merely by such a process of dovetailing; for the quotations in the Vinaya Pitaka, though not actually called quotations, bear the unmistakable stamp of being taken from some pre-existing work. The cause which led to the Pâtimokkha, and the

[1] For instance, regulations as to the conduct of Brethren towards Sisters come together in Pâkittiya 21–30; those about meal-times in Pâkittiya 31–40; about conduct in relation to armies in Pâkittiya 48–50.

[2] For instance, Pâkittiya 5, 6, and 43–45; and again, Pâkittiya 20 and 62, &c.

Upasampadâ-kammavâ*k*a, being separately preserved at all, is the same as the cause which led to their exclusion from the lists of the Pi*t*aka texts—the fact, that is, of their being liturgical compositions.

We turn now to the consideration of the question how a series of further literary productions were gradually developed out of, or added to the Pâtimokkha[1].

Whoever reads through the Mahâvagga will at once be struck by one section of it which differs completely both in contents and in form from the rest of the work. This is the section in the Second Book, Chapter III, paragraphs 4–8.

This passage is preceded by the opening words of the Pâtimokkha; and in the passage itself those words are separately paraphrased or explained. But the explanation does not appear to be put into the mouth of the Buddha; it bears rather, without any historical or conversational form, the impersonal shape of a simple commentary: and it only differs from the later commentaries by peculiar solemn diffuseness and rhetorical tautology.

If we were to consider the Mahâvagga only, the sudden and unexplained appearance in this connection, and in this connection only, of an isolated passage of this kind, would have to remain an insoluble puzzle. But when we look further into the other parts of the Vinaya Pi*t*aka, an answer immediately suggests itself. In the portion of that Pi*t*aka which is better called the Sutta-vibhaṅga, but is divided in the MSS. into two divisions, under the somewhat misleading titles of Pârâ*g*ika and Pâ*k*ittiya, we find, at regularly recurring intervals, passages of an exactly similar character, and without any doubt of the same origin, as the isolated passage in the Mahâvagga.

The Sutta-vibhaṅga is occupied with laying down and explaining all the Rules which are contained in the Pâtimokkha. Now, immediately after the text of each of these Rules, there is found a word for word commentary upon

[1] With the following paragraphs should be compared H. Oldenberg in the Introduction to his edition of the Pâli text of the Vinaya, vol. i. pp. xvi and following.

them—precisely as a word for word commentary follows, in the passage above cited in the Mahâvagga, upon the quoted words of the Introductory Formular of the Pâtimokkha service. Here then lies the explanation. This Introductory Formular is the only passage contained in the Pâtimokkha which is not found also in the Sutta-vibhaṅga. And with the explanation of the curiously isolated passage in the Mahâvagga we have also a new fact of very great importance. Not only does the Vinaya Piṭaka contain, word for word, the whole of the Pâtimokkha, but it contains also, and again word for word, the whole of an ancient Commentary on the Pâtimokkha.

This commentary no longer exists as a separate work, and it would indeed be strange if it did. It was not required in the simple liturgical services of Ordination and Confession in use in the Order: and if any one wished to refer to it, in order to refresh his memory as to the explanation of any passage in the Pâtimokkha, he had only to repeat, or to get repeated over to him, the corresponding passage from the Sutta-vibhaṅga. There he would find the Old Commentary (as we shall hereafter call it) word for word, together with the additional commentary by which it had been supplemented in later times.

A question may then possibly occur to the reader whether we can be really sure that the Old Commentary has been preserved complete, or whether what we have is a fragment only. We think there can be but little doubt as to the right answer. The Pâtimokkha, which the Old Commentary deals with word by word, has been separately preserved to us, and we know that no one phrase of it remains uncommented upon. And further it is clear from several passages that the words of the old commentator were considered so sacred or authoritative that they have been kept intact even in cases where they are in contradiction to the later parts of the Vinaya Piṭaka[1]. It should however be noted that this Old Commentary is philological

[1] See, for instance, the comparison made by Oldenberg in the Introduction to his edition of the text, vol. i. p. xviii. The Old Commentary follows of course the passage there referred to in the Pâtimokkha.

and exegetical throughout, containing nothing of a legendary or quasi-historical nature. It is just possible to suggest that it may have originally contained not only such an explanation of the meaning of each Rule, but an account also of the occasion on which the Rule was laid down. But it is difficult to see why greater sacredness should have been attached to one part of the work than to another; or to explain how it was that, if any part was changed, the contradictory passages above referred to were not also altered. Every probability therefore points to the conclusion that we have the complete work still before us, and not fragments of it only.

It seems to us to have been precisely the absence of any such historical account in the older Commentary which probably led to the formation of what was practically the new edition of the Pâtimokkha which now lies before us in the first part of the Vinaya Piṭaka.

In the earliest books of the Sutta Piṭaka, which contains the statement of Buddhist belief, we find—just as in the Gospels and in the Socratic dialogues—that that belief is not stated directly. The books profess to give, not simply the belief itself, but the belief as the Buddha uttered it, with an account of the time when, and the place at which, he uttered it. The Buddha's new method of salvation, his new doctrine of what salvation was, did not present itself to the consciousness of the early Buddhist community as an idea, a doctrine, standing alone, and merely on its own merits. In their minds it was indissolubly bound up with the memory of the revered and striking personality of him who had proclaimed it. So in the Sutta Piṭaka the actor and speaker is almost throughout the Buddha himself: (occasionally, but very seldom, one of his disciples.) Introductions—often indeed short and tending in later times to disappear—give a full account of where, and when, he spoke; what was the occasion which led to his uttering that particular speech; and to whom he uttered it. But, throughout, the principal thing is what the Buddha said.

It is only natural that this distinguishing mark of the

literature of the Buddhist Dhamma—much of which was no doubt in existence at a very early date—should have reacted upon the literature of the Buddhist Vinaya. The members of the Order were no longer contented to learn, and to understand the meaning of, the various Rules of the Pâtimokkha. A desire sprang up to have, for each one of them also, a kind of historical basis; to know the story of how the Buddha himself came to lay down the Rule to his disciples. And it was only the Brother who was properly acquainted with all this who was accounted a real 'Doctor of the Law.'

So it is said in the *K*ullavagga (IX, 5, 1):—'If a Brother, Upâli, has not received gladly both the Pâtimokkhas in their full extent, has not well divided them, well established them, well investigated them, both sutta by sutta, and in every detail; if when asked, "Where was this spoken by the Blessed One?" he fail to solve the question: then there will be some who will say to him, "But then, let the venerable one still devote himself to learning the Vinaya!" thus will they say[1].'

It is evident from this passage that, at the time when it was written, such a tradition regarding each Rule was in existence; and that the knowledge of these traditions was held in high esteem. It is therefore a reasonable conjecture that steps were taken to amalgamate these traditions with the Text and the Old Commentary in a complete work, which should also contain what we may call Notes on the Rules—that is, decisions on points of Law involved, though not expressed in so many words, in the Rules; discussions on what cases were really included and what were not, in particular regulations; enumeration of exceptions to the Rules; and so on.

Whether this conjecture be right or not, it is precisely such a work that we have now before us in that part of the Vinaya Pi*t*aka called the Sutta-vibhaṅga, and divided

[1] No *k*e Upâli bhikkhuno ubhayâni Pâtimokkhâni vitthârena svâgatâni honti suvibhattâni suppavattîni suvini*kkh*itâni suttato anuvya*ñ*ganaso, idam pan' âvuso kattha vutta*m* Bhagavatâ 'ti iti pu*tth*o na sampâyati, tassa bhavanti vattâro: Iṅgha tâva âyasmâ Vinaya*m* pariyâpu*n*assû 'ti: iti 'ssa bhavanti vattâro.

in the present MSS., as above pointed out, into two books called respectively—after the class of Rules with which they begin—Pârâgika and Pâkittiya. And it is possible throughout, without the possibility of mistake, to distinguish between the three portions of which the present work is built up. The historical basis comes first, leading up to the extract from the Pâtimokkha, which is always placed in the Buddha's own mouth; then comes the Old Commentary, with its verbal explanations; and then, finally, the Notes giving the exceptions to, and the extensions of, the Rule in the Pâtimokkha.

The foregoing paragraphs show the way in which the Sutta-vibhaṅga grew up on the basis of the Pâtimokkha. The following books—the Khandhakas—give a detailed and connected account of the admission into the Saṃgha; of the ceremony of the Uposatha; of the annually recurring observances connected with the beginning and the end of the rainy season; of the principal disciplinary proceedings; and of miscellaneous details regarding the medicine, food, dwelling-places, and daily life of the members of the Order (Bhikkhus). As in the Sutta-vibhaṅga, so here also, the outward form is arranged in such a way that in the case of every regulation a history was given of the occasion upon which the Buddha was supposed to have made it. These histories again lead up, in most cases, to a liturgical formulary by which the regulation was to be carried out.

While, however, in the case of the Sutta-vibhaṅga the liturgy on which it has been founded has been preserved in a separate shape, the formularies in the Khandhakas have not as yet, except in some instances, been found in existence apart from the Khandhakas. The principal exception is the Upasampadâ-kammavâka (The Words of the Act of Ordination), which recurs in its entirety in the First Khandhaka of the Mahâvagga (I, 76, 3 to I, 78, 5). It is impossible therefore as yet to trace the history of the gradual formation of the Khandhakas as we think it already possible to do in the case of the Sutta-vibhaṅga.

In the Khandhakas too, no doubt, the introductory

histories are the latest part. But while some of the formularies and regulations to which they lead up may well be very old, others are probably additions to, or modifications of, those older ones; and it is difficult to attempt to show, even with regard to the exceptions above mentioned, which are the older and which are the later. The misfortune that these forms are not all now separately extant[1] is probably simply due to the fact that the formularies separately preserved (including the Pâtimokkha) are the only ones which continued to be used in actual services among the members of the Order.

Such being the nature and contents, and such—so far as it can be traced—being the origin of the Sutta-vibhaṅga and of the Khandhakas respectively, it follows that in all probability they were composed, or put into their present shape, at about the same period in the development of early Buddhism—it is even possible that both works arose in immediate connection.

The kind of narrative setting with which, in both cases, the older material has been surrounded is alike in both. Here and there in both works are included real fragments of ancient legend or tradition—as, for instance, the account of the events from the attainment of Buddhahood down to the conversion of Sâriputta and Moggallâna (Mahâvagga I, 1–24), the story of Devadatta (*K*ullavagga VII), the story of the conversion and the sin of Sudinna (Vibhaṅga, First Pârâ*g*ika). But the greater number of these narratives are of the most meagre description, and have altogether the appearance of being mere inventions.

There is little doubt that this is what they, in fact, were. Actual remembrance of the Buddha, and of his time, could have sufficed only in the rarest instances to give a correct historical basis for the Rules or Ceremonies, which had to be explained. We find a precisely similar

[1] Mr. Dickson has given us an excellent text of the Upasampadâ-kammavâ*k*â; and it were much to be wished that the rest of them should also be published. Mr. Clough has given a translation of six others in 'Miscellaneous Translations from Oriental Languages,' London, 1834; and the Liverpool Free Library has MSS. of others.

state of things leading, in the Introductions to the *G*âtaka Stories, to what were unquestionably inventions: and it must be acknowledged that the compilers have not taken the slightest trouble to conceal the evidently unsubstantial character of most of these summary introductions. But it does not follow that they were invented at the time when the Sutta-vibhaṅga and the Khandhakas were compiled. They may possibly have formed part of the traditional explanatory teaching of the schools.

As to the time when the Sutta-vibhaṅga and the Khandhakas were compiled, we have important evidence in their silence regarding the well-known Ten Points.

The long-continued struggle on that question—as important for the history of Buddhism as the Arian controversy for that of Christianity—agitated the whole Buddhist world to its very centre; and the attempted settlement of it, at the Council of Vesâlî, led to a most serious schism in the Buddhist Church. Now the ten expressions in which the question was summarised or catalogued[1] are (as was pointed out in the Introduction to the Pâli Text of the Mahâvagga) conspicuous by their absence from the Vibhaṅga, and from all, except the last, of the Khandhakas[2]. The first mention of most of them, and the first use of any one of them as a distinctive war-cry, is found in those last books, which are evidently an appendix to the rest of the Khandhakas, and of an entirely different nature from the earlier ones; for they contain a regular historical account of the two Councils, that of Râ*g*agaha, and that of Vesâlî[3].

---

1 Siṅgilo*n*a, dvaṅgula, &c. (*K*ullavagga XII, 1, 10).

2 That is, as war-cries; *g*âtarûparaga*t*a occurs in the sense of the precious metals.

3 In the present division of the Khandhakas into two parts, called the Larger and Smaller Divisions (Mahâ- and *K*ulla-vagga), there are ten Khandhakas in the first Division, and ten, apart from this appendix, in the second Division. Without the appended two last Khandhakas the so-called smaller Division is really considerably smaller than the larger Division; and there is therefore a good reason for the name which was given to it. With the two last Khandhakas the difference in length of the two Divisions as a whole is not sufficiently striking to account satisfactorily for the choice of their names; and the smaller

But the Ten Points in dispute were all matters of ecclesiastical law, they all related to observances of the brotherhood, they were in fact questions as to whether or not the ancient Rules should be relaxed or not in these ten respects. Is it possible that in a collection of works like the Vibhaṅga and the Khandhakas, which seek to set forth, down to the minutest detail, and even with hair-splitting diffuseness, all that has any relation to the daily life of the Brethren, and the regulations of the Buddhist Order—is it possible that in such a collection, if, when it was compiled, the struggle on the Ten Points had already burst into flame, there should be no reference at all, even in interpolations, to any one of these ten disputes? That the difference of opinion on the Ten Points remains altogether unnoticed in those parts of the collection where, in the natural order of things, it would be obviously referred to, and that it is only mentioned in an appendix where the Council held on its account is described, shows clearly, in our opinion, that the Vibhaṅga and the Khandhakas (save the two last) are older than the Council of Vesâlî—and, of course, a fortiori that the Pâtimokkha and the Kammavâ*k*âs are so too.

The Council of Vesâlî is said in the XIIth Khandhaka of the *K*ullavagga to have taken place a hundred years after the Buddha's death. This is no doubt a round number; and the exact year of the date of the Buddha's death is open to question. If it be placed, according to the Ceylon chronicles, at exactly 218 years before Asoka's coronation, it will fall in or about 483 B.C.

But the expression '218 years' can in no case be regarded as an absolutely reliable statement of actual fact, and the date of 483 B.C. must therefore be taken subject to a marginal allowance of some decades. And it appears to one of us, for various reasons which he has elsewhere stated at length, that the balance of probability leads to the conclusion that the date of the Buddha's Parinibbâna must be

Division actually contains two more Khandhakas than the larger. We lay no stress upon these facts, but it confirms the general argument to find little points of this kind tending in the same direction.

brought down to the period from 420–400 B.C.[1] We do not enter upon that question here, as the details are intricate, and the result uncertain; and it is sufficient for our present purpose to be able to fix the Council of Vesâlî, even after making allowance for all possibilities, at within thirty years of 350 B.C.

We would only point out that there is really no ground for discontent with a result which can be fixed, after all, within a few decades. For what difference does that make in this case? If we had to deal with Grecian history, such a result might well be deemed unsatisfactory. There are differences, both personal and political, between Greece in 480, in 440, and in 400—differences well known to us. But whether we fix the date of an event in India in 480, or in 440, what does it, at present, matter? Who would be bold enough to say that the mention of India in 480 B.C. calls up to his mind a condition of things different from that suggested by the mention of India in 440 B.C., or even in 400 B.C.? We need not therefore take too much to heart the uncertainty of this chronological result; though we may regret that our comfort is drawn from no better source than our want of knowledge.

The Vibhaṅga and the Twenty Khandhakas were at that time (*circa* 350 B.C.) already held in such high repute that no one ventured to alter them; a sanctity of this kind is not acquired without the lapse of a considerable time: and we think it is not going too far to say, Firstly, that these books must have been in existence, as we now have them, within thirty years, earlier or later, of, at least, 360 or 370 B.C.; Secondly, that the Old Commentary they have preserved must be considerably, perhaps fifty years, older; and Thirdly, that the Kammavâ*k*âs and the Pâtimokkha must be older still.

The reader will notice that in the foregoing discussion no mention has been made of the Fifth Book in the present

[1] See the dissertation on this subject in Rhys Davids's 'Ancient Coins and Measures of Ceylon;' and, more shortly, the close of the Introduction to his 'Buddhist Suttas from the Pâli.'

division of the Vinaya Pi*t*aka—the Parivâra-pâ*th*a. The reason is that this work, an abstract of the other parts of the Vinaya, is in fact a very much later compilation, and probably the work of a Ceylonese Thera. In some stanzas, which are found at the end of the Parivâra-pâ*th*a, it is stated to have been composed by 'the highly wise, learned, and skilful Dîpa, after he had inquired here and there into the methods (literally, the way) followed by former teachers[1].'

We have every hope that the foregoing argument will commend itself to our fellow workers as being, in the main, well founded. We now propose to test it by applying it in explanation of several difficult terms and phrases found in the Vinaya Pi*t*aka, which seem to have been hitherto incorrectly interpreted.

It has been pointed out that, in the Pâtimokkha, the offences are arranged in certain classes, called, with reference to the heinousness of the act committed, Pârâ*g*ika, Sa*m*ghâdisesa, Pâ*k*ittiya, Pâ*t*idesaniya, and Sekhiya. In other parts of the Vinaya, other offences are called Thulla*kk*aya and Dukka*t*a. On this nomenclature the Rev. S. Coles has founded a trenchant attack upon Buddhist morality. He says:

'Beside the Pârâjikas there are lesser faults, the nature of which is determined by various causes, as will subsequently appear. These are Saṅghâdisesa, Thullaccaya, and Dukka*t*a faults, and can all be easily remedied, the two latter especially; as, after a fault of this kind has been committed, the culprit has only to confess to his Upajjhâya (ordaining priest) without much delay, and is then exempted from all evil consequences; but the Saṅghâdisesa being more serious (about half a Pârâjikâ), a course of penance has to be submitted to, and confession without delay made to twenty-five superior Bhikkhus. The nature

[1] Pubbâ*k*ariyamaggañ *k*a pu*kkh*itvâ *k*a tahi*m* tahi*m*
Dîpo nâma mahâpa*ññ*o sutadharo vi*k*akkha*n*o
Ima*m* vitthârasa*m*khepa*m* sa*ggh*âmaggena ma*ggh*ime
*K*intayitvâ likhâpesi sissakâna*m* sukhâvaha*m*.

and extent of these penances are not defined in the first book of the Vinaya Pitaka, but in others, to which reference will be made when these books are brought under consideration. Suffice it to say, that they can possibly have no deterring effect on crime, but rather form loop-holes through which most enormous and disgusting misdeeds may be committed, and yet the perpetrator may remain not only as a Buddhist, but as a Bhikkhu[1].'

Mr. Coles then applies this argument to show that many offences against morality, being only called Dukka*t*a and not Pârâ*g*ika, must have been looked upon very leniently, not only by the Buddhists, but by Gotama himself; and that therefore his system of morality was not of the lofty kind it has usually been supposed to be, but was, in fact, a mere cloak and encouragement to wickedness and crime!

If Mr. Coles had looked at the Pi*t*aka he was discussing from a historical, instead of from a controversial, point of view, he would scarcely have advanced this argument. The use of the term Dukka*t*a does not arise from, nor is it evidence of, a weakness in moral feeling; but merely of a difference in point of time. It occurs only in what we have ventured above to call the Notes: that is to say, in the latest portion of the Pi*t*aka. When the author or authors of the final recension of the Vinaya had to speak of an offence not actually mentioned, though implied, in the text before them, they did not presume to call it by any of the names applied in the Pâtimokkha itself to the classification of offences. They no more dared to add to the number of Pârâ*g*ikâs, for instance, than a clergyman would now venture seriously to propose an addition to the Ten Commandments. They made use of two technical terms (both entirely new ones), namely, Thulla*kk*aya and Dukka*t*a (literally, Serious Transgression and Bad-deed), using the former more sparingly, and for graver misdemeanours. No argument based on passages where the word Dukka*t*a occurs can therefore have any force as to the teaching of Gotama himself; and the Bhikkhus, who did use the

[1] Journal of the Ceylon Asiatic Society, 1867-1870, p. 155.

word, were restrained from using the older term Pârâgika by a feeling of reverence towards their sacred books—a feeling surely deserving, not of censure, but of sympathy.

Again, there are certain terms applied to various parts of the Vinaya itself on which the above historical analysis may throw some light. When Asoka, in the Edict of Bhabra, addressed to the Buddhist Order, exhorted them to take as their authority, among other works, the Vinaya-Samukase, or Abstract of the Vinaya, he may fairly be supposed to have referred to the Pâtimokkha, which that epithet would very appropriately describe. If it be asked why he did not then call it the Pâtimokkha, the explanation may be either that that word is more especially a term for the act to be performed, than for the liturgy which shows the way to perform it (though it was also undoubtedly used as a name of the liturgy), or else that the work was known under both designations.

We would just add, in passing, that, in the passage in question, the reading samukase (samutkarsha), instead of the formerly accepted samâkase, is quite clear in General Cunningham's lithograph[1]; and the generally accepted view that the Edict was addressed to a council, and is therefore an authoritative confirmation of the Ceylon traditions regarding the Council of Patna, ought to be reconsidered. The Edict merely says: 'King Devânampiya of Mâgadha salutes the Sa*m*gha' (that is, the Order, or the Community, of Bhikkhus)[2]. Without desiring to throw any doubt upon the reality of the Council of Patna, we are driven to the conclusion that such an expression as 'the Sa*m*gha' could not have been meant to describe a formal

[1] 'Corpus Inscriptionum Indicarum,' pl. xv.

[2] Burnouf translated 'à l'assemblée du Magadha,' and Wilson, 'to the venerable assembly of Mâgadha' (see 'Corpus,' &c., p. 131); but the reading is clearly Mâgadhe in the 'Corpus,' while the older facsimile in the Journal of the Bengal Asiatic Society (ix. 618) had the impossible form Mâgdhe*m*. Even if we could read Mâgadha*m* sa*m*gha*m* (an expression for which we know no parallel), the above remarks would still hold good. Compare further Professor Kern in the 'Jaartelling der Zuidelijke Buddhisten,' pp. 30-35.

council. Surely, if the Edict had been addressed to such a council, the fact would have been plainly intimated.

It is just possible that Vinaya-Samukase may refer to the Old Commentary as well as to the Pâtimokkha; but this is not probable, for there is no reason to believe that in Asoka's time the Old Commentary any longer existed apart from its setting in the Vibhaṅga. And Vinaya-Samukase cannot for the reasons above stated mean, as has been supposed, the Parivâra-pâ*th*a.

As regards the meaning of the word Pâtimokkha we have the explanation of the Old Commentator in that single passage of his work found, as above pointed out, in the Khandhakas[1]. He there describes it as 'the origin, the front (mukha), the chief of the good Dhammas;' where the word Dhammâ means 'qualities,' and where the evident inference is that the commentator[2] derived Pâtimokkha from mukha. But, on the other hand, the tradition of the Northern Buddhists, in whose Sanskrit works the word is replaced by Prâtimoksha, points to a derivation from the root mu*k*.

It seems scarcely open to doubt that we must, in accordance with this last interpretation, connect the word with mu*k*, and not with mukha. 'Pratimukha' means in Sanskrit 'over against, standing close in front.' How is it possible to derive from that any meaning appropriate as a title for the liturgy of confession called Pâtimokkha? On the other hand, the derivation from mu*k* is straightforward and simple. Prati-mu*k* (âtmanep.) means 'to free oneself, to get rid of;' and it is precisely through the recitation of this formular, and the answering of the questions contained in it, that the conscience of the member of the Brotherhood

---

[1] Pâtimokkhan ti âdi*m* eta*m* mukha*m* eta*m* pamukha*m* eta*m* kusalâna*m* dhammâna*m*, tena vu*kk*ati pâtimokkhan ti. Mahâvagga II, 3, 4.

[2] We use the phrase 'Old Commentator' for convenience only. The commentary was, no doubt, handed down by tradition in the Buddhist schools; and there is no reason to believe that it was the work of any one mind.

was set free from the sense of the offence he had incurred[1]. Pâtimokkha or Prâtimoksha means therefore 'Disburdening, Getting free.' The lengthening of the first vowel in the Pâli word is not without analogies which have been already adduced by Childers. It is certain that the word is older than the present shape of the Formulary now so called; for it is used several times in the Formulary itself, as well as in many of the oldest Suttas.

The Old Commentator makes the Pâtimokkha 'the head of the good Dhammas.' There is a curious passage in the Pâtimokkha where the Dhammas are said to be included in the Suttas:

'If a Bhikkhu at the half-monthly recitation of the Pâtimokkha should say, "Now for the first time do I notice that this Dhamma, as one handed down in the Suttas, embraced in the Suttas, gets recited every half-month!" then' &c.[2]

It is plain here that neither Dhamma nor Sutta is used in the sense to which we are accustomed from the later books. The Dhammas recited half-monthly are those contained in the scheme of offences given in the Pâtimokkha, and the Suttas must therefore mean the separate clauses of that Formulary.

The fact is that the use of the word Sutta is by no means confined in the oldest Pâli to the texts of what was afterwards the Sutta Pi*t*aka, nor is it exclusively used either in earlier or later times[3] in opposition to Vinaya. Thus we find it used again, as we think, of the Rules of the Pâtimokkha; and in contrast, as in the rule above quoted, to Dhamma, in *K*ullavagga IV, 14, 22, 23:

'This Bhikkhu, of such and such a name, is a preacher

---

[1] Compare Mahâvagga II, 3, 3.

[2] Yo pana bhikkhu anvaddhamâsa*m* Pâtimokkhe uddissamâne eva*m* vadeyya; idân' eva kho aha*m* *g*ânâmi, ayam pi kira dhammo suttâgato suttapariyâpanno anvaddhamâsa*m* uddesa*m* âga*kkh*atîti, ta*ñ* *k*e . . . (the 73rd Pâ*k*ittiya, quoted in *K*ullavagga III, 34, 2).

[3] Though more especially concerned here with the earlier use of the word Sutta, it may be well to remind our readers of the name Suttadharâ applied in the Sumaṅgala Vilâsinî to secular lawyers (see Alwis, 'Introd.' &c., p. 100).

of the Dhamma; but the Suttas have not been handed down to him, nor the Sutta-Vibhaṅga.'

'This Bhikkhu, of such and such a name, is a preacher of the Dhamma, and the Suttas have been handed down to him, but not the Sutta-Vibhaṅga[1].'

So again in the constantly repeated phrase above referred to—

'If the two Pâtimokkhas are (or are not, as the connection requires) thoroughly known to a Bhikkhu in their entirety with all their divisions and explanations, if he have (or have not) thoroughly mastered them Sutta by Sutta, and Detail by Detail; then' &c.[2]

—the word Sutta evidently refers to the clauses of the two Pâtimokkhas; and we find also in the immediate context the mention of Dhamma or of Vinaya, or of both.

It is no doubt true that in one passage of the Mahâ-parinibbâna Sutta (IV, 8–11 = pp. 39, 40), Sutta is opposed to Vinaya in much the same way as Sutta Pi*t*aka was afterwards opposed to Vinaya Pi*t*aka; yet the contrast between these two ideas is usually expressed by the apposition of Dhamma to Vinaya[3], and the passage in the Mahâ-parinibbâna Sutta stands, so far as we yet know, quite alone. Indeed in the oldest tradition the discourses or conversations now called Suttas seem not to have been called by that name, but are referred to as Suttantas.

So in the Mahâvagga III, 5, 9, 12 mention is made of devout men, or of devout women, who may have been accustomed to recite some well-known Suttanta[4]; and in the next Khandhaka (IV, 15, 4) we find Suttanta, Dhamma, and Vinaya all occurring in one context:

'It may happen, Brethren, that in some district on the day of Pavâra*n*â the night may have become far spent

[1] Sutta*m* tassa âgata*m* na Suttavibhaṅga*m*. On the latter term see below.

[2] Ubhayâni nu kho Pâtimokkhâni vitthârena svâgatâni suvibhattâni suppavattîni suvini*kk*hitâni suttato anuvya*ñ*ganaso (Mahâvagga I, 36, 14; I, 37, 14; *K*ullavagga IV, 14, 19; IX, 5, 1). Anuvya*ñ*gana may perhaps refer here to the Old Commentary.

[3] Compare H. Oldenberg's Introduction to his edition of the Mahâvagga, pp. 7 and following.

[4] Abhi*ññ*âta*m* vâ Suttanta*m* bha*n*ati.

while the Brethren are in confusion—some reciting the Dhamma, those versed in the Suttantas intoning some Suttanta together, the custodians of the Vinaya discussing the Vinaya, and the preachers of the Dhamma discoursing about the Dhamma.'

The whole of these expressions recur in *K*ullavagga IV, 4, 4; and are found again, with others of a similar character, in *K*ullavagga VI, 6, 2. This last passage is in the Introduction to a fable which of course recurs, as a *G*âtaka, in the *G*âtaka collection, and with an introduction in almost the same words. We should therefore expect to find there also the epithet suttantika ('versed in the Suttantas'), if that expression had remained in use as late as the fifth century A.D.; but it is omitted, the Suttantikas having been then long since replaced by those entrusted, not with the whole, but with special portions only, of the Dhamma literature. The word Suttanta was however still in common use at the time when the presumably later books now contained in the Pi*t*akas were composed; for it occurs in the Aṅguttara Nikâya [1], and in a constantly recurring verse in the Buddhava*m*sa in which it is opposed to Vinaya [2], and the word is still used in the MSS. as the title of the more important Suttas.

In the passage quoted above from the *K*ullavagga IV, 14, 22, 23 there is a term Sutta-vibhaṅga used as the name of some part of the Vinaya literature apparently distinct

---

[1] The Aṅguttara Nikâya, Pañ*k*aka Nipâta (Phayre MS. vol. ii. fol. gâ*h*): Ye te Suttantâ Tathâgatassa bhâvitâ gambhîrâ gambhîratthâ lokuttarâ suñ-ñatapa*t*isa*m*yuttâ tesu bhaññamânesu na sussissanti no sota*m* odahissanti na aññâ*k*itta*m* upa*tth*âpessanti na *k*a te dhamme uggahetabba*m* pariyâpu*n*itabba*m* maññissanti; ye pana te suttantâ kathitâ kâveyyâ *k*ittakkharâ *k*ittabyañ*g*anâ bahirakâ sâvakabhâsitâ tesu bhaññamânesu sussissanti sota*m* odahissanti; &c.

Ibid. fol. ṅa*h*: Ye te bhikkhû bahussutâ âgatâgamâ dhammadharâ vinayadharâ mâtikâdharâ te na sakka*kk*am suttanta*m* para*m* vâ*k*enti, tesam a*kk*ayena *kh*in-namûlako suttanto hoti apa*t*isara*n*o.

On the form compare the Sanskrit d*r*ish*t*ânta, v*r*ittânta, and siddhânta.

[2] Suttanta*m* Vinayañ *k*âpi navaṅga*m* Satthusâsana*m*
Sabba*m* pariyâpu*n*itvâna sobhayi *G*inasâsana*m*.

The phrase is used of various Buddhas in verses 317, 348, 594, 627, and 786 of the Buddhava*m*sa. This reference we owe to Dr. Morris.

from the Suttas of the Pâtimokkha. 'The Suttas have been handed down to him, but not the Suttavibhaṅga.'

The word recurs only in one other passage[1], and that is in the appended Khandhakas of the *K*ullavagga, in the account of the Council of Vesâlî[2]. Seven passages are there quoted from the Pâtimokkha in condemnation of seven out of the Ten Points raised by the heretics; and in answer to the question, 'Where was it condemned?' and before the passages are quoted, the place where the passage was uttered is mentioned, and condemnation is stated to be 'in the Suttavibhaṅga.' Thus

Revata says, 'Is it right, Lord, to drink *g*alogi?'

Sabbakâmî replies, 'What, Friend, is this *g*alogi?'

Revata: 'Is it right, Lord, to drink strong drink which not being fermented, is not yet intoxicating?'

Sabbakâmî: 'No, my friend, it is not right.'

Revata: 'Where has it been condemned?'

Sabbakâmî: 'At Kosambî in the Suttavibhaṅga.'

Revata: 'What does he (who drinks *g*alogi) commit?'

Sabbakâmî: 'He commits the Pâ*k*ittiya offence of drinking strong drink and of drinking intoxicating liquors.'

This is a quotation of the Pâ*k*ittiya Rule, No. 51; but the words quoted do not in fact condemn the drinking of toddy, and neither the Pâtimokkha nor the Old Commentary contains any reference to the place, Kosambî, where the words are here said to have been uttered.

It is only in the introduction afterwards appended (in what is now called the Vibhaṅga) to the two older works, that Kosambî is mentioned; and in the appendix following the Rule 51 in the Vibhaṅga there are no exceptions which would include *g*alogi. But Kosambî is mentioned in the Introductory History. It is therefore most probable that the term Sutta-vibhaṅga refers to what is now called the Vibhaṅga; or, if not, at least to that body of traditional teaching (including the Pâtimokkha and the Old Commentary) out of which the present Vibhaṅga was composed.

---

[1] That is, of the Vinaya Pi*t*aka. We are not certain that it may not be found in the Sutta Pi*t*aka.

[2] *K*ullavagga XII, 2, 8.

It may be convenient to make some reference here to the question whether the literature above discussed was handed down by memory only, or by writing. We are justified in expecting to find, in texts dealing in such minute detail with the daily life of the members of the Buddhist Order, some distinct evidence—and it will be equally distinct whether it consists in actual statement, or in silence—as to writing, and the use of written books. And this expectation is not disappointed.

In the first place, there are several passages which confirm in an indisputable manner the existence of the art of writing at the time when the Vinaya texts were put into their present shape.

'A certain man, who had committed a theft, ran away, and got ordained among the Bhikkhus. Now he was written up in the king's palace with an injunction that he should be slain wheresoever he should be found[1].'—

'But there occurred to the parents of Upâli this consideration: "If Upâli should learn writing[2], Upâli might thus after our decease live at ease, and not be troubled."'

And in the Vibhaṅga we find an interesting explanation of the Third Pârâ*g*ika Rule, which lays down that whosoever wilfully kills a man, or brings about his death, must be expelled from the Order.

In the Notes on this Rule the Sutta-vibhaṅga discusses the case of some one causing the death of another by persuading him that suicide is glorious, or that it results in salvation. And in this connection the possibility is considered of these representations being made to the proposed victim, not by word of mouth, and not by a messenger, but by writing.

'He engraves a writing to this effect: "Who so dies, he acquires wealth, or acquires fame, or goes to heaven." By that writing he is guilty of a Dukka*t*a offence. The other sees the writing, and, determining to die, is filled

[1] A*ññ*ataro puriso *k*orika*m* katvâ palâyitvâ bhikkhûsu pabba*g*ito hoti. So *k*a ra*ññ*o antepure likhito hoti yattha passitabbo tattha hantabbo 'ti (Mahâvagga I, 43).

[2] Sa*k*e kho Upâli lekha*m* sikkheyya (Mahâvagga I, 49, 1).

with painful feelings. (The writer is) guilty of a Thullakkaya offence. He does die. (The writer is) guilty of a Pârâgika offence[1].'

And again with respect to the injunction addressed to the Sisters of the Order not to devote themselves to worldly wisdom (tirakkhâna-viggâ), the Vibhaṅga makes an exception in favour of learning to write[2].

It is evident therefore that writing was in vogue in the time when the Notes on the Rules were put into their present form, that it was made use of for the publication of official announcements, and for the drawing up of written communications in private life; and that while the knowledge of the art was a possible source of livelihood, it was not confined to 'clerks,' but was acquired by ordinary persons, and even by women.

But it is a long step from the use of writing for such public or private notifications to the adoption of it for the purpose of recording an extensive and sacred literature: and our texts show—and show, as it seems to us, in an equally indisputable manner—that for this latter purpose writing, however well known, had not yet come into use.

Had the sacred texts been written down and read, books, manuscripts, and the whole activity therewith connected, must have necessarily played a very important part in the daily life of the members of the Buddhist Order. Now the texts of the Vinaya place clearly enough before our eyes the whole of the 'personal property,' so to speak, of the Buddhist Ârâmas and Vihâras. Every movable thing, down to the smallest and least important domestic utensils, is in some way or other referred to, and its use pointed out; while the use of other articles, not usually found in the Vihâras, is mentioned, and condemned. But nowhere do we find the least trace of any reference to manuscripts;

[1] Lekham *kh*indati yo evam marati so dhanam vâ labhati yasam vâ labhati saggam vâ ga*kkh*atîti. Akkharakkharâya âpatti dukka*t*assa. Lekham passitvâ marissâmîti dukkham vedanam uppâdeti. Âpatti thulla*kk*ayassa. Marati. Âpatti pârâgikassa.

[2] Anâpatti lekham pariyâpu*n*âti (Bhikkhunî-Pâtimokkha, Pâ*k*ittiya 49).

much less of inks, or pens, or styles, or leaves, or other writing materials.

And we do find, on the contrary, passages which show the difficulties which arose every time that the memorial tradition by word of mouth of any of the sacred texts was interrupted, or threatened to be interrupted.

So, for instance, we find the case discussed of no one Bhikkhu, among all the Brethren dwelling in some particular place, knowing the Pâtimokkha. There was no other way out of the difficulty, save that of one of the Bhikkhus being sent out to some neighbouring fraternity, with the commission there to learn the Pâtimokkha by heart, either in its full extent (that is, as we take it, all the rules being learnt in full) or at least in abstract[1].

And again, in a passage already quoted, we hear of the case of an Upâsaka, who knows some important Suttanta, and is afraid that the knowledge of it will fade away. So he sends to a fraternity of Bhikkhus, and invites the Brethren to come over to him; and in that case an exception is made to the Rule forbidding the Brethren to travel in the rainy season, provided only that they do not stay away from home longer than seven days[2].

We may quote in this connection a passage of the same tendency from the Aṅguttara Nikâya, in which, among the circumstances hurtful to the security and the propagation of the Buddhist faith, the possibility is mentioned of the well-instructed Bhikkhus neglecting to take pains to hand on to others the Suttantas which they know. Then, when they have passed away, 'the root of that Suttanta is cut off, and it finds no place of refuge[3].'

It is very plain from these last passages that the Buddhist community in its earliest days did not think of the

---

[1] Mahâvagga II, 17, 5. 6. On this meaning of vitthârena and sa*m*khittena see also Mahâvagga II, 15, 1. 2.

[2] Mahâvagga III, 5, 9.

[3] *K*atukka-Nipâta (Phayre MS. vol. i. fol. *n*â); and repeated in the Pañ*k*aka-Nipâta (ibid. vol. ii. fol. ṅâ*h*): Ye te bhikkhû bahussutâ âgatâgamâ dhammadharâ vinayadharâ mâtikâdharâ te na sakka*kk*am suttanta*m* para*m* vâ*k*enti tesa*m* a*kk*ayena *kh*innamûlako suttanto hoti apa*t*isara*n*o.

possibility of using writing as a means of guarding against such painful accidents. Can this have arisen from any belief that writing the books would have been an irreverent treatment of them? We cannot think that among such a community as that of the Buddhists—who were so advanced in their views that they deliberately adopted the language of the people, and even took no thought, within the ranks of their community, of caste—any such consideration would have prevailed. It seems much more probable that, at the date referred to, the art of writing had not been taken advantage of for the purposes of any kind of literature; but that its use was wholly confined to recording short messages or notes, or private letters, or advertisements of a public character—a result which may well have been due to the want of any practical material on which to engrave the letters that were nevertheless evidently known[1].

On the texts above quoted, and the inferences which may fairly be drawn from them, we would base two remarks. Firstly, that there can be no reasonable ground for doubting the correctness of the ancient tradition preserved in the well-known verse of the Ceylon Chroniclers, when, speaking of the time of Va*tt*a Gâma*n*i, who began to reign 88 B.C., they say,

'The text of the Three Pi*t*akas, and the Commentary too thereon,
The wise Bhikkhus of former time had handed down by word of mouth:
The then Bhikkhus, perceiving how all beings do decay,
Meeting together, wrote them in books, that the Dhamma might last long[2].'

But, secondly, though we must therefore believe that the

[1] Compare Burnell, 'Elements of South Indian Palaeography,' p. 10.

[2] Dîpava*m*sa XX, 20, 21; Mahâva*m*sa, p. 207. As the stanza is common to both works it is taken in all probability, word for word, from the Old Commentary in Si*m*halese, the Sîhala*tth*akathâ, preserved in the Mahâvihâra in Anurâdhapura. See H. Oldenberg's Introduction to his edition of the Dîpava*m*sa.

Vinaya, before it was reduced to writing, was handed down for about three hundred years solely by memory, and that it lived only in the minds of the Vinayadharâ, the Bhikkhus 'who were versed in the Vinaya,' we do not think it is at all necessary, or even possible, to impugn the substantial accuracy of the texts handed down in a manner that seems, to moderns, so unsafe. The Text, as it lies before us, stands so well against all proofs, whether we compare its different parts one with another, or with the little that is yet known of its northern counterparts[1], that we are justified in regarding these Pâli books as in fact the authentic mirror of the old Mâgadhî text as fixed in the central schools of the most ancient Buddhist Church. That text, in the dialect of Magadha, may have been lost to us, once for all; and we can scarcely hope, unless some isolated sentences may hereafter be found preserved here and there in Inscriptions, that this loss will ever be, even partially, made good. But we may well be thankful that the faithful zeal and industry of these old monks has preserved for us a translation, in a dialect so nearly allied to the original, and in so perfect and trustworthy a state as the Pâli version of the Vinaya still undoubtedly presents.

We trust that the choice we have made from the literature of the Vinaya Pi*t*aka for insertion in this Collection of Translations from the Sacred Books of the East will be considered to need little justification. As the oldest and in many respects most important material of the Vinaya literature we have included a version of the Pâtimokkha; though confining ourselves to the Bhikkhu-Pâtimokkha,

---

[1] How little this is, is apparent from the fact that Burnouf, who had studied all those that were then accessible, did not even find the words pârâgika and sa*m*ghâdisesa (Introduction, &c., p. 301). To the Tibetan texts Csoma Körösi has devoted a few pages ('Analysis of the Dulva' in Asiatic Researches, vol. xx. pp. 45 and foll.) Of the Chinese we have only the brief notices of M. Rémusat (Foe Koue Ki, pp. 104 and foll.) and of Mr. Beal (in H. Oldenberg's Introduction to the Vinaya, vol. i. pp. xliv, xlv). The last scholar also mentions several Vinaya works, of the contents of which however nothing further is known, in his Catalogue of Chinese Buddhist Works now in the India Office Library (pp. 67–71).

as our predecessors, Mr. Dickson and Professor Minayeff, have done before us. We could not consider, even after their labours, that a new translation of this difficult text would be superfluous. And of the younger literature we have confined ourselves to the Khandhakas, both because these books, in their variety, and in the fulness of their contents, are better calculated to afford a correct view of the conditions, and the life, of that oldest and most influential of the many monkish orders, the Buddhist Sa*m*gha; and also because the Sutta-vibhaṅga is little more than an expansion of the Pâtimokkha, which we have already, for the reasons just stated, determined to include[1].

T. W. RHYS DAVIDS.
H. OLDENBERG.

November, 1880.

[1] For the Upasampadâ-kammavâ*k*a see the passages recurring in the Khandhakas as pointed out above, p. xix.

Additional Note on Mahâvagga III, 2, 2 (vassupanâyikâ).

As entering upon Vassa is called vassa*m* upaga*kkh*ati or vassa*m* upeti, we believe that upanâyikâ, the final member of the compound vassupanâyikâ (entrance upon Vassa), must not be derived from upa-nî, but from upa-i (upan-i). Comp. *S*atapatha-Brâhma*n*a II, 3, 2, 2: ahar-ahar vai Na*d*o Naishidho Yama*m* râ*g*âna*m* dakshi*n*ata upanayati (Sâya*n*a: upaga*kkh*ati). The preposition upan contained in upan-ayati will be treated of by Professor Joh. Schmidt in the 26th volume of Kuhn's Zeitschrift.

THE PÂTIMOKKHA

THE WORDS OF DISBURDENMENT.

REVERENCE TO THE BLESSED ONE, THE HOLY ONE, THE FULLY ENLIGHTENED ONE.

NIDÂNA[1].

INTRODUCTION.

May the Chapter[2], reverend Sirs, hear me!

To-day is the sacred day (of the full, or new, moon), the fifteenth day of the half-month[3]. If it be convenient to the Chapter, let the Chapter hold Uposatha, let it repeat the Pâtimokkha. How is it with respect to the necessary preliminaries to a meeting of the Order? Let the reverend brethren announce their purity[4], and I will rehearse the Pâtimokkha!

We all gladly give ear and do attend[5]!

---

[1] The whole of this Introduction, with the ancient commentary upon it (referred to above, in the Introduction), recurs in the Mahâvagga II, 3, where further notes will be found. The previous chapter in Dickson entitled the Pu*kkh*âvissa*gg*ana is not part of the ancient text of the Pâtimokkha.

[2] Sa*m*gho: of course not the whole Order, but those members then present, spoken of collectively.

[3] Uposatho pa*nn*araso. See below, Mahâvagga, Book II, and especially chap. 14.

[4] That is, their freedom from any of those disabilities which are declared below, Book II, to incapacitate a member of the Order from assembling at a formal meeting on the Uposatha day.

[5] On sabbe 'va santâ compare ubho 'va santâ in the ninth Nissaggiya, and the Old Commentary loc. cit.

Whosoever have incurred a fault, let him declare it! If no fault have been incurred it is meet to keep silence!

Now, venerable Sirs, it is by your silence, that I shall know whether you are pure. As to each one question put there must be an answer, so, in such a meeting as this, each question is put[1] as many as three times. Then if any Bhikkhu, when it has been three times put, knowingly omit to declare a fault incurred, he is guilty of uttering a conscious lie. Venerable Sirs, the uttering of a deliberate lie has been declared by the Blessed One to be a condition hurtful (to spiritual progress)[2]. Therefore a fault, if there be one, should be declared by that Bhikkhu who remembers it, and desires to be cleansed therefrom. For a fault, when declared, shall be light to him.

Venerable Sirs, the Introduction is now recited.

Thus do I question you, venerable Sirs, 'Are you pure in this matter?'

A second time do I question you, 'Are you pure in this matter?'

A third time do I question you, 'Are you pure in this matter?'

The venerable ones are pure herein. Therefore do they keep silence. Thus I understand.

Here endeth the recitation of the Introduction.

---

[1] The spelling of the Pâli word in the text should be anussâvita*m*, and so below, anussâviyamâne. By 'the text' we refer throughout to Mr. Dickson's very careful edition, all the necessary corrections in which—they are mostly only misprints—will be noticed in the following notes.

[2] See Mahâvagga II, 3, 7.

PÂRÂ*G*IKÂ DHAMMÂ.

THE PÂRÂ*G*IKA RULES[1].

Here these four Rules, concerning those acts which bring about Defeat[2], come into recitation.

1. Whatsoever Bhikkhu who has taken upon

[1] The whole of the following portion of the Pâtimokkha, together with the ancient commentary upon it, is contained in the first book of the Vibhaṅga, also called the Pârâ*g*ika*m*.

Dickson translates throughout Dhammâ by 'offences.' He is no doubt right in taking the word, not in its ordinary sense of condition or quality, but in a more strictly technical, legal, sense. 'Offences' is however not the right direction in which to limit the general sense. Dhammâ must here be 'Rules,' in accordance with the passages quoted in our Introduction, pp. xxviii–xxx.

[2] Childers (sub voce) follows Burnouf (Introduction, &c., p. 301) in deriving the word Pârâ*g*ika from A*G* with parâ prefixed, taking that compound in the sense of 'to expel.' Dickson's translation 'deadly sin' rests upon the same basis. The Buddhist commentators refer the word to the passive of *G*I with parâ prefixed, in the sense of 'to suffer defeat.' So the Samanta-Pâsâdikâ: Pârâ*g*iko hotîti parâ*g*ito parâ*g*aya*m* âpanno. Now the root A*G* belongs to the Vedic dialect only, and is not met with in any Buddhist expressions, and even in the Vedas it does not occur with parâ prefixed. The Buddhist forms of speech have quite different and settled terms with which to convey the idea of expulsion. On the other hand, there was a considerable group of words in use in the Buddhist community with which pârâ*g*ika stands in close connection: parâ*g*i, 'to suffer defeat;' parâ*g*ita, 'defeated;' parâ*g*aya, 'defeat.' We cannot therefore but think that the native commentators are right in associating pârâ*g*ika also with this group, and that the word really means 'involving defeat.' This may mean specifically defeat in the struggle with Mâra the Evil One; but more probably defeat in the struggle against evil generally, defeat in the effort to accomplish the object for which the Bhikkhu entered the Order, in the effort to reach the 'supreme goal' of Arahatship.

himself the Bhikkhus' system of self-training and rule of life, and has not thereafter withdrawn from the training, or declared his weakness, shall have carnal knowledge of any one, down even to an animal, he has fallen into defeat, he is no longer in communion[1].

2. Whatsoever Bhikkhu shall take, from village or from wood, anything not given—what men call 'theft[2]'—in such manner of taking as kings would seize the thief for, and slay, or bind, or banish him, saying, 'Thou art a thief, thou art stupid, thou art a fool, thou art dishonest,'—the Bhikkhu who in that manner takes the thing not given, he, too, has fallen into defeat, he is no longer in communion.

3. Whatsoever Bhikkhu shall knowingly deprive of life a human being, or shall seek out an assassin against a human being, or shall utter the praises of death, or incite another to self-destruction, saying, 'Ho! my friend! what good do you get from this sinful, wretched life? death is better to thee than life!'—if, so thinking, and with such an aim, he, by various argument, utter the praises of death or incite another to self-destruction—he, too, is fallen into defeat, he is no longer in communion[3].

---

[1] 'Declared his weakness' refers to the permission (on the ground that it was better to leave the Order than to burn) for a Bhikkhu to acknowledge himself unfit for the discipline, and throw off the robe. 'Withdrawn from the training' is the formal expression for thus throwing off the Robes. See below, Mahâvagga II, 22, 3.

On sikkhâsâ*g*îva*m*, which is by no means only 'Rules of the Order,' see the Vibhaṅga (Pâr. I, 8, 1).

[2] The Vibhaṅga (Pâr. II, 3) takes theyya-sa*m*khâta*m* as meaning 'with dishonest intent.'

[3] The deviations here from Mr. Dickson's version will, we hope, justify themselves. There is no commentary on hâraka, though

4. Whatsoever Bhikkhu, without being clearly conscious of extraordinary qualities, shall give out regarding himself that insight into the knowledge of the noble ones has been accomplished, saying, 'Thus do I know,' 'Thus do I perceive:' and at some subsequent time whether on being pressed, or without being pressed, he, feeling guilty, shall be desirous of being cleansed from his fault, and shall say, 'Brethren! when I knew not, I said that I knew; when I saw not, I said that I saw—telling a fruitless falsehood;' then, unless he so spake through undue confidence he, too, has fallen into defeat, he is no longer in communion[1].

Venerable Sirs, the four Conditions of Defeat have been recited, of which when a Bhikkhu has fallen into one or other, he is no longer allowed to be in co-residence with the Bhikkhus. As before, so afterwards, he is defeated, he is not in communion[2].

---

the Vibhaṅga (Pâr. III, 3, 1) explains the different kinds of Sattha. Pâpaka must be 'sinful,' not merely 'poor;' the suggestion is 'by destroying your life you will escape from the possibility of sinning.'

[1] The extraordinary qualities (literally, 'superhuman qualities') are defined to be the Vimokkhas, Samâdhis, the Samâpattis, the *Ñâṇa*-dassana, the having experienced the Noble Path, and having realised the Fruit thereof; that is to say, Arahatship and the highest forms of spiritual emotion and intelligence which can accompany Arahatship. They are in fact, therefore, superhuman only in the sense of extraordinary; as it is precisely human beings, and only human beings, who were supposed to be able to acquire these qualities.

Uddha*kk*a, 'Self-righteousness,' is also the last but one of the ten Sa*m*yo*g*anas, or 'Fetters,' which the Arahat has to break.

[2] The sentences which follow in the text, but are not here translated, and in which it is declared that all the following portions of the Pâtimokkha have already been heard, do not occur in the Vibhaṅga. They are not part of the Pâtimokkha; but only the

In respect of them I ask the venerable ones, 'Are you pure in this matter?'

A second time I ask, 'Are you pure in this matter?'

A third time I ask, 'Are you pure in this matter?'

The venerable ones are pure herein. Therefore do they keep silence. Thus I understand.

Here endeth the recitation of the Pârâ*g*ikas.

---

form to be used, when the Pâtimokkha cannot be recited in full, and all the remaining Rules are to be omitted. According to Mahâvagga II, 15, 1, 4 this abridged recital may be used in certain cases of danger.

On Yathâ pure tatha pa*kkh*â there is no explanation in the Old Commentary. The phrase probably means that the Bhikkhu is irrevocably defeated. He must remain for ever in the condition (of permanent exclusion from the Order) into which he has brought himself.

SA*M*GHÂDISESÂ DHAMMÂ.

RULES WHICH REQUIRE, AS WELL IN THEIR EARLIER AS IN THEIR LATER STAGES, FORMAL MEETINGS OF THE ORDER[1].

Here, venerable Sirs, the thirteen matters, which, as well in their earlier as in their later stages, require formal meetings of the Order, come into recitation.

1. The emission of semen by design, except by a person sleeping, is a Sa*m*ghâdisesa.

2. Whatsoever Bhikkhu, being degraded[2], shall, with perverted[3] mind, come into bodily contact with a woman, by taking hold of her hand, or by taking hold of her hair, or by touching any part of her body—that is a Sa*m*ghâdisesa.

3. Whatsoever Bhikkhu, being degraded, shall, with perverted mind, address a woman with wicked words, exciting to passion as those of a young man to a maid—that is a Sa*m*ghâdisesa[4].

---

[1] The expression is curious, but the authorities given by Childers (sub voce) are decisive as to its meaning. Whereas the Pârâ*g*ika offences were dealt with in one meeting of the Order, these thirteen offences gave rise to the various Sa*m*ghakammas (formal resolutions or proceedings at meetings of the Order), which are explained in detail in the third Khandhaka of the *K*ullavagga.

The text of, and the ancient commentary on this portion of the Pâtimokkha will be found in the Vibhaṅga in the Book on the Sa*m*ghâdisesas.

[2] Oti*nn*o, literally, 'having gone down,' which the old commentator in the Vibhaṅga explains as 'lustfully, or with a mind bound by desire.' Our word 'degraded' has often a very similar connotation.

[3] Vipari*n*atena, literally, 'changed;' here 'changed for the worse.' Compare Mahâ-sudassana Sutta II, 39, and the Old Comment at Minayeff, p. 64.

[4] Compare the second Aniyata.

4. Whatsoever Bhikkhu, being degraded, shall, with perverted mind, magnify, in the hearing of a woman, ministration to himself[1] (by saying), 'This, Sister, would be the noblest of ministrations, that to so righteous and exalted a religious person as myself you should ministrate by that act,' (meaning) sexual intercourse—that is a Sa*m*ghâdisesa.

5. Whatsoever Bhikkhu shall act as a go-between for a woman to a man, or for a man to a woman, or for a wife, or for a paramour, or even for a harlot—that is a Sa*m*ghâdisesa.

6. A Bhikkhu who, begging (the materials) together, is having a hut put up for his own use, to belong to no one (else), must have it made of due measurement. And herein this is the measurement—in length twelve spans according to the accepted span[2], in breadth seven spans (measured) inside.

---

[1] Attakâmapâri*k*ariyâ, perhaps 'to his lusts;' but we follow the old commentator.

[2] Sugata-vidatthiyâ. Dickson translates 'of the span of Buddha,' Sugata being one of the many epithets applied to the Buddha in poetry, or poetical prose. Mr. James D'Alwis in the Ceylon Asiatic Society's Journal for 1874 has a long article to show that this cannot be the correct meaning of the word 'Sugata' in this connection; and we think he is right, though his discussion as to what it does mean (evidently more than a simple span) seems to lead to no certain conclusion. The older Ceylon commentators take the expression as being equal to one and a half carpenter's cubits, a 'carpenter's cubit' (Si*m*halese Wa*d*u-riyana) being two ordinary cubits, so that 'the Buddha's span' (as they translate it) would be four feet and a half! But the Bhikkhus of the present day in Ceylon take it to be equal to the length of the supposed foot-print of the Buddha on Adam's Peak; that is, four ordinary cubits, or six feet. See Dickson's note; and compare Nissaggiya 15, and Pâ*k*ittiya 87–92.

There is no comment on the phrase in the Old Commentary,

The Bhikkhus must be brought to the place to approve the site; and those Bhikkhus shall approve a site free from danger[1], and with an open space around it[2]. If a Bhikkhu shall, at his own request, have a hut put up on a dangerous site, without the open space around it, or shall not bring the Bhikkhus to approve the site, or shall exceed the (due) measure—that is a Samghâdisesa.

7. A Bhikkhu who is having a large[3] residence made for his own use, and to belong (also) to others, shall bring the Bhikkhus to the place to approve the site; and those Bhikkhus shall approve a site free from danger, and with an open space around it. If a Bhikkhu shall have a large residence made on a dangerous site, without the open space around it, or shall not bring the Bhikkhus to the place to approve the site—that is a Samghâdisesa.

8. Whatsoever Bhikkhu[4], in harshness, malice, or anger, shall harass (another) Bhikkhu by a groundless (charge of having committed) a Pârâgika offence, thinking to himself, 'Perchance I may (thus) get him to fall from this religious life[5]'—and then at some later time, either when he is pressed, or without his being pressed, the case turns out to be groundless,

---

which is especially curious if the word Sugata meant 'the Buddha's,' that is to say, the Buddha's span, when that work was composed.

[1] That is, either to living creatures (birds, ants, and so on) by clearing the site; or to the future resident after it is built. See the old commentator's note on Sârambha at Minayeff, p. 71.

[2] 'Sufficient for a cart drawn by a yoke of oxen to pass round it,' according to the old commentator.

[3] Mahallaka. Compare Kullavagga VI, 11, 1.

[4] In the text read, of course, Bhikkhu, not Bhikkhû.

[5] I. e. to throw off the robes, to leave the Order.

and the Bhikkhu confesses his malice[1]—that is a Sa*m*ghâdisesa.

9. Whatsoever Bhikkhu, in harshness, malice, or anger, shall harass another Bhikkhu by a groundless charge of having committed a Pârâ*g*ika offence, supporting himself by some point or other of no importance in a case that really rests on something of a different kind; thinking to himself, 'Perchance I may thus get him to fall from this religious life'—and then at some later time, either when he is pressed, or without his being pressed, the case turns out to rest on something of a different kind, and that Bhikkhu confesses his malice—that is a Sa*m*ghâdisesa[2].

10. Whatsoever Bhikkhu shall go about to cause division in a community[3] that is at union, or shall persist in calling attention to some matter calculated to cause division, that Bhikkhu should thus be addressed by the Bhikkhus: 'Sir, go not about to cause division in a community that is at union;' or, 'Persist not in calling attention to a matter calculated to cause division;' 'Be, Sir, at one with the community, for the community, being at unity, in harmony, without dispute, dwells pleasantly under

[1] Dosa*m* was probably meant here to refer to the doso at the beginning of the rule.

[2] For instance, the Bhikkhu has seen that A, who is a Khattiya, has committed some offence. He says either that he has seen a Khattiya commit that offence, and thus harasses an innocent person; or he says that A has committed a Pârâ*g*ika offence, whereas the offence is of a lesser nature.

For *k*aveyyan in the text read *k*âveyyan.

[3] Sa*m*gha; that is, the company of the Brethren dwelling in one place, or in one district.

one authority[1].' If that Bhikkhu, when he has thus been spoken to by the Bhikkhus, should persist as before, then let that Bhikkhu be (formally) admonished about it by the Bhikkhus as a body[2], even to the third time, to the intent that he abandon that course. If, while being so admonished up to the third time, he abandon that course, it is well: if he abandon it not—that is a Sa*m*ghâdisesa.

11. Now if other Bhikkhus, one, or two, or three, become adherents of that Bhikkhu, and raise their voices on his side; if they should say thus: 'Say not, Sirs, anything against that Bhikkhu! That Bhikkhu both speaks according to the Dhamma, and he speaks according to the Vinaya; it is our wish, too, and desire, that he adopts, and gives expression to; and he speaks, knowing that what he says appears to us also to be right:'—then let those Bhikkhus be addressed by the Bhikkhus thus: 'Say not so, Sirs! That Bhikkhu speaks not according to the Dhamma, neither does he speak according to the Vinaya. Let not, Sirs, the causing of division in the community be pleasing to you! Be, Sirs, at one with the community! for the community, being at unity, in harmony, without dispute, dwells pleasantly under one discipline.' If those Bhikkhus, when they have thus been spoken to by the Bhikkhus, should persist as before, those Bhikkhus should be

[1] Ekuddeso; that is, the authority of the rules recited in the Pâtimokkha.

[2] Samanubhâsitabbo. We think 'admonish' is not too strong a rendering of this term; and not inconsistent with the equality of the fraternity, as the admonition comes from the united body. The preposition sam need not imply a Sa*m*ghakamma, which appears to have been necessary only after the Sa*m*ghâdisesa offence had been completed. We occasionally render the word by 'adjure.'

(formally) adjured by the Bhikkhus, as a body, even to the third time, to the end that they abandon that course. If, while being so adjured, up to the third time, they abandon that course, it is well: if they abandon it not—that is a Sa*m*ghâdisesa.

12. Should a Bhikkhu refuse to listen to what is said to him[1]; and when spoken to by the Bhikkhus, in accordance with the Dhamma[2], touching the precepts handed down in the body of recited law[3], will allow nothing to be said to him (objecting), 'Say nothing to me, Sirs, either good or bad: and I will say nothing, either good or bad, to you. Be good enough, Sirs, to refrain from speaking to me!'—then let that Bhikkhu be addressed by the Bhikkhus thus: 'Do not, Sir, make yourself a person who cannot be spoken to: make yourself rather, Sir, a person to whom we can speak. Speak to the Bhikkhus, Sir, in accordance with the Dhamma; and the Bhikkhus, Sir, will speak in accordance with the Dhamma to you. For thus has the church[4] of the Blessed One grown large; that is to say, by mutual converse, and by mutual help[5].' If that Bhikkhu, when he has thus been spoken to by the Bhikkhus, should persist as before, then let that Bhikkhu be

---

[1] Dubba*k*o is not 'unruly,' as Dickson has, following Childers, who gives 'abusive, unruly, violent.' It means rather 'difficult to reason with, averse to instruction.' Compare *G*âtaka I, 151, 152.

[2] Sahadhammika*m*, which is here adverbial; and where the Dhamma refers to the Rules, as is pointed out in the Introduction.

[3] Uddesa-pariyâpannesu; uddesa being here practically the same as Pâtimokkha.

[4] Parisâ, 'the retinue, the followers, the adherents,' referring here to the Sa*m*gha only.

[5] In the text read vu*tth*âpanena.

(formally) adjured by the Bhikkhus as a body, even to the third time, to the end that he abandon that course. If, while being so adjured, up to the third time, he abandon that course, it is well: if he abandon it not—that is a Samghâdisesa.

13. Should a Bhikkhu dwell near a certain village or town, leading a life hurtful to the laity, and devoted to evil, (so that) his evil deeds are seen and heard, and the families led astray by him are seen and heard, let that Bhikkhu be spoken to by the Bhikkhus thus: 'Your life, Sir, is hurtful to the laity, and evil; your evil deeds, Sir, are seen and heard; and families are seen and heard to be led astray by you. Be so good, Sir, as to depart from this residence; you have dwelt here, Sir, long enough.' If, when that Bhikkhu is thus addressed by the Bhikkhus he should answer the Bhikkhus thus: 'The Bhikkhus are walking in longing, the Bhikkhus are walking in malice, the Bhikkhus are walking in delusion, the Bhikkhus are walking in fear; and, for a fault of a like nature, they send some away, and some they send not away[1]:'—then that Bhikkhu should be spoken to by the Bhikkhus thus: 'Say not so, Sir! The Bhikkhus walk not in longing, the Bhikkhus walk not in malice, the Bhikkhus walk not in delusion, the Bhikkhus walk not in fear; and they send not some away, for a fault of a like nature, while they send others not away. Your life, Sir, is hurtful to the laity, and evil; your evil deeds, Sir, are seen and heard, and families are seen and heard, Sir, to be led astray by you. Be so good, Sir, as to depart from this residence; you have dwelt

[1] On the use of Pabbâgeti in this sense comp. the 2nd Pâr.

here, Sir, long enough.' If that Bhikkhu, when thus spoken to by the Bhikkhus should persist as before, that Bhikkhu should be (formally) adjured by the Bhikkhus as a body, even to the third time, to the end that he abandon that course. If, while being so adjured, up to the third time, he abandon that course, it is well: if he abandon it not—that is a Sa*m*ghâdisesa.

Venerable Sirs, the thirteen matters which require, as well in their earlier as in their later stages, formal meetings of the Order, have been recited; nine which become offences at once, and four which are not completed until the third admonition.

If a Bhikkhu have committed either one or other of these[1], for as many days as he knowingly conceals his sin, for so many days must that Bhikkhu, even against his will, remain in probation[2]. When the probation is over, that Bhikkhu must, for six further days, undergo the Mânatta discipline[3] (Penance). When the Penance has been removed, that Bhikkhu must be reinstated in some place where the community of the Bhikkhus forms a body of twenty. If a community of Bhikkhus forming a body of less than twenty, even by one, should reinstate that Bhikkhu, he is not reinstated, and that community is blameworthy. This is the proper course in that case.

---

[1] Literally, 'of which.' In the text there should be no full stop after yâvatatiyakâ.

[2] On the regulations respecting Parivâsa (Probation), see *K*ullavagga II, 1–3.

[3] On the regulations respecting Mânatta (Penance), see *K*ullavagga II, 6–8.

In respect of them I ask the venerable ones, 'Are you pure in this matter?'

A second time I ask the venerable ones, 'Are you pure in this matter?'

A third time I ask the venerable ones, 'Are you pure in this matter?'

The venerable ones are pure herein. Therefore do they keep silence. Thus I understand.

Here endeth the recitation of the Samghâdisesas.

ANIYATÂ DHAMMÂ[1].

Rules regarding Undetermined Matters.

Here, venerable Sirs, the two Rules regarding undetermined matters come into recitation.

1. Whatsoever Bhikkhu shall take a seat with a woman, one man with one woman, in secret, on a secluded seat, suitable[2] (for sexual intercourse); and if a believing woman, trustworthy of speech, who has seen (them so), shall lay it to his charge under one or other of three Rules, either under the Pârâ*g*ika[3], or under the Sa*m*ghâdisesa[4], or under the Pâ*k*ittiya[5] Rules:—let then that Bhikkhu, if he acknowledge that he has so sat, be dealt with (according to the circumstances reported) for a Pârâ*g*ika, or for a Sa*m*ghâdisesa, or for a Pâ*k*ittiya; or let that Bhikkhu be dealt with under that one of those three Rules under which the believing woman, trustworthy in speech, shall lay it to his charge.

This rule relates to a matter undetermined.

2. And furthermore, even if the seat be not secluded, and not convenient (for sexual intercourse), but be convenient for addressing a woman with wicked words[6], then whatsoever Bhikkhu shall take

[1] The whole of the following portion of the Pâtimokkha, together with the Old Commentary on it, recurs in the Vibhaṅga, Book III.

[2] Ala*m*kammaniye, an expression found only in this passage. The Vibhaṅga interprets it as above (Aniyata I, 2, 1).

[3] The 1st Pârâ*g*ika. [4] The 2nd Sa*m*ghâdisesa.

[5] Pâ*k*ittiya 44, 45; and compare also 7, 27.

[6] Compare the 3rd Sa*m*ghâdisesa, and probably the 4th is also referred to.

a seat with a woman, one man with one woman, in secret, on such a seat, and a believing woman, trustworthy in speech, who has seen (them so), shall lay it to his charge under one or other of two Rules, either under the Sa*m*ghâdisesa, or under the Pâ*k*ittiya Rule—let then that Bhikkhu, if he acknowledge that he has so sat, be dealt with (according to the circumstances reported) for a Sa*m*ghâdisesa, or for a Pâ*k*ittiya; or let that Bhikkhu be dealt with under that one of those two Rules under which the believing woman, trustworthy in speech, shall lay it to his charge.

This rule relates to a matter undetermined.

Venerable Sirs, the two Rules regarding uncertain matters have been recited.

In respect of them I ask the venerable ones, 'Are you pure in this matter?'

A second time I ask the venerable ones, 'Are you pure in this matter?'

A third time I ask the venerable ones, 'Are you pure in this matter?'

The venerable ones are pure herein. Therefore do they keep silence. Thus I understand.

Here endeth the recitation of the Aniyatas.

NISSAGGIYÂ PÂ*K*ITTIYÂ DHAMMÂ.

Pâ*k*ittiya Rules involving Forfeiture.

Here, venerable Sirs, the thirty Pâ*k*ittiya Rules involving forfeiture come into recitation.

1. When the robes have been settled, when the Ka*th*ina has been taken up by the Bhikkhu, an extra robe may be kept up to the end of a period of ten days. To him who goes beyond that there is a Pâ*k*ittiya offence involving forfeiture[1].

[1] The following Rules, most of which have long ago fallen into abeyance, depend in great measure upon communistic customs of the ancient Fraternity, which are now somewhat difficult to understand. The following explanation of this rule, and more especially of the first few words of it, is therefore submitted with diffidence. At the end of the Vassa period (see below, Mahâvagga, Books III and VII) the Sa*m*gha, or community of brethren in any place, was accustomed to give over to some one of the Bhikkhus such store of robes (Ka*th*ina-dussa) as it possessed; and it should here be observed that no Bhikkhu had a separate personal ownership over his robes, though nominally given to him for his own use, and really his own subject to the rules, they were, technically speaking, the property of the whole Sa*m*gha (that is, here, of the Order as a whole, not of the community residing together at that place). The Bhikkhu above referred to then spread the store of robes out to dry (suriye attharati); and afterwards satisfied out of it the wants of any brother whose robes, through the dampness of the season or other causes, had become spoiled. Meanwhile, each of the Bhikkhus had, of course, to wear something—it being one of the points most frequently insisted upon that a Bhikkhu should be decently clad, in direct contradiction to certain then popular views as to the sanctity of nakedness—but, during the interval, some of the rules about the robes were temporarily relaxed.

Now the Mahâvagga (VII, 1, 7) gives eight reasons by which the Ka*th*ina license would be extinguished for any one particular Bhikkhu alone—as it would be for the community at that place

2. When the robes have been settled, after the taking up of the Ka*th*ina by the Bhikkhu, if a Bhikkhu be without his three robes, even for a single night, unless with the permission of the Bhikkhus—that is a Pâ*k*ittiya offence involving forfeiture[1].

---

by the formal 'taking up of the store of robes' (Ka*th*inuddhâra or Ka*th*inassa ubbhâra);—and with it that Bhikkhu's claim to a share in the common store. These eight reasons are merely eight ways in which that particular Bhikkhu's wants are already amply supplied; and the necessity, in his case, for a relaxation of the rules no longer exists.

One of these reasons is that his set of robes is settled or done for (*k*îvara*m* ni*tth*ita*m*); which, according to the old commentator on our rule here, means that his set has been made, or spoiled, or destroyed, or burnt, or that his hope of receiving one from the laity has been disappointed (ni*tth*ita*k*îvarasmin ti *k*îvara*m* kata*m* vâ hoti na*tth*a*m* vâ vina*tth*a*m* vâ da*ddh*a*m* vâ *k*îvarâsâ vâ upa*kkh*innâ, according to which the Scholion in Dickson's note must be corrected). In each of these cases his wants are already supplied by the set of robes he has retained for wear during the process of drying: only the case of those Bhikkhus remains to be settled who have not had new robes made, and whose old ones were still good enough to wear during that process.

After the Ka*th*inuddhâra, either particular or general, no Bhikkhu can retain for his own use an atireka-*k*îvara, a spare robe. He must give it up to any brother who has need of it.

As to the 'ten days,' the Sutta Vibhaṅga has the following story. Ânanda, after the Ka*th*inuddhâra, has a spare robe. He wants to give it to Sâriputta; but the latter is in Sâketa, and is not expected back till the ninth or tenth day. So the Buddha, to meet such cases, establishes the rule that the spare robe may be kept up to the tenth day.

The words 'a Pâ*k*ittiya offence involving forfeiture,' repeated at the end of each of the Nissaggiyas, are intended to mean that that offence involves, firstly, all that a Pâ*k*ittiya involves; and secondly, forfeiture.

[1] To this Rule there is the following story in the Sutta Vibhaṅga. Certain Bhikkhus left their robes in charge of the other Bhikkhus,

3. When the robes have been settled, when the Ka*th*ina has been taken up by the Bhikkhu, if a set of robes should be offered to a Bhikkhu out of season, it may be accepted by that Bhikkhu, should he so wish. But when he has accepted it, it must be made up at once; and if it be not sufficient for him, it may be kept up to the end of a month by that Bhikkhu should he have any hope that the deficiency may be supplied. If he keep it beyond that time, even if there be hope of (the deficiency) being supplied—that is a Pâ*k*ittiya offence requiring forfeiture.

4. Whatsoever Bhikkhu shall have his soiled robe[1] washed, or dyed, or beaten by a Bhikkhunî (sister)[2] who is not related to him—that is a Pâ*k*ittiya offence involving forfeiture[3].

5. Whatsoever Bhikkhu shall receive a robe from the hands of a Bhikkhunî not related to him, except in exchange—that is a Pâ*k*ittiya offence involving forfeiture.

6. Whatsoever Bhikkhu shall ask a householder, or a householder's wife[4], not being related to him,

and went on a journey. The robes, being laid by for a long time, became spoilt. The Buddha thereupon forbad a Bhikkhu, under the circumstances stated in this Rule, to separate himself from his robes (ti-*k*îvara).

As regards the permission we have the story that a sick Bhikkhu was invited home that his friends might nurse him. He answers, 'The Blessed One has forbidden us to separate ourselves from our robes. I am sick, and unable to travel in my robes.' Then the Blessed One allows a sick brother to obtain leave to dispense with the Rule.

[1] Literally, 'an old robe,' which the Vibhaṅga (Nissaggiya IV, 2, 1) explains as one that has been once worn.

[2] And so, frequently, below.

[3] Compare the 17th Nissaggiya.

[4] Householder is here gahapati; that is, pater familias. See Rh. D.'s note on Mahâ-sudassana Sutta I, 41.

for a robe, except at the right season—that is a Pâ*k*ittiya offence involving forfeiture.

Here the right season means when the Bhikkhu has been robbed of his robe, or when his robe has been destroyed. This is the right season in this connection.

7. If the householder, or the householder's wife, should offer him a choice[1] from (the materials for) many robes, that Bhikkhu may have robes made out of it up to the (due portion of) inner and outer robes. If he has robes made beyond this limit—that is a Pâ*k*ittiya offence involving forfeiture.

8. In case the value in barter of a set of robes has been laid by, for a particular Bhikkhu, by a householder who is not a relative of his, or a householder's lady, with the intention 'I will get a set of robes in exchange for this robe-fund, and so provide a dress for such and such a Bhikkhu:'—in that case,

---

[1] One MS. of the Vibhaṅga reads abhiha*t*u*m*; but another reads abhiha*tth*u*m*, as does Minayeff; while the Samanta-Pâsâdikâ makes it equal to abhiharitu*m*. The right reading is probably abhiha*tth*u*m*. In any case, the unusual form and grammatical construction throw some doubt on the exact meaning of the phrase. The Samanta-Pâsâdikâ, which explains it philologically as just mentioned, goes on in the next words to explain it syntactically as abhiharitvâ, which it refers to the subject of pavâreyya, and states could be done either actually, or by words. Dickson's rendering, 'arrange to supply him,' does not accurately convey the force of pavâreyya; but the right rendering may be 'should offer to bring forth for him (whatever he chose) from (amongst the material for) many robes.' The only possible alternative is 'should make him an offer to take whatever he chose from amongst the material for many robes.' Compare the 34th Pâ*k*ittiya.

Santar-uttara-parama*m* is meant, according to the Vibhaṅga, to imply 'to the extent of one inner, and one outer robe;' but we preserve the ambiguity of the text.

if that Bhikkhu, before the offer has been made to him, go and give directions as to the make of the robe, saying, 'It would be well, Sir, to get in exchange such and such a sort of robe with that robe-fund to clothe me with;' desiring something fine—that is a Pâ*k*ittiya offence involving forfeiture[1].

9. In case two persons, householders or householders' ladies, have each laid by for a particular Bhikkhu the value in barter of a set of robes, with the intention, 'We will each get a set of robes in exchange for this robe-fund, and so provide a dress for such and such a Bhikkhu:'—in that case, if that Bhikkhu, before the offer has been made to him, go and give directions as to the make of the robe, saying, 'It would be well, Sirs, to get in exchange, with the value in barter you have each laid by, such and such a sort of robe to clothe me with, the two becoming one:' desiring something fine—that is a Pâ*k*ittiya offence involving forfeiture.

10. In case a Râ*g*a, or a Khattiya, or a Brâhman, or a Gahapati should send by messenger, for a particular Bhikkhu, the value in barter of a set of robes, saying, 'Get a set of robes in exchange for this robe-fund, and provide a dress for such and such a Bhikkhu!' if then that messenger should go to that Bhikkhu and say, 'I have brought, Sir, this robe-fund for your reverence. May your reverence

[1] Both Dickson and Childers have gone too far in rendering *k*etâpetvâ by 'purchase.' The Samanta-Pâsâdikâ (Minayeff, 78) explains it by parivattetvâ. So Rh. D., 'Ancient Coins and Measures of Ceylon,' p. 6.

In the text read *K*etâpana*m* (compare Ka*kk*âyana, p. 322 of Senart's edition); and it should not be rendered 'money;' see Rh. D., loc. cit. The 'Robe-fund' consisted of things for barter.

In the text the vâ after a*ññ*âtakassa should be omitted.

accept the robe-fund!' let then that monk answer that messenger thus: 'We do not, my friend, accept the value in barter for a set of robes; but we may accept a set of robes, at the right time, and of the suitable kind.' If then that messenger shall answer that Bhikkhu thus: 'Has then your reverence a person who attends (to such matters for you)?' then, Bhikkhus[1], let the Bhikkhu, to whom the robes are to belong, point out, as his agent, the man who keeps the ârâma in order[2], or some believer, saying, 'This man, my friend, is the Bhikkhus' agent.' If then that messenger, when he has made an appointment with that agent, shall come to that Bhikkhu, and say, 'I have made an appointment, Sir, with that agent whom your reverence pointed out. Let your reverence come, and he will clothe you with the set of robes betimes!' then, Bhikkhus[1], let that Bhikkhu, to whom the set of robes is to belong, go to the agent and warn him and remind him two or three times, saying, 'Sir, I have need of a set of robes!' If, while so warning and reminding[3] two or three times, he should succeed in obtaining

[1] This word of address is most noteworthy as standing quite isolated in the Pâtimokkha. It must be meant as an address by the Buddha himself to the Brethren; for, if it were the address of the Bhikkhu reciting the Pâtimokkha, the expression used would necessarily be âyasmanto, as in the closing words of each chapter, or other words to that effect. That it should have been left in is a striking proof of the faithfulness with which the Pâtimokkha has been preserved. Is it a survival of some form of words older even than the Pâtimokkha? or is it merely an ancient blunder?

[2] The ârâma is, literally, the grove or pleasure-ground in which the monks' residence stood; but it had probably before this already come to include the residence, or vihâra, itself.

[3] In the text read *k*odayamâno, sârayamâno; the medial participle with active sense, as often.

the robes, it is well. Should he not succeed in obtaining them, let him up to the fourth, fifth, or sixth time go and stand silently on that matter[1]. If, while so standing silently on that matter up to the fourth, fifth, or sixth time, he should succeed in obtaining the set of robes, it is well. Should he not succeed in obtaining them (so), and then, exerting himself beyond that point succeed in obtaining them—that is a Pâkittiya offence involving forfeiture. (But) if he should not succeed in obtaining them, let him either go himself, or send a messenger (to the place) whence the robe-fund was brought to him, and say, 'The robe-fund which your reverences sent for a Bhikkhu, that has in no wise advantaged that Bhikkhu. Take heed, your reverences, of your own, that your own go not to ruin!' This is the proper course in that case[2].

Here ends the first section,
the 'Robe-section.'

11. Whatsoever Bhikkhu shall have a rug or mat made with silk in it—that is a Pâkittiya offence involving forfeiture[3].

[1] In the text read *kh*akkhattuparama*m*. This silent standing is the only mode of asking for food permitted to a Bhikkhu.

[2] Both here, and in the Conclusion of the Sa*m*ghâdisesa, and further below in the 22nd Nissaggiya, where the same phrase occurs, Mr. Dickson takes it to mean, 'This is the way to Nirvâ*n*a.' We are unable to see any foundation for such a rendering.

[3] The following rules were for use in a tropical climate, and refer not to bed coverings, but to materials spread over a hard seat or couch. The word translated 'rug or mat' is a more general term, meaning 'a thing spread;' but there is no corres-

12. Whatsoever Bhikkhu shall have a rug or mat made of pure black wool of goats' hair[1]—that is a Pâkittiya offence involving forfeiture.

13. In case a Bhikkhu is having a new rug made, two parts should be taken of pure black wool of goats' hair, the third part of white wool, and the fourth of the colour of oxen (reddish brown). If a Bhikkhu should have a new rug made without taking two parts of pure black wool, the third of white, and the fourth of tawny—that is a Pâkittiya offence involving forfeiture[2].

14. When a Bhikkhu has had a new rug made, he should use it for six years. If he should have another new rug made within the six years, whether he has got rid, or has not got rid of the former one, unless with the permission of the Bhikkhus[3]—that is a Pâkittiya offence involving forfeiture.

15. When a Bhikkhu is having a new rug made to sit upon, a piece of the breadth of the accepted span[4] must be taken from all round the old one in

---

ponding word in English, as 'coverlet' or 'counterpane' would imply a different state of things.

[1] The Sutta Vibhaṅga says that kâlaka is of two kinds, either gâtiyâ kâlaka or ragana-kâlaka; that is, that the wool is either naturally black, or dyed of that colour. Elaka is a goat, not a sheep.

[2] This is deliberately chosen as an ugly mixture, which would lessen the commercial value of the rug, by making it unfashionable.

[3] Regarding this permission the Vibhaṅga gives the following story. A sick monk was asked by his relatives to come home, that they might nurse him. He answered that he was too ill to carry his rug, could not get on without one, and could not have a new one made within six years. Then the Blessed One established this exception to the general Rule.

[4] See the note on the 6th Samghâdisesa.

order to disfigure it. If a Bhikkhu should have a new seat-rug made without taking a span's width from all round the old one—that is a Pâkittiya offence involving forfeiture.

16. In case a Bhikkhu should get some goats' wool whilst he is on a journey [1], let him accept it, if he likes; and when he has accepted it, he may carry it in his own hand, if there are no porters, for the distance of three leagues [2]. Should he carry it further than that, even if there are no porters—that is a Pâkittiya offence involving forfeiture.

17. Whatsoever Bhikkhu shall get goats' wool washed, or dyed, or combed out by a Bhikkhunî who is not related to him—that is a Pâkittiya offence involving forfeiture [3].

18. Whatsoever Bhikkhu shall receive gold or silver, or get some one to receive it for him, or allow it to be kept in deposit for him [4]—that is a Pâkittiya offence involving forfeiture.

---

[1] Addhâna-magga-patipanno; which the Kaṅkhâ Vitaranî (Minayeff, p. 80) explains as being on a long road, called addhâna (high-road). But one may be on a high-road without going a long journey.

[2] Yoganas; a yogana being a trifle under eight miles. See Rh. D., 'Ancient Coins and Measures' &c., pp. 16, 17.

[3] Compare the 4th Nissaggiya.

[4] Upanikkhittam vâ sâdiyeyya; which cannot possibly mean 'if he thinks to appropriate money entrusted to him,' as Mr. Dickson translates. See Rh. D., 'Ancient Coins' &c., p. 7.

The method of procedure on a breach of this rule, or of the next, is thus described in the Vibhaṅga. The guilty Bhikkhu has to give up the gold or silver to the community (Samgha, not here, as elsewhere in sentences concerning forfeiture, 'or to a gana or to a puggala'). Then when an ârâmika or an upâsaka comes, it is to be given to him, to buy ghee or oil with it for the Samgha; and whatever is bought is the common property of all the Samgha, save the guilty Bhikkhu. Should the layman object to undertake the

19. Whatsoever Bhikkhu shall engage in any one of the various transactions in which silver is used—that is a Pâ*k*ittiya offence involving forfeiture.

20. Whatsoever Bhikkhu shall engage in any one of the various kinds of buying and selling—that is a Pâ*k*ittiya offence involving forfeiture.

End of the second section,
the 'Silk-section.'

21. A spare bowl may be kept up to the limit of ten days. To him who exceeds that there is a Pâ*k*ittiya offence involving forfeiture.

22. Whatsoever Bhikkhu shall get another new bowl in exchange for an (old) one broken in less than five places—that is a Pâ*k*ittiya offence involving forfeiture.

That bowl must be forfeited by that Bhikkhu to the company of Bhikkhus; and whichever in that company of Bhikkhus shall be the worst bowl, that shall be given to that Bhikkhu with the words, 'This, Bhikkhu, is thy bowl; it must be kept until it breaks.' This is the right course in that case.

23. Now those medicines which may be used by the sick Bhikkhus—to wit, ghee, butter, oil, honey, molasses—when they have received them, they may enjoy them, storing them up to the seventh day. To him who exceeds that there is a Pâ*k*ittiya offence involving forfeiture.

spending of the gold or silver, he is to be asked to throw it away. Or, if this cannot be managed, then, as a last resource, some Bhikkhu is to be formally appointed 'Bullion-remover' (Rûpiya-*kkh*a*dd*aka), and he is to go and throw it away somewhere, 'animitta*m* katvâ,' (without making any mark at the place!)

24. When he sees that a month of the hot days has yet to run, let a Bhikkhu provide himself with the materials for robes for the rainy season: when he sees that half a month of the hot days has yet to run, let him make them, and wear them. Should he provide himself with the materials for robes for the rainy season when more than a month of the hot days has yet to run; or should he make them, and wear them, when more than half a month of the hot days has yet to run—that is a Pâkittiya offence involving forfeiture.

25. Whatsoever Bhikkhu, when he has himself given a set of robes to another Bhikkhu, shall thereafter, being angry or displeased with him, take them away, or get them taken away—that is a Pâkittiya offence involving forfeiture.

26. Whatsoever Bhikkhu shall himself ask for yarn, and have it woven up by weavers into cloth for a set of robes—that is a Pâkittiya offence involving forfeiture.

27. In case a householder, who is not related to him, or a householder's lady, shall have the cloth for a set of robes woven for a particular Bhikkhu by weavers; in that case, if that Bhikkhu, before the offer has been made to him, shall go to the weavers, and give directions as to the make of the robe, saying, 'This robe-cloth, my friends, is being woven for me. Make it long and broad, and make it thick, and well woven, and evenly woven[1], and with even lines, and well carded. If you do so, ourselves will

[1] Suppavâyita*m*, literally, 'well woven forth.' We follow the Samanta-Pâsâdikâ in its explanation of this word, but with considerable hesitation. Çompare the relation between Sanskrit ota and prota; and between English 'web' and 'woof.'

make it up to you, friends, in some way or other!' If that Bhikkhu[1], having thus spoken, should make it up[2] to them in any way, even by the contents of a begging bowl—that is a Pâ*k*ittiya offence involving forfeiture.

28. In case a robe should fall to the lot of a Bhikkhu, as a special gift[3], ten days before the Kattika-temâsa[3] full moon, that Bhikkhu may take it, considering it as a special gift: and when he has it, he may keep it up till the robe time[3].

---

[1] In the text read Evañ *k*a so bhikkhu.

[2] Anupada*gg*eyya is a double potential. Da*gg*âma would be equal to Sanskrit dadyâma; and to that a second potential termination has been added.

[3] The expression in the Pâli is literally 'should a special robe come to a Bhikkhu,' &c.; where 'special robe' is a*kk*eka-*k*îvara*m*, explained in the Samanta-Pâsâdikâ (Minayeff, 83) as equal to a*kk*âyika-kîvara*m*. The Vibhaṅga says, 'If a man wants to join the army or to emigrate, or if a man has fallen sick, or a woman is with child, or an unbeliever has come to believe, or a believer is edified (pasâdo uppanno hoti); then, if such a one send a messenger to the Bhikkhus, saying, "Let their reverences come hither, I will give a gift for the rainy season" (vassâvâsika*m*; perhaps, "such a gift as the laity are wont to give to the Bhikkhus who have spent the vassa among them")—that is an a*kk*eka-*k*îvara*m*' (Minayeff, 82, 83). A*kk*aya is an immediate, threatening, danger: compare the expression 'donatio mortis causâ.' 'Special robe' is, no doubt, an inadequate rendering; but we have chosen it in reference to the special circumstances under which the donation is made, and in default of a better translation. Compare the 85th Pâ*k*ittiya.

The Kattika-temâsi-pu*nn*amâ is, according to the Vibhaṅga (Minayeff, p. 82), the close of the Pavâra*n*â, the ceremony at the end of Vassa (see below, Book IV).

The robe time is the time when the robes were settled. The Vibhaṅga says, 'Robe time is, if the robes have not been laid out to dry (see the note to the first rule in this division of the Pâtimokkha), the last month of the rains; if they have, it is five months.'

Should he keep it beyond that—that is a Pâkittiya offence involving forfeiture.

29. When vassa is completed up to the full moon in Kattika[1] in case a Bhikkhu, who is dwelling in a place belonging to the class of those forest dwellings which are held to be insecure and dangerous, should desire to do so, he may leave one or other of his three robes in a hut inside a village, and if there is any ground for that Bhikkhu being separated from that robe, he may be separated from it up to the sixth night. Should he separate himself from it more than that, except by permission from the Bhikkhus—that is a Pâkittiya offence involving forfeiture.

30. Whatsoever Bhikkhu shall cause to be diverted to himself any benefit already dedicated to the Samgha—that is a Pâkittiya offence involving forfeiture.

Here ends the third section,
the 'Bowl-section.'

Venerable Sirs, the thirty Pâkittiya Rules involving forfeiture have been recited.

In respect of them I ask the venerable ones, 'Are you pure in this matter?'

[1] This is a different date from that mentioned in the last rule, and one month later. The Vibhaṅga explains the date here as Kattika-kâtumâsinî, whereas the date in Rule 28 is temâsinî, and is called by the Samanta-Pâsâdikâ (Minayeff, p. 82) pathama-kattika-punnamâ.

The same distinction is evident, from Mahâvagga IV, 14, 7–11, between Pavâranâ and the Kâtumâsinî. But how both these full moons came to be called Kattika is not clear.

A second time I ask the venerable ones, 'Are you pure in this matter?'

A third time I ask the venerable ones, 'Are you pure in this matter?'

The venerable ones are pure herein. Therefore do they keep silence. Thus I understand.

Here ends the recitation of the Nissaggiyas.

PÂ*K*ITTIYÂ DHAMMÂ.

THE PÂ*K*ITTIYA[1] RULES.

Now here, venerable Sirs, the ninety-two Pâ*k*ittiya Rules (Rules regarding matters requiring expiation) come into recitation.

1. There is Pâ*k*ittiya in a deliberate lie.

2. There is Pâ*k*ittiya in abusive language.

3. There is Pâ*k*ittiya in slander of a Bhikkhu.

4. Whatsoever Bhikkhu shall cause one not received into the higher grade (of the Order[2]) to recite the Dhamma clause by clause[3]—that is a Pâ*k*ittiya.

5. Whatsoever Bhikkhu shall, for more than two or three nights, lie down (to sleep) in the same place with one not received into the higher grade (of the Order)—that is a Pâ*k*ittiya.

6. Whatsoever Bhikkhu shall lie down (to sleep) in the same place with a woman—that is a Pâ*k*ittiya[4].

7. Whatsoever Bhikkhu shall preach the Dhamma, in more than five or six words, to a woman,

[1] That is, 'requiring repentance.' Compare the Sanskrit terms Prâyas*k*ittika and Prâyas*k*ittîya.

[2] Literally, 'one who has not received the upasampadâ.'

[3] Anupasampanna*m* padaso dhamma*m* vâ*k*eyya. This rule is directed against a wrong method of teaching the Dhamma to a Sâma*n*era. See the extracts from the Old Commentary, and from the Samanta-Pâsâdikâ, given by Minayeff on p. 84. Read however in the second line osâpenti for âsâpenti; and then go on anvakkhara*m* nâma, rûpam ani*kk*an ti vu*kk*amâno ruppan ti opâteti: anuvya*ñ*gana*m* nâma, rûpam ani*kk*an ti vu*kk*amâno vedanâ ani*kk*â ti sadda*m* ni*kkh*âreti, &c.

[4] For the text read mâtugâmena.

without a man arrived at years of discretion[1] (being present)—that is a Pâkittiya.

8. Whatsoever Bhikkhu shall tell one not received into the higher grade (of the Order) that the (speaker or any other Bhikkhu) has extraordinary spiritual gifts, even when such is the case[2]—that is a Pâkittiya.

9. Whatsoever Bhikkhu shall tell one not received into the higher grade (of the Order) of a Bhikkhu having fallen into any grave offence—that is a Pâkittiya.

10. Whatsoever Bhikkhu shall dig the ground or have it dug[3]—that is a Pâkittiya.

Here ends the first section,
the 'Falsehood-section.'

11. There is Pâkittiya in destroying any vegetable.

12. There is Pâkittiya in prevarication, or in worrying (the assembled Bhikkhus; for instance, by refusing to answer[4]).

13. There is Pâkittiya in stirring up ill-will against, in speaking disrespectfully of (any Bhikkhu deputed to any official duty[5]).

[1] Viññu. The Vibhaṅga says, 'a man able to understand what is well said, and what is wrongly said; what is wicked, and what is not wicked.' Compare the use of viññutâ at Gâtaka I, 231.

[2] To do so when it was not the case, would be a Pârâgika. See the 4th Pârâgika, and our note there on the meaning of uttarimanussa-dhammam. The 'even' here means that the truth of the averment makes no excuse for it.

[3] Because doing so might bring some living thing into danger.

[4] Vihesake; which must be understood as being done in a formal meeting of the Samgha during an official enquiry.

[5] The words in parentheses are supplied from the explanations in the Vibhaṅga.

14. Whatsoever Bhikkhu who has put out, or got another to put out to air, a bedstead, or a chair, or a mat, or a stool[1], the common property of the Sa*m*gha; and when going away shall not put it back, or have it put back, but shall depart without saying anything to anybody—that is a Pâ*k*ittiya.

15. Whatsoever Bhikkhu has put out, or got another to put out, a bedstead in a dwelling-place common to a Sa*m*gha; and when going away shall not put it back, or have it put back, but shall depart without saying anything to anybody—that is a Pâ*k*ittiya.

16. Whatsoever Bhikkhu, in a dwelling-place common to a Sa*m*gha, shall lie down where he knows that he is encroaching on (the space occupied by) a Bhikkhu who arrived before him, thinking, 'If he become inconvenienced he may go away'—if he does it for that object, and for no other[2]—that is a Pâ*k*ittiya.

17. Whatsoever Bhikkhu, being angry or displeased with another Bhikkhu, shall drive him out, or get him driven out of a dwelling-place common to a Sa*m*gha—that is a Pâ*k*ittiya.

18. Whatsoever Bhikkhu shall hurriedly sit down, or lie down, in the upper story of a dwelling-place common to a Sa*m*gha[3], on a bedstead or chair with removable legs—that is a Pâ*k*ittiya.

---

[1] Ko*kkh*am, the meaning of which is not quite clear. The Vibhaṅga says there are four kinds, made of bark, of usîra roots, of mu*ñg*a grass, and of bulrushes. It is apparently therefore of wickerwork.

[2] That is, according to the Vibhaṅga, the rule does not apply to an invalid, or to one suffering from the heat, or the cold; and so on.

[3] Because if he does so, he might unwittingly upset the furniture,

19. In case a Bhikkhu is having a large dwelling-place put up, he may have the work rectified, in a place where straw is scarce, round the doors, and where the bolts are put in, and the openings for light are set, and till the roof has been twice or thrice covered in[1]. Should he go beyond that, even in such a place—that is a Pâkittiya.

20. Whatsoever Bhikkhu shall sprinkle water with living creatures in it, or shall cause such to be sprinkled on grass or on clay—that is a Pâkittiya.

Here ends the second section, the 'Bhûtagâma-section.'

---

21. Whatsoever Bhikkhu, not thereto deputed, shall exhort the Bhikkhunî's[2]—that is a Pâkittiya.

---

or fall himself, to the injury of some one who was rightfully on the ground floor.

[1] In the text read dvittikkhadanassa: *th*ite pi. This rule, directed against too great luxury in the matter of a perfectly finished dwelling, is somewhat obscure, owing to our want of information as to the mode in which such dwellings should be put up. It refers probably to a hut, albeit a large one, of wattel and daub (ku*dd*a: comp. Rh. D.'s note on the Mahâparinibbâna Sutta V, 41). The Samanta-Pâsâdikâ divides dvârakosa into dvâra-okâsa, and quotes various estimates from the old Sinhalese commentaries as to the proper extent of this space (see Minayeff, p. 87).

[2] Ovadeyya; that is, shall preach to them the eight Garudhammâ. On these see the passages mentioned in the Index appended to the text of the *K*ullavagga; and on the ovâda see *K*ullavagga X, 9, 2, and following. The mode of procedure is laid down in the Vibhaṅga as follows: 'The Bhikkhu asks the Bhikkhunî's, "Are you all present, sisters, and do none raise objections (that is, are you samaggâ)?" If they say, "That is so, Sir!" he asks, "Are the eight Garu-dhammâ being kept up?" If they say, "They are, Sir!" he is to say, "That, sisters, is the exhortation!" and so deliver it to them. If they say, "They are

22. If a Bhikkhu, even when thereto deputed, exhort the Bhikkhunî's after the sun has set—that is a Pâkittiya.

23. Whatsoever Bhikkhu shall go to the dwelling-place of Bhikkhunî's, and there exhort the Bhikkhunî's [1], except on the (right) occasion—that is a Pâkittiya.

Herein this is the right occasion: (to wit), when a Bhikkhunî is ill. This is the right occasion in this passage.

24. Whatsoever Bhikkhu shall speak thus: 'The Bhikkhus exhort the Bhikkhunî's for the sake of gain [2]!'—that is a Pâkittiya.

25. Whatsoever Bhikkhu shall give a robe to a Bhikkhunî who is not related to him, except in exchange—that is a Pâkittiya.

26. Whatsoever Bhikkhu shall make up a robe, or have it made up, for a Bhikkhunî who is not related to him—that is a Pâkittiya.

27. Whatsoever Bhikkhu, by appointment, shall travel along a high road in company with a Bhikkhunî, even to go as far as the village, except on the right occasion—that is a Pâkittiya.

---

not, Sir!" he should go all through them, saying, "A sister who has been received into the higher grade even one hundred years, &c. (and so on to the end of the Garu-dhammâ)."

'If he preach any other Dhamma to those who say, "We, Sir, are all present, and none raise objections!" he is guilty of a Dukkata. If he preach the eight Garu-dhammâ to those who say, "No, Sir, that is not so!" (vagg' amh' ayyâ ti, where vagga is vyagra, the opposite of samagga), he is guilty of a Dukkata. If he preach another Dhamma, when the eight Garu-dhammâ have not committed to their charge, he is guilty of a Dukkata.'

[1] Compare Kullavagga X, 6, 1.

[2] Âmisa-hetu; that is, in order that the sisters may be induced to supply the preachers with food, medicine, &c.

Herein this is the right occasion: (to wit), when the road is so insecure and dangerous that travellers on it have to carry arms. This is the right occasion in this passage.

28. Whatsoever Bhikkhu, by appointment, shall go on board the same boat, whether going up stream or down stream, in company with a Bhikkhunî, except for the purpose of crossing over to the other side—that is a Pâkittiya.

29. Whatsoever Bhikkhu, knowing it to be so, shall eat food procured by the intervention of a Bhikkhunî, unless the laity (who give the food) had already undertaken (to give it to him)[1]—that is a Pâkittiya.

30. Whatsoever Bhikkhu shall take a seat, one man with one woman, in company with a Bhikkhunî, in a secret place[2]—that is a Pâkittiya.

Here ends the third section,
the 'Bhikkhunovâda-section.'

---

31. A Bhikkhu who is not sick may take one meal at a public rest-house[3]. Should he take more than that—that is a Pâkittiya.

---

[1] The introductory story in the Vibhaṅga is of a Bhikkhu born in Râgagaha, who went to a relative's house, and a meal was there being prepared for him by his relatives. A kulupikâ bhikkhunî then arrives, and says, 'My friends, give the gentleman a meal!' Then the Bhikkhu was in doubt whether he ought not to refuse it as being Bhikkhunî-paripâkitam.

[2] Compare the Aniyatâ Dhammâ.

[3] Eko âvasatha-pindo bhuñgitabbo. An âvasatha is one of those 'chaultries,' or public resting-places, which good Buddhists were wont to put up in the villages or at cross roads. At some of

32. There is Pâ*k*ittiya in going in a body to receive a meal[1], except on the right occasion.

Herein the right occasion is this: (to wit), when there is sickness, when robes are being given, when robes are being made, when on a journey (on foot), when on board a boat, when (the influx of Bhikkhus) is great[2], when a general invitation is given to Sama*n*as[3]. This is right occasion in this passage.

33. There is Pâ*k*ittiya in taking food in turn[4], except on the right occasion.

Herein the right occasion is this: (to wit), when there is sickness, when robes are being given, when

---

these a constant supply of rice was provided for travellers. See the Mahâ-parinibbâna Sutta I, 10; II, 5 (pp. 10, 16); *G*âtaka, No. 31 ('Buddhist Birth Stories,' pp. 280–285); Mahâ-sudassana Sutta I, 63; Dhammapada Commentary apud Fausböll, 185. The Samanta-Pâsâdikâ on this rule (Minayeff, p. 88) says that âvasatha-pi*nd*o is a meal in such an âvasatha.

[1] On this rule compare *K*ullavagga VII, 3, 13. 'In a body' means four or more Bhikkhus going together to the same house.

[2] Mahâ-samayo. The Vibhaṅga relates how, when vassa was over, the Bhikkhus repaired in great numbers to visit the Buddha. On such occasions it was difficult or impossible for them all, if they adhered to the strict rule, to obtain their meals.

[3] Sama*n*a-bhatta-samayo. See the Vibhaṅga, and the Samanta-Pâsâdikâ, quoted by Minayeff, pp. 88, 89. 'Sama*n*as,' of course, includes others besides Buddhists.

[4] Parampara-bho*g*ane; that is, in picking and choosing with regard to food, or in regard to different invitations. The Bhikkhus were to eat straight on whatever was given, and to accept invitations in the order in which they were received. But a sick Bhikkhu might choose one morsel rather than another; and Bhikkhus in health might accept an invitation to a house where robes are going to be given, or made, rather than to a house where only a meal was offered. The last exception was simply to guard against the stock of robes falling short (Bhikkhû . . . nâdhivâsenti: *k*îvara*m* paritta*m* uppa*gg*ati, says the Vibhaṅga).

robes are being made. This is right occasion in this passage.

34. In case people should offer a Bhikkhu, who has gone to some house, to take as much as he chose of their sweetmeats and cakes, that Bhikkhu, should he so wish, may accept two or three bowls full[1]. If he should accept more than that—that is a Pâkittiya.

When he has accepted two or three bowls full[1], he must take them away, and divide them up among the Bhikkhus. That is the proper course in this case.

35. Whatsoever Bhikkhu, when he has once finished his meal, though still invited (to continue eating[2]), shall eat or partake of[3] food that has not been left over[4], whether hard or soft[5]—that is a Pâkittiya.

---

[1] In the text read dvittipattapurâ.

The word for sweetmeats, pûva, includes all those sweetmeats which it was then (as it is now) the custom to send as presents from one house to another at weddings, funerals, and such occasions.

'Cakes' (mantha) refers to those rice-cakes, &c., which were usually prepared as provision for a journey. Compare *G*âtaka I, 80.

'Should offer to take as much as he chose' is the phrase referred to above in our note on the 7th Nissaggiya. The Vibhaṅga says here, Abhiha*t*u*m* pavâreyyâ 'ti yâvataka*m* i*kkh*asi tâvataka*m* ga*n*hâhîti.

[2] Pavârito. The Vibhaṅga says, Pavârito nâma âsana*m* pa*ñ*-*ñ*âyati bhogana*m* pa*ññ*âyati hatthapâse *th*ito abhiharati pa*t*ikkhepo pa*ññ*âyati, which means, we think, 'A seat for him is there, food is there, (the host) standing near him still makes invitation, but there takes place a refusal (of the proferred food).'

[3] Khâdeyya vâ bhu*ñg*eyya vâ.

[4] The 'not left over' refers only to the case of a sick Bhikkhu. A Bhikkhu in health, when he has once finished his meal, ought not to eat what he has left.

[5] Khâdaniya*m* vâ bho*g*aniya*m* vâ. The former term is used of hard food, such as biscuits, cakes, meats, fruits, &c.; the latter

36. Whatsoever Bhikkhu shall offer a Bhikkhu who has finished his meal, though still invited to continue eating, his choice of food, whether hard or soft, that has not been left over, saying, 'Come, now, Bhikkhu; take and eat!' deliberately desiring to stir up longing (in that Bhikkhu); then if that Bhikkhu eats[1]—that is a Pâkittiya.

37. Whatsoever Bhikkhu shall take or eat any food, whether hard or soft, at the wrong time[2]—that is a Pâkittiya.

38. Whatsoever Bhikkhu shall eat food, whether hard or soft, that has been put by—that is a Pâkittiya.

39. Whatsoever Bhikkhu, when he is not sick, shall request, for his own use, and shall partake of delicacies—to wit, ghee, butter, oil, honey, molasses, fish, flesh, milk, curds[3]—that is a Pâkittiya.

40. Whatsoever Bhikkhu shall place, as food, within the door of his mouth, anything not given to him, save only water and a tooth-cleaner[4]—that is a Pâkittiya.

Here ends the fourth section,
the 'Bhogana-section.'

---

41. Whatsoever Bhikkhu shall, with his own

---

term of soft foods, such as boiled rice, curries, &c. The two words for eating correspond to these two ideas.

[1] Bhuttasmim pâkittiya; that is, the offence is completed when the eating has taken place; but the offer alone is not a Pâkittiya. So the Vibhaṅga.

[2] After sun-turn.

[3] In the text read tâni; madhu phânitam.

[4] Dantapona; doubtless the same, perhaps an older expression for, the dantakattha referred to in Kullavagga V, 31. It is a piece of fragrant root (cinnamon, betel, &c.) about eight inches long.

hand, give food, whether hard or soft, to an Akelaka or to a Paribbâgaka or to a Paribbâgikâ[1]—that is a Pâkittiya.

42. Whatsoever Bhikkhu shall address a Bhikkhu thus: 'Come, brother; let us go, for a meal, to the village, or the town!' and then, whether after he has got an alms for him, or without having got an alms for him, shall send him away, saying, 'Go away, brother! Talking with you, or sitting with you, is not pleasant to me. Talking, or sitting each one by himself, is more pleasant to me!'—if he does this for this cause, and for no other[2]—that is a Pâkittiya.

43. Whatsoever Bhikkhu shall force his way into a house where a meal is going on[3], and take a seat there—that is a Pâkittiya.

---

[1] These are the various non-Buddhist religious teachers or devotees, most of whom rejected the Vedas. The Paribbâgakas were mostly, though not always, wandering logicians, willing to maintain theses against all the world. Paribbâgikâ is merely the feminine of the last. Akelaka, which naturally has no feminine, were the naked ascetics.

The sect now called Gains are divided into two classes, Svetambaras and Digambaras, the latter of which eat naked. They are known to be the successors of the school called Niganthas in the Pâli Pitakas; and it is not certain whether the Niganthas are included in the Akelakas. It is probable that the Brâhman ascetics, the Vânaprasthas, were not included under the term Paribbâgakas; but our information on the exact meaning of these terms is, as yet, very imperfect.

[2] That is merely to get rid of him, in order to gain any purpose of his own. The Vibhaṅga gives as examples that the Bhikkhu sees some valuable things, and wants to get them; or sees some woman, and wants to speak to her.

[3] Sabhogane kule; the meaning of which is not quite clear. The Old Commentary says, 'A sabhogana kula is one where

44. Whatsoever Bhikkhu shall take a seat, in secret, with a woman, in a concealed place [1]—that is a Pâ*k*ittiya.

45. Whatsoever Bhikkhu shall take a seat, in secret, with a woman, one man with one woman—that is a Pâ*k*ittiya.

46. Whatsoever Bhikkhu, who has been invited (to a house), and has been (thus already) provided with a meal, shall, without having previously spoken about it to a Bhikkhu, if there is one there, go on his (begging) rounds among the families, either before meal-time or after meal-time [2], except on the right occasion—that is a Pâ*k*ittiya.

---

there is a husband and a wife; and they both, husband and wife, are not gone forth from, are not devoid of lust' (Minayeff, p. 89, under P.; but for anatikkantâ read anikkhantâ). Then the Samanta-Pâsâdikâ, doubtless to justify this suggested implication, makes sabho*g*ana*m* equal to saha ubhohi *g*anehi (!); or, in the alternative, to sabhoga*m*, since 'the wife is the bhoga of a man still given to passion, and the husband the bhoga of a wife.' The use of Bho*g*ana in any such sense is extremely forced, and was perhaps only suggested by the following rules; but it is just possible we should translate, 'a household still given to pleasure' (compare *K*ullavagga VIII, 5, 1), or 'fond of good food' (compare Milinda Pañha 76).

On anupakha*gg*a compare the 16th Pâ*k*ittiya.

[1] Compare the 30th Pâ*k*ittiya, and the two Aniyatâ Dhammâ.

[2] The Vibhaṅga has the following stories in regard to these two particulars. A family devoted to Upananda invited him and another Bhikkhu. Before meal-time he went to attend on other families (purebhatta*m* kulâni payirupâsati). The people delayed giving his meal to the other Bhikkhu till Upananda should arrive. He came late; and the other Bhikkhu was thereby discomforted.

The family devoted to Upananda sent him food for his use; saying it was to be given to the Sa*m*gha, with special reference to him. He had gone for an alms to the village. The messengers delivered the food and the message, and asked where Upananda was.

Herein the right occasion is this: (to wit), a time of giving of robes, a time of making of robes. That is right occasion in this passage.

47. A Bhikkhu who is not sick may accept a (standing) invitation with regard to the requisites [1] for four months. If he accept it for a period longer than that—unless there be a second invitation, or a perpetual invitation—that is a Pâkittiya.

48. Whatsoever Bhikkhu shall go to see an army drawn up in battle-array, except for a cause thereto sufficient—that is a Pâkittiya.

49. And if there be any reason for that Bhikkhu's going to the army, that Bhikkhu may remain there for two or three nights. If he remain longer than that—that is a Pâkittiya.

50. And if while remaining there for two or three nights he should go to the battle-array, or to the numbering of the forces, or to the drawing up of the forces, or to a review [2]—that is a Pâkittiya.

End of the fifth section,
the 'Akelaka-section.'

The Bhikkhus told the matter to the Blessed One. He directed the present to be accepted, and laid by till Upananda should return. After Upananda returned, he nevertheless went out again to attend on other families, and the food so sent went bad.

The Bhikkhu is to tell a resident Bhikkhu before, on account of this rule, giving up his usual rounds, in order that he may still go if a sick Bhikkhu wants medicine.

The exceptions are, as above, to prevent the stock of robes falling short.

[1] These are usually four—clothing, food, residence, and medicine. This rule refers more especially to medicine, as appears from the explanation in the Vibhaṅga.

[2] On this rule compare the third section of the Maggհima-Sîla,

51. There is Pâkittiya in the drinking of fermented liquors, or strong drinks[1].

52. There is Pâkittiya in poking (another person) with the finger.

53. There is Pâkittiya in sporting in the water[2].

54. There is Pâkittiya in disrespect[3].

55. Whatsoever Bhikkhu shall frighten a Bhikkhu[4]—that is a Pâkittiya.

56. Whatsoever Bhikkhu, who is not sick, shall, desiring to warm himself[5], kindle a fire, or have a fire kindled, without cause sufficient thereto—that is a Pâkittiya.

57. Whatsoever Bhikkhu shall bathe at intervals of less than half a month, except on the proper occasion—that is a Pâkittiya.

Herein this is proper occasion: (to wit), the two and a half months during which there is hot weather, and during which there is fever; namely, the last month and a half of the heats, and the first month

---

and the third section of the Mahâ-Sîla (translated in Rh. D.'s 'Buddhist Suttas from the Pâli,' pp. 192, 198). We follow the Vibhaṅga in the interpretation of the various terms.

[1] The Old Commentary (quoted by Minayeff, p. 90) distinguishes between surâ and meraya by the former being derived from flour, water, &c., and the latter from flowers, fruits, &c.

[2] Throwing water over one another, and chasing one another, were common amusements at the public and private bathing-places. Our MSS. read throughout hâsa-dhamme.

[3] Anâdariye. That is, according to the Vibhaṅga, paying no heed, when one's attention is drawn by an upasampanna to the fact that this or that action is against the rule laid down (paññattam). But compare also Kullavagga VIII, 8, 1.

[4] In the text read bhimsâpeyya.

[5] H. O.'s MS. reads visibbanâpekho. At Mahâvagga I, 20, 15, visibbesum occurs in the sense of 'they warmed themselves.' Trenckner at p. 47 of the Milinda Pañha reads aggim galetvâ visîvetvâ; and at p. 102, samsibbitavisibbitattâ sâkhânam.

of the rains[1]: when sick; when there is work; when on a journey; when there has been wind and rain. This is right occasion in this connection.

58. A Bhikkhu who receives a new robe must choose one or other mode of disfigurement out of the three modes of disfigurement; either (making part of it) dark blue, or (marking part of it with) mud, or (making part of it) black. If a Bhikkhu should make use of a new robe without choosing one or other mode of disfigurement out of the three modes of disfigurement[2]—that is a Pâkittiya.

59. Whatsoever Bhikkhu who has made over[3] his robe to a Bhikkhu, or to a Bhikkhunî, or to a probationer, or to a Sâmanera, or to a Sâmanerî, shall continue to make use of it as a thing not (formally) given—that is a Pâkittiya.

---

[1] The Vibhaṅga refers the first of these periods to the hot weather, and the second to the fever weather.

[2] In the text insert a full stop after kâlasâmam vâ. The object of this rule, according to the Vibhaṅga, is to enable a Bhikkhu to trace his robe should it get lost by being mixed up with others. Compare the 15th Nissaggiya.

[3] The Vibhaṅga says, 'There are two ways of appointment (in making over, vikappanâ), promising in the presence, and promising in the absence (of the person to whom the appointment is made). Promise in the presence is by the words, "I make over this robe to you, or to such and such a one (then present)!" Promising in the absence is by the words, "I give this robe to you for you to appoint (to some one else)." Then the person spoken to should say, "Who is your friend, or intimate acquaintance?" "Such a one, or such a one." Then the other should say, "I give this to them. This is their property. Wear it, or part with it, or do with it as you like!"'

These last are the formal words used on presenting a robe; and by their use the property in the robe is transferred. After that the original owner, in spite of the formal words, may not, according to our rule, continue to use the robe.

On apakkuddhârakam see Childers, sub voce pakkuddhâro.

60. Whatsoever Bhikkhu shall hide, or cause another to hide, a Bhikkhu's bowl, or his robe, or the mat on which he sits, or his needle-case[1], or his girdle, even though in fun—that is a Pâkittiya.

End of the sixth section,
the 'Surâpâna-section.'

61. Whatsoever Bhikkhu shall deliberately deprive any living thing of life—that is a Pâkittiya.

62. Whatsoever Bhikkhu shall, knowingly, drink water with living things in it—that is a Pâkittiya.

63. Whatsoever Bhikkhu shall stir up for decision again a matter which he knows to have been settled according to the Dhamma[2]—that is a Pâkittiya.

64. Whatsoever Bhikkhu, who knows of it, shall conceal a serious offence[3] committed by a Bhikkhu—that is a Pâkittiya.

65. Whatsoever Bhikkhu shall admit a person under twenty years of age to the higher grade in the Order, knowing him (or her) to be so—(while) the person is not admitted to the higher grade, and the other Bhikkhus (who assist) are blameworthy—this is in him[4] a Pâkittiya.

66. Whatsoever Bhikkhu shall, by appointment, journey along the same route with a caravan of

[1] In the text read sûkigharam.

[2] Compare the 79th Pâkittiya, and Kullavagga IV, 14 passim.

[3] That is, a Pârâgika, or a Samghâdisesa.

[4] The upagghâya is guilty of a Pâkittiya; the âkariya, and the gana, of a Dukkata, says the Vibhanga.

robbers, knowing it to be such, even as far as the next village[1]—that is a Pâ*k*ittiya.

67. Whatsoever Bhikkhu shall, by appointment, journey along the same route with a woman[2], even as far as the next village—that is a Pâ*k*ittiya.

68. Whatsoever Bhikkhu shall speak thus: 'In this wise do I understand that the Dhamma has been proclaimed by the Blessed One: that to him who cultivates those Qualities which have been called "dangerous" by the Blessed One, there is not sufficient danger (to prevent his acquiring spiritual gifts)[3];' then that Bhikkhu should be addressed by the Bhikkhus thus: 'Say not so, brother! bear not false witness against the Blessed One! For neither is it seemly to bring a false accusation against the Blessed One, nor could the Blessed One speak so. By many a figure[4], brother, have the Dangerous Qualities been declared by the Blessed One to be full of danger[5], and also to be sufficient to prevent him who cultivates them (from attaining spiritual gifts)[3].' If that Bhikkhu, when he has thus been spoken to by the Bhikkhus, should persist as before, then let that Bhikkhu be (formally) admonished about it by the Bhikkhus as a body, even to the third time, to the intent that he abandon that course.

---

[1] Compare the 27th Pâ*k*ittiya. A caravan that sets out with intent to steal or rob on the way is meant.

[2] Compare the 27th and 28th Pâ*k*ittiyas.

[3] These are specified in detail in Mahâvagga II, 3, 7.

[4] Pariyâya; fulness, extent, of illustration and explanation. Not merely manner, or method, of statement. Much of this pariyâya will be found in the various similes used in the *K*ullavagga loc. cit.

[5] In the text here, and in the corresponding clause of No. 70, read anekapariyâyena âvuso antarâyikâ dhammâ antarâyikâ vuttâ bhagavatâ, as in *K*ullavagga I, 32.

If, while being so admonished, up to the third time, he abandon that course, it is well. If he abandon it not—that is a Pâkittiya[1].

69. Whatsoever Bhikkhu, knowing him to be so, shall eat in company with, or dwell together with[2], or sleep in one place with a Bhikkhu who talks thus (as in 68), and has not been dealt with according to the law[3], and has not laid aside his delusion—that is a Pâkittiya.

70. If a Sâmanera[4] even should say thus: 'In this wise do I understand that the Dhamma has been proclaimed by the Blessed One: that to him who cultivates those Qualities which have been called "dangerous" by the Blessed One there is not sufficient danger (to prevent his attaining to spiritual gifts);' then that Sâmanera should be addressed by the Bhikkhus thus: 'Say not so, good Sâmanera! Bear not false witness against the Blessed One. For neither is it seemly to bring a false accusation against the Blessed One, nor could the Blessed One speak so. By many a figure, good Sâmanera, have the

[1] This rule is directed against the delusion that sin, to a very holy man, loses its danger and its sinfulness. Compare the 4th Samghâdisesa; and, on the method of procedure here laid down, the 10th to the 13th Samghâdisesas. At Kullavagga I, 32 lust is declared to be an antarâyiko dhammo; and falsehood another at Mahâvagga II, 3, 3. The Samanta-Pâsâdikâ (quoted by Minayeff, p. 92) gives five divisions of these 'dangerous qualities.'

[2] This the Vibhaṅga explains as holding Uposatha, or Pavâranâ, or a Samghakamma with him.

[3] Ukkhitto anosârito, says the Vibhaṅga. Compare Mahâvagga IX, 4, 10, 11.

[4] Samanuddeso; which is explained by the Old Commentary as equal to Sâmanera. Why, in the Pâtimokkha, now one and now the other expression should be used, is not clear. In the later texts Sâmanera is the usual form, but samanuddeso is found also in a few passages.

Dangerous Qualities been declared by the Blessed One to be full of danger, and also to be sufficient to prevent him who cultivates them (from attaining to spiritual gifts).' And if that Sâma*n*era, when so addressed by the Bhikkhus, shall persist in that course, that Sâma*n*era should be addressed by the Bhikkhus thus: 'From this day forth, good Sâma*n*era, neither can that Blessed One be referred to[1] by you as your Teacher, nor can the privilege, which the other Sâma*n*eras enjoy, of sleeping in the same place with the Bhikkhus for two or three nights[2], any longer be yours! Depart! away with you[3]!'

Whatsoever Bhikkhu shall encourage[4], or support[5], or eat with, or sleep in the same place with, a Sâma*n*era thus expelled—that is a Pâ*k*ittiya.

End of the seventh section,
the 'Sappâ*n*aka[6]-section.'

[1] Apadisitabbo. Compare the four Mahâpadesâ in the Mahâ-parinibbâna Sutta IV, 7–11.

[2] Compare the 5th Pâ*k*ittiya.

[3] In the text read *k*ara pi re; that is, *k*ara api re, instead of *k*ara pare. On vinassa compare Mahâvagga I, 61, 1.

[4] Upalâpeyya. Compare Mahâvagga I, 59, and Mahâ-parinibbâna Sutta I, 5, and the passages quoted in Rh. D.'s version of the latter passage. The Old Commentary says, 'Flatters him (talks him over, tassa upalâpeti) by saying, "I will give you a bowl, or a robe, or hear you repeat, or answer your questions."'

[5] Upa*tth*âpeyya. The Old Commentary says, 'by providing him with chunam, or clay, or a tooth-cleanser, or water to wash his face with.' No doubt upa*tth*âpeti is used in the sense of showing such personal attentions to another, as the upa*tth*âkâ did to the Buddha; and such services would very rightly come under this rule. Yet here, as often, the comment is rather a scholastic exegesis of the sentence, than a philologically exact explanation of the word.

[6] This title is taken from the second, not, as in all the other cases, from the first rule in the section.

71. Whatsoever Bhikkhu, when admonished by the Bhikkhus in respect of some precept in accordance with the Dhamma, shall speak thus: 'I cannot submit myself to that precept, brother, until I shall have enquired touching it of another Bhikkhu, an experienced master of the Vinaya'—that is a Pâkittiya.

A Bhikkhu desirous of training, Bhikkhus[1], should learn, and enquire, and settle in his own mind. This is the right rule in this connection.

72. Whatsoever Bhikkhu, when the Pâtimokkha is being recited, shall speak thus: 'What comes of these minor[2] precepts being here recited, save only that they tend to misgiving, and worry, and perplexity!'—there is Pâkittiya in thus throwing contempt on the precepts[3].

73. Whatsoever Bhikkhu, when at the half month the Pâtimokkha is being recited, should say thus: 'Now for the first time do I notice that this rule, they say, is handed down in the Suttas, is embraced in the Suttas!'—then, if the other Bhikkhus shall know concerning that Bhikkhu thus: 'This Bhikkhu has taken his place at the recitation of the Pâtimokkha once, or twice, not to say oftener[4]'—that Bhikkhu is not only not made free on account of his ignorance[5], but he is to be dealt with according to the Dhamma for the offence into which he has fallen, and furthermore he is to be charged with foolishness (in the words), 'This is loss to thee,

[1] On this strange allocution see the note to the 10th Nissaggiya.

[2] Khuddânukhuddakehi. Compare the Mahâ-parinibbâna Sutta VI, 3, and the passages quoted there in Rh. D.'s note.

[3] In the text read vivannake.

[4] In the text read ko pana vâdo bhiyyo.

[5] In the text read aññânakena.

brother, this is an evil to thee, in that when the Pâtimokkha is being recited you fail to take it to your heart, and attend to it with care.' There is Pâ*k*ittiya in such foolish conduct.

74. Whatsoever Bhikkhu, being angry or displeased with another Bhikkhu, shall give a blow—that is a Pâ*k*ittiya.

75. Whatsoever Bhikkhu, being angry or displeased with another Bhikkhu, shall make use of any threatening gesture[1]—that is a Pâ*k*ittiya.

76. Whatsoever Bhikkhu shall harass a Bhikkhu with a (charge of) Sa*m*ghâdisesa without ground—that is a Pâ*k*ittiya.

77. Whatsoever Bhikkhu shall intentionally suggest difficulties of conscience to a Bhikkhu, with the idea of causing him uneasiness, even for a moment; if he does it to that end alone—that is a Pâ*k*ittiya.

78. Whatsoever Bhikkhu shall stand by overhearing when Bhikkhus are quarrelling, or making a disturbance, or engaged in a dispute, hoping to hear what they shall utter; if he does it to that end alone—that is a Pâ*k*ittiya.

79. Whatsoever Bhikkhu, when he has declared his consent to formal proceedings conducted according to the Dhamma, shall thereafter grumble (about those proceedings)[2]—that is a Pâ*k*ittiya.

---

[1] Talasattika*m* uggireyya. The Old Commentary says, Kâya*m* vâ kâyapa*t*ibaddha*m* vâ antamaso uppalapatta*m* pi u*kk*âreti. Compare âvudhâni uggiritvâ at *G*âtaka I, 150.

[2] If he should raise any formal objections so as to re-open the question, that would fall under the 63rd Pâ*k*ittiya. On 'declaring one's consent' in this and the following rule, see below, Mahâvagga II, 23. The whole rule, as well as on No. 63, is repeatedly referred to in *K*ullavagga IV, 14.

80. Whatsoever Bhikkhu, when the Sa*m*gha is engaged in conducting a (formal) enquiry, shall rise from his seat, and go away, without having declared his consent—that is a Pâ*k*ittiya.

81. Whatsoever Bhikkhu, when, in a regularly constituted Sa*m*gha[1], he has given away a robe, shall thereafter grumble about it, saying, 'The Bhikkhus appropriate the property of the Sa*m*gha according to friendship'—that is a Pâ*k*ittiya.

82. Whatsoever Bhikkhu shall divert to the use of any individual property dedicated to the Sa*m*gha, knowing it to be so—that is a Pâ*k*ittiya.

Here ends the eighth section,
the 'Sahadhammika-section.'

---

83. Whatsoever Bhikkhu shall cross the threshold of an anointed *K*hattiya king, when the king has not gone forth, and the queen has not withdrawn, without first having had himself announced[2]—that is a Pâ*k*ittiya.

---

[1] Samaggena sa*m*ghena. See the note to the 21st Pâ*k*ittiya.

[2] Indakhîla, the word translated 'threshold,' is explained in the Old Commentary by sayani-ghara, 'sleeping chamber;' but this is rather a didactic gloss on the rule. Compare the note above on the 43rd Pâ*k*ittiya. The phrase 'when the queen has not gone in' is somewhat doubtful. H. O.'s MS. of the Vibhaṅga reads (as Minayeff does) aniggata-ratanake, instead of Dickson's anîhata-ratanake. The former is the better reading; nîhata is impossible, it must be either nihata or nîha*t*a. But ratanaka, though the queen is one of the seven Ratanas of a king, is not found elsewhere used absolutely for a queen: the use of râ*g*ake, too, immediately after rañño, instead of rañ*ñ*e or râ*g*ini, is curious. A possible alternative rendering would be 'when the court has not departed, and the regalia not laid aside:' but we prefer on

84. Whatsoever Bhikkhu shall pick up, or cause another to pick up, except in a grove or in a dwelling-place, a jewel, or anything deemed a jewel[1]—that is a Pâkittiya.

Should a Bhikkhu have picked up, either in a grove or in a dwelling-place, a jewel, or anything deemed a jewel, it is to be laid aside, that he to whom it may belong may take it away. This is the right course in such a case.

85. Whatsoever Bhikkhu shall, out of hours[2], enter a village, without having informed a Bhikkhu if one is present[3], except on account of business of a special nature[4] thereto sufficient—that is a Pâkittiya.

86. Whatsoever Bhikkhu shall have a needle-case made of bone, or ivory, or horn, it shall be broken up—and that is a Pâkittiya.

87. When a Bhikkhu is having a new bedstead or chair made, it should be made with legs eight inches in height, according to the accepted inch[5], exclusive of the lowermost piece of the bed frame[6]. To him who exceeds that limit there is a Pâkittiya,

---

the whole the Old Commentator's explanation of râgaka and ratanaka.

[1] Ratanasammatam; that is, a thing made of one of those substances ranked with gems, such as jade, coral, &c.

[2] Vikâle; that is, says the Old Commentary, from sun-turn in one day till sun-rise in the next.

[3] Santam bhikkhum. If one is not present, he may go without. The Old Commentary gives no such definition of being present, as Mr. Dickson has supplied.

[4] Akkâyika. Compare the note on the 28th Nissaggiya.

[5] Sugatangulena. See the note on the 6th Samghâdisesa.

[6] Atani. There is no explanation of this term, either in the Old Commentary, or in the Samanta-Pâsâdikâ.

and (the legs of the piece of furniture) shall be cut down (to the proper size).

88. Whatsoever Bhikkhu shall have a bedstead or a chair made, stuffed with cotton[1], the stuffing shall be torn out—and that is a Pâ*k*ittiya.

89. When a Bhikkhu is having a rug or mat to sit upon made, it must be made of the right measure. Herein this is the measure: in length two spans, according to the accepted span; in breadth one span; the border one span. To him who exceeds that limit there is a Pâ*k*ittiya, and (the article) shall be cut down (to the proper size).

90. When a Bhikkhu is having an itch-cloth[2] made, it must be made of the right measure. Herein this is the measure: in length four spans, according to the accepted span; in width two spans. To him who exceeds that limit there is a Pâ*k*ittiya, and (the cloth) shall be cut (down to the proper size).

91. When a Bhikkhu is having a garment made for the rainy season, it must be made of the right measure. Herein this is the right measure: in length six spans, according to the accepted span; in breadth two spans and a half. To him who exceeds that limit there is a Pâ*k*ittiya, and (the garment) shall be cut (down to the proper size).

92. Whatsoever Bhikkhu shall have a robe made of the dimensions of a Sugata's robe[3], or larger—

---

[1] Tûla*m*; which the Old Commentary expands into three kinds—tûla*m* from a tree, tûla*m* from a creeper, and tûla*m* from a young fowl.

[2] When a Bhikkhu had a boil, or running sore, or any such disease, the use of an itch-cloth (so called from the first in the list of skin complaints there mentioned) is laid down in Mahâvagga VIII, 17.

[3] On the doubtful meaning of Sugata, see the note above on

that is a Pâkittiya, and (the robe) shall be cut down to the proper size.

Herein this is the measure of the Sugata robe of a Sugata: in length nine spans, according to the accepted span; in breadth six spans. This is the measure of the Sugata robe of a Sugata.

End of the ninth section,
the 'Ratana-section.'

Venerable Sirs, the ninety-two rules regarding matters requiring expiation have been recited.

In respect of them I ask the venerable ones, 'Are you pure in this matter?'

A second time I ask the venerable ones, 'Are you pure in this matter?'

A third time I ask the venerable ones, 'Are you pure in this matter?'

The venerable ones are pure herein. Therefore do they keep silence. Thus I understand.

Here endeth the recitation of the Pâkittiyas.

---

the 28th Nissaggiya. There is no reason whatever to believe that Gotama's robe was larger, in proportion, than those worn by the other members of his order. He exchanged robes with Mahâ Kassapa. Of the two sets of robes brought by Pukkusa, one was given to Ânanda, and one was reserved for the Buddha himself; and no one can read the account in the Mahâ-parinibbâna Sutta without feeling that both are supposed to be of the same size.

PÂ*T*IDESANIYÂ DHAMMÂ.

RULES REGARDING MATTERS WHICH OUGHT TO BE CONFESSED.

Here, venerable Sirs, the four rules regarding matters which ought to be confessed come into recitation.

1. Whatsoever Bhikkhu, when a Bhikkhunî not related to him has entered within the houses [1], shall, with his own hand, accept at her hands food, either hard or soft, and eat or enjoy it—that is a matter which ought to be confessed by that Bhikkhu, saying, 'I have fallen, Brethren, into a blameworthy offence, unbecoming, which ought to be confessed; and I confess it!'

2. Now Bhikkhus, when they have been invited to laymen's houses, eat. If the Bhikkhunî stay there giving directions, saying, 'Here give curry, give rice here!' the Bhikkhunî ought to be rebuked by those Bhikkhus, saying, 'Stand aside, Sister, as long as the Bhikkhus are eating!' If it should not occur to a single Bhikkhu to rebuke the Bhikkhunî, saying, 'Stand aside, Sister, as long as the Bhikkhus are eating!'—that is a matter that ought to be confessed by those Bhikkhus, saying, 'We have fallen, Brethren, into a blameworthy offence, unbecoming, which ought to be confessed; and we confess it!'

3. Whatsoever Bhikkhu shall accept, with his

[1] Antaraghara*m* pavi*tth*â; that is, during her alms-visit to the village. Compare the 3rd Sekhiya; Mahâvagga I, 23, 3; and *K*ullavagga VIII, 5, 2.

own hand, food, either hard or soft, in such households as have been (by a formal sammuti) declared to be households, under discipline[1], without having been previously invited, and without being sick, and eat it or enjoy it—that is a matter that ought to be confessed by that Bhikkhu, saying, 'I have fallen, Brethren, into a blameworthy offence, unbecoming, which ought to be confessed; and I confess it!'

4. Whatsoever Bhikkhu, while he is dwelling in a place belonging to the class of those forest dwellings which are held to be insecure and dangerous[2], shall accept, with his own hand, at his home, food, either hard or soft, without having previously given notice (of the danger incurred by people that enter that forest), unless he is sick, and shall eat it or enjoy it—that is a matter that ought to be confessed by that Bhikkhu, saying, 'I have fallen, Brethren, into a blameworthy offence, unbecoming, which ought to be confessed; and I confess it!'

Here end the Pâ*t*idesaniyas.

Venerable Sirs, the four rules regarding matters which require confession have been recited.

In respect of them I ask the venerable ones, 'Are you pure in this matter?'

---

[1] Sekha-sammatâni kulâni; which the Vibhaṅga explains as a household grown rich in faith, but poor in goods; where whatever they get is given away to the Order, though the family may be some days in want of it. Compare what is said of Anâthapi*nd*ika in the Introduction to the 40th *G*âtaka (*G*âtaka I, 228); though his lot had not reached the very lowest limit.

[2] Compare the 29th Nissaggiya.

A second time I ask the venerable ones, 'Are you pure in this matter?'

A third time I ask the venerable ones, 'Are you pure in this matter?'

The venerable ones are pure herein. Therefore do they keep silence. Thus I understand.

Here endeth the recitation of the Pâ*t*idesaniyas.

SEKHIYÂ DHAMMÂ.

Rules regarding Matters connected with Discipline.

Here, venerable Sirs, the rules regarding matters connected with discipline come into recitation.

1. 'I will put on my under garment all around me[1].' This is a discipline which ought to be observed.

2. 'I will put on my robe all around me.' This is a discipline which ought to be observed.

3. 'Properly clad will I go amidst the houses[2].' This is a discipline which ought to be observed.

4. 'Properly clad will I take my seat amidst the houses.' This is a discipline which ought to be observed.

5. '(With my body) under proper control[3] will I go amidst the houses.' This is a discipline which ought to be observed.

6. '(With my body) under proper control will I take my seat amidst the houses.' This is a discipline which ought to be observed.

7. 'With downcast eye[4] will I go amidst the

---

[1] Parima*nd*ala*m*: 'so as to cover the navel-ma*nd*ala, and the knee-ma*nd*ala,' says the Old Commentary. Compare Childers sub voce Tima*nd*ala*m*; and *K*ullavagga VIII, 5, 2.

[2] Antaraghare. The antaraghara*m* is the space in a village between the huts; not exactly the same, and yet in the following rules practically the same, as the village (gâma).

[3] Not, for instance, with dirty hands or feet, according to the Vibhaṅga.

[4] The practical rule is for a Bhikkhu to look at a spot in the ground about a plough's length in front of him.

houses.' This is a discipline which ought to be observed.

8. 'With downcast eye will I take my seat amidst the houses.' This is a discipline which ought to be observed.

9. 'With robes not pulled up[1] will I go amidst the houses.' This is a discipline which ought to be observed.

10. 'With robes not pulled up will I take my seat amidst the houses.' This is a discipline which ought to be observed.

End of the first section.

---

11. 'Not with loud laughter will I go amidst the houses.' This is a discipline which ought to be observed.

12. 'Not with loud laughter will I take my seat amidst the houses.' This is a discipline which ought to be observed.

13. 'Making but a little sound will I go amidst the houses.' This is a discipline which ought to be observed.

14. 'Making but a little sound will I take my seat amidst the houses.' This is a discipline which ought to be observed.

15. 'Without swaying my body about will I go amidst the houses.' This is a discipline which ought to be observed.

16. 'Without swaying my body about will I take

[1] Or perhaps 'thrown off.' He is to be fully dressed as laid down in the 1st and 2nd Sekhiyas.

my seat amidst the houses.' This is a discipline which ought to be observed.

17. 'Without swaying my arms about will I go amidst the houses.' This is a discipline which ought to be observed.

18. 'Without swaying my arms about will I take my seat amidst the houses.' This is a discipline which ought to be observed.

19. 'Without swaying my head about will I go amidst the houses.' This is a discipline which ought to be observed.

20. 'Without swaying my head about will I take my seat amidst the houses.' This is a discipline which ought to be observed.

End of the second section.

21. 'With my arms not akimbo[1] will I go amidst the houses.' This is a discipline which ought to be observed.

22. 'With my arms not akimbo will I take my seat amidst the houses.' This is a discipline which ought to be observed.

23. 'With my head uncovered[2] will I go amidst the houses.' This is a discipline which ought to be observed.

24. 'With my head uncovered will I take my seat amidst the houses.' This is a discipline which ought to be observed.

[1] Nakkhambhakato: 'putting the hands on the hips,' says the Old Commentary.

[2] Na ogu*nth*ito: which the Old Commentary applies to the head.

25. 'Without walking on my heels or my toes[1] will I go amidst the houses.' This is a discipline which ought to be observed.

26. 'Without lolling[2] will I take my seat amidst the houses.' This is a discipline which ought to be observed.

27. 'With mind alert[3] will I receive an alms.' This is a discipline which ought to be observed.

28. 'Paying attention to my bowl will I receive an alms.' This is a discipline which ought to be observed.

29. 'With equal curry[4] will I receive an alms.' This is a discipline which ought to be observed.

30. 'Equally full[5] will I receive an alms.' This is a discipline which ought to be observed.

End of the third section.

---

31. 'With mind alert will I eat the alms placed in my bowl.' This is a discipline which ought to be observed.

32. 'Paying attention to my bowl will I eat the

---

[1] Na ukku*t*ikâya; an unusual sense of the word; but it is so explained here by the Old Commentary.

[2] Na pallatthikâya. 'Without making a rest with his hands, or with a cloth,' according to the Old Commentary. Compare the Tipallattha-miga *G*âtaka, and No. 65 below.

[3] Sakka*kk*am. Sati*m* upa*tth*âpetvâ, says the Samanta-Pâsâdikâ. See also No. 31.

[4] Samasûpaka*m*. 'When the curry is in quantity one-fourth of the rice' explains the Samanta-Pâsâdikâ. See No. 34.

[5] Samatittika*m*. 'Equally full, equally heaped up (samabhârita*m*)' explains the Samanta-Pâsâdikâ. Compare the several passages quoted in Rh. D.'s note on Tevi*gg*a Sutta I, 24.

alms placed in my bowl.' This is a discipline which ought to be observed.

33. 'Begging straight on from house to house[1] will I eat the alms placed in my bowl.' This is a discipline which ought to be observed.

34. 'With equal curry will I eat the alms placed in my bowl.' This is a discipline which ought to be observed.

35. 'Without pressing down from the top[2] will I eat the alms placed in my bowl.' This is a discipline which ought to be observed.

36. 'Neither the curry nor the condiment will I cover up with the rice, desiring to make it nicer[3].' This is a discipline which ought to be observed.

37. 'Neither curry nor rice will I ask for, for my own particular use, unless I am sick.' This is a discipline which ought to be observed.

38. 'Not with envious thoughts will I look at others' bowls.' This is a discipline which ought to be observed.

39. 'Not into too large balls will I make (up my food).' This is a discipline which ought to be observed.

40. 'Into round mouthfuls will I make up my food.' This is a discipline which ought to be observed.

End of the fourth section.

[1] Sapadâna*m*. See Childers sub voce. The Vibhaṅga says, *Kh*abbaggiyâ bhikkhû taha*m* taha*m* omadditvâ pi*nd*apâta*m* bhuñ-*g*anti. The Samanta-Pâsâdikâ says, Sapadânan ti tattha tattha odhi*m* akatvâ anupa*t*ipâ*t*iyâ.

[2] Na thûpato omadditvâ; on which the Samanta-Pâsâdikâ has 'matthakato vemaggh*a*to ti.' He is not to pick and choose what morsel he takes.

[3] Compare the 8th Nissaggiya. In the text read upâdâya.

41. 'Not till the ball is brought close will I open the door of my mouth.' This is a discipline which ought to be observed.

42. 'Not the whole hand, when eating, will I put into my mouth.' This is a discipline which ought to be observed.

43. 'When the food is in my mouth will I not talk.' This is a discipline which ought to be observed.

44. 'Without tossing the food into my mouth will I eat[1].' This is a discipline which ought to be observed.

45. 'Without nibbling at the balls of food will I eat.' This is a discipline which ought to be observed.

46. 'Without stuffing my cheeks out will I eat[2].' This is a discipline which ought to be observed.

47. 'Without shaking my hands about[3] will I eat.' This is a discipline which ought to be observed.

48. 'Without scattering the lumps of boiled rice will I eat.' This is a discipline which ought to be observed.

49. 'Without putting out my tongue will I eat.' This is a discipline which ought to be observed.

50. 'Without smacking my lips[4] will I eat.' This is a discipline which ought to be observed.

End of the fifth section.

---

[1] Pi*nd*ukkhepakan ti pi*ndam* ukkhipitvâ ukkhipitvâ, says the Samanta-Pâsâdikâ.

[2] Avaga*nd*akârakan ti makka*t*o viya ga*nd*e katvâ, says the Samanta-Pâsâdikâ (Minayeff, p. 93).

[3] That is, to disengage particles of the rice, to shake them off on to the ground.

[4] Literally, without making the sound '*K*apu-*k*apu.'

51. 'Without making a hissing sound will I eat[1].' This is a discipline which ought to be observed.

52. 'Without licking my fingers will I eat.' This is a discipline which ought to be observed.

53. 'Without licking my bowl will I eat.' This is a discipline which ought to be observed.

54. 'Without licking my lips will I eat.' This is a discipline which ought to be observed.

55. 'Not with a hand soiled with food will I take hold of the water-jar.' This is a discipline which ought to be observed.

56. 'The rinsings of the bowl mixed with lumps of boiled rice will I not throw into the inner court[2].' This is a discipline which ought to be observed.

57. 'Not to a person with a sunshade in his hand, unless he is sick, will I preach the Dhamma.' This is a discipline which ought to be observed.

58. 'Not to a person with a staff in his hand, unless he is sick, will I preach the Dhamma.' This is a discipline which ought to be observed.

59. 'Not to a person with a sword in his hand, unless he is sick, will I preach the Dhamma.' This is a discipline which ought to be observed.

60. 'Not to a person with a weapon in his hand, unless he is sick, will I preach the Dhamma.' This is a discipline which ought to be observed.

End of the sixth section.

61. 'Not to a person wearing slippers, unless he

[1] Literally, without making the sound 'Suru-suru.'

[2] Antaraghare, which here means the space, or small open square in the middle of the house.

is sick, will I preach the Dhamma.' This is a discipline which ought to be observed.

62. 'Not to a person wearing sandals, unless he is sick, will I preach the Dhamma.' This is a discipline which ought to be observed.

63. 'Not to a person seated in a cart, unless he is sick, will I preach the Dhamma.' This is a discipline which ought to be observed.

64. 'Not to a person lying on a couch, unless he is sick, will I preach the Dhamma.' This is a discipline which ought to be observed.

65. 'Not to a person lolling, unless he is sick, will I preach the Dhamma.' This is a discipline which ought to be observed.

66. 'Not to a person with a turban on his head, unless he is sick, will I preach the Dhamma.' This is a discipline which ought to be observed.

67. 'Not to a person with his head covered, unless he is sick, will I preach the Dhamma.' This is a discipline which ought to be observed.

68. 'Not to a person seated on a seat, unless he is sick, will I, seated on the earth, preach the Dhamma.' This is a discipline which ought to be observed.

69. 'Not to a person seated on a high seat, unless he is sick, will I, seated on a low seat, preach the Dhamma.' This is a discipline which ought to be observed.

70. 'Not to a person sitting, unless he is sick, will I, standing, preach the Dhamma.' This is a discipline which ought to be observed.

End of the seventh section.

71. 'Not to a person walking in front of me, unless he is sick, will I, walking behind, preach the Dhamma.' This is a discipline which ought to be observed.

72. 'Not to a person walking on a path, unless he is sick, will I, walking by the side of the path, preach the Dhamma.' This is a discipline which ought to be observed.

73. 'Not standing will I ease myself, unless I am sick.' This is a discipline which ought to be observed.

74. 'Not on growing grass will I ease myself, or spit.' This is a discipline which ought to be observed.

75. 'Not into water will I ease myself, or spit.' This is a discipline which ought to be observed.

Venerable Sirs, the rules regarding matters of discipline have been recited.

In respect of them I ask the venerable ones, 'Are you pure in this matter?'

A second time I ask the venerable ones, 'Are you pure in this matter?'

A third time I ask the venerable ones, 'Are you pure in this matter?'

The venerable ones are pure herein. Therefore do they keep silence. Thus I understand.

Here endeth the recitation of the Sekhiyas.

THE ADHIKARAṆA-SAMATHÂ DHAMMÂ.

THE RULES REGARDING THE SETTLEMENT OF CASES.

Here, venerable Sirs, the seven rules regarding the settlement of cases come into recitation.

For the decision and settlement of cases as they from time to time arise, the Proceeding in presence[1] must be performed, or the Proceeding for the consciously innocent[2], or the Proceeding in the case of those who are no longer out of their mind[3], or the Proceeding on confession of guilt[4], or the Proceeding by majority of the chapter[5], or the Proceeding for the obstinate[6], or the Proceeding by covering over as with grass[7].

Venerable Sirs, the seven rules regarding the settlement of cases have been recited.

In respect of them I ask the venerable ones, 'Are you pure in this matter?'

A second time I ask the venerable ones, 'Are you pure in this matter?'

A third time I ask the venerable ones, 'Are you pure in this matter?'

---

[1] Sammukhâ-vinaya. See *K*ullavagga IV, 14, 16. and following.

[2] Sati-vinaya. See *K*ullavagga IV, 14, 27.

[3] Amû*lh*a-vinaya. See *K*ullavagga IV, 5, and following, and IV, 14, 28.

[4] Pa*t*iññâya. See *K*ullavagga IV, 7, 8.

[5] Yebhuyyasikâ. See *K*ullavagga IV, 9, and IV, 14, 24.

[6] Tassapâpiyyasikâ. See *K*ullavagga IV, 11.

[7] Ti*n*avatthâraka. See *K*ullavagga IV, 13.

The venerable ones are pure herein. Therefore do they keep silence. Thus I understand.

Here endeth the recitation of the Adhikara*n*a-samathas.

Venerable Sirs! Recited is the Introduction.
Recited are the four Pârâ*g*ika Rules.
Recited are the thirteen Sa*m*ghâdisesa Rules.
Recited are the two Aniyata Rules.
Recited are the thirty Nissaggiya-Pâ*k*ittiya Rules.
Recited are the ninety-two Pâ*k*ittiya Rules.
Recited are the four Pâ*t*idesaniya Rules.
Recited are the Sekhiya Rules.
Recited are the seven Adhikara*n*a-samatha Rules.

So much (of the words) of the Blessed One, handed down in the Suttas, embraced in the Suttas, comes into recitation every half month. It behoveth all to train themselves according thereto in concord, in pleasantness, without dispute!

Here endeth the recitation of the Pâtimokkha for the use of the Bhikkhus.

MAHÂVAGGA.

THE MAHÂVAGGA.

REVERENCE TO THE BLESSED ONE, THE HOLY ONE, THE FULLY ENLIGHTENED ONE.

FIRST KHANDHAKA.

(THE ADMISSION TO THE ORDER OF BHIKKHUS.)

1[1].

1. At that time the blessed Buddha dwelt at

[1] To this book is prefixed, as introduction, an account of the first events after Gotama's attaining Buddhahood, down to the conversion of his two chief disciples, Sâriputta and Moggallâna (chaps. 1–24). Among the elements of historical or legendary character with which, in the Vinaya Pi*t*aka, the discussion of the monastic discipline is interwoven, this account occupies by far the first place, both in extent and in importance. For it contains the oldest version accessible to us now and, most probably, for ever, of what the Buddhist fraternity deemed to be the history of their Master's life in its most important period.

The connection in which this legendary narration stands with the main subject of the first Khandhaka is not difficult to account for. The regulations regarding the admission to the fraternity, which are discussed in this Khandhaka, could not but present themselves to the redactors of the Pi*t*aka as being the very basis of their religious discipline and monastic life. It was possible to fancy the existence of the Sa*m*gha without the Pâtimokkha rules, or without the regulations about the Pavâra*n*â festival, but it was impossible to realise the idea of a Sa*m*gha without rules showing who was to be regarded as a duly admitted member of the fraternity, and who was not. It is quite natural, therefore, that the stories or legends concerning the ordination of Bhikkhus were put in connection with the record of the very first events of the history of the Sa*m*gha.

Nor is it difficult to account for the theory formulated by the

Uruvelâ, on the bank of the river Nerañgarâ[1], at the foot of the Bodhi tree (tree of wisdom), just after he had become Sambuddha. And the blessed Buddha sat cross-legged at the foot of the Bodhi tree uninterruptedly during seven days, enjoying the bliss of emancipation[2].

---

historians of the Buddhist ecclesiastical law, of different successive forms in which the ordination of Bhikkhus had been performed. In the beginning, of course, there was nobody but the Buddha himself who could ordain Bhikkhus; to him those who desired to be received, expressed their wish, and he conferred on them the pabbaggâ and upasampadâ ordinations by the formula: 'Ehi bhikkhu,' &c. (see I, 6, 32, 34, &c.) It was a very natural conception that afterwards, as the Samgha grew larger, the Buddha should have transferred the power of admitting new members to the Bhikkhus themselves, and should have instituted that form of ordination which the redactors of the Piṭaka found valid at their own time.

The transition, however, from the supposed oldest form of ordination (the so-called ehi-bhikkhu-upasampadâ) to that latter form is in the Vinaya legends not represented as immediate. There is described an intermediate stage between the two, the ordination by the three saranagamanas, or by the candidate's three times repeated declaration of his taking refuge in the Buddha, the Dhamma, and the Samgha (see Mahâvagga I, 12). The reason which has led the redactors of the Vinaya Piṭaka to this construction, was most probably the important part which in the upasampadâ service of the later time devolved upon the preceptor (upagghâya) of the candidate. As only learned Bhikkhus, who had completed the tenth year after their own upasampadâ, could perform the function of upagghâya at the upasampadâ ordination of other Bhikkhus (Mahâvagga I, 31, 8), it was natural that the redactors of the Vinaya found it impossible to ascribe this form of upasampadâ service to the first times of Buddha's teaching. For these times, therefore, they recorded another form, the upasampadâ by the three saranagamanas, the introduction of which they assigned, very naturally, to the time soon after the conversion of Yasa's friends, by which event the number of Bhikkhus had been augmented at once from seven to sixty-one.

[1] The Lilayan or Phalgu river in Behar; see General Cunningham's map, Archaeological Reports, vol. i. plate iii.

[2] After having reached the sambodhi and before preaching to

2. Then the Blessed One (at the end of these seven days) during the first watch of the night fixed his mind upon the Chain of Causation[1], in direct and in reverse order: 'From Ignorance[2] spring the sa*m*-

---

the world the truth he has acquired, the Buddha remains, according to the tradition, during some weeks at Uruvelâ, 'enjoying the bliss of emancipation.' The Mahâvagga, which contains these legends in their oldest forms, assigns to this stay a period of four times seven days; the later tradition is unanimous in extending it to seven times seven days (Buddhaghosa in the commentary on the Mahâvagga; *G*âtaka Atthav. vol. i. p. 77 seq.; Dîpava*m*sa I, 29, 30; Lalita Vistara, p. 488 seq.; Beal, Romantic Legend, p. 236 seq., &c.)

[1] The Chain of Causation, or the doctrine of the twelve nidânas (causes of existence), contains, as has often been observed, in a more developed form an answer to the same problem to which the second and third of the four Noble Truths (ariyasa*kk*a) also try to give a solution, viz. the problem of the origin and destruction of suffering. The Noble Truths simply reduce the origin of suffering to Thirst, or Desire (Ta*n*hâ), in its threefold form, thirst for pleasure, thirst for existence, thirst for prosperity (see I, 6, 20). In the system of the twelve nidânas Thirst also has found its place among the causes of suffering, but it is not considered as the immediate cause. A concatenation of other categories is inserted between ta*n*hâ and its ultimate effect; and on the other hand, the investigation of causes is carried on further beyond ta*n*hâ. The question is here asked, What does ta*n*hâ come from? and thus the series of causes and effects is led back to avi*gg*â (Ignorance), as its deepest root. We may add that the redactors of the Pi*t*akas, who of course could not but observe this parallelity between the second and third ariyasa*kk*as and the system of the twelve nidânas, go so far, in one instance (Aṅguttara-Nikâya, Tika-Nipâta, fol. *k*e of the Phayre MS.), as to directly replace, in giving the text of the four ariyasa*kk*as, the second and third of them by the twelve nidânas, in direct and reverse order respectively. Professor Childers has furnished a valuable note on the nidânas; see Colebrooke, Miscellaneous Essays (second edition), II, 453 seq.

[2] In the Sammâdi*tth*isuttanta (Ma*gg*hima-Nikâya, fol. khû of Turnour's MS.) we find the following explanation of what Ignorance is: 'Not to know Suffering, not to know the Cause of suffering,

khâras[1], from the saṃkhâras springs Consciousness, from Consciousness spring Name-and-Form, from Name-and-Form spring the six Provinces (of the

not to know the Cessation of suffering, not to know the Path which leads to the cessation of suffering, this is called Ignorance.' The same is repeated in the explanation of the nidâna formula, which is given in the Vibhaṅga (Abhidhamma-Piṭaka, Paṭikkasamuppâda-vibhaṅga, fol. ki of the Phayre MS.), and we must accept it, therefore, as the authentic expression of Buddhistical belief. It is obvious, however, that this explanation leaves room for another question. Ignorance, we are told, is the source of all evil and of all suffering, and the subject ignored is stated to be the four Truths. But who is the subject that ignores them? All attributes (as the viññâṇa, &c.), that constitute sentient beings and enable them to know or to ignore, are said to be first produced by Ignorance, and we should conclude, therefore, that they cannot exist before Ignorance has begun to act. Or are we to understand that it is the Ignorance incurred by a sentient being in a preceding existence, that causes the saṃkhâras and Consciousness, the connecting links between the different existences, to act and to bring about the birth of a new being?

As is well known, this Ignorance (Avidyâ) plays a great part also in the Brahmanical philosophy of the Upanishads; and the Buddhist belief is, no doubt, founded to a considerable extent on older theories. But we cannot venture in a note to touch upon one of the most difficult and interesting questions which await the research of Indianists.

[1] It is very frequently stated that there are three saṃkhâras or productions: kâyasaṃkhâra, vakîsaṃkhâra, and kittasaṃkhâra, or, productions of body, of speech, and of thought (see, for instance, the Sammâdiṭṭhisuttanta, Magghima-Nikâya, fol. khû of Turnour's MS.) The kâyasaṃkhâra consists, according to the Saṃkhâra-Yamaka (Abhidhamma-Piṭaka), in inhalation and expiration (assâsapassâsâ); the vakîsaṃkhâra in attention and investigation (vitakkavikârâ); the kittasaṃkhâra in ideas, sensations, and all attributes of mind except attention and investigation (saññâ ka vedanâ ka ṭhapetvâ vitakkavikâre sabbe pi kittasampayuttakâ dhammâ). The Vibhaṅga (Abhidhamma-Piṭaka, Paṭikkasamuppâdavibhaṅga, l.l.) gives, when discussing the saṃkhâras, six categories instead of the three: 'Now which are

six senses[1]), from the six Provinces springs Contact, from Contact springs Sensation, from Sensation springs Thirst (or Desire), from Thirst springs Attachment, from Attachment springs Existence, from Existence springs Birth, from Birth spring Old Age and Death, grief, lamentation, suffering, dejection, and despair. Such is the origination of this whole mass of suffering. Again, by the destruction of Ignorance, which consists in the complete absence of lust, the sa*m*khâras are destroyed, by the destruction of the sa*m*khâras Consciousness is destroyed, by the destruction of Consciousness Name-and-Form are destroyed, by the destruction of Name-and-Form the six Provinces are destroyed, by the destruction of the six Provinces Contact is destroyed, by the destruction of Contact Sensation is destroyed, by the destruction of Sensation Thirst is destroyed, by the destruction of Thirst Attachment is destroyed, by the destruction of Attachment Existence is destroyed, by the destruction of Existence Birth is destroyed, by the destruction of Birth Old Age and Death, grief, lamentation, suffering, dejection, and despair are

---

the sa*m*khâras that are produced by Ignorance? Sa*m*khâras (or, productions) that lead to righteousness, sa*m*khâras that lead to sinfulness, sa*m*khâras that lead to immovability, productions of body, of speech, and of thought.' The Pâli words are: 'Tattha katame avi*gg*âpa*kk*ayâ sa*m*khârâ? pu*ññ*âbhisa*m*khâro apu*ññ*âbhisa*m*khâro â*n*a*ñg*âbhisa*m*khâro kâyasa*m*khâro va*k*îsa*m*khâro *k*ittasa*m*khâro.' The list of fifty-five categories belonging to the sa*m*khâra-khandha, which Sp. Hardy gives in his Manual (p. 404 seq.; comp. also Rh. D., 'Buddhism,' p. 91 seq., and 'Buddhist Suttas from the Pâli,' p. 242), is not founded, as far as we know, on the authority of the Pi*t*akas themselves, but on later compendia and commentaries.

[1] I. e. eye, ear, nose, tongue, body (or the faculty of touch), and mind.

destroyed. Such is the cessation of this whole mass of suffering.'

3. Knowing this the Blessed One then on that occasion pronounced this solemn utterance: 'When the real nature of things becomes clear to the ardent, meditating Brâhma*n*a, then all his doubts fade away, since he realises what is that nature and what its cause.'

4. Then the Blessed One during the middle watch of the night fixed his mind upon the Chain of Causation, in direct and reverse order: 'From Ignorance spring the sa*m*khâras, &c. . . . . . . Such is the origination of this whole mass of suffering, &c. . . . . . . Such is the cessation of this whole mass of suffering.'

5. Knowing this the Blessed One then on that occasion pronounced this solemn utterance: 'When the real nature of things becomes clear to the ardent, meditating Brâhma*n*a, then all his doubts fade away, since he has understood the cessation of causation.'

6. Then the Blessed One during the third watch of the night fixed his mind, &c.

7. Knowing this the Blessed One then on that occasion pronounced this solemn utterance: 'When the real nature of things becomes clear to the ardent, meditating Brâhma*n*a, he stands, dispelling the hosts of Mâra, like the sun that illuminates the sky.'

Here ends the account of what passed under the Bodhi tree.

2.

1. Then the Blessed One, at the end of those seven days, arose from that state of meditation, and went from the foot of the Bodhi tree to the A*g*apâla banyan tree (banyan tree of the goat-herds[1]). And when he had reached it, he sat cross-legged at the foot of the A*g*apâla banyan tree uninterruptedly during seven days, enjoying the bliss of emancipation.

2. Now a certain Brâhma*n*a, who was of a haughty disposition[2], went to the place where the Blessed One was; having approached him, he exchanged greeting with the Blessed One; having exchanged with him greeting and complaisant words, he stationed himself near him; then standing near him that Brâhma*n*a thus spoke to the Blessed One: 'By what, Gotama, does one become a Brâhma*n*a, and what are the characteristics that make a man a Brâhma*n*a?'

3. And the Blessed One, having heard that, on this occasion pronounced this solemn utterance: 'That Brâhma*n*a who has removed (from himself) all sinfulness, who is free from haughtiness, free from impurity, self-restrained, who is an accomplished master of knowledge (or, of the Veda), who has fulfilled the duties of holiness, such a Brâhma*n*a may

[1] Buddhaghosa: 'The goat-herds used to go to the shadow of that banyan tree and to sit there; therefore it was called the banyan tree of the goat-herds.' The northern Buddhists say that this tree had been planted by a shepherd boy, during the Bodhisatta's six years' penance, in order to shelter him; see Beal, Rom. Legend, pp. 192, 238, and the Mahâvastu.

[2] 'Huhuṅka*g*âtiko.' Buddhaghosa: 'Because he was di*tth*amaṅgalika, he became filled with haughtiness and wrath, and went about uttering the sound "huhu*m*."' Di*tth*amaṅgalika (having seen something auspicious?) is obscure to us.

justly call himself a Brâhma*n*a, whose behaviour is uneven to nothing in the world.'

Here ends the account of what passed under the A*g*apâla tree.

3.

1. Then the Blessed One, at the end of those seven days, arose from that state of meditation, and went from the foot of the A*g*apâla banyan tree to the Mu*k*alinda tree. And when he had reached it, he sat cross-legged at the foot of the Mu*k*alinda tree uninterruptedly during seven days, enjoying the bliss of emancipation.

2. At that time a great cloud appeared out of season, rainy weather which lasted seven days, cold weather, storms, and darkness. And the Nâga (or Serpent) king Mu*k*alinda came out from his abode, and seven times encircled the body of the Blessed One with his windings, and kept extending his large hood over the Blessed One's head, thinking to himself: 'May no coldness (touch) the Blessed One! May no heat (touch) the Blessed One! May no vexation by gadflies and gnats, by storms and sunheat and reptiles (touch) the Blessed One!'

3. And at the end of those seven days, when the Nâga king Mu*k*alinda saw the open, cloudless sky, he loosened his windings from the body of the Blessed One, made his own appearance disappear, created the appearance of a youth, and stationed himself in front of the Blessed One, raising his clasped hands, and paying reverence to the Blessed One.

4. And the Blessed One, perceiving that, on this occasion, pronounced this solemn utterance: 'Happy is the solitude of him who is full of joy, who has learnt the Truth, who sees (the Truth). Happy is freedom from malice in this world, (self-)restraint towards all beings that have life. Happy is freedom from lust in this world, getting beyond all desires; the putting away of that pride which comes from the thought "I am!" This truly is the highest happiness!'

Here ends the account of what passed under the Mu*k*alinda tree.

4.

1. Then the Blessed One, at the end of those seven days, arose from that state of meditation, and went from the foot of the Mu*k*alinda tree to the Râ*g*âyatana (tree[1]); when he had reached it, he sat cross-legged at the foot of the Râ*g*âyatana tree uninterruptedly during seven days, enjoying the bliss of emancipation.

2. At that time Tapussa and Bhallika, two merchants, came travelling on the road from Ukkala (Orissa) to that place. Then a deity who had been (in a former life) a blood-relation of the merchants Tapussa and Bhallika, thus spoke to the merchants

[1] Buddhaghosa says that Râ*g*âyatana (lit. a royal apartment) was the name of a tree. It is the same tree which in the Lalita Vistara (p. 493, ed. Calcutta) is called Târâya*n*a, and in the Dîpava*m*sa (II, 50) Khîrapâla. The place where the two merchants met Buddha, is thus described in the Mahâvastu: kshîrikâvanasha*nd*e bahudevatake *k*etiye.

Tapussa and Bhallika: 'Here, my noble friends, at the foot of the Râ*g*âyatana tree, is staying the Blessed One, who has just become Sambuddha. Go and show your reverence to him, the Blessed One, by (offering him) rice-cakes and lumps of honey. Long will this be to you for a good and for a blessing.'

3. And the merchants Tapussa and Bhallika took rice-cakes and lumps of honey, and went to the place where the Blessed One was; having approached him and respectfully saluted the Blessed One, they stationed themselves near him; standing near him, the merchants Tapussa and Bhallika thus addressed the Blessed One: 'May, O Lord, the Blessed One accept from us these rice-cakes and lumps of honey, that that may long be to us for a good and for a blessing!'

4. Then the Blessed One thought: 'The Tathâgatas[1] do not accept (food) with their hands. Now

[1] The term Tathâgata is, in the Buddhistical literature, exclusively applied to Sammâsambuddhas, and it is more especially used in the Pi*t*akas when the Buddha is represented as speaking of himself in the third person as 'the Tathâgata.' The meaning 'sentient being,' which is given to the word in the Abhidhânappadîpikâ, and in Childers's Dictionary, is not confirmed, as far as we know, by any passage of the Pi*t*akas. This translation of the word is very possibly based merely on a misunderstanding of the phrase often repeated in the Sutta Pi*t*aka: hoti tathâgato para*m* mara*n*â, which means, of course, 'does a Buddha exist after death?' In the *G*aina books we sometimes find the term tatthagaya (tatragata), 'he who has attained that world, i.e. emancipation,' applied to the *G*inas as opposed to other beings who are called ihagaya (idhagata), 'living in this world.' See, for instance, the *G*ina*k*aritra, § 16. Considering the close relation in which most of the dogmatical terms of the *G*ainas stand to those of the Bauddhas, it is difficult to believe that tathâgata and tatthagaya

with what shall I accept the rice-cakes and lumps of honey?' Then the four Mahârâga gods[1], understanding by the power of their minds the reflection which had arisen in the mind of the Blessed One, offered to the Blessed One from the four quarters (of the horizon) four bowls made of stone (saying), 'May, O Lord, the Blessed One accept herewith the rice-cakes and the lumps of honey!' The Blessed One accepted those new stone bowls; and therein he received the rice-cakes and honey lumps, and those, when he had received, he ate.

5. And Tapussa and Bhallika, the merchants, when they saw that the Blessed One had cleansed[2] his bowl and his hands, bowed down in reverence

---

should not originally have conveyed very similar ideas. We think that on the long way from the original Mâgadhî to the Pâli and Sanskrit, the term tatthagata or tatthâgata (tatra + âgata), 'he who has arrived there, i. e. at emancipation,' may very easily have undergone the change into tathâgata, which would have made it unintelligible, were we not able to compare its unaltered form as preserved by the Gainas.

[1] The four guardian gods of the quarters of the world; see Hardy's Manual, p. 24. Their Pâli names, as given in the Abhidhânappadîpikâ, vv. 31, 32, the Dîpavamsa XVI, 12, &c., were, Dhataraṭṭha, Virûḷhaka, Virûpakkha, and Vessavaṇa or Kuvera.

[2] Onîtapattapâni, which is said very frequently of a person who has finished his meal, is translated by Childers, 'whose hand is removed from the bowl' (comp. also Trenckner, Pali Miscellany, p. 66). We do not think this explanation right, though it agrees with, or probably is based on, a note of Buddhaghosa ('pattato ka apanîtapânim'). Onîta, i. e. avanîta, is not apanîta, and the end of the dinner was marked, not by the Bhikkhu's removing his hand from the bowl, but by his washing the bowl (see Kullavagga VIII, 4, 6), and, of course, his hands. In Sanskrit the meaning of ava-nî is, to pour (water) upon something; see the Petersburg Dictionary. We have translated, therefore, onîtapattapâni accordingly.

at the feet of the Blessed One and thus addressed the Blessed One: 'We take our refuge, Lord, in the Blessed One and in the Dhamma; may the Blessed One receive us as disciples who, from this day forth while our life lasts, have taken their refuge (in him).' These were the first in the world to become lay-disciples (of the Buddha) by the formula which contained (only) the dyad[1].

Here ends the account of what passed under the Râgâyatana tree.

5.

1. Then the Blessed One, at the end of those seven days, arose from that state of meditation, and went from the foot of the Râgâyatana tree to the Agapâla banyan tree. And when he had reached it, the Blessed One stayed there at the foot of the Agapâla banyan tree.

2. Then in the mind of the Blessed One, who was alone, and had retired into solitude, the following thought arose: 'I have penetrated this doctrine which is profound, difficult to perceive and to understand, which brings quietude of heart, which is exalted, which is unattainable by reasoning, abstruse, intelligible (only) to the wise. This people, on the other hand, is given to desire, intent upon desire, delighting in desire. To this people, therefore, who

[1] Because there was no Samgha at that time, their declaration of taking refuge, by which they became upâsakas, could refer only to the dyad (the Buddha and the Dhamma), instead of to the triad of the Buddha, the Dhamma, and the Samgha.

are given to desire, intent upon desire, delighting in desire, the law of causality and the chain of causation will be a matter difficult to understand; most difficult for them to understand will be also the extinction of all sa*m*khâras, the getting rid of all the substrata (of existence[1]), the destruction of desire, the absence of passion, quietude of heart, Nirvâ*n*a! Now if I proclaim the doctrine, and other men are not able to understand my preaching, there would result but weariness and annoyance to me.'

3. And then the following ....[2] stanzas, unheard before, occurred to the Blessed One: 'With great pains have I acquired it. Enough! why should I now proclaim it? This doctrine will not be easy to understand to beings that are lost in lust and hatred.

'Given to lust, surrounded with thick darkness, they will not see what is repugnant (to their minds), abstruse, profound, difficult to perceive, and subtle.'

4. When the Blessed One pondered over this matter, his mind became inclined to remain in quiet, and not to preach the doctrine. Then Brahmâ

---

[1] The upadhis (substrata of existence) are specified in the commentary on the Sutta-Nipâta, ap. Dhammapada, p. 433: 'sabbûpadhinam parikkhayâ 'ti sabbesa*m* khandhakâmagu*n*akilesâbhisa*m*khârabhedâna*m* upadhîna*m* parikkhî*n*attâ.' Probably abhisa*m*khâra is not co-ordinate with the other members of the compound, but is determined by them, comp. pabba*gg*âbhisa*m*khâra, iddhâbhisa*m*khâra, gamikâbhisa*m*khâra. The upadhis, therefore, according to this passage, consist: firstly, in the actions of mind that are directed towards the khandhas (i. e. that have the effect of propagating and augmenting the dominion of the khandhas); secondly, in the actions tending to the fivefold pleasures of sense; and thirdly, in those connected with kilesa (evil passion).

[2] Buddhaghosa explains ana*kkh*ariya by anua*kkh*ariya, which is alike unintelligible to us. The Lalita Vistara (p. 515, ed. Calcutta) has abhîksh*n*am ('repeatedly').

Sahampati[1], understanding by the power of his mind the reflection which had arisen in the mind of the Blessed One, thought: 'Alas! the world perishes! Alas! the world is destroyed! if the mind of the Tathâgata, of the holy, of the absolute Sambuddha inclines itself to remain in quiet, and not to preach the doctrine.'

5. Then Brahmâ Sahampati disappeared from Brahma's world, and appeared before the Blessed One (as quickly) as a strong man might stretch his bent arm out, or draw back his out-stretched arm.

6. And Brahmâ Sahampati adjusted his upper robe so as to cover one shoulder, and putting his right knee on the ground, raised his joined hands towards the Blessed One, and said to the Blessed One: 'Lord, may the Blessed One preach the doctrine! may the perfect One preach the doctrine! there are beings whose mental eyes are darkened by scarcely any dust; but if they do not hear the doctrine, they cannot attain salvation. These will understand the doctrine.'

7. Thus spoke Brahmâ Sahampati; and when he had thus spoken, he further said: 'The Dhamma hitherto manifested in the country of Magadha has been impure, thought out by contaminated men. But do thou now open the door of the Immortal[2]; let them hear the doctrine discovered by the spotless One!

'As a man standing on a rock, on mountain's

[1] It is difficult to believe that the Pâli name of Brahmâ Sahampati, the ruler of the Brahma worlds (see Spence Hardy's Manual, pp. 43, 56), is not connected with the Brahman svayambhû of the Brahmanical literature. Perhaps the Sanskrit equivalent of sahampati might be svayampati.

[2] Amata, an epithet of Arahatship, which may perhaps mean simply ambrosia. See Rh. D., Buddhism, pp. 60, 111, 184.

top, might overlook the people all around, thus, O wise One, ascending to the highest palace of Truth, look down, all-seeing One, upon the people lost in suffering, overcome by birth and decay,—thou, who hast freed thyself from suffering!

'Arise, O hero; O victorious One! Wander through the world, O leader of the pilgrim band, who thyself art free from debt. May the Blessed One preach the doctrine; there will be people who can understand it!'

8. When he had spoken thus, the Blessed One said to Brahmâ Sahampati: 'The following thought, Brahmâ, has occurred to me: "I have penetrated this doctrine, ... (&c., down to end of § 2)." And also, Brahmâ, the following . . . . [1] stanzas have presented themselves to my mind, which had not been heard (by me) before: "With great pains, ... (&c., down to end of § 3)." When I pondered over this matter, Brahmâ, my mind became inclined to remain in quiet, and not to preach the doctrine.'

9. And a second time Brahmâ Sahampati said to the Blessed One: 'Lord, may the Blessed One preach the doctrine, ... (&c., as in §§ 6, 7).' And for the second time the Blessed One said to Brahmâ Sahampati: 'The following thought . . . . (&c., as before).'

10. And a third time Brahmâ Sahampati said to the Blessed One: 'Lord, may the Blessed One preach the doctrine, ... (&c., as before).'

Then the Blessed One, when he had heard Brahmâ's solicitation, looked, full of compassion towards sentient beings, over the world, with his (all-perceiving) eye of a Buddha. And the Blessed One, looking over the world with his eye of a Buddha,

[1] See § 3 with our note for this omitted word.

saw beings whose mental eyes were darkened by scarcely any dust, and beings whose eyes were covered by much dust, beings sharp of sense and blunt of sense, of good disposition and of bad disposition, easy to instruct and difficult to instruct, some of them seeing the dangers of future life and of sin.

11. As, in a pond of blue lotuses, or water-roses, or white lotuses, some blue lotuses, or water-roses, or white lotuses, born in the water, grown up in the water, do not emerge over the water, but thrive hidden under the water; and other blue lotuses, or water-roses, or white lotuses, born in the water, grown up in the water, reach to the surface of the water; and other blue lotuses, or water-roses, or white lotuses, born in the water, grown up in the water, stand emerging out of the water, and the water does not touch them,—

12. Thus the Blessed One, looking over the world with his eye of a Buddha, saw beings whose mental eyes were darkened, ... (&c., the text repeats § 10); and when he had thus seen them, he addressed Brahmâ Sahampati in the following stanza: 'Wide opened is the door of the Immortal to all who have ears to hear; let them send forth faith to meet it. The Dhamma sweet and good I spake not, Brahmâ, despairing of the weary task, to men.'

13. Then Brahmâ Sahampati understood: 'The Blessed One grants my request that He should preach the doctrine.' And he bowed down before the Blessed One, and passed round him with his right side towards him; and then he straightway disappeared.

Here ends the story of Brahmâ's request.

6.

1. Now the Blessed One thought: 'To whom shall I preach the doctrine first? Who will understand this doctrine easily?' And the Blessed One thought: 'There is Â*l*âra Kâlâma[1]; he is clever, wise, and learned; long since have the eye of his mind been darkened by scarcely any dust. What if I were to preach the doctrine first to Â*l*âra Kâlâma? He will easily understand this doctrine.'

2. Then an invisible deity said to the Blessed One: 'Â*l*âra Kâlâma has died, Lord, seven days ago.' And knowledge sprang up in the Blessed One's mind that Â*l*âra Kâlâma had died seven days ago. And the Blessed One thought: 'Highly noble was Â*l*âra Kâlâma. If he had heard my doctrine, he would easily have understood it.'

3. Then the Blessed One thought: 'To whom shall I preach the doctrine first? Who will understand this doctrine easily?' And the Blessed One thought: 'There is Uddaka Râmaputta[1]; he is clever, wise, and learned; long since have the eye of his mind been darkened by scarcely any dust. What if I were to preach the doctrine first to Uddaka Râmaputta? He will easily understand this doctrine.'

4. Then an invisible deity said to the Blessed One: 'Uddaka Râmaputta has died, Lord, yesterday evening.' And knowledge arose in the Blessed One's mind that Uddaka Râmaputta had died the previous evening. And the Blessed One thought:

[1] Â*l*âra Kâlâma and Uddaka Râmaputta were the two teachers to whom Gotama had attached himself first after his pabba*gg*â. See Fausböll's *G*âtaka, vol. i. p. 66; Rh. D., Buddhism, p. 34.

'Highly noble was Uddaka Râmaputta. If he had heard my doctrine, he would easily have understood it.'

5. Then the Blessed One thought: 'To whom shall I preach the doctrine first? Who will understand this doctrine easily?' And the Blessed One thought: 'The five Bhikkhus[1] have done many services to me[2]; they attended on me during the time of my exertions (to attain sanctification by undergoing austerities). What if I were to preach the doctrine first to the five Bhikkhus?'

6. Now the Blessed One thought: 'Where do the five Bhikkhus dwell now?' And the Blessed One saw by the power of his divine, clear vision, surpassing that of men, that the five Bhikkhus were living at Benares, in the deer park Isipatana[3]. And the Blessed One, after having remained at Uruvelâ as long as he thought fit, went forth to Benares.

7. Now Upaka, a man belonging to the Â*g*îvaka sect (i. e. the sect of naked ascetics), saw the Blessed One travelling on the road, between Gayâ and the Bodhi tree; and when he saw him, he said to the Blessed One: 'Your countenance, friend, is serene; your complexion is pure and bright. In whose

---

[1] See about the five companions of Buddha's self-mortification, in the time before the sambodhi, the *G*âtaka, vol. i. p. 67; Hardy, Manual, p. 165; Rh. D., Buddhism, p. 35. The names of the five Bhikkhus were, Ko*nd*aññа, Vappa, Bhaddiya, Mahânâma, Assa*g*i.

[2] Perhaps instead of kho 'me (=kho ime) we should read kho me.

[3] 'The Mrigadâwa, or Deer Park, is represented by a fine wood, which still covers an area of about half a mile, and extends from the great tower of Dhamek on the north, to the Chaukundi mound on the south.' Cunningham, Arch. Reports, I, p. 107.

name, friend, have you retired from the world? Who is your teacher? Whose doctrine do you profess?'

8. When Upaka the Âgîvaka had spoken thus, the Blessed One addressed him in the following stanzas: 'I have overcome all foes; I am all-wise; I am free from stains in every way; I have left everything; and have obtained emancipation by the destruction of desire. Having myself gained knowledge, whom should I call my master? I have no teacher; no one is equal to me; in the world of men and of gods no being is like me. I am the holy One in this world, I am the highest teacher, I alone am the absolute Sambuddha; I have gained coolness (by the extinction of all passion) and have obtained Nirvâ*n*a. To found the Kingdom of Truth I go to the city of the Kâsîs (Benares); I will beat the drum of the Immortal in the darkness of this world.'

9. (Upaka replied): 'You profess then, friend, to be the holy, absolute *G*ina[1].'

(Buddha said): 'Like me are all *G*inas who have reached extinction of the Âsavas[2]; I have overcome (*g*itâ me) all states of sinfulness; therefore, Upaka, am I the *G*ina.'

When he had spoken thus, Upaka the Âgîvaka replied: 'It may be so, friend;' shook his head, took another road, and went away.

10. And the Blessed One, wandering from place to place, came to Benares, to the deer park Isipatana, to the place where the five Bhikkhus were. And

[1] *G*ina, or the victorious One, is one of the many appellations common to the founders of the Bauddha and *G*aina sects.

[2] Sensuality, individuality, delusion, and ignorance (Kâma, Bhava, Di*tth*i, and Avi*gg*â).

the five Bhikkhus saw the Blessed One coming from afar; when they saw him, they concerted with each other, saying, 'Friends, there comes the sama*n*a Gotama, who lives in abundance, who has given up his exertions, and who has turned to an abundant life. Let us not salute him; nor rise from our seats when he approaches; nor take his bowl and his robe from his hands. But let us put there a seat; if he likes, let him sit down.'

11. But when the Blessed One gradually approached near unto those five Bhikkhus, the five Bhikkhus kept not their agreement. They went forth to meet the Blessed One; one took his bowl and his robe, another prepared a seat, a third one brought water for the washing of the feet, a foot-stool, and a towel[1]. Then the Blessed One sat down on the seat they had prepared; and when he was seated, the Blessed One washed his feet. Now they addressed the Blessed One by his name, and with the appellation 'Friend.'

12. When they spoke to him thus, the Blessed One said to the five Bhikkhus: 'Do not address, O Bhikkhus, the Tathâgata by his name, and with the appellation "Friend." The Tathâgata, O Bhikkhus, is the holy, absolute Sambuddha. Give ear, O Bhikkhus! The immortal (Amata) has been won (by me); I will teach you; to you I preach the doctrine. If you walk in the way I show you, you will, ere long, have penetrated to the truth, having yourselves known it and seen it face to face; and you

[1] Buddhaghosa, in a note on *K*ullavagga II, 1, 1, says that pâdapî*th*a is a stool to put the washed foot on, pâdakathalika (or pâdakathalikâ?), a stool to put the unwashed foot on, or a cloth to rub the feet with (pâdagha*m*sana).

will live in the possession of that highest goal of the holy life, for the sake of which noble youths fully give up the world and go forth into the houseless state.'

13. When he had spoken thus, the five monks said to the Blessed One: 'By those observances, friend Gotama, by those practices, by those austerities, you have not been able to obtain power surpassing that of men, nor the superiority of full and holy knowledge and insight. How will you now, living in abundance, having given up your exertions, having turned to an abundant life, be able to obtain power surpassing that of men, and the superiority of full and holy knowledge and insight?'

14. When they had spoken thus, the Blessed One said to the five Bhikkhus: 'The Tathâgata, O Bhikkhus, does not live in abundance, he has not given up exertion, he has not turned to an abundant life. The Tathâgata, O Bhikkhus, is the holy, absolute Sambuddha. Give ear, O Bhikkhus; the immortal has been won (by me); I will teach you, to you I will preach the doctrine. If you walk in the way I show you, you will, ere long, have penetrated to the truth, having yourselves known it and seen it face to face; and you will live in the possession of that highest goal of the holy life, for the sake of which noble youths fully give up the world and go forth into the houseless state.'

15. And the five Bhikkhus said to the Blessed One a second time (as above). And the Blessed One said to the five Bhikkhus a second time (as above). And the five Bhikkhus said to the Blessed One a third time (as above).

16. When they had spoken thus, the Blessed One

said to the five Bhikkhus: 'Do you admit, O Bhikkhus, that I have never spoken to you in this way before this day?'

'You have never spoken so, Lord.'

'The Tathâgata, O Bhikkhus, is the holy, absolute Sambuddha. Give ear, O Bhikkhus, &c. (as above).'

And the Blessed One was able to convince the five Bhikkhus; and the five Bhikkhus again[1] listened willingly to the Blessed One; they gave ear, and fixed their mind on the knowledge (which the Buddha imparted to them).

17. And the Blessed One thus addressed the five Bhikkhus[2]: 'There are two extremes, O Bhikkhus, which he who has given up the world, ought to avoid. What are these two extremes? A life given to pleasures, devoted to pleasures and lusts: this is degrading, sensual, vulgar, ignoble, and profitless; and a life given to mortifications: this is painful, ignoble, and profitless. By avoiding these two extremes, O Bhikkhus, the Tathâgata has gained the knowledge of the Middle Path which leads to insight, which leads to wisdom, which conduces to calm, to knowledge, to the Sambodhi, to Nirvâ*n*a.

18. 'Which, O Bhikkhus, is this Middle Path the knowledge of which the Tathâgata has gained, which leads to insight, which leads to wisdom, which con-

---

[1] As they had done before when they underwent austerities together with the Bodhisatta at Uruvelâ.

[2] Of the literature that exists referring to the discourse which follows now (the Dhamma*k*akkappavattana Sutta), it will suffice to quote M. Feer's Études Bouddhiques, I, p. 189 seq., and Rh. D., 'Buddhist Suttas from the Pâli,' pp. 137–155, and in the Fortnightly Review for December 1879.

duces to calm, to knowledge, to the Sambodhi, to Nirvâ*n*a? It is the holy eightfold Path, namely, Right Belief, Right Aspiration, Right Speech, Right Conduct, Right Means of Livelihood, Right Endeavour, Right Memory, Right Meditation. This, O Bhikkhus, is the Middle Path the knowledge of which the Tathâgata has gained, which leads to insight, which leads to wisdom, which conduces to calm, to knowledge, to the Sambodhi, to Nirvâ*n*a.

19. 'This, O Bhikkhus, is the Noble Truth of Suffering: Birth is suffering; decay is suffering; illness is suffering; death is suffering. Presence of objects we hate, is suffering; Separation from objects we love, is suffering; not to obtain what we desire, is suffering. Briefly, the fivefold clinging to existence[1] is suffering.

20. 'This, O Bhikkhus, is the Noble Truth of the Cause of suffering: Thirst, that leads to re-birth, accompanied by pleasure and lust, finding its delight here and there. (This thirst is threefold), namely, thirst for pleasure, thirst for existence, thirst for prosperity.

21. 'This, O Bhikkhus, is the Noble Truth of the Cessation of suffering: (it ceases with) the complete cessation of this thirst,—a cessation which consists in the absence of every passion,—with the abandoning of this thirst, with the doing away with it, with the deliverance from it, with the destruction of desire.

22. 'This, O Bhikkhus, is the Noble Truth of the Path which leads to the cessation of suffering:

[1] Clinging to the five elements of existence, rûpa, vedanâ, saññâ, sa*m*khârâ, viññâ*n*a. See § 38 seq.

that holy eightfold Path, that is to say, Right Belief, Right Aspiration, Right Speech, Right Conduct, Right Means of Livelihood, Right Endeavour, Right Memory, Right Meditation.

23. '"This is the Noble Truth of Suffering;"—thus, O Bhikkhus, of this doctrine, which formerly had not been heard of, have I obtained insight, knowledge, understanding, wisdom, intuition. "This Noble Truth of Suffering must be understood," thus, O Bhikkhus, of this doctrine, ... (&c., down to intuition). "This Noble Truth of Suffering I have understood," thus, O Bhikkhus, of this doctrine, ... (&c., down to intuition).

24. '"This is the Noble Truth of the Cause of suffering," thus, O Bhikkhus, (&c.) "This Noble Truth of the Cause of suffering must be abandoned[1] . . . . has been abandoned by me," thus, O Bhikkhus, (&c.)

25. '"This is the Noble Truth of the Cessation of suffering," thus, O Bhikkhus, (&c.) "This Noble Truth of the Cessation of suffering must be seen face to face . . . . has been seen by me face to face," thus, O Bhikkhus, (&c.)

26. '"This is the Noble Truth of the Path which leads to the cessation of suffering," thus, O Bhikkhus, (&c.) "This Noble Truth of the Path which leads to the cessation of suffering, must be realised . . . . has been realised by me," thus, O Bhikkhus, (&c.)

27. 'As long, O Bhikkhus, as I did not possess with perfect purity this true knowledge and insight into these four Noble Truths, with its three modifi-

[1] I. e. the thirst (ta*n*hâ), which is declared in this Noble Truth to be the cause of suffering, must be abandoned.

cations and its twelve constituent parts[1]; so long, O Bhikkhus, I knew that I had not yet obtained the highest, absolute Sambodhi in the world of men and gods, in Mâra's and Brahma's world, among all beings, Sama*n*as and Brâhma*n*as, gods and men.

28. 'But since I possessed, O Bhikkhus, with perfect purity this true knowledge and insight into these four Noble Truths, with its three modifications and its twelve constituent parts, then I knew, O Bhikkhus, that I had obtained the highest, universal Sambodhi in the world of men and gods, ... (&c., as in § 27).

29. 'And this knowledge and insight arose in my mind: "The emancipation of my mind cannot be lost; this is my last birth; hence I shall not be born again!"'

Thus the Blessed One spoke. The five Bhikkhus were delighted, and they rejoiced at the words of the Blessed One. And when this exposition was propounded, the venerable Ko*nd*añña obtained the pure and spotless Eye of the Truth (that is to say, the following knowledge): 'Whatsoever is subject to the condition of origination, is subject also to the condition of cessation.'

30. And as the Blessed One had founded the Kingdom of Truth (by propounding the four Noble Truths), the earth-inhabiting devas shouted: 'Truly the Blessed One has founded at Benares, in the deer park Isipatana, the highest kingdom of Truth, which may be opposed neither by a Sama*n*a nor by a Brâhma*n*a, neither by a deva, nor by Mâra, nor by Brahma, nor by any being in the world.'

---

[1] The three modifications and twelve constituent parts are those specified in §§ 23–26.

Hearing the shout of the earth-inhabiting devas, the *k*âtumahârâ*g*ika devas (gods belonging to the world of the four divine mahârâ*g*as) shouted, ... (&c., as above). Hearing the shout of the *k*âtumahârâ*g*ika devas, the tâvati*m*sa devas[1], ... the yâma devas, ... the tusita devas, ... the nimmânarati devas, ... the paranimmitavasavatti devas, ... the brahmakâyika devas shouted: 'Truly the Blessed One, ...' (&c., as above).

31. Thus in that moment, in that instant, in that second the shout reached the Brahma world; and this whole system of ten thousand worlds quaked, was shaken, and trembled; and an infinite, mighty light was seen through the world, which surpassed the light that can be produced by the divine power of the devas.

And the Blessed One pronounced this solemn utterance: 'Truly Ko*nd*a*ññ*a has perceived it ("a*ññ*âsi"), truly Ko*nd*a*ññ*a has perceived it!' Hence the venerable Ko*nd*a*ññ*a received the name A*ññ*âtako*nd*a*ññ*a (Ko*nd*a*ññ*a who has perceived the doctrine).

32. And the venerable A*ññ*âtako*nd*a*ññ*a, having seen the Truth, having mastered the Truth, having understood the Truth, having penetrated the Truth, having overcome uncertainty, having dispelled all doubts, having gained full knowledge, dependent on nobody else for knowledge of the doctrine of the Teacher, thus spoke to the Blessed One: 'Lord, let

[1] The thirty-three devas of the Vedic mythology. This enumeration gives the gods who reside in the different worlds, beginning from the lowest (the bhummâ devâ, who inhabit the earth), and gradually ascending to the higher devalokas. See Hardy, Manual, p. 25.

me receive the pabba*gg*â and upasampadâ ordinations from the Blessed One.'

'Come, O Bhikkhu,' said the Blessed One, 'well taught is the doctrine; lead a holy life for the sake of the complete extinction of suffering.' Thus this venerable person received the upasampadâ ordination.

33. And the Blessed One administered to the other Bhikkhus exhortation and instruction by discourses relating to the Dhamma. And the venerable Vappa, and the venerable Bhaddiya, when they received from the Blessed One such exhortation and instruction by discourses relating to the Dhamma, obtained the pure and spotless Eye of the Truth (that is to say, the following knowledge): 'Whatsoever is subject to the condition of origination is subject also to the condition of cessation.'

34. And having seen the Truth, having mastered the Truth, ... (&c., as in § 32), they thus spoke to the Blessed One: 'Lord, let us receive the pabba*gg*â and upasampadâ ordinations from the Blessed One.'

'Come, O Bhikkhus,' said the Blessed One, 'well taught is the doctrine; lead a holy life for the sake of the complete extinction of suffering.' Thus these venerable persons received the upasampadâ ordination.

35. And the Blessed One, living on what the Bhikkhus brought him, administered to the other Bhikkhus exhortation and instruction by discourse relating to the Dhamma; in this way the six persons lived on what the three Bhikkhus[1] brought home from their alms pilgrimage.

[1] Those three Bhikkhus of the five, who had been converted,

36, 37. And the venerable Mahânâma and the venerable Assa*g*i, when they received from the Blessed One, ... (&c., as in §§ 33, 34, down to :). Thus these venerable persons received the upasampadâ ordination.

38. And the Blessed One thus spoke to the five Bhikkhus: 'The body (Rûpa), O Bhikkhus, is not the self. If the body, O Bhikkhus, were the self, the body would not be subject to disease, and we should be able to say: "Let my body be such and such a one, let my body not be such and such a one." But since the body, O Bhikkhus, is not the self, therefore the body is subject to disease, and we are not able to say: "Let my body be such and such a one, let my body not be such and such a one."

39–41. 'Sensation (Vedanâ), O Bhikkhus, is not the self, ... (&c.[1]) Perception (Sa*ññ*â) is not the self, ... The Sa*m*khâras[2] are not the self, ... Consciousness (Vi*ññ*â*n*a) is not the self, ... (&c.[1])

42. 'Now what do you think, O Bhikkhus, is the body permanent or perishable?'

---

went about for alms; while the Buddha remained with their two companions, and instructed them.

[1] This is shown exactly in the same way and with the same words that are used in § 38 with regard to the body. Body, sensations, perceptions, sa*m*khâras, and consciousness are the well-known five classes (khandha) of bodily and mental parts and powers; see Rh. D., 'Buddhism,' p. 90 seq. The self (attâ), which, if it exists at all, must be permanent and imperishable, is not to be found in any one of these five classes, which are all subject to origin and decay. This discourse of the Buddha's, which is frequently called the Anattalakkha*n*a Sutta (Sutta of the not having the signs of self), shows the perishable nature of the five khandhas, and that the khandhas are not the self. But it does not deal with the question, whether the self exists or not, in any other way.

[2] See the note on chap. 1. 2.

'It is perishable, Lord.'

'And that which is perishable, does that cause pain or joy?'

'It causes pain, Lord.'

'And that which is perishable, painful, subject to change, is it possible to regard that in this way: 'This is mine, this am I, this is my self?'

'That is impossible, Lord.'

43. 'Is sensation permanent or perishable?' . . . . (&c.[1])

44. 'Therefore, O Bhikkhus, whatever body has been, will be, and is now, belonging or not belonging to sentient beings, gross or subtle, inferior or superior, distant or near, all that body is not mine, is not me, is not my self: thus it should be considered by right knowledge according to the truth.

45. 'Whatever sensation, ... (&c.[2])

46. 'Considering this, O Bhikkhus, a learned, noble hearer of the word becomes weary of body, weary of sensation, weary of perception, weary of the Sa*m*khâras, weary of consciousness. Becoming weary of all that, he divests himself of passion; by absence of passion he is made free; when he is free, he becomes aware that he is free; and he realises that re-birth is exhausted; that holiness is completed; that duty is fulfilled; and that there is no further return to this world[3].'

47. Thus the Blessed One spoke; the five Bhikkhus were delighted, and rejoiced at the words of the Blessed One. And when this exposition had been

---

[1] Here follow the same questions, answers, and rejoinders, with regard to sensation, perception, the sa*m*khâras, and consciousness.

[2] The same with regard to the other four khandhas.

[3] Compare Burnouf, 'Lotus de la bonne Loi,' p. 481.

propounded, the minds of the five Bhikkhus became free from attachment to the world, and were released from the Âsavas[1].

At that time there were six Arahats (persons who had reached absolute holiness) in the world.

End of the first Bhânavâra.

7[2].

1. At that time there was in Benares a noble youth, Yasa by name, the son of a *setth*i (or treasurer[3]) and delicately nurtured. He had three palaces, one for winter, one for summer, one for the rainy season. In the palace for the rainy season he lived during the four months (of that season), surrounded with female musicians among whom no

[1] See the note on § 9.

[2] A well-known scene in the life of the Bodhisatta has evidently been represented after the model of this story. See *G*âtaka I, p. 61; Lalita Vistara, p. 251; Bigandet, Life of Gaudama, p. 55. Nowhere in the Pâli Pi*t*akas is the story told about the Bodhisatta himself.

[3] This was a position of honour among the merchants. In the later literature we hear of an office of se*tth*i (se*tth*i-*tth*âna) in a city, to which any one with the requisite wealth and talent was eligible (*G*âtaka I, 120–122); and, according to the Mahâva*m*sa, the king appointed to an office called se*tth*itâ, apparently at his court (Mah. p. 69). The Gahapati, or Treasurer, one of the seven jewels of a king, is explained by Buddhaghosa to be se*tth*i-gahapati (see Rh. D.'s note on Mahâ-sudassana Sutta I, 41). 'The Se*tth*i,' standing alone, or 'the Mahâ-se*tth*i,' means Anâtha Pi*nd*ika (*G*âtaka I, 95, 227–230; Dhammapada Commentary, p. 395). Below, in chapter 9, § 1, it would seem that the rank of se*tth*i was hereditary, and this is confirmed by the later literature; but this applies to the social rank only, and not to the office.

man was, and he did not descend from that palace (all that time). Now one day Yasa, the noble youth, who was endowed with, and possessed of the five pleasures of sense[1], while he was attended (by those female musicians), fell asleep sooner than usual; and after him his attendants also fell asleep. Now an oil lamp was burning through the whole night.

2. And Yasa, the noble youth, awoke sooner than usual; and he saw his attendants sleeping; one had her lute leaning against her arm-pit; one had her tabor leaning against her neck; one had her drum leaning against her arm-pit; one had dishevelled hair; one had saliva flowing from her mouth; and they were muttering in their sleep. One would think it was a cemetery one had fallen into[2]. When he saw that, the evils (of the life he led) manifested themselves to him; his mind became weary (of worldly pleasures). And Yasa, the noble youth, gave utterance to this solemn exclamation: 'Alas! what distress; alas! what danger!'

3. And Yasa, the noble youth, put on his gilt slippers, and went to the gate of his house. Non-human beings opened the gate, in order that no being might prevent Yasa the noble youth's leaving the world, and going forth into the houseless state. And Yasa, the noble youth, went to the gate of the city. Non-human beings opened the gate, in order that no being might prevent Yasa the noble youth's leaving the world, and going forth into the houseless state. And Yasa, the noble youth, went to the deer park Isipatana.

---

[1] Pleasures of the eye, ear, nose, tongue, and touch.

[2] Hatthappatta*m* susâna*m* mañ*ñ*e, literally, 'one would think a cemetery had (suddenly) come to one's hand.'

4. At that time the Blessed One, having arisen in the night, at dawn was walking up and down in the open air. And the Blessed One saw Yasa, the noble youth, coming from afar. And when he saw him, he left the place where he was walking, and sat down on a seat laid out (for him). And Yasa, the noble youth, gave utterance near the Blessed One to that solemn exclamation: 'Alas! what distress; alas! what danger!' And the Blessed One said to Yasa, the noble youth: 'Here is no distress, Yasa, here is no danger. Come here, Yasa, sit down; I will teach you the Truth (Dhamma).'

5. And Yasa, the noble youth, when he heard that there was no distress, and that there was no danger, became glad and joyful; and he put off his gilt slippers, and went to the place where the Blessed One was; having approached him and having respectfully saluted the Blessed One, he sat down near him. When Yasa, the noble youth, was sitting near him, the Blessed One preached to him in due course: that is to say, he talked about the merits obtained by alms-giving, about the duties of morality, about heaven, about the evils, the vanity, and the sinfulness of desires, and about the blessings of the abandonment of desire[1].

6. When the Blessed One saw that the mind of Yasa, the noble youth, was prepared, impressible, free from obstacles (to understanding the Truth), elated, and believing, then he preached what is the principal doctrine of the Buddhas, namely, Suffering,

[1] Nekkhamma is neither naishkramya nor naishkarmya, but naishkâmya. Itivuttaka, fol. khi (Phayre MS.): kâmânam eta*m* nissara*n*a*m* yad ida*m* nekkhamma*m*, rûpânam eta*m* nissara*n*a*m* yad ida*m* aruppa*m*.

the Cause of suffering, the Cessation of suffering, the Path. Just as a clean cloth free from black specks properly takes the dye, thus Yasa, the noble youth, even while sitting there, obtained the pure and spotless Eye of the Truth (that is, the knowledge): 'Whatsoever is subject to the condition of origination is subject also to the condition of cessation.'

7. Now the mother of Yasa, the noble youth, having gone up to his palace, did not see Yasa, the noble youth, and she went to the se*tth*i, the householder (her husband), and having approached him, she said to the se*tth*i, the householder: 'Your son Yasa, O householder, has disappeared.' Then the se*tth*i, the householder, sent messengers on horseback to the four quarters of the horizon; and he went himself to the deer park Isipatana. Then the se*tth*i, the householder, saw on the ground the marks of the gilt slippers; and when he saw them, he followed them up.

8. And the Blessed One saw the se*tth*i, the householder, coming from afar. On seeing him, he thought: 'What if I were to effect such an exercise of miraculous power, that the se*tth*i, the householder, sitting here, should not see Yasa, the noble youth, who is sitting here also.' And the Blessed One effected such an exercise of his miraculous power.

9. And the se*tth*i, the householder, went to the place where the Blessed One was; having approached him, he said to the Blessed One: 'Pray, Lord, has the Blessed One seen Yasa, the noble youth?'

'Well, householder, sit down. Perhaps, sitting here, you may see Yasa, the noble youth, sitting here also.'

And the se*tth*i, the householder, who thought: 'Indeed, sitting here I shall see Yasa, the noble youth, sitting here also!' became glad and joyful, and having respectfully saluted the Blessed One, he sat down near him.

10. When the se*tth*i, the householder, was sitting near him, the Blessed One preached to him in due course; that is to say, he talked about the merits obtained by alms-giving, ... (&c., as at end of § 5). And the se*tth*i, the householder, having seen the Truth, having mastered the Truth, having penetrated the Truth, having overcome uncertainty, having dispelled all doubts, having gained full knowledge, dependent on nobody else for the knowledge of the doctrine of the Teacher, said to the Blessed One: 'Glorious, Lord! glorious, Lord! Just as if one should set up, Lord, what had been overturned, or should reveal what had been hidden, or should point out the way to one who had lost his way, or should bring a lamp into the darkness, in order that those who had eyes might see visible things, thus has the Blessed One preached the doctrine in many ways. I take my refuge, Lord, in the Blessed One, and in the Dhamma, and in the fraternity of Bhikkhus; may the Blessed One receive me from this day forth while my life lasts as a disciple who has taken his refuge in Him.'

This was the first person in the world who became a lay-disciple by the formula of the holy triad.

11. And Yasa, the noble youth, while instruction was administered (by the Buddha) to his father, contemplated the stage of knowledge which he had seen with his mind and understood; and his mind became free from attachment to the world, and was

released from the Âsavas. Then the Blessed One thought: 'Yasa, the noble youth, while instruction was administered to his father, has contemplated the stage of knowledge which he had seen with his mind and understood; and his mind has become free from attachment to the world, and has become released from the Âsavas. It is impossible that Yasa, the noble youth, should return to the world and enjoy pleasures, as he did before, when he lived in his house. What if I were now to put an end to that exertion of my miraculous power.' And the Blessed One put an end to that exertion of his miraculous power.

12. Then the se*tth*i, the householder, saw Yasa, the noble youth, sitting there. On seeing him he said to Yasa, the noble youth: 'My son Yasa, your mother is absorbed in lamentation and grief; restore your mother to life.'

13. Then Yasa, the noble youth, looked at the Blessed One. And the Blessed One said to the se*tth*i, the householder: 'What do you think then, O householder? That Yasa has (first) won only an imperfect[1] degree of knowledge and insight into the Truth, as you have yourself? Or that rather he was contemplating the stage of knowledge which he had seen with his mind and understood; and that his mind has thus become free from attachment to the world, and has become released from the Âsavas? Now would it then be possible, O householder, that Yasa should return to the world and enjoy pleasures as he did before, when he lived in his house?'

'Not so, Lord.'

[1] The stage of a sekha, i. e. a person who has attained to any stage in the Noble Eightfold Path (such as sotâpattiphala, &c.) inferior to the highest (Arahatship).

'Yasa, the noble youth, O householder, had (first) won, like yourself, an imperfect degree of knowledge and insight into the Truth. But when he was contemplating the stage of knowledge which he had seen with his mind and understood, his mind has become free from attachment to the world, and has become released from the Âsavas. It is impossible, O householder, that Yasa, the noble youth, should return to the world and enjoy pleasures as he did before, when he lived in his house.'

14. 'It is all gain, Lord, to Yasa, the noble youth, it is high bliss, Lord, for Yasa, the noble youth, that the mind of Yasa, the noble youth, has become free from attachment to the world, and has become released from the Âsavas. Might, Lord, the Blessed One consent to take his meal with me to-day together with Yasa, the noble youth, as his attendant?'

The Blessed One expressed his consent by remaining silent. Then the se*tth*i, the householder, when he understood that the Blessed One had accepted his invitation, rose from his seat, respectfully saluted the Blessed One, and passing round him with his right side towards him, departed thence.

15. And Yasa, the noble youth, soon after the se*tth*i, the householder, was gone, said to the Blessed One: 'Lord, let me receive the pabba*gg*â and upasampadâ ordinations from the Blessed One.'

'Come, O Bhikkhu,' said the Blessed One, 'well taught is the doctrine; lead a holy life for the sake of the complete extinction of suffering.'

Thus this venerable person received the upasampadâ ordination. At that time there were seven Arahats in the world.

End of the story of Yasa's pabba*gg*â.

8.

1. And in the forenoon the blessed One, having put on his under-robes[1], took his alms-bowl, and, with his *k*îvara on, went with the venerable Yasa as his attendant to the house of the se*tth*i, the householder. When he had arrived there, he sat down on a seat laid out for him. Then the mother and the former wife of the venerable Yasa went to the place where the Blessed One was; having approached him and having respectfully saluted the Blessed One, they sat down near him.

2. Then the Blessed One preached to them in due course; that is to say, he talked about the merits obtained by alms-giving, ... (&c., as in chap. 7. 5, 6, down to:); thus they obtained, while sitting there, the pure and spotless Eye of the Truth (that is, the knowledge): 'Whatsoever is subject to the condition of origination is subject also to the condition of cessation.'

3. And having seen the Truth, ... (&c., as above, §§ 5, 6, down to:), dependent on nobody else for knowledge of the Teacher's doctrine, they thus spoke to the Blessed One: 'Glorious, Lord! glorious Lord! Just as if one should set up (&c., as in chap. 7. 10, down to:). We take our refuge, Lord, in the Blessed One, and in the Dhamma, and in the fraternity of Bhikkhus; may the Blessed One receive us from this day forth, while our life lasts, as disciples who have taken their refuge in Him.'

These were the first females in the world who became lay-disciples by the formula of the holy triad.

[1] The rules about the dress of a Bhikkhu who is going to the village are given in the *K*ullavagga VIII, 4, 3; 5, 2. Compare Rh. D.'s note on the Mahâ-parinibbâna Sutta V, 45.

4. And the mother and the father and the former wife of the venerable Yasa with their own hands served and offered[1] excellent food, both hard and soft, to the Blessed One and to the venerable Yasa; and when the Blessed One had finished his meal, and cleansed his bowl and his hands, they sat down near him. Then the Blessed One taught, incited, animated, and gladdened the mother, and father, and the former wife of the venerable Yasa by religious discourse; and then he rose from his seat and went away.

9.

1. Now four lay persons, friends of the venerable Yasa, belonging to the se*tth*i families of Benares, and to the highest after the se*tth*i families, by name Vimala, Subâhu, Pu*nn*a*g*i, and Gavampati, heard: 'Yasa, the noble youth, has cut off his hair and beard, and has put on yellow robes, and has given up the world, and gone forth into the houseless state.' When they had heard that, they thought: 'Surely that cannot be a common doctrine and discipline, that cannot be a common renunciation of the world, if Yasa, the noble youth, has cut off his hair and beard, and has put on yellow robes, and has given up the world, and gone forth into the houseless state.'

[1] According to Subhûti (in Childers's Dictionary) sampavâreti means that the host hands dishes to the guest until the latter says, 'I have had enough.' Childers accordingly translates sampavâreti, 'to cause to refuse.' But as pavâreti means, 'to cause to accept,' it is impossible that sampavâreti should have exactly the opposite meaning. We prefer, therefore, to take it as an emphatic synonym of pavâreti.

2. Those four persons went to the place where the venerable Yasa was; having approached him and having respectfully saluted the venerable Yasa, they stood by his side. And the venerable Yasa went with his four lay-friends to the place where the Blessed One was; having approached him and having respectfully saluted the Blessed One, he sat down near him. Sitting near him the venerable Yasa said to the Blessed One: 'Lord, here are four lay-friends of mine, belonging to the se*tth*i families of Benares and to the highest after the se*tth*i families; their names are Vimala, Subâhu, Pu*nn*a*g*i, and Gavampati. May the Blessed One administer exhortation and instruction to these four persons.'

3. Then the Blessed One preached to them, ... (&c., as in chap. 8. 2).

4. And having seen the Truth, ... (&c., down to:) dependent on nobody else for the knowledge of the Teacher's doctrine, they thus spoke to the Blessed One: 'Lord, let us receive the pabba*gg*â and upasampadâ ordinations from the Blessed One.'

'Come, O Bhikkhus,' said the Blessed One, 'well taught is the doctrine; lead a holy life for the sake of the complete extinction of suffering.'

Thus these venerable persons received the upasampadâ ordination. And the Blessed One administered to these Bhikkhus exhortation and instruction by discourse relating to the Dhamma. While they received exhortation and instruction from the Blessed One by discourse relating to the Dhamma, their minds became free from attachment to the world, and were released from the Âsavas.

At that time there were eleven Arahats in the world.

Here ends the story of the ordination of the four laymen.

10.

Now fifty lay persons, friends of the venerable Yasa, belonging to the highest families in the country and to those next to the highest, heard, ... (&c., as in chap. 9, §§ 1, 2, 3, 4, down to:). While they received exhortation and instruction from the Blessed One by discourse relating to the Dhamma, their minds became free from attachment to the world, and were released from the Âsavas.

At that time there were sixty-one Arahats in the world.

11.

1. And the Blessed One said to the Bhikkhus: 'I am delivered, O Bhikkhus, from all fetters, human and divine. You, O Bhikkhus, are also delivered from all fetters, human and divine. Go ye now, O Bhikkhus, and wander, for the gain of the many, for the welfare of the many, out of compassion for the world, for the good, for the gain, and for the welfare of gods and men. Let not two of you go the same way[1]. Preach, O Bhikkhus, the doctrine

[1] This cannot be understood as a general rule, for it is repeated nowhere where precepts for wandering Bhikkhus are given, and, on the contrary, numerous instances occur in the Sacred Texts

which is glorious in the beginning, glorious in the middle, glorious at the end, in the spirit and in the letter; proclaim a consummate, perfect, and pure life of holiness. There are beings whose mental eyes are covered by scarcely any dust, but if the doctrine is not preached to them, they cannot attain salvation. They will understand the doctrine. And I will go also, O Bhikkhus, to Uruvelâ, to Senâninigama[1], in order to preach the doctrine.'

2. And Mâra the wicked One went to the place where the Blessed One was; having approached him, he addressed the Blessed One in the following stanza: 'Thou art bound by all fetters, human and divine. Thou art bound by strong fetters. Thou wilt not be delivered from me, O Sama*n*a.'

Buddha replied: 'I am delivered from all fetters, human and divine. I am delivered from the strong fetters. Thou art struck down, O Death.'

(Mâra said): 'The fetter which pervades the sky, with which mind is bound, with that fetter I will bind thee. Thou wilt not be delivered from me, O Sama*n*a.'

(Buddha replied): 'Whatever forms, sounds, odours, flavours, or contacts there are which please the

---

in which two or more Bhikkhus are mentioned as wandering together, without any expression of disapproval being added. The precept given here evidently is intended to refer only to the earliest period in the spread of the new doctrine; just as in chap. 12 a form of upasampadâ is introduced by Buddha which was regarded as inadmissible in later times.

[1] The correct spelling of this name appears to be Senâninigama ('the General's Town'), and not Senânigama ('the Army's Town'); the *G*âtaka Atthava*nn*anâ (vol. i. p. 68) and the Paris MS. of the Mahâvagga (manu secunda) read Senâninigama. The Lalita Vistara has Senâpatigrâma.

senses, in me desire for them has ceased. Thou art struck down, O Death.'

Then Mâra the wicked One understood: 'The Blessed One knows me, the perfect One knows me,' and, sad and afflicted, he vanished away.

Here ends the story of Mâra.

12.

1. At that time the Bhikkhus brought (to Buddha), from different regions and different countries, persons who desired to obtain the pabba*gg*â and upasampadâ ordinations, thinking: 'The Blessed One will confer on them the pabba*gg*â and upasampadâ ordinations.' Thus both the Bhikkhus became tired (from the journey), and also those who desired to obtain the pabba*gg*â and upasampadâ ordinations. Now when the Blessed One was alone and had retired into solitude, the following consideration presented itself to his mind: 'The Bhikkhus now bring to me from different regions and different countries persons who desire to obtain the pabba*gg*â and upasampadâ ordinations, thinking: "The Blessed One will confer on them the pabba*gg*â and upasampadâ ordinations." Now both the Bhikkhus become tired, and also those who desire to obtain the pabba*gg*â and upasampadâ ordinations. What if I were to grant permission to the Bhikkhus, saying: "Confer henceforth, O Bhikkhus, in the different regions, and in the different countries, the pabba*gg*â and upasampadâ ordinations yourselves (on those who desire to receive them)."'

2. And the Blessed One, having left the solitude

in the evening, in consequence of that, and on this occasion, after having delivered a religious discourse, thus addressed the Bhikkhus: 'When I was alone, O Bhikkhus, and had retired into solitude, the following consideration, &c. What if I were to permit, ...' (&c., as in § 1).

3. 'I grant you, O Bhikkhus, this permission: Confer henceforth in the different regions and in the different countries the pabba*gg*â and upasampadâ ordinations yourselves (on those who desire to receive them). And you ought, O Bhikkhus, to confer the pabba*gg*â and upasampadâ ordinations in this way: Let him (who desires to receive the ordination), first have his hair and beard cut off; let him put on yellow robes, adjust his upper robe so as to cover one shoulder, salute the feet of the Bhikkhus (with his head), and sit down squatting; then let him raise his joined hands and tell him to say:

4. '"I take my refuge in the Buddha, I take my refuge in the Dhamma, I take my refuge in the Sa*m*gha. And for the second time I take (&c. . . . . Sa*m*gha). And for the third time I take my refuge in the Buddha, and for the third time I take my refuge in the Dhamma, and for the third time I take my refuge in the Sa*m*gha."

'I prescribe, O Bhikkhus, the pabba*gg*â and upasampadâ ordinations consisting in the three times repeated declaration of taking refuge (in the holy triad).'

End of the account of the upasampadâ ordination by the threefold declaration of taking refuge[1].

---

[1] On this ceremony, which is still gone through before the regular ordination, see the remarks in the note on chapter 1, § 1.

13.

1. And the Blessed One, after having kept the vassa residence[1], thus addressed the Bhikkhus: 'By wise contemplation, O Bhikkhus, and by wise firmness of exertion have I attained the highest emancipation, have I realised the highest emancipation. Attain ye also, O Bhikkhus, the highest emancipation, realise the highest emancipation, by wise contemplation and by wise firmness of exertion.'

2. And Mâra the wicked One went to the place where the Blessed One was; having approached him, he addressed the Blessed One by the following stanza: 'Thou art bound by Mâra's fetters, human and divine. Thou art bound by strong fetters. Thou wilt not be delivered from me, O Sama*n*a.'

(Buddha replied): 'I am delivered from Mâra's fetters, human and divine. I am delivered from the strong fetters. Thou art struck down, O Death.'

Then Mâra the wicked One understood: 'The Blessed One knows me, the perfect One knows me;' and, sad and afflicted, he vanished away.

14.

1. And the Blessed One, after having dwelt at Benares as long as he thought fit, went forth to Uruvelâ. And the Blessed One left the road and went to a certain grove; having gone there, and having entered it, he sat down at the foot of a tree. At that time there was a party of thirty friends, rich young men, who were sporting in that same grove

[1] See about the vassa residence the rules given in Book III.

together with their wives. One of them had no wife; for him they had procured a harlot. Now while they did not pay attention, and were indulging in their sports, that harlot took up the articles belonging to them, and ran away.

2. Then those companions, doing service to their friend, went in search of that woman; and, roaming about that grove, they saw the Blessed One sitting at the foot of a tree. Seeing him they went to the place where the Blessed One was; having approached him, they said to the Blessed One: 'Pray, Lord, has the Blessed One seen a woman passing by?'

'What have you to do, young men, with the woman?'

'We were sporting, Lord, in this grove, thirty friends, rich young men, together with our wives. One of us had no wife; for him we had procured a harlot. Now, Lord, while we did not pay attention, and were indulging in our sports, that harlot has taken up the articles belonging to us, and has run away. Therefore, Lord, we companions, doing service to our friend, go in search of that woman, and roam about this grove.'

3. 'Now what think you, young men? Which would be the better for you; that you should go in search of a woman, or that you should go in search of yourselves?'

'That, Lord, would be the better for us, that we should go in search of ourselves.'

'If so, young men, sit down, I will preach to you the Truth (Dhamma).'

The rich young companions replied: 'Yes, Lord,' and respectfully saluted the Blessed One, and sat down near him.

4. Then the Blessed One preached to them, ... (&c., as in chap. 8. 2, or 9. 3).

5. And having seen the Truth, ... (&c., as in chap. 9. 4 down to:). Thus these venerable persons received the upasampadâ ordination.

Here ends the story of the thirty rich young companions.

End of the second Bhâ*n*avâra.

15.

1. And the Blessed One, wandering from place to place, came to Uruvelâ. At that time there lived in Uruvelâ three *Ga*t*ilas*[1], Uruvelâ Kassapa, Nadî Kassapa (Kassapa of the River, i. e. the Nera*ñg*arâ), and Gayâ Kassapa (Kassapa of the village Gayâ). Of these the *Ga*t*ila* Uruvelâ Kassapa was chief, leader, foremost, first, and highest over five hundred *Ga*t*ilas*; Nadî Kassapa was chief . . . . (&c., down to highest over) three hundred *Ga*t*ilas*, Gayâ Kassapa was chief . . . . (&c., down to highest over) two hundred *Ga*t*ilas*.

2. And the Blessed One went to the hermitage of

---

[1] The *Ga*t*ilas* (i. e. ascetics wearing matted hair) are Brahmanical vânaprasthas. The description of their ascetic life given in many passages of the *G*âtaka Atthava*nn*anâ and of the Apadâna exactly agrees with the picture of the forest life of the ὑλόβιοι which so frequently occurs in the Mahâbhârata. In the Mahâvagga (VI, 35, 2) it is expressly stated that the *Ga*t*ilas* recognised the authority of the Veda, and it is in keeping with this that the usual term for adopting the state of a *Ga*t*ila* is 'isipabba*gg*am pabba*g*ati' (frequently in the *G*ât. Atth.), i. e. leaving the world and becoming a *R*ishi.

the *Gat*ila Uruvelâ Kassapa; having gone there, he said to the *Gat*ila Uruvelâ Kassapa: 'If it is not disagreeable to you, Kassapa, let me spend one night in the room where your (sacred) fire is kept.'

'It is not disagreeable to me, great Sama*n*a, but there is a savage Nâga (or Serpent) king of great magical power[1], a dreadfully venomous serpent; let him do no harm to you.'

And a second time the Blessed One said to the *Gat*ila Uruvelâ Kassapa: 'If it is not disagreeable,' &c. . . . .

'It is not disagreeable,' &c.

And a third time the Blessed One said: 'If it is not disagreeable,' &c. . . . .

'It is not disagreeable,' &c. . . . .

'He is not likely to do any harm to me. Pray, Kassapa, allow me a place in the room where your fire is kept.'

'Stay there, great Sama*n*a, as you wish it.'

3. Then the Blessed One entered the room where the fire was kept, made himself a couch of grass, and sat down cross-legged, keeping the body erect and surrounding himself with watchfulness of mind[2]. And the Nâga saw that the Blessed One had entered; when he saw that, he became annoyed, and irritated, and sent forth a cloud of smoke. Then the Blessed One thought: 'What if I were to leave intact the skin, and hide, and flesh, and ligaments, and bones,

---

[1] Iddhi. Compare the passages referred to by Rh. D. in 'Buddhist Suttas from the Pâli,' pp. 2, 40, 259; and further Mahâvagga VI, 15, 8, and *K*ullavagga VII, 1, 4, and VII, 2, 1.

[2] Sati*m* upa*tth*âpetvâ. Sati is here a more precise idea than memory.

and marrow of this Nâga; but were to conquer the fire, which he will send forth, by my fire.'

4. And the Blessed One effected the appropriate exercise of miraculous power and sent forth a cloud of smoke. Then the Nâga, who could not master his rage[1], sent forth flames. And the Blessed One, converting his body into fire[2], sent forth flames. When they both shone forth with their flames, the fire room looked as if it were burning and blazing, as if it were all in flames. And the *G*a*t*ilas, surrounding the fire room, said: 'Truly the countenance of the great Sama*n*a is beautiful, but the Nâga will do harm to him[3].'

5. That night having elapsed, the Blessed One, leaving intact the skin and hide and flesh and ligaments and bones and marrow of that Nâga, and conquering the Nâga's fire by his fire, threw him into his alms-bowl, and showed him to the *G*a*t*ila Uruvelâ Kassapa (saying), 'Here you see the Nâga, Kassapa; his fire has been conquered by my fire.'

Then the *G*a*t*ila Uruvelâ Kassapa thought: 'Truly the great Sama*n*a possesses high magical powers and great faculties, in that he is able to conquer by his fire the fire of that savage Nâga king, who is possessed of magical power, that dreadfully venomous serpent. He is not, however, holy (arahâ) as I am.'

6[4]. Near the Nera*ñg*arâ river the Blessed One

---

[1] Buddhaghosa explains makkha by kodha.

[2] Compare *K*ullavagga IV, 4, 4, where Dabba also te*g*odhâtu*m* samâpa*gg*ati, that is, his finger is on fire.

[3] Compare the Editor's corrections at *K*ullavagga, p. 363.

[4] In §§ 6, 7 (excepting the last clause of § 7) the story related in §§ 1–5 is repeated in a more popular style. This appears to us to be a more archaic redaction than the preceding. We do not know

said to the *Gatila* Uruvelâ Kassapa: 'If it is not disagreeable to you, Kassapa, let me dwell this moonlight night in your fire room.'

'It is not disagreeable to me, great Sama*n*a, but in your own behalf I warn you off. There is a savage Snake king there possessed of magical power, a dreadfully venomous serpent; let him do no harm to you.'

'He is not likely to do any harm to me; pray, Kassapa, allow me a place in your fire room.'

When he saw that Kassapa had given his permission, fearlessly He, who had overcome all fear, entered. When the chief of Serpents saw that the Sage had entered, he became irritated, and sent forth a cloud of smoke. Then the chief of men[1], joyful and unperplexed, also sent forth a cloud of smoke. Unable to master his rage, the chief of Serpents sent forth flames like a burning fire. Then the chief of men[1], the perfect master of the element of fire, also sent forth flames. When they shone forth both with their flames, the *Gatilas* looked at the fire room (saying), 'Truly the countenance of the great Sama*n*a is beautiful, but the Nâga will do harm to him.'

7. And when that night had elapsed, the flames of the Nâga were extinguished, but the various-coloured flames of Him who is possessed of magical powers remained. Dark blue and red, light red, yellow, and crystal-coloured flames of various colours

---

any other instance in the Pâli Pi*t*akas of a similar repetition, excepting a short passage at the end of chap. 24. 3; and one other in the Mahâ-padhâna Sutta.

[1] Literally, 'the Snake among men,' or 'the Elephant among men' (manussanâgo).

appeared on the Aṅgirasa's[1] body. Having put the chief of Serpents into his alms-bowl, he showed him to the Brâhmaṇa (saying), 'Here you see the Nâga, Kassapa; his fire has been conquered by my fire.'

And the *Gaṭ*ila Uruvelâ Kassapa, having conceived an affection for the Blessed One in consequence of this wonder, said to the Blessed One: 'Stay with me, great Sama*n*a, I will daily provide you with food.'

End of the first Wonder.

16.

1. And the Blessed One resided in a certain grove near the hermitage of the *Gaṭ*ila Uruvelâ Kassapa. And on a beautiful night the four Mahârâ*g*as[2], filling the whole grove with light by the brilliancy of their complexion, went to the place where the Blessed One was; having approached him and respectfully saluted the Blessed One, they stood in the four directions like great firebrands.

2. And when that night had elapsed, the *Gaṭ*ila Uruvelâ Kassapa went to the place where the Blessed One was; having approached him, he said to the Blessed One: 'It is time, great Sama*n*a, the meal is ready. Who were they, great Sama*n*a, who came, this beautiful night, filling the whole grove with light by the brilliancy of their complexion, to

[1] According to Vedic tradition the Gautamas, as is well known, belong to the Âṅgirasa tribe.

[2] See chap. 4. 4.

the place where you were, and having approached you and respectfully saluted you, stood in the four directions like great firebrands?'

'They were the four Mahârâgas, Kassapa, who came to me in order to hear my preaching.'

Then the *G*a*t*ila Uruvelâ Kassapa thought: 'Truly the great Sama*n*a possesses high magical powers and great faculties, since even the four Mahârâ*g*as come to hear his preaching. He is not, however, holy like me.'

And the Blessed One ate the food offered by the *G*a*t*ila Uruvelâ Kassapa, and continued to stay in that same grove.

End of the second Wonder.

17.

1. And on a beautiful night Sakka (*S*akra or Indra) the king of the devas, filling the whole grove with light by the brilliancy of his complexion, went to the place where the Blessed One was; having approached him and respectfully saluted the Blessed One, he stood near him like a great firebrand, surpassing in beauty and brilliancy the splendour of the former appearances.

2. And when that night had elapsed (&c., as in chap. 16. 2).

End of the third Wonder.

18.

And on a beautiful night Brahmâ Sahampati (&c., as in chap. 17).

End of the fourth Wonder.

19.

1. At that time a great sacrifice which the *Gat*ila Uruvelâ Kassapa used to celebrate was approaching, and all the people of Aṅga and Magadha wished to go to that sacrifice carrying abundant food, both hard and soft. Now the *Gat*ila Uruvelâ Kassapa thought: 'Presently my great sacrifice is approaching, and all the people of Aṅga and Magadha will come and bring with them abundant food, both hard and soft. If the great Sama*n*a should perform a wonder before that great assembly, gain and honour would increase to the great Sama*n*a, and my gain and honour would diminish. Well, the great Sama*n*a shall not appear here to-morrow.'

2. Then the Blessed One, understanding by the power of his mind this reflection which had arisen in the mind of the *Gat*ila Uruvelâ Kassapa, went to Uttara Kuru; having begged alms there, he took the food (he had received) to the Anotatta lake[1]; there he took his meal and rested during the heat of the day at the same place.

And when the night had elapsed, the *Gat*ila Uruvelâ Kassapa went to the place where the Blessed One was; having approached him, he said to the

[1] One of the supposed seven great lakes in the Himavant.

Blessed One: 'It is time, great Samana, the meal is ready. Why did you not come yesterday, great Samana? We have thought of you: "Why does the great Samana not come?" and your portions of food, both hard and soft, were served up for you.'

3. (Buddha replied): 'Did you not think, Kassapa: "Presently my great sacrifice (&c., as above down to:). Well, the great Samana shall not appear here to-morrow?"

4. 'Now I understood, Kassapa, by the power of my mind this reflection which had arisen in your mind, and I went to Uttara Kuru; having begged alms there, I took the food to the Anotatta lake; there I took my meal and rested during the heat of the day at the same place.'

Then the *Gat*ila Uruvelâ Kassapa thought: 'Truly the great Samana possesses high magical powers and great faculties, since he is able to understand by the power of his mind the thoughts of other people. He is not, however, holy like me.'

And the Blessed One ate (&c., as in chap. 16. 2).

End of the fifth Wonder.

20.

1. At that time the Blessed One had rags taken from a dust heap (of which he was going to make himself a dress). Now the Blessed One thought: 'Where shall I wash these rags?' Then Sakka the king of the devas, understanding in his mind the thought which had arisen in the mind of the Blessed One, dug a tank with his own hand,

and said to the Blessed One: 'Lord, might the Blessed One wash the rags here.'

And the Blessed One thought: 'What shall I rub the rags upon?' Then Sakka the king of the devas, understanding, &c., put there a great stone and said: 'Lord, might the Blessed One rub the rags upon this stone.'

2. And the Blessed One thought: 'What shall I take hold of when going up (from the tank)?' Then a deity that resided in a Kakudha tree, understanding, &c., bent down a branch and said: 'Lord, might the Blessed One take hold of this branch when going up (from the tank).'

And the Blessed One thought: 'What shall I lay the rags upon (in order to dry them)?' Then Sakka the king of the devas, understanding, &c., put there a great stone and said: 'Lord, might the Blessed One lay the rags upon this stone.'

3. And when that night had elapsed, the *G*a*t*ila Uruvelâ Kassapa went to the place where the Blessed One was; having approached him, he said to the Blessed One: 'It is time, great Sama*n*a, the meal is ready. What is this, great Sama*n*a? Formerly there was here no tank, and now here is this tank. Formerly no stone was put here; by whom has this stone been put here? Formerly this Kakudha tree did not bend down its branch, and now this branch is bent down.'

4. 'I had rags, Kassapa, taken from a dust heap; and I thought, Kassapa: "Where shall I wash these rags?" Then, Kassapa, Sakka the king of the devas, understanding in his mind the thought which had arisen in my mind, dug a tank with his hand and said to me: "Lord, might the Blessed One wash the

rags here." Thus this tank has been dug by the hand of a non-human being.

'And I thought, Kassapa: "What shall I rub the rags upon?" Then, Kassapa, Sakka, &c. Thus this stone has been put here by a non-human being.

5. 'And I thought, Kassapa: "What shall I take hold of when going up (from the tank)?" Then, Kassapa, a deity, &c. Thus this Kakudha tree has served me as a hold for my hand.

'And I thought, Kassapa: "Where shall I lay the rags upon (in order to dry them)?" Then, Kassapa, Sakka, &c. Thus this stone has been put here by a non-human being.'

6. Then the *Gat*ila Uruvelâ Kassapa thought: 'Truly the great Sama*n*a possesses high magical powers and great faculties, since Sakka the king of the devas does service to him. He is not, however, holy like me.'

And the Blessed One ate (&c., as in chap. 16. 2).

7. And when that night had elapsed, the *Gat*ila Uruvelâ Kassapa went to the place where the Blessed One was; having approached him, he announced to the Blessed One that it was time, by saying, 'It is time, great Sama*n*a, the meal is ready.'

(Buddha replied): 'Go you, Kassapa; I will follow you.'

Having thus sent away the *Gat*ila Uruvelâ Kassapa, he went to pluck a fruit from the *g*ambu tree after which this continent of *G*ambudîpa (the *G*ambu Island, or India) is named[1]; then arriving before

[1] See about this *g*ambu tree, which grows in the forest of Himavant, Hardy's Manual, p. 18 seq.

Kassapa he sat down in the room where Kassapa's (sacred) fire was kept[1].

8. Then the *Gat*ila Uruvelâ Kassapa saw the Blessed One sitting in the fire room; seeing him he said to the Blessed One: 'By what way have you come, great Sama*n*a? I have departed before you, and you have arrived before me and are sitting in the fire room.'

9. 'When I had sent you away, Kassapa, I went to pluck a fruit from the *g*ambu tree after which this continent of *G*ambudîpa is named; then I arrived before you and sat down in the fire room. Here is the *g*ambu fruit, Kassapa, it is beautiful, fragrant, and full of flavour; you may eat it, if you like.'

'Nay, great Sama*n*a, to you alone it is becoming to eat it; eat it yourself.'

And the *Gat*ila Uruvelâ Kassapa thought: 'Truly the great Sama*n*a possesses high magical powers and great faculties, since he is able, having sent me away before him, to go and pluck a fruit from the *g*ambu tree after which this continent of *G*ambudîpa is named, and then to arrive before me and to sit down in the fire room. He is not, however, holy like me.'

And the Blessed One ate (&c., as in chap. 16. 2).

10. And when that night had elapsed (&c., as in § 7, down to:). Having thus sent away the *Gat*ila Uruvelâ Kassapa, he went to pluck a fruit from a mango tree growing near the *g*ambu tree after which this continent of *G*ambudîpa is named, &c. He

[1] Very probably it is this story in which a similar legend has originated that the Ceylonese tell about Mahinda, the converter of their island; see Dîpava*m*sa XII, 75.

went to pluck a fruit from an emblic myrobalan tree, &c., from a yellow myrobalan tree growing near the *g*ambu tree, &c. He went to the Tâvati*m*sa heaven to pluck a pâri*kkh*attaka (or pâri*g*âtaka) flower; then arriving before Kassapa he sat down in the fire room. Then the *G*a*t*ila Uruvelâ Kassapa saw (&c., as in § 8).

11. 'When I had sent you away, Kassapa, I went to the Tâvati*m*sa heaven to pluck a pâri*kkh*attaka flower; then I arrived before you and sat down in the fire room. Here is the pâri*kkh*attaka flower, Kassapa; it is beautiful and fragrant; you may take it, if you like.'

'Nay, great Sama*n*a, to you alone it is becoming to keep it; keep it yourself.'

And the *G*a*t*ila (&c., as in § 9). 'He is not, however, holy as I am.'

---

12. At that time one day the *G*a*t*ilas, who wished to attend on their sacred fires, could not succeed in splitting fire-wood. Now these *G*a*t*ilas thought: 'Doubtless this is the magical power and the high faculty of the great Sama*n*a that we cannot succeed in splitting fire-wood.' Then the Blessed One said to the *G*a*t*ila Uruvelâ Kassapa: 'Shall the fire-wood be split, Kassapa?'

'Let it be split, great Sama*n*a.'

Then in a moment the five hundred pieces of fire-wood[1] were split. And the *G*a*t*ila Uruvelâ

[1] Bigandet (Life of Gaudama, p. 135) translates this passage from the Burmese version: 'Gaudama split it in a moment, in five hundred pieces.' Doubtless the true meaning is, that there were five hundred pieces of wood, one for each of the five hundred *G*a*t*ilas over whom was Kassapa chief. In the following two stories (§§ 13, 14) we have five hundred sacred fires.

Kassapa thought: 'Truly the great Samana possesses high magical powers and great faculties, since even the fire-wood splits itself (at his command). He is not, however, holy like me.'

13. At that time the Gatilas who wished to attend on their sacred fires, could not succeed in lighting up the fires (&c., as in the preceding story).

14. At that time the Gatilas, after having attended on their sacred fires, could not succeed in extinguishing the fires (&c., as above).

15. At that time in the cold winter nights, in the time between the ashtakâ festivals[1], when snow falls, the Gatilas plunged into the river Nerañgarâ, and emerged again, and repeatedly plunged into the water and emerged. And the Blessed One created five hundred vessels with burning fire[2]; at those the Gatilas coming out of the river warmed themselves. And the Gatilas thought: 'Doubtless this is the magical power and the high faculty of the great Samana that these vessels with fire have been caused to appear here.' And the Gatila Uruvelâ Kassapa thought: 'Truly the great Samana possesses high magical powers and great faculties, since he can create such great vessels with fire. He is not, however, holy like me.'

16. At that time a great rain fell out of season; and a great inundation arose. The place where the Blessed One lived was covered with water. Then

[1] The ashtakâ festivals, about which accurate details are given in the Grihya Sûtras, were celebrated about the wane of the moon of the winter months mârgasîrsha, taisha, and mâgha; see Weber, Die vedischen Nachrichten von den Naxatra, II, p. 337, and H. O.'s note on the Sâṅkhâyana Grihya, 3, 12, ap. Indische Studien, XV, p. 145.

[2] Buddhaghosa explains mandâmukhiyo by aggibhâganâni.

the Blessed One thought: 'What if I were to cause the water to recede round about, and if I were to walk up and down in the midst of the water on a dust-covered spot.' And the Blessed One caused the water to recede round about, and he walked up and down in the midst of the water on a dust-covered spot.

And the *Gaṭ*ila Uruvelâ Kassapa, who was afraid that the water might have carried away the great Sama*n*a, went with a boat together with many *Gaṭ*ilas to the place where the Blessed One lived. Then the *Gaṭ*ila Uruvelâ Kassapa saw the Blessed One, who had caused the water to recede round about, walking up and down in the midst of the water on a dust-covered spot. Seeing him, he said to the Blessed One: 'Are you there, great Sama*n*a?'

'Here I am, Kassapa,' replied the Blessed One, and he rose in the air and stationed himself in the boat.

And the *Gaṭ*ila Uruvelâ Kassapa thought: 'Truly the great Sama*n*a possesses high magical powers and great faculties, since the water does not carry him away. He is not, however, holy like me.'

17. Then the Blessed One thought: 'This foolish man will still for a long time think thus: "Truly the great Sama*n*a possesses high magical powers and great faculties; he is not, however, holy like me." What if I were to move the mind of this *Gaṭ*ila (in order to show him my superiority).'

And the Blessed One said to the *Gaṭ*ila Uruvelâ Kassapa: 'You are not holy (arahâ), Kassapa, nor have you entered the path of Arahatship, nor do you walk in such a practice as will lead you to Arahatship, or to entering the path of Arahatship.'

Then the *Ga/t/*ila Uruvelâ Kassapa prostrated himself, inclining his head to the feet of the Blessed One, and said to the Blessed One: 'Lord, let me receive the pabba*gg*â and upasampadâ ordinations from the Blessed One.'

18. (Buddha replied): 'You, Kassapa, are chief, leader, foremost, first, and highest of five hundred *Ga/t/*ilas; go first and inform them of your intention, and let them do what they think fit.'

Then the *Ga/t/*ila Uruvelâ Kassapa went to those *Ga/t/*ilas; having gone to them, he said to those *Ga/t/*ilas: 'I wish, Sirs, to lead a religious life under the direction of the great Sama*n*a; you may do, Sirs, what you think fit.'

(The *Ga/t/*ilas replied): 'We have conceived, Sir, an affection for the great Sama*n*a long since; if you will lead, Sir, a religious life under the great Sama*n*a's direction, we will all lead a religious life under the great Sama*n*a's direction.'

19. Then the *Ga/t/*ilas flung their hair[1], their braids, their provisions[2], and the things for the agnihotra sacrifice into the river, and went to the place where the Blessed One was; having approached him and prostrated themselves before him, inclining their heads to the feet of the Blessed One, they said to the Blessed One: 'Lord, let us receive the pabba*gg*â and upasampadâ ordinations from the Blessed One.'

---

[1] Which they had cut off in order to receive the pabba*gg*â ordination, see chap. 12. 3.

[2] We are extremely doubtful about the meaning of khârikâ*g*a, which Buddhaghosa explains by khâribhâra. Perhaps it may mean provisions of any description of which each *Ga/t/*ila used to keep one khârî (a certain dry measure).

'Come, O Bhikkhus,' said the Blessed One, 'well taught is the doctrine; lead a holy life for the sake of the complete extinction of suffering.'

Thus these venerable persons received the upasampadâ ordination.

20. And the *G*a*t*ila Nadî Kassapa saw the hair the braids, the provisions, the things for the agnihotra sacrifice, which were carried down by the river; when he saw that, he became afraid that some misfortune might have befallen his brother. He sent some *G*a*t*ilas, saying, 'Go and look after my brother,' and went himself with his three hundred *G*a*t*ilas to the venerable Uruvelâ Kassapa; having approached him, he said to the venerable Uruvelâ Kassapa: 'Now, Kassapa, is this bliss?'

(Uruvelâ Kassapa replied): 'Yes, friend, this is bliss.'

21. And the *G*a*t*ilas (who had come with Nadî Kassapa (&c., as in § 19).

22. And the *G*a*t*ila Gayâ Kassapa saw (&c., as in § 20); when he saw that, he became afraid that some misfortune might have befallen his brothers. He sent some *G*a*t*ilas, saying, 'Go and look after my brothers,' and went himself with his two hundred *G*a*t*ilas to the venerable Uruvelâ Kassapa (&c., as above).

23. And the *G*a*t*ilas (who had come with Gayâ Kassapa (&c., as in § 19).

24. [1] At the command of the Blessed One the five hundred pieces of fire-wood could not be split and were split, the fires could not be lit up and

[1] This is evidently a remark added to the text by a reader or commentator.

were lit up, could not be extinguished and were extinguished; besides he created five hundred vessels with fire. Thus the number of these miracles amounts to three thousand five hundred.

21.

1. And the Blessed One, after having dwelt at Uruvelâ as long as he thought fit, went forth to Gayâsîsa[1], accompanied by a great number of Bhikkhus, by one thousand Bhikkhus who all had been *Ga*t*ilas before. There near Gayâ, at Gayâsîsa, the Blessed One dwelt together with those thousand Bhikkhus.

2. There the Blessed One thus addressed the Bhikkhus: 'Everything, O Bhikkhus, is burning. And how, O Bhikkhus, is everything burning?

'The eye, O Bhikkhus, is burning; visible things are burning; the mental impressions based on the eye are burning; the contact of the eye (with visible things) is burning; the sensation produced by the contact of the eye (with visible things), be it pleasant, be it painful, be it neither pleasant nor painful, that also is burning. With what fire is it burning? I declare unto you that it is burning with the fire of lust, with the fire of anger, with the fire of ignorance; it is burning with (the anxieties of) birth, decay, death, grief, lamentation, suffering, dejection, and despair.

3. 'The ear is burning, sounds are burning, &c. . . . . The nose is burning, odours are burning, &c.

[1] According to General Cunningham, Gayâsîsa ('the head of Gayâ') is the mountain of Brahmâyoni near Gayâ. Arch. Rep. III, 107.

. . . . The tongue is burning, tastes are burning, &c. . . . . The body is burning, objects of contact are burning, &c. . . . . The mind is burning, thoughts are burning, &c. . . . .[1]

4. 'Considering this, O Bhikkhus, a disciple learned (in the scriptures), walking in the Noble Path, becomes weary of the eye, weary of visible things, weary of the mental impressions based on the eye, weary of the contact of the eye (with visible things), weary also of the sensation produced by the contact of the eye (with visible things), be it pleasant, be it painful, be it neither pleasant nor painful. He becomes weary of the ear (&c. . . . . , down to . . . . thoughts[1]). Becoming weary of all that, he divests himself of passion; by absence of passion he is made free; when he is free, he becomes aware that he is free; and he realises that re-birth is exhausted; that holiness is completed; that duty is fulfilled; and that there is no further return to this world.'

When this exposition was propounded, the minds of those thousand Bhikkhus became free from attachment to the world, and were released from the Âsavas.

Here ends the sermon on 'The Burning.'

End of the third Bhâ*n*avâra concerning the Wonders done at Uruvelâ.

---

[1] Here the same exposition which has been given relating to the eye, its objects, the sensations produced by its contact with objects, &c., is repeated with reference to the ear and the other organs of sense.

22.

1. And the Blessed One, after having dwelt at Gayâsîsa as long as he thought fit, went forth to Râ*g*agaha, accompanied by a great number of Bhikkhus, by one thousand Bhikkhus who all had been *G*a*t*ilas before. And the Blessed One, wandering from place to place, came to Râ*g*agaha. There the Blessed One dwelt near Râ*g*agaha, in the La*tth*ivana pleasure garden, near the sacred shrine of Supati*tth*a[1].

2. Then the Magadha king Seniya Bimbisâra heard: 'The Sama*n*a Gotama Sakyaputta, an ascetic of the Sakya tribe, has just arrived at Râ*g*agaha and is staying near Râ*g*agaha, in the La*tth*ivana pleasure garden, near the sacred shrine of Supati*tth*a. Of Him the blessed Gotama such a glorious fame is spread abroad: "Truly he is the blessed, holy, absolute Sambuddha, endowed with knowledge and conduct, the most happy One, who understands all worlds, the highest One, who guides men as a driver curbs a bullock, the teacher of gods and men, the blessed Buddha. He makes known the Truth, which he has understood himself and seen face to face, to this world system with its devas, its Mâras, and its Brahmâs; to all beings, Sama*n*as and Brâhma*n*as,

[1] La*tth*ivana (Sansk. yash*t*ivana), literally, 'stick forest,' means a forest consisting of bambus. General Cunningham has the following note about this bambu forest: 'In 1862, when I was at Râjgir (i.e. Râ*g*agaha), I heard the bambu forest always spoken of as Jaktiban; . . . I fixed the position of the bambu forest to the south-west of Râjgir on the hill lying between the hot-springs of Tapoban and old Râ*g*agr*i*ha.' Reports, III, 140.

The word we have rendered sacred shrine is *K*etiya.

gods and men; he preaches that Truth (Dhamma) which is glorious in the beginning, glorious in the middle, glorious at the end, in the spirit and in the letter; he proclaims a consummate, perfect, and pure life." It is good to obtain the sight of holy men (Arahats) like that.'

3. And the Magadha king Seniya Bimbisâra, surrounded by twelve myriads of Magadha Brâhma*n*as and householders[1], went to the place where the Blessed One was; having approached him and respectfully saluted the Blessed One, he sat down near him. And of those twelve myriads of Magadha Brâhma*n*as and householders some also respectfully saluted the Blessed One and sat down near him; some exchanged greeting with the Blessed One, having exchanged with him greeting and complaisant words, they sat down near him; some bent their clasped hands towards the Blessed One and sat down near him; some shouted out their name and their family name before the Blessed One and sat down near him; some silently sat down near him.

4. Now those twelve myriads of Magadha Brâhma*n*as and householders thought: 'How now is this? has the great Sama*n*a placed himself under the spiritual direction of Uruvelâ Kassapa, or has Uruvelâ Kassapa placed himself under the spiritual direction of the great Sama*n*a?'

And the Blessed One, who understood in his mind the reflection which had arisen in the minds of those twelve myriads of Magadha Brâhma*n*as and householders, addressed the venerable Uruvelâ Kassapa

[1] The word householder (gahapati) is used here, as is the case not unfrequently, to denote householders of the third caste. Compare Rh. D.'s note on Mahâ-sudassana Sutta, p. 260.

in this stanza: 'What knowledge have you gained, O inhabitant of Uruvelâ, that has induced you, who were renowned for your penances[1], to forsake your sacred fire? I ask you, Kassapa, this question: How is it that your fire sacrifice has become deserted?'

(Kassapa replied): 'It is visible things and sounds, and also tastes, pleasures and woman that the sacrifices speak of[2]; because I understood that whatever belongs to existence[3] is filth, therefore I took no more delight in sacrifices and offerings[4].'

5. 'But if your mind, Kassapa (said the Blessed One[5]), found there no more delight,—either in visible things, or sounds, or tastes,—what is it in the world of men or gods in which[6] your mind, Kassapa, now finds delight? Tell me that.'

(Kassapa replied): 'I have seen the state of peace (i. e. Nirvâ*n*a) in which the basis of existence (upadhi[3]) and the obstacles to perfection (ki*ñ*-

---

[1] Literally, 'who is known as emaciate.' This is said with reference to the mortifications practised by the *G*a*t*ilas or Vânaprasthas. The Mahâbhârata (III, 1499) uses the same adjective (k*ris*a) of a *G*a*t*ila. Vadâno we take for a participle, but it is possible also to read vadâ no, 'tell us,' which Professor Jacobi (Zeitschrift der Deutschen Morg. Ges., XXXIV, p. 187) prefers. Buddhaghosa takes kisakovadâno for a compound of kisaka and ovadâna: tâpasâna*m* ovâdako anusâsako.

[2] The meaning is: The mantras which are recited at the sacrifices contain praises of visible things, &c., and the rewards that are promised to him who offers such sacrifices do not extend beyond that same sphere.

[3] The Pâli word is upadhi, which is translated by Childers, 'substratum of being.' See our note on chap. 5. 2. In this passage upadhi is said to refer to the Khandhas (Buddhaghosa).

[4] Here we have the Vedic distinction of greater and smaller sacrifices (ya*g*atayas and *g*uhotayas).

[5] The words 'said the Blessed One' (ti Bhagavâ avo*k*a) are probably interpolated from a gloss, as they destroy the metre.

[6] Doubtless Buddhaghosa is right in explaining ko by kva.

*k*ana[1]) have ceased, which is free from attachment to sensual existence, which cannot pass over into another state, which cannot be led to another state; therefore I took no more delight in sacrifices and offerings.'

6. Then the venerable Uruvelâ Kassapa rose from his seat, adjusted his upper robe so as to cover one shoulder, prostrated himself, inclining his head to the feet of the Blessed One, and said to the Blessed One: 'My teacher, Lord, is the Blessed One, I am his pupil; my teacher, Lord, is the Blessed One, I am his pupil.' Then those twelve myriads of Magadha Brâhma*n*as and householders understood: 'Uruvelâ Kassapa has placed himself under the spiritual direction of the great Sama*n*a.'

7, 8. And the Blessed One, who understood in his mind the reflection that had arisen in the minds of those twelve myriads of Magadha Brâhma*n*as and householders, preached to them in due course (&c., as in chap. 7, §§ 5, 6, down to:). Just as a clean cloth free from black specks properly takes the dye, thus eleven myriads of those Magadha Brâhma*n*as and householders with Bimbisâra at their head, while sitting there, obtained the pure and spotless Eye of the Truth (that is, the knowledge): 'Whatsoever is subject to the condition of origination is subject

---

[1] Aki*ñk*ana here, and elsewhere, used as an epithet of Arahatship, refers to the state of mind in which the ki*ñk*anas, that is, lust, malice, and delusion (so in the Sa*m*giti Sutta of the Dîgha Nikâya), have ceased to be. It is literally 'being without the somethings,' which are the things that stand in the way, the obstacles to Buddhist perfection; and Buddhaghosa (in the Sumaṅgala Vilâsinî on the passage in the Sa*m*gîti Sutta) explains accordingly ki*ñk*ana by pa*l*ibodha.

also to the condition of cessation.' One myriad announced their having become lay-pupils.

9. Then the Magadha king Seniya Bimbisâra, having seen the Truth (&c. . . . . down to) dependent on nobody else for the knowledge of the Teacher's doctrine, said to the Blessed One: 'In former days, Lord, when I was a prince, I entertained five wishes; these are fulfilled now. In former days, Lord, when I was a prince, I wished: "O that I might be inaugurated as king." This was my first wish, Lord; this is fulfilled now. "And might then the holy, absolute Sambuddha come into my kingdom." This was my second wish, Lord; this is fulfilled now.

10. '"And might I pay my respects to Him, the Blessed One." This was my third wish, Lord; this is fulfilled now. "And might He the Blessed One preach his doctrine (Dhamma) to me." This was my fourth wish, Lord; this is fulfilled now. "And might I understand His, the Blessed One's doctrine." This was my fifth wish, Lord; this is fulfilled now. These were the five wishes, Lord, which I entertained in former days when I was a prince; these are fulfilled now.

11. 'Glorious, Lord! (&c., as in chap. 7. 10, down to:) who has taken his refuge in Him. And might the Blessed One, Lord, consent to take his meal with me to-morrow together with the fraternity of Bhikkhus.'

The Blessed One expressed his consent by remaining silent.

12. Then the Magadha king Seniya Bimbisâra, when he understood that the Blessed One had accepted his invitation, rose from his seat, respectfully saluted the Blessed One, and, passing round him with his right side towards him, went away.

And when the night had elapsed, the Magadha king Seniya Bimbisâra ordered excellent food, both hard and soft, to be prepared, and had dinner-time announced to the Blessed One in the words: 'It is time, Lord, the meal is ready.' And in the forenoon the Blessed One, having put on his under-robes, took his alms-bowl, and with his *k*îvara on entered the city of Râ*g*agaha accompanied by a great number of Bhikkhus, by one thousand Bhikkhus who all had been *G*a*t*ilas before.

13. At that time Sakka the king of the devas, assuming the appearance of a young Brâhman, walked in front of the Bhikkhu fraternity with Buddha at its head, singing the following stanzas: 'The self-controlled One with the self-controlled, with the former *G*a*t*ilas, the released One with the released, the Blessed One, gold-coloured like an ornament of siṅgî gold[1], has entered Râ*g*agaha.

'The emancipated One with the emancipated, with the former *G*a*t*ilas, &c.

'He who has crossed (the ocean of passion) with them who have crossed (it), with the former *G*a*t*ilas, the released One with the released, the Blessed One, gold-coloured like an ornament of siṅgî gold, has entered Râ*g*agaha.

'He who is possessed of the ten Noble States[2]

---

[1] Gold colour is one (the 17th) of the thirty-two lakkha*n*a which form the characteristics of Buddha as a mahâpurisa.

[2] The ten ariyavâsas. Buddhaghosa says: dasasu ariyavâsesu vutthavâso. The Sa*m*gîti Sutta gives the ten Noble States, as follows: 1. being free from the five bad qualities (pa*ñk*aṅga), 2. being possessed of the six good qualities (*kh*a*l*aṅga), 3. being guarded in the one thing (ekârakkha), 4. observing four things (*k*aturâpassena), 5. rejecting each of the four false truths (panunna pa*kk*eka-sa*kk*a), 6. seeking right things (samavayasa-

and of the ten Powers[1], who understands the ten Paths of Kamma[2] and possesses the ten (attributes of Arahatship)[3], the Blessed One, surrounded by ten hundred of followers, has entered Râgagaha.'

14. The people when they saw Sakka the king of the devas, said: 'This youth indeed is handsome; this youth indeed has a lovely appearance; this youth indeed is pleasing. Whose attendant may this youth be?'

When they talked thus, Sakka the king of the devas addressed those people in this stanza: 'He who is wise, entirely self-controlled, the unrivalled Buddha, the Arahat, the most happy upon earth: his attendant am I.'

15. And the Blessed One went to the palace of the Magadha king Seniya Bimbisâra. Having gone there, he sat down with the Bhikkhus who followed him, on seats laid out for them. Then the Magadha king Seniya Bimbisâra with his own hands served and offered excellent food, both hard and soft, to the fraternity of Bhikkhus with the Buddha at

dhesana), 7. having pure aims (anâvila-samkappa), 8. being full of ease (passaddhakâya-samkhâra), 9. being emancipated in heart (suvimuttakitta), 10. being emancipated in ideas (suvimuttapañña). The Samgîti then further enlarges on the meaning of each of these ten.

[1] The ten Balas, which are ten kinds of knowledge (ñâna); see Burnouf, Lotus, p. 781 and following, and compare Gâtaka I, 78.

[2] Buddhaghosa explains dasadhammavidû by dasakammapathavidû.

[3] Buddhaghosa explains dasabhi k'ûpeto by supplying asekhehi dhammehi. The first eight of the ten asekhâ dhammâ consist in the full perfection of sammâditthi (right belief) and the other categories enumerated in the formula of the Noble Eightfold Path; the ninth and tenth are the perfection of sammâñâna (right knowledge) and sammâvimutti (right emancipation).

its head; and when the Blessed One had finished his meal and cleansed his bowl and his hands, he sat down near him.

16. Sitting near him the Magadha king Seniya Bimbisâra thought: 'Where may I find a place for the Blessed One to live in, not too far from the town and not too near, suitable for going and coming, easily accessible for all people who want (to see him), by day not too crowded, at night not exposed to much noise and alarm, clean of the smell of people, hidden from men, well fitted for a retired life?'

17. And the Magadha king Seniya Bimbisâra thought: 'There is the Ve*l*uvana[1], my pleasure garden, which is not too far from the town and not too near, suitable for going and coming, ... (&c., down to a retired life). What if I were to make an offering of the Ve*l*uvana pleasure garden to the fraternity of Bhikkhus with the Buddha at its head?'

18. And the Magadha king Seniya Bimbisâra took a golden vessel (with water in it, to be poured over the Buddha's hand); and dedicated (the garden) to the Blessed One (by saying), 'I give up this Ve*l*uvana pleasure garden, Lord, to the fraternity of Bhikkhus with the Buddha at its head.' The Blessed One accepted the ârâma (park). Then the Blessed One, after having taught, incited, animated, and gladdened the Magadha king Seniya

[1] The site of the Ve*l*uvana ('bambu forest') near Râ*g*agaha has not yet been discovered. 'It must have occupied about the position where the ancient basements, marked K. K. K. and G. in Cunningham's map of Râ*g*ag*ri*ha (pl. xiv, Reports, vol. i), were found by him' (Rh. D., 'Buddhism,' p. 62 note).

Bimbisâra by religious discourse, rose from his seat and went away.

And in consequence of this event the Blessed One, after having delivered a religious discourse, thus addressed the Bhikkhus: 'I allow you, O Bhikkhus, to receive the donation of an ârâma (a park).'

23.

1. At that time Sañgaya, a paribbâgaka (wandering ascetic), resided at Râgagaha with a great retinue of paribbâgakas, with two hundred and fifty paribbâgakas. At that time Sâriputta and Moggallâna (two young Brâhmanas) led a religious life as followers of Sañgaya the paribbâgaka; these had given their word to each other: 'He who first attains to the immortal (amata, i.e. Nirvâna) shall tell the other one.'

2. Now one day the venerable Assagi in the forenoon, having put on his under-robes, and having taken his alms-bowl, and with his kîvara on, entered the city of Râgagaha for alms; his walking, turning back, regarding, looking, drawing (his arms) back, and stretching (them) out was decorous; he turned his eyes to the ground, and was dignified in deportment. Now the paribbâgaka Sâriputta saw the venerable Assagi, who went through Râgagaha for alms, whose walking, &c., was decorous, who kept his eyes on the ground, and was dignified in deportment. Seeing him he thought: 'Indeed this person is one of those Bhikkhus who are the worthy ones (Arahats) in the world, or who have entered the path of Arahatship. What if I were to approach this Bhikkhu and

to ask him: "In whose name, friend, have you retired from the world? Who is your teacher? Whose doctrine do you profess?"'

3. Now the paribbâ*g*aka Sâriputta thought: 'This is not the time to ask this Bhikkhu; he has entered the interior yard of a house, walking for alms. What if I were to follow this Bhikkhu step by step, according to the course recognised by those who want something[1].'

And the venerable Assa*g*i, having finished his alms-pilgrimage through Râ*g*agaha, went back with the food he had received. Then the paribbâ*g*aka Sâriputta went to the place where the venerable Assa*g*i was; having approached him, he exchanged greeting with the venerable Assa*g*i; having exchanged with him greeting and complaisant words, he stationed himself at his side; standing at his side the paribbâ*g*aka Sâriputta said to the venerable Assa*g*i: 'Your countenance, friend, is serene; your complexion is pure and bright. In whose name, friend, have you retired from the world? Who is your teacher? Whose doctrine do you profess[2]?'

4. (Assa*g*i replied): 'There is, friend, the great Sama*n*a Sakyaputta, an ascetic of the Sakya tribe; in His, the Blessed One's, name have I retired from the world; He, the Blessed One, is my teacher; and His, the Blessed One's, doctrine do I profess.'

---

[1] This seems to us the meaning of atthikehi upaññâta*m* magga*m*. Sâriputta followed Assa*g*i as suppliants are accustomed to follow their proposed benefactor till a convenient season arrives for preferring their request.

[2] The same words as are put in the mouth of Upaka, when addressing the Buddha, above, chap. 6, § 7 (and see below, § 6).

'And what is the doctrine, Sir, which your teacher holds, and preaches to you?'

'I am only a young disciple, friend; I have but recently received the ordination; and I have newly adopted this doctrine and discipline. I cannot explain to you the doctrine in detail; but I will tell you in short what it means.'

Then the paribbâ*g*aka Sâriputta said to the venerable Assa*g*i: 'Well, friend, tell me much or little as you like, but be sure to tell me the spirit (of the doctrine); I want but the spirit; why do you make so much of the letter?'

5. Then the venerable Assa*g*i pronounced to the paribbâ*g*aka Sâriputta the following text of the Dhamma: 'Of all objects which proceed from a cause, the Tathâgata has explained the cause, and He has explained their cessation also; this is the doctrine of the great Sama*n*a[1].'

And the paribbâ*g*aka Sâriputta after having heard this text obtained the pure and spotless Eye of the Truth (that is, the following knowledge): 'Whatsoever is subject to the condition of origination is subject also to the condition of cessation.' (And he said): 'If this alone be the Doctrine (the Dhamma), now you have reached up to the state where all sorrow ceases (i. e. Nirvâ*n*a), (the state) which has remained unseen

[1] This famous stanza doubtless alludes to the formula of the twelve Nidânas (see chap. 1. 2) which explains the origination and cessation of what are called here 'dhammâ hetuppabhavâ.' Hetu and pa*kk*aya (the word so frequently used in the formula of the Nidânas) are nearly synonymous. Colebrooke (Life and Essays, vol. ii. p. 419) says that the Bauddhas distinguish between hetu, 'proximate cause,' and pa*kk*aya (pratyaya), 'concurrent occasion;' but, in practical use, this slight difference of meaning, if it really existed, has but little weight attached to it.

through many myriads of Kappas (world-ages) of the past.'

6. Then the paribbâ*g*aka Sâriputta went to the place where the paribbâ*g*aka Moggallâna was. And the paribbâ*g*aka Moggallâna saw the paribbâ*g*aka Sâriputta coming from afar; seeing him he said to the paribbâ*g*aka Sâriputta: 'Your countenance, friend, is serene; your complexion is pure and bright. Have you then really reached the immortal, friend?'

'Yes, friend, I have attained to the immortal.'

'And how, friend, have you done so?'

7-9. 'I saw, friend, the Bhikkhu Assa*g*i who went through Râ*g*agaha for alms (&c.[1], down to:); "But I will tell you in short what it means."

'"Tell me much or little as you like, but be sure to tell me the spirit (of the doctrine); I want but the spirit; why do you make so much of the letter?"

10. 'Then, friend, the Bhikkhu Assa*g*i pronounced the following Dhamma sentence: "Of all objects which proceed from a cause, the Tathâgata has explained the cause, and He has explained their cessation also; this is the doctrine of the great Sama*n*a."'

And the paribbâ*g*aka Moggallâna, after having heard (&c., as in § 5, down to the end).

24.

1. Then the paribbâ*g*aka Moggallâna said to the paribbâ*g*aka Sâriputta: 'Let us go, friend, and join

[1] See §§ 2-4. Instead of 'The paribbâ*g*aka Sâriputta,' of course, the pronoun of the first person is to be read; instead of 'The venerable Assa*g*i' read, 'The Bhikkhu Assa*g*i;' and further, the vocative 'Friend' (âvuso), addressed to Moggallâna, is inserted three or four times in the course of this narration.

the Blessed One; that He, the Blessed One, may be our teacher.'

(Sâriputta replied): 'It is on our account, friend, that these two hundred and fifty paribbâgakas live here (as followers of Sañgaya), and it is we whom they regard; let us first inform them also of our intention; then they may do what they think fit.'

Then Sâriputta and Moggallâna went to the place where those paribbâgakas were; having approached them, they said to the paribbâgakas: 'Friends, we are going to join the Blessed One; that He, the Blessed One, may be our teacher.'

(The paribbâgakas replied): 'It is on your account, Sirs, that we live here, and it is you whom we regard; if you, Sirs, are about to place yourselves under the spiritual direction of the great Samana, we all will place ourselves also under the spiritual direction of the great Samana.'

2. Then Sâriputta and Moggallâna went to the place where the paribbâgaka Sañgaya was; having approached him, they said to the paribbâgaka Sañgaya: 'Friend, we are going to join the Blessed One; that He, the Blessed One, may be our teacher.'

(Sañgaya replied): 'Nay, friends, do not go; let us all three share in the leadership of this body (of disciples).'

And a second time Sâriputta and Moggallâna said, &c. And a third time Sâriputta and Moggallâna said, &c. (And a third time he replied): 'Nay, friends, do not go; let us all three share in the leadership of this body (of disciples).'

3. But Sâriputta and Moggallâna took with them those two hundred and fifty paribbâgakas and went to the Veluvana. But the paribbâgaka Sañgaya

began, on the spot, to vomit hot blood from his mouth[1].

And the Blessed One saw them, Sâriputta and Moggallâna, coming from afar; on seeing them he thus addressed the Bhikkhus: 'There, O Bhikkhus, two companions arrive, Kolita and Upatissa[2]; these will be a pair of (true) pupils, a most distinguished, auspicious pair.'

When[3] (Sâriputta and Moggallâna), who had reached emancipation in the perfect destruction of the substrata (of existence), which is a profound subject accessible only to knowledge, came to the Ve*l*uvana, the Teacher, who saw them, foretold about

---

[1] The later Burmese and Chinese works translated by Bigandet (Life of Gaudama, p. 152) and by Beal (Romantic Legend, p. 330) add that he died. This is not in the Pâli text, and the Sinhalese account given by Hardy (Manual, p. 197) is directly opposed to that statement.

[2] Upatissa was called Sâriputta after his mother ('The Son of Sârî'); Kolita had the family name Moggallâna (compare Beal, Romantic Legend, pp. 324, 331). The name Upatissa occurs in Asoka's well-known edict which has been found at Bairât. The king there quotes 'The Question of Upatissa' among the texts, the study of which he recommends to the brethren and sisters of the fraternity and to the laymen of either sex. This very probably refers to the dialogue between Assa*g*i and Sâriputta.

[3] As to this repetition of what had been related before, comp. the note on chap. 15. 6, 7. The words from gambhîre down to upadhisa*m*khaye form a *s*loka. This is one of several instances where an older passage in verse, and probably first composed in some nearly related dialect, appears in the Pâli Pi*t*akas in prose. It is this which explains the extraordinary grammatical construction of the first seven words. Compare Rh. D.'s note on the similar instance at Mahâ-parinibbâna Sutta V, 62. The exclamation put into the mouth of Sâriputta, and afterwards of Moggallâna (above, chap. 23, §§ 5, 10), ought also, perhaps, to be included in the same category.

them: 'These two companions who are now coming—Kolita and Upatissa—these will be a pair of (true) pupils, a most distinguished, auspicious pair.'

4. Then Sâriputta and Moggallâna went to the place where the Blessed One was; having approached him, they prostrated themselves, inclining their heads to the feet of the Blessed One, and said to the Blessed One: 'Lord, let us receive the pabba*gg*â and upasampadâ ordinations from the Blessed One.'

'Come, O Bhikkhus,' said the Blessed One, 'well taught is the doctrine; lead a holy life for the sake of the complete extinction of suffering.' Thus these venerable persons received the upasampadâ ordination.

5. At that time many distinguished young Magadha noblemen led a religious life under the direction of the Blessed One. The people were annoyed, murmured, and became angry (saying), 'The Sama*n*a Gotama causes fathers to beget no sons; the Sama*n*a Gotama causes wives to become widows; the Sama*n*a Gotama causes families to become extinct. Now he has ordained one thousand *G*a*t*ilas, and he has ordained these two hundred and fifty paribbâ*g*akas who were followers of Sa*ñg*aya; and these many distinguished young Magadha noblemen are now leading a religious life under the direction of the Sama*n*a Gotama.' And moreover, when they saw the Bhikkhus, they reviled them in the following stanza: 'The great Sama*n*a has come to Giribba*g*a (i.e. Râ*g*agaha) of the Magadha people, leading with him all the followers of Sa*ñg*aya; who will be the next to be led by him?'

6. Some Bhikkhus heard those people that were

annoyed, murmured, and had become angry; these Bhikkhus told this thing to the Blessed One. (He replied): 'This noise, O Bhikkhus, will not last long; it will last only seven days; after seven days it will be over. And if they revile you, O Bhikkhus, in this stanza: "The great Sama*n*a has come, &c.," you should reply to the revilers in the following stanza: "It is by means of the true doctrine that the great heroes, the Tathâgatas, lead men. Who will murmur at the wise, who lead men by the power of the Truth?"'

7. At that time the people, when seeing the Bhikkhus, reviled them in the following stanza: 'The great Sama*n*a has come, &c.'

Then the Bhikkhus replied to the revilers in the following stanza: 'It is by means of the true doctrine, &c.'

Then the people understood: 'It is by truth, and not by wrong, that the Sakyaputtiya Sama*n*as lead men;' and thus that noise lasted only seven days, and after seven days it was over.

Here ends the narration of the ordination of Sâriputta and Moggallâna.

End of the fourth Bhâ*n*avâra.

25[1].

1. At that time some Bhikkhus, as they had no upa*ggh*âyas (preceptors) and received no exhorta-

---

[1] The chief object of the first book being to discuss the regulations for the upasampadâ ordination, at which the preceptor

tion and instruction, went on their rounds for alms wearing improper under and upper garments (or, wearing their under and upper garments improperly), and in an improper attire. While people were eating, they held out their alms-bowls in which were leavings of food[1], over the hard food (which the people were eating), and held them out over soft food, and held them out over savoury food, and held them out over drinks. They asked for soup and boiled rice themselves, and ate it; in the dining halls they made a great and loud noise.

2. The people were annoyed, murmured, and became angry (saying), 'How can the Sakyaputtiya Sama*n*as go on their rounds for alms wearing improper under and upper garments, ... (&c., as in § 1, down to drinks)? How can they make so great and loud a noise in the dining halls? They behave like Brâhma*n*as at the dinners given to them.'

3. Some Bhikkhus heard those people that were annoyed, murmured, and had become angry. Those Bhikkhus who were moderate, frugal, modest, con-

(upa*ggh*âya) of the candidate has a principal part, the text now goes on to relate the institution of the office and upa*ggh*âyas, and to explain the mutual duties incumbent on upa*ggh*âyas and pupils (saddhivihârikas).

[1] Buddhaghosa has the following note on utti*tth*apatta: 'utti*tth*apattan ti pi*nd*âya *k*ara*n*akapatta*m*, tasmi*m* hi manussâ u*kk*i*tth*asaññino (this word is spelt so in the Paris MS. as well as in the Berlin MS. of the Samanta Pâsâdikâ; the usual spelling is u*kkh*i*tth*a), tasmâ utti*tth*apattan ti vutta*m*. athavâ u*tth*ahitvâ patta*m* upanâmentîti evam ettha attho da*tth*abbo.' We take the word, as the former of Buddhaghosa's two explanations implies, for a composition of u*kkh*i*tth*a. For the conversion of palatal consonants into dentals, see E. Kuhn, Beiträge zur Pali-Grammatik, p. 36, and on the use of the word compare Trenckner's Milinda Pañho, pp. 213, 214.

scientious, anxious for training, were annoyed, murmured, and became angry: 'How can the Bhikkhus go on their rounds for alms wearing improper under and upper garments, &c.? How can they make so great and loud a noise in the dining halls?'

4. These Bhikkhus told this thing to the Blessed One.

In consequence of that and on this occasion the Blessed One, having ordered the fraternity of Bhikkhus to assemble, questioned the Bhikkhus: 'Is it true, O Bhikkhus, that some Bhikkhus go on their rounds, ... (&c., down to), that they make a great and loud noise in the dining halls?'

'It is true, Lord.'

5. Then the Blessed Buddha rebuked those Bhikkhus: 'It is improper, O Bhikkhus, what these foolish persons are doing, it is unbecoming, indecent, unworthy of Sama*n*as, unallowable, and to be avoided. How can these foolish persons, O Bhikkhus, go on their rounds, &c.? How can they make so great and loud a noise in the dining halls? This will not do, O Bhikkhus, for converting the unconverted, and for augmenting the number of the converted; but it will result, O Bhikkhus, in the unconverted being repulsed (from the faith), and in many of the converted being estranged.'

6. And the Blessed One rebuked those Bhikkhus in many ways, spoke against unfrugality, ill-nature, immoderation, insatiableness, delighting in society, and indolence; spoke in many ways in praise of frugality, good-nature, of the moderate, contented, who have eradicated (sin), who have shaken off (sin), of the gracious, of the reverent, and of the energetic. And having delivered before the Bhikkhus a religious

discourse in accordance to, and in conformity with these subjects, he thus addressed the Bhikkhus: 'I prescribe, O Bhikkhus, (that young Bhikkhus choose) an upa*ggh*âya (or preceptor).

'The upa*ggh*âya, O Bhikkhus, ought to consider the saddhivihârika (i.e. pupil) as a son; the saddhivihârika ought to consider the upa*ggh*âya as a father. Thus these two, united by mutual reverence, confidence, and communion of life, will progress, advance, and reach a high stage in this doctrine and discipline.

7. 'And let them choose, O Bhikkhus, an upa*ggh*âya in this way: Let him (who is going to choose an upa*ggh*âya) adjust his upper robe so as to cover one shoulder, salute the feet (of the intended upa*ggh*âya), sit down squatting, raise his joined hands, and say: "Venerable Sir, be my upa*ggh*âya; venerable Sir, be my upa*ggh*âya; venerable Sir, be my upa*ggh*âya." (If the other answer): "Well," or, "Certainly," or, "Good," or, "All right," or, "Carry on (your work) with friendliness (towards me)," or should he express this by gesture (lit. by his body), or by word, or by gesture and word, then the upa*ggh*âya has been chosen. If he does not express this by gesture, nor by word, nor by gesture and word, the upa*ggh*âya has not been chosen.

8. 'The saddhivihârika, O Bhikkhus, ought to observe a strict conduct towards his upa*ggh*âya. And these are the rules for his conduct: Let him arise betimes, and having taken off his shoes[1] and adjusted his upper robe so as to cover one shoulder,

[1] If he had put on shoes for having a walk early in the morning or for keeping his feet clean (Buddhaghosa).

let him give (to the upa*ggh*âya) the teeth-cleanser and water to rinse his mouth with. Then let him prepare a seat (for the upa*ggh*âya). If there is rice-milk, let him rinse the jug and offer the rice-milk (to the upa*ggh*âya). When he has drunk it, let him give water (to the upa*ggh*âya), take the jug, hold it down, rinse it properly without (damaging it by) rubbing, and put it away. When the upa*ggh*âya has risen, let him take away the seat. If the place is dirty, let him sweep the place.

9. 'If the upa*ggh*âya wishes to go into the village, let (the saddhivihârika) give (to the upa*ggh*âya) his under garment, take (from him) his second under garment (i.e. his house-dress?), give him his girdle, lay the two upper garments upon each other[1] and give them (to the upa*ggh*âya), rinse the alms-bowl, and give it him with some water in it. If the upa*ggh*âya wishes (to go with) an attendant Bhikkhu, let him put on his under garment so as to conceal the three circles (viz. the navel and the two knees) and as to cover the body all around; then let him put on his girdle, lay the two upper garments upon each other and put them on, tie the knots, take his alms-bowl, after having it rinsed, and follow the upa*ggh*âya as his attendant. Let him not go too far (from the upa*ggh*âya) nor too near. Let him take (from the upa*ggh*âya) what has been put into his alms-bowl[2].

10. 'When the upa*ggh*âya speaks, let (the sad-

---

[1] Buddhaghosa explains sagu*n*a*m* katvâ by ekato katvâ.

[2] According to Buddhaghosa the meaning of these words is: If the alms-bowl of the upa*ggh*âya has become too heavy or hot by the food put into it, the saddhivihârika ought to take it and give his own bowl to the upa*ggh*âya.

dhivihârika) not interrupt him. If the upagghâya is in danger of committing an offence by the words he says, let (the saddhivihârika) keep him back. When (the upagghâya) turns back (from his alms-pilgrimage), let the saddhivihârika go back (to the Vihâra) before (the upagghâya), prepare a seat, get water for the washing of his feet, a foot-stool, and a towel[1]; then let him go to meet the upagghâya, take his bowl and his robe, give him his second under garment (his house-dress ?), and take his under garment. If the robe (of the upagghâya) is wet with perspiration, let him dry it a while in a hot place, but let him not leave the robe in a hot place. Let him fold up the robe. When folding up the robe, let him fold it up so as to leave (every day) four inches (more than the day before) hanging over at the corners, in order that no fold may arise in the middle of it[2]. Let him . . . . the girdle[3]. If there is any food received in the alms-bowl, and the upagghâya desires to eat it, let him give water (to the upagghâya) and then offer him the food.

11. 'Let him offer to the upagghâya (water) to drink. When the upagghâya has finished his meal, let (the saddhivihârika) give him water, take his alms-bowl, hold it down, rinse it properly without (damaging it by) rubbing, pour the water out, and dry (the bowl) a while in some hot place, but let

---

[1] See Chap. 6. 11, with the note.

[2] I. e. in order that the folds might not fall upon the same place every day, and the robe might be worn out at that place (Buddhaghosa).

[3] The Pâli text is : 'Obhoge kâyabandhana*m* kâtabba*m*.' Buddhaghosa's note runs as follows: 'Kâyabandhana*m* sa*m*gharitvâ (read sa*m*haritvâ) *k*îvarabhoge pakkhipitvâ *th*apetabba*m*.' We do not venture to offer any conjectures as to the meaning of this passage.

him not leave the bowl in the hot place. Let him put away the alms-bowl and the robe. When he puts away the alms-bowl, let him do so holding the alms-bowl with one hand, and first feeling with the other hand under the bed or under the chair (where he is going to put the bowl), and let him not put the bowl on the bare ground. When he hangs up the robe, let him take the robe with one hand and stroke with the other hand along the bambu peg or rope on which the robe is to be hung up, and hang up the robe so that the border is turned away from him (and turned to the wall), and the fold is turned towards him. When the upa*ggh*âya has risen, let him take away the seat and put away the water for the washing of the feet, the foot-stool, and the towel[1]. If the place is dirty, let him sweep the place.

12. 'If the upa*ggh*âya wishes to bathe, let him prepare a bath. If he wants cold water, let him get cold water; if he wants hot water, let him get hot water. If the upa*ggh*âya wishes to go to the *g*antâghara[2], let (the saddhivihârika) knead the powder[3], moisten the clay[4], take up the chair belonging to the *g*antâghara, follow the upa*g*-*gh*âya from behind, give him the chair, take his

[1] See Chap. 6. 11, with the note.

[2] A *g*antâghara (Sansk. yantrag*ri*ha, according to Dr. Bühler's conjecture) is a bathing-place for hot sitting baths. See *K*ullavagga V, 14, 3; VIII, 8; Kuhn's Zeitschrift für vergleichende Sprachf., XXV, 325.

[3] It is first moistened by water and then kneaded into lumps (Buddhaghosa),—no doubt to be rubbed over the person who is bathing.

[4] The face was besmeared with moistened clay in order to protect it from the heat. See *K*ullavagga V, 14, 3.

robe and put it aside, give him the powder and the clay. If he is able[1], let him also enter the *g*antâghara. When he is going to enter the *g*antâghara, let him besmear his face with clay, cover himself from before and behind, and thus enter the *g*antâghara.

13. 'Let him not sit down so as to encroach on senior Bhikkhus, nor let him dislodge junior Bhikkhus from their seats. Let him wait upon the upa*ggh*âya in the *g*antâghara. When he is going to leave the *g*antâghara, let him take up the chair belonging to the *g*antâghara, cover himself from before and behind, and thus leave the *g*antâghara. Let him wait upon the upa*ggh*âya also in the water. When he has bathed, let (the saddhivihârika) go out of the water first, let him dry his own body, put on his dress, then wipe off the water from his upa*ggh*âya's body, give him his under garment and his upper garment, take the chair belonging to the *g*antâghara, go before the upa*ggh*âya, prepare a seat for him, and get water for the washing of his feet, a foot-stool, and a towel[2]. Let him offer to the upa*ggh*âya (water) to drink.

14. 'If (the upa*ggh*âya) likes being called upon to deliver a discourse, let him call upon (the upa*ggh*âya to do so). If (the upa*ggh*âya) likes questions being put to him, let him put questions (to the upa*ggh*âya).

'If the Vihâra, in which the upa*ggh*âya dwells, is dirty, let him clean that Vihâra, if he is able to do so. When cleaning the Vihâra, let him first take away the alms-bowl and the robe (of the upa*ggh*âya)

[1] I. e. if he is not prevented by indisposition (Buddhaghosa).

[2] See Chap. 6. 11, with the note.

and lay them aside. Let him take away the mat and the sheet[1] and lay them aside. Let him take away the mattress and the pillow and lay them aside.

15. 'Let him turn down the bed, take it away properly without rubbing it (against the floor) and without knocking it against door or doorpost, and put it aside. Let him turn down the chair, take it away properly without rubbing it (against the floor) and without knocking it against door or doorpost, and put it aside. Let him take away the supporters of the bed[2] and put them aside. Let him take away the spitting-box and put it aside. Let him take away the board to recline on[3] and put it aside. Let him take away the carpet, after having noticed how it was spread out, and put it aside. If there are cobwebs in the Vihâra, let him remove them as soon as he sees them. Let him wipe off the casements[4] and the corners of the room. If a wall which is coated with red chalk, is dirty, let him moisten the mop, wring it out, and scour the wall. If the floor is coated black and is dirty, let him moisten the mop, wring it out, and scour the floor. If the floor is not blacked, let him sprinkle it with water and scrub it in order that the Vihâra may not become dusty. Let him heap up the sweepings and cast them aside.

16. 'Let him bask the carpet in the sunshine, clean it, dust it by beating, take it back, and spread it out as it was spread before. Let him put the supporters of the bed in the sunshine, wipe them,

---

[1] See VIII, 16, 3. 4.

[2] The bedstead rested on movable supporters. See *K*ullavagga VI, 2, 5.

[3] See *K*ullavagga VI, 20, 2.

[4] See the Samanta Pâsâdikâ, ap. Minayeff, Prâtimoksha, p. 87.

take them back, and put them in their place. Let him put the bed in the sunshine, clean it, dust it by beating, turn it down, take it back properly without rubbing it (against the floor) and without knocking it against door and doorpost, and put it in its place. Let him put the chair in the sunshine, &c.[1] Let him put mattress and pillow in the sunshine, clean them, dust them by beating, take them back, and lay them out as they were laid out before. Let him put the mat and sheet in the sunshine, &c.[1] Let him put the spittoon in the sunshine, wipe it, take it back, and put it in its place. Let him put in the sunshine the board to recline on, &c.[1]

17. 'Let him put away the alms-bowl and the robe. When he puts them away (&c., as in § 11, down to:), and hang up the robe so that the border is turned away from him and the fold is turned towards him.

18. 'If dusty winds blow from the East, let him shut the windows on the East. If dusty winds blow from the West, let him shut the windows on the West, &c.[2] If it is cold weather, let him open the windows by day and shut them at night. If it is hot weather, let him shut the windows by day and open them at night.

19. 'If the cell is dirty, let him sweep the cell. If the store-room is dirty, let him sweep the store-room. If the refectory, &c. If the fire room, &c. If the privy is dirty, let him sweep the privy. If there is no drinkable water, let him provide drinkable water. If there is no food, let him provide food. If there is no water in the waterpot for rinsing the mouth with, let him pour water into the pot.

---

[1] As in the preceding clause.

[2] The same for North and South.

20. 'If discontent has arisen within the upagghâya's heart, let the saddhivihârika appease him[1], or cause him to be appeased (by another), or compose him by religious conversation. If indecision has arisen in the upagghâya's mind, let the saddhivihârika dispel it, or cause it to be dispelled, or compose him by religious conversation. If the upagghâya takes to a false doctrine, let the saddhivihârika discuss it, or cause another to discuss it, or compose (the upagghâya) by religious conversation.

21. 'If the upagghâya is guilty of a grave offence, and ought to be sentenced to parivâsa discipline[2], let the saddhivihârika take care that the Samgha sentence the upagghâya to parivâsa discipline. If the upagghâya ought to be sentenced to recommence his penal discipline, let the saddhivihârika take care that the Samgha may order the upagghâya to recommence his penal discipline. If the mânatta discipline ought to be imposed on the upagghâya, let the saddhivihârika take care that the Samgha impose the mânatta discipline on the upagghâya. If the upagghâya is to be rehabilitated (when his penal discipline has been duly undergone), let the saddhivihârika take care that the Samgha rehabilitate the upagghâya.

[1] Literally, make it (the discontentedness) clear. Buddhaghosa reads vûpakâsetabbo vûpakâsâpetabbo, which he explains thus: 'vûpakâsetabbo means, "Let (the saddhivihârika) lead him to another place;" vûpakâsâpetabbo means, "Let him tell another Bhikkhu to take the Thera and go with him elsewhere."'

[2] The second and third books of the *K*ullavagga contain a detailed explanation of parivâsa and of the other technical terms contained in this paragraph.

22. 'If the Sa*m*gha wishes to proceed against the upa*ggh*âya by the ta*gg*aniyakamma[1], or the nissaya, or the pabbâ*g*aniyakamma, or the pa*t*isâra*n*iyakamma, or the ukkhepaniyakamma, let the saddhivihârika do what he can in order that the Sa*m*gha may not proceed against the upa*ggh*âya or may mitigate the proceeding. Or if the Sa*m*gha has instituted a proceeding against him, the ta*gg*aniyakamma, &c., or the ukkhepaniyakamma, let the saddhivihârika do what he can in order that the upa*ggh*âya may behave himself properly, live modestly, and aspire to get clear of his penance, and that the Sa*m*gha may revoke its sentence.

23. 'If the robe of the upa*ggh*âya must be washed, let the saddhivihârika wash it or take care that the upa*ggh*âya's robe is washed. If a robe must be made for the upa*ggh*âya, let the saddhivihârika make it or take care that the upa*ggh*âya's robe is made. If dye must be boiled for the upa*ggh*âya, &c. If the robe of the upa*ggh*âya must be dyed, &c. When he dyes the robe, let him dye it properly and turn it whenever required, and let him not go away before the dye has ceased to drop.

24. 'Let him not give his alms-bowl to any one without the permission of his upa*ggh*âya. Let him not accept an alms-bowl from any one else without the permission of his upa*ggh*âya. Let him not give his robe to any one else, &c. Let him not accept a robe from any one else; let him not give articles

[1] The discussion about the ta*gg*aniyakamma and the other disciplinary proceedings alluded to in this paragraph is given in the first book of the *K*ullavagga.

(required for a Bhikkhu) to any one else; let him not receive (such) articles from any one else; let him not shave the hair of any one else; let him not have his hair shaven by any one else; let him not wait upon any one else; let him not have done service by any one else; let him not execute commissions for any one else; let him not have commissions executed by any one else; let him not go with any one else as his attendant; let him not take any one else with him as his attendant; let him not carry any one's food received by him in alms (to the Vihâra); let him not have the food received by himself in alms carried by any one (to the Vihâra) without the permission of his upa*ggh*âya. Let him not enter the village, or go to a cemetery, or go abroad on journeys without the permission of his upa*ggh*âya. If his upa*ggh*âya is sick, let him nurse him as long as his life lasts, and wait until he has recovered.'

End of the duties towards an upa*ggh*âya.

26.

1. 'The upa*ggh*âya, O Bhikkhus, ought to observe a strict conduct towards his saddhivihârika. And these are the rules for his conduct: Let the upa*ggh*âya, O Bhikkhus, afford (spiritual) help and furtherance to the saddhivihârika by teaching, by putting questions to him, by exhortation, by instruction. If the upa*ggh*âya has an alms-bowl and the saddhivihârika has not, let the upa*ggh*âya give the alms-bowl to the saddhivihârika or take care

that the saddhivihârika gets an alms-bowl. If the upa*gg*h*â*ya has a robe and the saddhivihârika has not, let the upa*ggh*âya give the robe, &c. If the upa*ggh*âya has the articles (required for a Bhikkhu) and the saddhivihârika has not, &c.

2–6. 'If the saddhivihârika is sick, let (the upa*ggh*âya) arise betimes and give him the teeth-cleanser and water to rinse his mouth with. Then let him prepare a seat (for the saddhivihârika). If there is rice-milk (&c., as in chap. 25. 8, 9, down to :), and give it him with some water in it. When he expects: "Now he must be about to return," let him prepare a seat, get water for the washing of his feet (&c., as in chap. 25. 10–13[1], down to :). Let him offer to the saddhivihârika water to drink.

7–10. 'If the Vihâra in which the saddhivihârika dwells, is dirty (&c., as in chap. 25. 14–22).

11. 'If the robe of the saddhivihârika must be washed, let the upa*ggh*âya tell the saddhivihârika: "Thus must you wash your robe," or let him take care that the saddhivihârika's robe is washed. If a robe must be made for the saddhivihârika, let the upa*ggh*âya tell the saddhivihârika: "Thus must you make the robe," or let him take care that the saddhivihârika's robe is made. If dye must be boiled for the saddhivihârika, &c. If the robe of the saddhivihârika must be dyed, let the upa*ggh*âya tell, &c. When he dyes the robe, let him dye it properly, and turn it whenever required, and let him not go away before the dye has ceased to drop. If the saddhivihârika

[1] Instead of, 'Follow the upa*ggh*âya from behind' (chap. 25. 12), read here, 'Go (with the saddhivihârika).'

is sick, let him nurse him as long as his life lasts, and wait until he has recovered.'

End of the duties towards a saddhivihârika.

27.

1. At that time the saddhivihârikas did not observe a proper conduct towards their upa*ggh*âyas. The moderate Bhikkhus[1] were annoyed, murmured, and became angry, saying, 'How can the saddhivihârikas not observe a proper conduct towards their upa*ggh*âyas?' These Bhikkhus told this thing to the Blessed One.

(Then Buddha questioned the Bhikkhus): 'Is it true, O Bhikkhus, that the saddhivihârikas do not observe a proper conduct towards their upa*ggh*âyas?'

(They replied): 'It is true, Lord.'

Then the blessed Buddha rebuked those Bhikkhus: 'How can the saddhivihârikas, O Bhikkhus, not observe a proper conduct towards their upa*ggh*âyas?' Having rebuked them and delivered a religious discourse, he thus addressed the Bhikkhus[2]: 'Let a saddhivihârika, O Bhikkhus, not forbear to observe a proper conduct towards

[1] We believe that the words 'The moderate Bhikkhus' are intended here and throughout the whole work as an abbreviation of the fuller phrase, 'Those Bhikkhus who were moderate, frugal, modest, conscientious, anxious for training' (chap. 25. 3).

[2] All this is an abbreviation of what has been given at full length in chap. 25. 4–6.

his upa*ggh*âya. He who does not observe it, is guilty of a dukka*t*a[1] offence.'

2. Notwithstanding this, they did not observe a proper conduct. They told this thing to the Blessed One.

'I ordain, O Bhikkhus, to turn away (a saddhivihârika) who does not observe a proper conduct. And he ought, O Bhikkhus, to be turned away in this way: (The upa*ggh*âya is to say): "I turn you away," or, "Do not come back hither," or, "Take away your alms-bowl and robe," or, "I am not to be attended by you any more." Whether he express this by gesture, or by word, or by gesture and word, the saddhivihârika has then been turned away. If he does not express this by gesture, nor by word, nor by gesture and word, the saddhivihârika has not been turned away.'

3. At that time saddhivihârikas who had been turned away did not beg pardon (of their upa*ggh*âyas). They told this thing to the Blessed One.

'I prescribe, O Bhikkhus, that (a saddhivihârika who has been turned away) should beg pardon (of his upa*ggh*âya).'

They did not beg pardon notwithstanding. They told, &c.

'I prescribe, O Bhikkhus, that (a saddhivihârika) who has been turned away shall not forbear to beg pardon (of his upa*ggh*âya). If he does not beg pardon, it is a dukka*t*a offence.'

[1] Those slight offences which were not embodied in the Pâtimokkha are called dukka*t*a offences. They range, as to their gravity, with the pâ*k*ittiya offences of the Pâtimokkha. For him who had committed a dukka*t*a offence, no further penance was required than a simple confession of his fault. See *K*ullavagga XI, 1, 10.

4. At that time upagghâyas, when the saddhivihârikas begged their pardon, would not forgive them. They told, &c.

'I prescribe, O Bhikkhus, forgiving.'

Notwithstanding this they did not forgive. The saddhivihârikas went away, or returned to the world, or went over to other schools. They told, &c.

'Let him who is asked for his pardon, not withhold it. He who does not forgive, is guilty of a dukkata offence.'

5. At that time upagghâyas turned away (a saddhivihârika) who observed a proper conduct, and did not turn away one who did not observe it. They told, &c.

'Let no one, O Bhikkhus, who observes a proper conduct, be turned away. He who turns him away is guilty of a dukkata offence. And let no one, O Bhikkhus, who does not observe a proper conduct, not be turned away. (An upagghâya) who does not turn him away is guilty of a dukkata offence.

6. 'In five cases, O Bhikkhus, a saddhivihârika ought to be turned away: when he does not feel great affection for his upagghâya, nor great inclination (towards him), nor much shame, nor great reverence, nor great devotion (towards the upagghâya). In these five cases, O Bhikkhus, a saddhivihârika ought to be turned away.

'In five cases, O Bhikkhus, a saddhivihârika ought not to be turned away: when he feels great affection for his upagghâya, great inclination (towards him), &c. In these five cases, O Bhikkhus, a saddhivihârika ought not to be turned away.

7. 'In five cases, O Bhikkhus, it is right to turn away a saddhivihârika: when he does not feel

great affection, &c. In these five cases, O Bhikkhus, it is right to turn away a saddhivihârika.

'In five cases, O Bhikkhus, it is not right, &c.

8. 'In five cases, O Bhikkhus, an upa*ggh*âya who does not turn away a saddhivihârika, trespasses (against the law), and an upa*ggh*âya who turns him away, does not trespass: when he does not feel great affection, &c. In these five cases, &c.

'In five cases, O Bhikkhus, an upa*ggh*âya who turns away a saddhivihârika, trespasses (against the law), and an upa*ggh*âya who does not turn him away, does not trespass, &c.'

28.

1. At that time a certain Brâhma*n*a came to the Bhikkhus and asked them for the pabba*gg*â ordination. The Bhikkhus were not willing to ordain him. As he did not obtain the pabba*gg*â ordination from the Bhikkhus, he became emaciated, lean, discoloured, more and more livid, and the veins became visible all over his body.

And the Blessed One saw this Brâhma*n*a, who had become emaciated, &c. When he had seen him, he said to the Bhikkhus: 'How is it, O Bhikkhus, that this Brâhma*n*a has become emaciated, &c.?'

'This Brâhma*n*a, Lord, came to the Bhikkhus and asked them for the pabba*gg*â ordination (&c., as above, down to:), and the veins became visible all over his body.'

2. Then the Blessed One said to the Bhikkhus: 'Now, O Bhikkhus, who remembers anything about this Brâhma*n*a?'

When he had spoken thus, the venerable Sâriputta said to the Blessed One: 'I remember something, Lord, about this Brâhma*n*a.'

'And what is it you remember, Sâriputta, about this Brâhma*n*a?'

'This Brâhma*n*a, Lord, one day, when I went through Râ*g*aga*h*a for alms, ordered a spoonful of food to be given to me; this is what I remember, Lord, about this Brâhma*n*a.'

3. 'Good, good, Sâriputta; pious men, Sâriputta, are grateful and remember what has been done to them. Therefore, Sâriputta, confer you the pabba*gg*â and upasampadâ ordinations on that Brâhma*n*a.'

'Lord, how shall I confer the pabba*gg*â and upasampadâ ordinations on this Brâhma*n*a?'

Then the Blessed One on this occasion, after having delivered a religious discourse, thus addressed the Bhikkhus: 'I abolish, O Bhikkhus, from this day the upasampadâ ordination by the threefold declaration of taking refuge[1], which I had prescribed. I prescribe, O Bhikkhus, that you confer the upasampadâ ordination by a formal act of the Order in which the announcement (*ñ*atti) is followed by three questions[2].

4. 'And you ought, O Bhikkhus, to confer the

---

[1] See chap. 12 and the note on chap. 1. 1.

[2] The form for bringing a formal motion before the Order is the following: The mover first announces to the assembled Bhikkhus what resolution he is going to propose; this announcement is called *ñ*atti (see, for instance, § 4). After the *ñ*atti follows the question put to the Bhikkhus present if they approve the resolution. This question is put either once or three times; in the first case we have a *ñ*attidutiya kamma (see, for instance, II, chap. 6); in the second case, a *ñ*atti*k*atuttha kamma (as in this chapter).

upasampadâ ordination in this way: Let a learned, competent Bhikkhu proclaim the following *ñ*atti before the Sa*m*gha:

'Let the Sa*m*gha, reverend Sirs, hear me. This person N. N. desires to receive the upasampadâ ordination from the venerable N. N. (i. e. with the venerable N. N. as his upa*ggh*âya). If the Sa*m*gha is ready, let the Sa*m*gha confer on N. N. the upasampadâ ordination with N. N. as upa*ggh*âya. This is the *ñ*atti.

5, 6. 'Let the Sa*m*gha, reverend Sirs, hear me. This person N. N. desires to receive the upasampadâ ordination from the venerable N. N. The Sa*m*gha confers on N. N. the upasampadâ ordination with N. N. as upa*ggh*âya. Let any one of the venerable brethren who is in favour of the upasampadâ ordination of N. N. with N. N. as upa*ggh*âya, be silent, and any one who is not in favour of it, speak.

'And for the second time I thus speak to you: Let the Sa*m*gha (&c., as before).

'And for the third time I thus speak to you: Let the Sa*m*gha, &c.

'N. N. has received the upasampadâ ordination from the Sa*m*gha with N. N. as upa*ggh*âya. The Sa*m*gha is in favour of it, therefore it is silent. Thus I understand[1].'

29.

1. At that time a certain Bhikkhu shortly after having received the upasampadâ ordination, aban-

[1] With this and the following chapters should be compared the corresponding ordinance laid down in chapters 74–76.

doned himself to bad conduct. The Bhikkhus said to him: 'You ought not to do so, friend; it is not becoming.'

He replied: 'I never asked you, Sirs, saying, "Confer on me the upasampadâ ordination." Why have you ordained me without your being asked?'

They told this thing to the Blessed One.

'Let no one, O Bhikkhus, ordain a person unless he has been asked to do so. He who does, commits a dukka*t*a offence. I prescribe, O Bhikkhus, that you ordain only after having been asked.

2. 'And (a Bhikkhu) ought to be asked in this way: Let him who desires to receive the upasampadâ ordination, go to the Sa*m*gha, adjust his upper robe so as to cover one shoulder, salute the feet of the Bhikkhus with his head, sit down squatting, raise his joined hands, and say: "I ask the Sa*m*gha, reverend Sirs, for the upasampadâ ordination; might the Sa*m*gha, reverend Sirs, draw me out (of the sinful world) out of compassion towards me." And for the second time, &c.; and for the third time let him ask, &c.

3. 'Then let a learned, competent Bhikkhu proclaim the following *ñ*atti before the Sa*m*gha: "Let the Sa*m*gha, reverend Sirs, hear me. This person N. N. desires to receive the upasampadâ ordination from the venerable N. N.; N. N. asks the Sa*m*gha for the upasampadâ ordination with N. N. as upa*ggh*âya. If the Sa*m*gha is ready, &c.[1]"'

[1] Here follows the complete formula of a *ñ*atti*k*atuttha kamma, as in chap. 28. 4–6. The only difference is, that here in the *ñ*atti, as well as in the three questions, the words 'N. N. asks the Sa*m*gha for the upasampadâ ordination with N. N. as upa*ggh*âya' are inserted after the words 'desires to receive the upasampadâ ordination from the venerable N. N.'

30.

1. At that time an arrangement had been made at Râ*g*agaha that the Bhikkhus were to receive excellent meals successively (in the houses of different rich upâsakas). Now (one day) a certain Brâhma*n*a thought: 'Indeed the precepts which these Sakyaputtiya Sama*n*as keep and the life they live are commodious; they have good meals and lie down on beds protected from the wind[1]. What if I were to embrace the religious life among the Sakyaputtiya Sama*n*as?' Then this Brâhma*n*a went to the Bhikkhus and asked them for the pabba*gg*â ordination; the Bhikkhus conferred the pabba*gg*â and upasampadâ ordinations on him.

2. When he had been ordained, the arrangement of successive meals (with the rich upâsakas) came to an end. The Bhikkhus said to him: 'Come, friend, let us now go on our rounds for alms.'

He replied: 'I have not embraced the religious life for that purpose—to going about for alms; if you give me (food), I will eat; if you do not, I will return to the world'

(The Bhikkhus said): 'What, friend! have you indeed embraced the religious life for your belly's sake?'

'Yes, friends.'

3. The moderate Bhikkhus were annoyed, murmured, and became angry: 'How can a Bhikkhu embrace the religious life in so well-taught a doctrine and discipline for his belly's sake?'

[1] On this curious expression, compare *K*ullavagga IV, 4, 8. It is frequently repeated below.

These Bhikkhus told this thing to the Blessed One.

(The Buddha said): 'Is it true, O Bhikkhu, that you have embraced the religious life for your belly's sake?'

(He replied): 'It is true, Lord.'

Then the blessed Buddha rebuked that Bhikkhu: 'How can you, foolish person that you are, embrace the religious life in so well-taught a doctrine and discipline for your belly's sake? This will not do, O foolish one, for converting the unconverted and for augmenting the number of the converted.'

Having rebuked him and delivered a religious discourse, he thus addressed the Bhikkhus:

4. 'I prescribe, O Bhikkhus, that he who confers the upasampadâ ordination (on a Bhikkhu), tell him the four Resources:

'The religious life has morsels of food given in alms for its resource. Thus you must endeavour to live all your life. Meals given to the Sa*m*gha, to certain persons, invitations, food distributed by ticket, meals given each fortnight, each uposatha day (i. e. the last day of each fortnight), or the first day of each fortnight, are extra allowances.

'The religious life has the robe made of rags taken from a dust heap for its resource. Thus you must endeavour to live all your life. Linen, cotton, silk, woollen garments, coarse cloth, hempen cloth are extra allowances.

'The religious life has dwelling at the foot of a tree for its resource. Thus you must endeavour to live all your life. Vihâras, a*ddh*ayogas, storied dwellings, attics, caves[1] are extra allowances.

[1] These are the five kinds of dwellings (pa*ñk*a lenâni) which are declared to be allowable, *K*ullavagga VI, 1, 2. The single expres-

'The religious life has decomposing urine as medicine[1] for its resource. Thus you must endeavour to live all your life. Ghee, butter, oil, honey, and molasses are extra allowances.'

Here ends the fifth Bhâ*n*avâra, which contains the duties towards upa*ggh*âyas.

31.

1. At that time a certain youth came to the Bhikkhus and asked them to be ordained. The Bhikkhus told him the (four) Resources before his ordination. Then he said: 'If you had told me the Resources, venerable Sirs, after my ordination, I should have persisted (in the religious life); but now, venerable Sirs, I will not be ordained; the Resources are repulsive and loathsome to me.'

The Bhikkhus told this thing to the Blessed One.

'You ought not, O Bhikkhus, to tell the Resources (to the candidates) before their ordination. He who does, is guilty of a dukka*t*a offence. I prescribe, O Bhikkhus, that you tell the Resources (to the newly-ordained Bhikkhus) immediately after their upasampadâ.'

---

sions are explained by Buddhaghosa in his note on *K*ullavagga I. I. as follows: 'a*ddh*ayogo 'ti suva*nn*avaṅgageha*m*, pâsâdo 'ti dîgha-pâsâdo, hammiyan ti upariâkâsatale pati*tth*itakû*t*âgâro pâsâdo yeva, guhâ 'ti i*tth*akaguhâ silâguhâ dâruguhâ pa*m*suguhâ,' i. e. 'A*ddh*ayoga is a gold-coloured Bengal house. Pâsâda is a long storied mansion (or, the whole of an upper storey). Hammiya is a Pâsâda, which has an upper chamber placed on the topmost storey. Guhâ is a hut made of bricks, or in a rock, or of wood.'

[1] Compare Mahâvagga VI, 14, 6.

2. At that time some Bhikkhus performed the upasampadâ service with a chapter of two or three Bhikkhus.

They told this thing to the Blessed One.

'Let no one, O Bhikkhus, receive the upasampadâ ordination before a chapter of less than ten Bhikkhus. He who performs the upasampadâ service (with a smaller number of Bhikkhus), is guilty of a dukka*t*a offence. I prescribe you, O Bhikkhus, the holding of upasampadâ services with a chapter of ten Bhikkhus or more than ten.'

3. At that time some Bhikkhus conferred the upasampadâ ordination on their saddhivihârikas one or two years after their own upasampadâ. [1] Thus also the venerable Upasena Vaṅgantaputta conferred the upasampadâ ordination on a saddhivihârika of his one year after his own upasampadâ. When he had concluded the vassa residence, after two years from his own upasampadâ had elapsed, he went with his saddhivihârika, who had completed the first year after his upasampadâ, to the place where the Blessed One was; having approached him and respectfully saluted the Blessed One, he sat down near him.

4. Now it is the custom of the blessed Buddhas to exchange greeting with incoming Bhikkhus. And the Blessed One said to the venerable Upasena Vaṅgantaputta: 'Do things go well with you, Bhikkhu? Do you get enough to support your life? Have you made your journey with not too great fatigue?'

'Things go pretty well with us, Lord; we get

[1] This story recurs in the *G*âtaka Commentary II, 449.

enough, Lord, to support our life, and we have made our journey, Lord, with not too great fatigue.'

The Tathâgatas sometimes ask about what they know; sometimes they do not ask about what they know. They understand the right time when to ask, and they understand the right time when not to ask. The Tathâgatas put questions full of sense, not void of sense; to what is void of sense the bridge is pulled down for the Tathâgatas. For two purposes the blessed Buddhas put questions to the Bhikkhus, when they intend to preach the doctrine or when they intend to institute a rule of conduct to their disciples.

5. And the Blessed One said to the venerable Upananda Vaṅgantaputta: 'How many years have you completed, O Bhikkhu, since your upasampadâ?'

'Two years, Lord.'

'And how many years has this Bhikkhu completed?'

'One year, Lord.'

'In what relation does this Bhikkhu stand to you?'

'He is my saddhivihârika, Lord.'

Then the blessed Buddha rebuked him: 'This is improper, O foolish one, unbecoming, unsuitable, unworthy of a Sama*n*a, unallowable, and to be avoided. How can you, O foolish one, who ought to receive exhortation and instruction from others, think yourself fit for administering exhortation and instruction to another Bhikkhu? Too quickly, O foolish one, have you abandoned yourself to the ambition of collecting followers. This will not do (&c., as in chap. 30. 3). Let no one, O Bhikkhus, confer the upasampadâ ordination who has not completed ten years. He who does, is guilty of a dukka*t*a offence. I prescribe, O Bhikkhus, that only he who has completed ten years, or more than ten years, may confer the upasampadâ ordination.'

6. At that time ignorant, unlearned Bhikkhus (who said), 'We have completed ten years (since our upasampadâ), we have completed ten years,' conferred the upasampadâ ordination; (thus) ignorant upa*ggh*âyas were found and clever saddhivihârikas; unlearned upa*ggh*âyas were found and learned saddhivihârikas; upa*ggh*âyas were found who had small knowledge, and saddhivihârikas who had great knowledge; foolish upa*ggh*âyas were found and wise saddhivihârikas. And a certain Bhikkhu who had formerly belonged to a Titthiya school, when his upa*ggh*âya remonstrated with him (on certain offences) according to the Dhamma, brought his upa*ggh*âya (by reasoning) to silence and went back to that same Titthiya school[1].

7. The moderate Bhikkhus were annoyed, murmured, and became angry: 'How can those ignorant, unlearned Bhikkhus confer the upasampadâ ordination (saying), "We have completed ten years, we have completed ten years?" (Thus) ignorant upa*ggh*âyas are found and clever saddhivihârikas (&c., down to:), foolish upa*ggh*âyas are found and wise saddhivihârikas.'

These Bhikkhus told, &c.

'Is it true, O Bhikkhus, &c.?'

'It is true, Lord.'

8. Then the blessed Buddha rebuked those Bhikkhus: 'How can these foolish persons, O Bhikkhus,

[1] See the conclusion of this in chapter 38.

confer the upasampadâ ordination (saying), "We have, &c?" (Thus) ignorant upa*ggh*âyas are found, &c. This will not do, O Bhikkhus, for converting the unconverted and for augmenting the number of the converted.'

Having rebuked those Bhikkhus and delivered a religious discourse, he thus addressed the Bhikkhus: 'Let no ignorant, unlearned Bhikkhu, O Bhikkhus, confer the upasampadâ ordination. If he does, he is guilty of a dukka*t*a offence. I prescribe, O Bhikkhus, that only a learned, competent Bhikkhu who has completed ten years, or more than ten years, may confer the upasampadâ ordination.'

32.

1. At that time some Bhikkhus whose upa*ggh*âyas were gone away, or had returned to the world, or had died, or were gone over to a (schismatic) faction[1], as they had no â*k*ariyas and received no exhortation and instruction, went on their rounds for alms wearing improper under and upper garments (&c., as in chap. 25. 1–6, down to:), he thus addressed the Bhikkhus: 'I prescribe, O Bhikkhus, (that young Bhikkhus choose) an â*k*ariya[2].

---

[1] Buddhaghosa can scarcely be right in explaining pakkhasa*m*kanta by titthiyapakkhasa*m*kanta.

[2] Â*k*ariya as well as upa*ggh*âya means 'teacher,' or 'preceptor.' It is very difficult or rather impossible to draw a sharp line of distinction between â*k*ariya and upa*ggh*âya. The duties of an â*k*ariya towards his antevâsika, and of an antevâsika towards his â*k*ariya, as indicated in chaps. 32, 33 (=*K*ullavagga VIII, 13, 14), are exactly the same as those of an upa*ggh*âya

'The â*k*ariya, O Bhikkhus, ought to consider the antevâsika (i.e. disciple) as a son; the antevâsika ought to consider the â*k*ariya as a father. Thus these two, united by mutual reverence, confidence, and communion of life, will progress, advance, and reach a high stage in this doctrine and discipline.

'I prescribe, O Bhikkhus, that you live (the first) ten years in dependence (on an â*k*ariya); he who has completed his tenth year may give a nissaya[1] himself.

towards his saddhivihârika and vice versa (chaps. 25, 26 = *K*ullavagga VIII, 11, 12). The position of an upa*ggh*âya, however, was considered as the more important of the two; at the upasampadâ service the upa*ggh*âya had a more prominent part than the â*k*ariya, as we may infer from chaps. 28, 29, and from the explanations on the 65th pâ*k*ittiya rule which are given in the Sutta Vibhaṅga. There it is said that, if the upasampadâ ordination had been conferred, against the rule, on a person that has not yet attained his twentieth year, the upa*ggh*âya has made himself guilty of a pâ*k*ittiya offence, the â*k*ariya and the other present Bhikkhus only of a dukka*t*a offence. We may add that the succession of Vinaya teachers from Upâli down to Mahinda, which is given in the Dîpava*m*sa (Bhâ*n*avâras IV and V), is a succession of upa*ggh*âyas and saddhivihârikas (see IV, 36, 42, 43, &c.), not of â*k*ariyas and antevâsikas; the duty of instructing the young Bhikkhus in the holy doctrines and ordinances seems, therefore, to belong to the upa*ggh*âya rather than to the â*k*ariya; compare also Dîpava*m*sa VII, 26. So among the Brâhma*n*as, on the contrary, the â*k*ârya is estimated higher than the upâdhyâya; see Manu II, 145; Yâ*gñ*avalkya I, 35. Compare also chap. 36. 1 (end of the paragraph), and Buddhaghosa's explanation of that passage.

[1] Nissaya (i.e. dependence) is the relation between â*k*ariya and antevâsika. The antevâsika lives 'nissâya' with regard to the â*k*ariya, i.e. dependent on him; the â*k*ariya gives his nissaya to the antevâsika, i.e. he receives him into his protection and care. At chap. 36. 1, 'nissaya' is said also of the relation between upa*ggh*âya and saddhivihârika.

2. 'And let (the antevâsika), O Bhikkhus, choose his â*k*ariya in this way: Let him adjust his upper robe so as to cover one shoulder, salute the feet (of the â*k*ariya), sit down squatting, raise his joined hands, and say: "Venerable Sir, be my â*k*ariya, I will live in dependence on you, Sir."' (This formula is repeated thrice.)

'(If the other answers): "Well" (&c., as in chap. 25. 7).

3. 'The antevâsika, O Bhikkhus, ought to observe a strict conduct towards his â*k*ariya' (&c., as in chap. 25. 8–24).

End of the duties towards an â*k*ariya.

33.

'The â*k*ariya, O Bhikkhus, ought to observe a strict conduct towards his antevâsika' (&c., as in chap. 26).

End of the duties towards an antevâsika.

End of the sixth Bhâ*n*avâra.

34.

At that time the antevâsikas did not observe a proper conduct towards their â*k*ariyas (&c., as in chap. 27. 1–8).

35.

1, 2. At that time ignorant, unlearned Bhikkhus (who said), 'We have completed ten years (since our upasampadâ), we have completed ten years,' gave a nissaya (i. e. they received young Bhikkhus as their antevâsikas); (thus) ignorant â*k*ariyas were found and clever antevâsikas; unlearned â*k*ariyas were found and learned antevâsikas; â*k*ariyas were found who had small knowledge, and antevâsikas who had great knowledge; foolish â*k*ariyas were found and wise antevâsikas. The moderate Bhikkhus were annoyed (&c., as in chap. 31. 7, 8).

'Let no ignorant, unlearned Bhikkhu, O Bhikkhus, give a nissaya. If he does, he is guilty of a dukka*t*a offence. I prescribe, O Bhikkhus, that only a learned, competent Bhikkhu who has completed ten years, or more than ten years, may give a nissaya.'

36.

1. At that time the Bhikkhus whose â*k*ariyas and upa*ggh*âyas were gone away, or had returned to the world, or had died, or were gone over to a (schismatic) faction, were not acquainted with (the rules about) the cessation of their nissayas[1].

They told this thing to the Blessed One.

'There are five cases of cessation of a nissaya, O Bhikkhus, between (saddhivihârika and) upa*g*-

[1] That is, 'did not know how to decide whether their nissaya was destroyed, or not.'

ghâya: When the upagghâya is gone away, or he has returned to the world, or has died, or is gone over to a (schismatic) faction; the fifth case is that of order (given by the upagghâya to the saddhivihârika[1]). These, O Bhikkhus, are the five cases of the cessation of a nissaya between (saddhivihârika and) upagghâya.

'There are six cases of cessation of a nissaya, O Bhikkhus, between (antevâsika and) âkariya: When the âkariya is gone away, &c.; the fifth case is that of order (given by the âkariya to the antevâsika); or (sixthly) when the âkariya and the upagghâya have come together at the same place[2]. These, O Bhikkhus, are the six cases of cessation of a nissaya between (antevâsika and) âkariya.

2. 'In five cases, O Bhikkhus, a Bhikkhu should not confer the upasampadâ ordination, nor give a nissaya, nor ordain a novice[3]: When he does not possess full perfection in what belongs to moral practices; or does not possess full perfection in what belongs to self-concentration; or does not possess full perfection in what belongs to wisdom; or does

[1] This refers, according to Buddhaghosa, to the panâmanâ (turning away of the saddhivihârika); see chap. 27. 2.

[2] Buddhaghosa: 'Coming together may be understood either by seeing or by hearing. If a saddhivihârika who lives in dependence (nissâya) on his âkariya sees his upagghâya paying homage to a sacred shrine in the same Vihâra, or going on his rounds in the same village, cessation of the nissaya (towards the âkariya) is the consequence. If he hears the voice of his upagghâya, who preaches the Dhamma or gladdens (lay-people by religious discourse), in the Vihâra or in the interior of a house, and if he recognises that it is his upagghâya's voice, cessation of the nissaya (towards the âkariya) is the consequence.'

[3] About the ordination of novices, see chap. 54. 3.

not possess full perfection in what belongs to emancipation; or does not possess full perfection in what belongs to knowledge and insight into emancipation. In these five cases, O Bhikkhus, a Bhikkhu should not confer the upasampadâ ordination, nor give a nissaya, nor ordain a novice.

3. 'In five cases, O Bhikkhus, a Bhikkhu may confer the upasampadâ ordination, give a nissaya, and ordain a novice: When he possesses full perfection in what belongs to moral practices, &c. In these five cases, O Bhikkhus, a Bhikkhu may, &c.

4. 'And also in other five cases, O Bhikkhus, a Bhikkhu should not confer, &c.: When he does not possess for himself full perfection in what belongs to moral practices, and is not able to help others to full perfection in what belongs to moral practices; or does not possess for himself full perfection in what belongs to self-concentration, and is not able to help others to full perfection in what belongs to self-concentration, &c.

5. 'In five cases, O Bhikkhus, a Bhikkhu may confer, &c.: When he possesses for himself full perfection in what belongs to moral practices, and is able to help others to full perfection, &c.

6. 'And also in other five cases, O Bhikkhus, a Bhikkhu should not confer, &c.: When he is unbelieving, shameless, fearless of sinning, indolent, forgetful. In these five cases, &c.

7. 'In five cases, O Bhikkhus, a Bhikkhu may confer, &c.: When he is believing, modest, fearful of sinning, strenuous, of ready memory. In these five cases, &c.

8. 'And also in other five cases, O Bhikkhus, a Bhikkhu should not confer, &c.: When as regards

moral practices he is guilty of moral transgressions; or when as regards the rules of conduct[1] he is guilty of transgressions in his conduct; or when as regards belief he is guilty of heresy; or when he is unlearned; or when he is foolish. In these five cases, &c.

9. 'In five cases, O Bhikkhus, a Bhikkhu may confer, &c.: When as regards moral practices he is not guilty of moral transgressions, &c.; when he is learned; and when he is wise. In these five cases, &c.

10. 'And also in other five cases, O Bhikkhus, a Bhikkhu should not confer, &c.: When he is not able to nurse or to get nursed an antevâsika or a saddhivihârika when he is sick, to appease him or to cause him to be appeased when discontent with religious life has sprung up within him, to dispel or to cause to be dispelled according to the Dhamma doubts of conscience which have arisen in his mind; when he does not know what is an offence; or does not know how to atone for an offence. In these five cases, &c.

11. 'In five cases, O Bhikkhus, a Bhikkhu may confer, &c.: When he is able (&c., down to:); when he knows what is an offence; and knows how to atone for an offence. In these five cases, &c.

12. 'And also in other five cases, O Bhikkhus, a Bhikkhu should not confer, &c.: When he is not able to train an antevâsika or a saddhivihârika in the precepts of proper conduct[2], to educate him

---

[1] According to Buddhaghosa, moral transgression (adhisîla) is said with regard to offences against the pârâgika and samghâdisesa rules, while transgressions in conduct (agghâkâra) consist in offences against the minor rules of the Pâtimokkha. Buddhaghosa's explanation is confirmed by the Mahâvagga IV, 16, 12.

[2] According to Buddhaghosa, this refers to instruction in the

in the elements of morality[1], to instruct him in what pertains to the Dhamma, to instruct him in what pertains to the Vinaya, to discuss or to make another discuss according to the Dhamma a false doctrine that might arise. In these five cases, &c.

13. 'In five cases, O Bhikkhus, a Bhikkhu may confer, &c.: When he is able, &c.

14. 'And also in other five cases, O Bhikkhus, a Bhikkhu should not confer, &c.: When he does not know what is an offence; or does not know what is no offence; or does not know what is a light offence; or does not know what is a grave offence; when the two Pâtimokkhas are not perfectly known to him in their entirety, with all their divisions and their whole course, and with the entire discussion according to the single rules and to the single parts of each rule. In these five cases, &c.

15. 'In five cases, O Bhikkhus, a Bhikkhu may confer, &c.: When he knows, &c.

16. 'And also in other five cases, O Bhikkhus, a Bhikkhu should not confer, &c.: When he does not know what is an offence; or does not know what is no offence; or does not know what is a light offence; or does not know what is a grave offence;

---

khandhakavatta (i.e. in the rules contained in the Khandhaka texts, Mahâvagga and *K*ullavagga?). See also Spence Hardy, Manual, p. 492.

[1] This means instructing him in the sekhapa*ññ*atti (Buddhaghosa). We cannot say what is the accurate meaning of the last term, which apparently, as its verbal meaning seems to imply, refers to ordinances for those Bhikkhus who have entered the path of sanctification, but have not yet attained Arahatship. Spence Hardy (Manual, p. 493) gives the term sekha-sîla, which he explains as the observance of precepts in order to become a sekha. See also Hardy's note on âdibrahma*k*ariya-sîla, l. l. p. 492.

or when he has not completed the tenth year (after his upasampadâ). In these five cases, &c.

17. 'In five cases, O Bhikkhus, a Bhikkhu may confer, &c.: When he knows (&c., down to:); when he has completed ten years or more than ten years (after his upasampadâ). In these five cases, &c.'

End of the sixteen times five cases concerning the admissibility of upasampadâ.

37.

'In six cases, O Bhikkhus, a Bhikkhu should not confer, &c.[1]'

End of the sixteen times[2] six cases concerning the admissibility of upasampadâ.

38.

1. At that time that Bhikkhu who, having formerly belonged to a Titthiya school, had (by reasoning) put to silence his upa*ggh*âya, when he remonstrated with him according to the Dhamma, and had returned to that same Titthiya school[3], came back again and asked the Bhikkhus for the upasampadâ ordination. The Bhikkhus told, &c.

'That Bhikkhu, O Bhikkhus, who having formerly

---

[1] Chap. 37 is exactly identical with chap. 36. 2–15, but for the sixth case, which, throughout chap. 37, is added each time at the end of the five cases given in chap. 36, 'When he has not completed the tenth year (after his upasampadâ);' and respectively, 'When he has completed ten years or more than ten years (after his upasampadâ).'

[2] It should be, 'Fourteen times.'

[3] See chap. 31, § 6.

belonged to a Titthiya school, has put to silence his upa*ggh*âya when he remonstrated with him according to the Dhamma, and has returned to that same Titthiya school, must not receive the upasampadâ ordination, if he comes back. On other persons, O Bhikkhus, who have formerly belonged to Titthiya schools and desire to receive the pabba*gg*â and upasampadâ ordinations in this doctrine and discipline, you ought to impose a parivâsa (a probation-time) of four months.

2. 'And you ought, O Bhikkhus, to impose it in this way: Let him (who desires to receive the ordination) first cut off his hair and beard; let him put on yellow robes, adjust his upper robe so as to cover one shoulder, salute the feet of the Bhikkhus (with his head), and sit down squatting; then let him raise his joined hands, and tell him to say: "I take my refuge in the Buddha, I take my refuge in the Dhamma, I take my refuge in the Sa*m*gha. And for the second time, &c. And for the third time take I my refuge in the Buddha, and for the third time take I my refuge in the Dhamma, and for the third time take I my refuge in the Sa*m*gha."

3. 'Let that person, O Bhikkhus, who has formerly belonged to a Titthiya school, approach the Sa*m*gha, adjust his upper robe so as to cover one shoulder, salute the feet of the Bhikkhus (with his head), sit down squatting, raise his joined hands, and say: "I, N. N., reverend Sirs, who have formerly belonged to a Titthiya school, desire to receive the upasampadâ ordination in this doctrine and discipline, and ask the Sa*m*gha, reverend Sirs, for a parivâsa of four months." Let him ask thus a second time. Let him ask thus a third time.

'Then let a learned, competent Bhikkhu proclaim the following *ñ*atti before the Sa*m*gha: "Let the Sa*m*gha, reverend Sirs, hear me. This person N. N., who has formerly belonged to a Titthiya school, desires to receive the upasampadâ ordination in this doctrine and discipline. He asks the Sa*m*gha for a parivâsa of four months. If the Sa*m*gha is ready, let the Sa*m*gha impose on N. N., who has formerly belonged to a Titthiya school, a parivâsa of four months. This is the *ñ*atti.

4. '"Let the Sa*m*gha, reverend Sirs, hear me. This person N. N., who has, &c. He asks the Sa*m*gha for a parivâsa of four months. The Sa*m*gha imposes on N. N., who has formerly belonged to a Titthiya school, a parivâsa of four months. Let any one of the venerable brethren who is in favour of imposing a parivâsa of four months on N. N., who has formerly belonged to a Titthiya school, be silent, and any one who is not in favour of it, speak. A parivâsa of four months has been imposed by the Sa*m*gha on N. N., who has formerly belonged to a Titthiya school. The Sa*m*gha is in favour of it, therefore it is silent. Thus I understand."

5. 'And this, O Bhikkhus, is the way in which a person that has formerly belonged to a Titthiya school, succeeds or fails in satisfying (the Bhikkhus and obtaining upasampadâ when the probation-time is over).

'What is the way, O Bhikkhus, in which a person that has formerly belonged to a Titthiya school, fails in satisfying (the Bhikkhus)?

'In case, O Bhikkhus, the person that has formerly belonged to a Titthiya school, enters the village too early, and comes back (to the Vihâra) too late, thus, O Bhikkhus, a person that has formerly belonged to a Titthiya school, fails in satisfying (the Bhikkhus).

'And further, O Bhikkhus, in case the person that has formerly belonged to a Titthiya school, frequents the society of harlots, or of widows, or of adult girls, or of eunuchs, or of Bhikkhunîs, thus also, O Bhikkhus, a person that has formerly belonged to a Titthiya school, fails in satisfying (the Bhikkhus).

6. 'And further, O Bhikkhus, in case the person that has formerly belonged to a Titthiya school, does not show himself skilled in the various things his fellow Bhikkhus have to do, not diligent, not able to consider how those things are to be done, not able to do things himself, not able to give directions to others, thus also, O Bhikkhus, &c.

'And further, O Bhikkhus, in case the person that has formerly belonged to a Titthiya school, does not show keen zeal, when the doctrine is preached to him or when questions are put, in what belongs to morality, to contemplation, and to wisdom, thus also, O Bhikkhus, &c.

7. 'And further, O Bhikkhus, in case the person that has formerly belonged to a Titthiya school, becomes angry, displeased, and dissatisfied, when people speak against the teacher, the belief, the opinions, the persuasion, the creed of the school he formerly belonged to; and is pleased, glad, and satisfied, when people speak against the Buddha, the Dhamma, and the Sa*m*gha; or he is pleased, glad, and satisfied, when people speak in praise of the teacher, &c.; and becomes angry, displeased, dissatisfied, when people speak in praise of the Buddha, the

Dhamma, and the Sa*m*gha; this, O Bhikkhus, is a decisive moment for the failure of a person that has formerly belonged to a Titthiya school (in obtaining admission to the Sa*m*gha).

'Thus, O Bhikkhus, a person that has formerly belonged to a Titthiya school, fails in satisfying (the Bhikkhus). When a person comes, O Bhikkhus, that has formerly belonged to a Titthiya school, and has thus failed in satisfying (the Bhikkhus), the upasampadâ ordination should not be conferred on him.

8–10. 'And what is the way, O Bhikkhus, in which a person that has formerly belonged to a Titthiya school, succeeds in satisfying (the Bhikkhus)?

'In case, O Bhikkhus, the person that has formerly belonged to a Titthiya school, does not enter the village too early (&c., point by point the contrary of the preceding).

'When a person comes, O Bhikkhus, that has formerly belonged to a Titthiya school, and has thus succeeded in satisfying (the Bhikkhus), the upasampadâ ordination ought to be conferred on him.

11. 'If a person, O Bhikkhus, that has formerly belonged to a Titthiya school, comes (to the Bhikkhus) naked, it is incumbent on his upa*ggh*âya to get a robe for him. If he comes with unshaven hair, the Sa*m*gha's permission ought to be asked for having his hair shaved[1].

'If fire-worshippers and *G*a*t*ilas come to you, O Bhikkhus, they are to receive the upasampadâ ordination (directly), and no parivâsa is to be imposed on them. And for what reason? These, O Bhikkhus, hold the doctrine that actions receive their

[1] Compare chap. 48.

reward, and that our deeds have their result (according to their moral merit).

'If a Sakya by birth, O Bhikkhus, who has belonged to a Titthiya school, comes to you, he is to receive the upasampadâ ordination (directly), and no parivâsa is to be imposed on him. This exceptional privilege, O Bhikkhus, I grant to my kinsmen.'

Here ends the exposition on the ordination of persons that have formerly belonged to Titthiya schools.

End of the seventh Bhâ*n*avâra.

39.

1. At that time these five diseases prevailed among the people of Magadha:—leprosy, boils, dry leprosy, consumption, and fits. The people who were affected with these five diseases went to *G*îvaka Komârabha*kk*a[1] and said: 'Pray, doctor, cure us.'

'I have too many duties, Sirs, and am too occupied. I have to treat the Magadha king Seniya Bimbisâra, and the royal seraglio, and the fraternity of Bhikkhus with the Buddha at their head. I cannot cure you.'

'All that we possess shall be yours, doctor, and we will be your slaves; pray, doctor, cure us!'

'I have too many duties, Sirs, &c.; I cannot cure you.'

2. Now those people thought: 'Indeed the precepts which these Sakyaputtiya Sama*n*as keep and

[1] *G*îvaka was physician to king Bimbisâra, and one of the chief partisans of Buddha at the court of Râ*g*agaha. See VIII, 1, the introduction of the Sâma*ññ*aphala Sutta, &c.

the life they live are commodious; they have good meals and lie down on beds protected from the wind. What if we were to embrace the religious life among the Sakyaputtiya Sama*n*as: then the Bhikkhus will nurse us, and *G*îvaka Komârabha*kk*a will cure us.'

Thus these persons went to the Bhikkhus and asked them for the pabba*gg*â ordination; the Bhikkhus conferred on them the pabba*gg*â and upasampadâ ordinations; and the Bhikkhus nursed them, and *G*îvaka Komârabha*kk*a cured them.

3. At that time the Bhikkhus, who had to nurse many sick Bhikkhus, began to solicit (lay people) with many demands and many requests: 'Give us food for the sick; give us food for the tenders of the sick; give us medicine for the sick.' And also *G*îvaka Komârabha*kk*a, who had to treat many sick Bhikkhus, neglected some of his duties to the king.

4. Now one day a man who was affected with the five diseases went to *G*îvaka Komârabha*kk*a and said: 'Pray, doctor, cure me.'

'I have too many duties, Sir, and am too occupied; I have to treat the Magadha king Seniya Bimbisâra, and the royal seraglio, and the fraternity of Bhikkhus with the Buddha at their head; I cannot cure you.'

'All that I possess shall be yours, doctor, and I will be your slave; pray doctor, cure me.'

'I have too many duties, Sir, &c.; I cannot cure you.'

5. Now that man thought: 'Indeed the precepts which these Sakyaputtiya Sama*n*as keep (&c., down to:): then the Bhikkhus will nurse me, and *G*îvaka Komârabha*kk*a will cure me. When I have become free from sickness, then I will return to the world.'

Thus that man went to the Bhikkhus and asked them for the pabba*gg*â ordination; the Bhikkhus conferred on him the pabba*gg*â and upasampadâ ordinations; and the Bhikkhus nursed him, and *G*îvaka Komârabha*kk*a cured him. When he had become free from sickness, he returned to the world. Now *G*îvaka Komârabha*kk*a saw this person that had returned to the world; and when he saw him he asked that person: 'Had you not embraced the religious life, Sir, among the Bhikkhus?'

'Yes, doctor.'

'And why have you adopted such a course, Sir?'

Then that man told *G*îvaka Komârabha*kk*a the whole matter.

6. Then *G*îvaka Komârabha*kk*a was annoyed, murmured, and became angry: 'How can the venerable brethren confer the pabba*gg*â ordination on a person affected with the five diseases?'

And *G*îvaka Komârabha*kk*a went to the place where the Blessed One was; having approached him and having respectfully saluted the Blessed One, he sat down near him. Sitting near him, *G*îvaka Komârabha*kk*a said to the Blessed One: 'Pray, Lord, let their reverences not confer the pabba*gg*â ordination on persons affected with the five diseases.'

7. Then the Blessed One taught, incited, animated, and gladdened *G*îvaka Komârabha*kk*a by religious discourse; and *G*îvaka Komârabha*kk*a, having been taught . . . . and gladdened by the Blessed One by religious discourse, rose from his seat, respectfully saluted the Blessed One, and passing round him with his right side towards him, went away.

In consequence of that and on this occasion the Blessed One, after having delivered a religious discourse, thus addressed the Bhikkhus: 'Let no one,

O Bhikkhus, who is affected with the five diseases, receive the pabba*gg*â ordination. He who confers the pabba*gg*â ordination (on such a person), is guilty of a dukka*t*a offence.'

40.

1. At that time the border provinces (of the kingdom) of the Magadha king Seniya Bimbisâra were agitated. Then the Magadha king Seniya Bimbisâra gave order to the officers who were at the head of the army: 'Well now, go and search through the border provinces[1].' The officers who were at the head of the army accepted the order of the Magadha king Seniya Bimbisâra (by saying), 'Yes, Your Majesty.'

2. Now many distinguished warriors thought: 'We who go (to war) and find our delight in fighting, do evil and produce great demerit. Now what shall we do that we may desist from evil-doing and may do good?'

Then these warriors thought: 'These Sakyaputtiya Sama*n*as lead indeed a virtuous, tranquil, holy life; they speak the truth; they keep the precepts of morality, and are endowed with all virtues. If we could obtain pabba*gg*â with the Sakyaputtiya Sama*n*as, we should desist from evil-doing and do good.'

Thus these warriors went to the Bhikkhus and

[1] On u*kk*inatha, compare the use of u*kkh*e*kkh*âmi at Mahâparinibbâna Sutta I, 1 (p. 1), which Buddhaghosa rightly explains by u*kkh*indissâmi. But we think it better to adhere here to the reading u*kk*inatha, in accordance with the MSS.

asked them for the pabba*gg*â ordination; the Bhikkhus conferred on them the pabba*gg*â and upasampadâ ordinations.

3. The officers at the head of the army asked the royal soldiers: 'Why, how is it that the warriors N. N. and N. N. are nowhere to be seen?'

'The warriors N. N. and N. N., Lords, have embraced religious life among the Bhikkhus.'

Then the officers at the head of the army were annoyed, murmured, and became angry: 'How can the Sakyaputtiya Sama*n*as ordain persons in the royal service?'

The officers who were at the head of the army told the thing to the Magadha king Seniya Bimbisâra. And the Magadha king Seniya Bimbisâra asked the officers of justice: 'Tell me, my good Sirs, what punishment does he deserve who ordains a person in the royal service?'

'The upa*ggh*âya, Your Majesty, should be beheaded; to him who recites (the kammavâ*k*â), the tongue should be torn out; to those who form the chapter, half of their ribs should be broken.'

4. Then the Magadha king Seniya Bimbisâra went to the place where the Blessed One was; having approached him and having respectfully saluted the Blessed One, he sat down near him. Sitting near him the Magadha king Seniya Bimbisâra said to the Blessed One: 'Lord, there are unbelieving kings who are disinclined (to the faith); these might harass the Bhikkhus even on trifling occasions. Pray, Lord, let their reverences not confer the pabba*gg*â ordination on persons in royal service.'

Then the Blessed One taught (&c., see chap. 39. 7,

down to:), thus addressed the Bhikkhus: 'Let no one, O Bhikkhus, who is in the royal service, receive the pabba*gg*â ordination. He who confers the pabba*gg*â ordination (on such a person), is guilty of a dukka*t*a offence.'

41.

At that time the robber Aṅgulimâla[1] had embraced religious life among the Bhikkhus. When the people saw that, they became alarmed and terrified; they fled away, went elsewhere, turned away their heads, and shut their doors. The people were annoyed, murmured, and became angry: 'How can the Sakyaputtiya Sama*n*as ordain a robber who openly wears the emblems (of his deeds)?'

Some Bhikkhus heard those people that were annoyed, murmured, and had become angry; these Bhikkhus told the thing to the Blessed One.

The Blessed One thus addressed the Bhikkhus: 'Let no robber, O Bhikkhus, who wears the emblems (of his deeds), receive the pabba*gg*â ordination. He who confers the pabba*gg*â ordination (on such a person), is guilty of a dukka*t*a offence.'

---

[1] The robber Aṅgulimâla (i. e. he who wears a necklace of fingers), whose original name was Ahi*m*saka, had received this surname from his habit of cutting off the fingers of his victims and wearing them as a necklace. See Spence Hardy, Manual, p. 249 seq.

42.

1. At that time the Magadha king Seniya Bimbisâra had issued the following decree: 'No one is to do any harm to those who are ordained among the Sakyaputtiya Sama*n*as; well taught is their doctrine; let them lead a holy life for the sake of the complete extinction of suffering.

Now at that time a certain person who had committed robbery was imprisoned in the jail. He broke out of the jail, ran away, and received the pabba*gg*â ordination with the Bhikkhus.

2. The people who saw him, said: 'Here is the robber who has broken out of jail; come, let us bring him (before the authorities).'

But some people replied: 'Do not say so, Sirs. A decree has been issued by the Magadha king Seniya Bimbisâra: 'No one is to do any harm to those who are ordained, &c.'

People were annoyed, murmured, and became angry, thinking: 'Indeed these Sakyaputtiya Sama*n*as are secure from anything; it is not allowed to do any harm to them. How can they ordain a robber who has broken out of jail?'

They told this thing to the Blessed One.

'Let no robber, O Bhikkhus, who has broken out of jail, receive the pabba*gg*â ordination. He who confers the pabba*gg*â ordination (on such a person), is guilty of a dukka*t*a offence.'

43.

At that time a certain person who had committed robbery had run away and had become ordained with the Bhikkhus. At the royal palace a proclamation was written: 'Wherever he is seen, he is to be killed.'

The people who saw him, said: 'Here is the proclaimed robber; come, let us kill him' (&c., as in chap. 42).

'Let no proclaimed robber, O Bhikkhus, receive the pabba*gg*â ordination. He who confers the pabba*gg*â ordination (on such a robber), is guilty of a dukka*t*a offence.'

44.

At that time a certain person who had been punished by scourging had been ordained with the Bhikkhus. People were annoyed, &c.: 'How can these Sakyaputtiya Sama*n*as ordain a person that has been punished by scourging?'

They told this thing to the Blessed One.

'Let no one, O Bhikkhus, who has been punished by scourging, receive the pabba*gg*â ordination. He who confers the pabba*gg*â ordination (on such a person), is guilty of a dukka*t*a offence.'

45.

At that time a certain person who had been punished by branding (&c., as in chap. 44, down to the end).

46.

At that time a certain person who was in debt, ran away and was ordained with the Bhikkhus. When his creditors saw him, they said: 'There is our debtor; come, let us lead him (to prison).' But some people replied: 'Do not say so, Sirs. A decree has been issued by the Magadha king Seniya Bimbisâra: 'No one is to do any harm to those who are ordained with the Sakyaputtiya Sama*n*as; well taught is their doctrine; let them lead a holy life for the sake of the complete extinction of suffering.'

People were annoyed, murmured, and became angry: 'Indeed these Sakyaputtiya Sama*n*as are secure from anything; it is not allowed to do anything to them. How can they ordain a debtor?'

They told this thing to the Blessed One.

'Let no debtor, O Bhikkhus, receive the pabba*gg*â ordination. He who confers the pabba*gg*â ordination (on a debtor), is guilty of a dukka*t*a offence.'

47.

At that time a slave ran away and was ordained with the Bhikkhus. When his masters saw him, they said: 'There is our slave; come, let us lead him away (back to our house),' (&c., as in chap. 46).

'Let no slave, O Bhikkhus, receive the pabba*gg*â ordination. He who confers the pabba*gg*â ordination (on a slave), is guilty of a dukka*t*a offence.'

48.

1. At that time a certain smith[1] who was bald-headed, having had a quarrel with his father and mother, had gone to the Ârâma and received pabbaggâ with the Bhikkhus. Now the father and mother of that bald-headed smith, searching after that bald-headed smith, came to the Ârâma and asked the Bhikkhus: 'Pray, reverend Sirs, have you seen such and such a boy?'

The Bhikkhus, who did not know him, said: 'We do not know him;' having not seen him, they said: 'We have not seen him.'

2. Now the father and mother of that bald-headed smith, searching after that bald-headed smith, found him ordained with the Bhikkhus; they were annoyed, &c.: 'These Sakyaputtiya Samanas are shameless, wicked, and liars. They knew him and said: "We do not know him;" they had seen him and said: "We have not seen him." This boy has been ordained with the Bhikkhus.'

Now some Bhikkhus heard the father and mother of that bald-headed smith, who were annoyed, &c. Those Bhikkhus told the thing to the Blessed One.

'I prescribe, O Bhikkhus, that the Samgha's permission is asked for having (the new coming Bhikkhus) shaved.'

---

[1] Buddhaghosa explains kammârabhandu by tulâtaramundako (read tulâdhâram.) suvannakâraputto. At Dhammapada, v. 239, kammâra is said of a silversmith. There was probably no distinction in these early times between gold, silver, copper, and iron smiths; the same man being an artificer in all kinds of metal.

49.

1. At that time there was in Râ*g*agaha a company of seventeen boys, friends of each other; young Upâli[1] was first among them. Now Upâli's father and mother thought: 'How will Upâli after our death live a life of ease and without pain?' Then Upâli's father and mother said to themselves: 'If Upâli could learn writing, he would after our death live a life of ease and without pain.' But then Upâli's father and mother thought again: 'If Upâli learns writing, his fingers will become sore. But if Upâli could learn arithmetic, he would after our death live a life of ease and without pain.'

2. But then Upâli's father and mother thought again: 'If Upâli learns arithmetic, his breast will become diseased[2]. But if Upâli could learn money-changing[3], he would after our death live a life of ease and comfort, and without pain.' But then Upâli's father and mother said to themselves: 'If Upâli learns money-changing, his eyes will suffer. Now here are the Sakyaputtiya Sama*n*as, who keep commodious precepts and live a commodious life; they have good meals and lie down on beds protected from the wind. If Upâli could be ordained with the

[1] This Upâli is different from the famous Upâli who belonged to the chief disciples of Buddha; the latter came not from Râ*g*agaha, but from the Sakya country.

[2] Buddhaghosa: 'He who learns arithmetic, must think much; therefore his breast will become diseased.'

[3] We prefer this translation of rûpa to translating it by 'painting,' on account of Buddhaghosa's note: 'He who learns the rûpa-sutta must turn over and over many kârshâpa*n*as and look at them.'

Sakyaputtiya Sama*n*as, he would after our death live a life of ease and without pain.'

3. Now young Upâli heard his father and mother talking thus. Then young Upâli went to the other boys; having approached them, he said to those boys: 'Come, Sirs, let us get ordained with the Sakyaputtiya Sama*n*as.' (They replied): 'If you will get ordained, Sir, we will be ordained also.' Then those boys went each to his father and mother and said to them: 'Give me your consent for leaving the world and going forth into the houseless state.' Then the parents of those boys, who thought, 'It is a good thing what all these boys are wishing so unanimously for,' gave their consent. They went to the Bhikkhus and asked them for the pabba*gg*â ordination. The Bhikkhus conferred the pabba*gg*â and upasampadâ ordinations on them.

4. In the night, at dawn, they rose and began to cry: 'Give us rice-milk, give us soft food, give us hard food!' The Bhikkhus said: 'Wait, friends, till day-time. If there is rice-milk, you shall drink; if there is food, soft or hard, you shall eat; if there is no rice-milk and no food, soft or hard, you must go out for alms, and then you will eat.'

But those Bhikkhus, when they were thus spoken to by the other Bhikkhus, threw their bedding about and made it wet, calling out: 'Give us rice-milk, give us soft food, give us hard food!'

5. Then the Blessed One, having arisen in the night, at dawn, heard the noise which those boys made; hearing it he said to the venerable Ânanda: 'Now, Ânanda, what noise of boys is that?'

Then the venerable Ânanda told the thing to the Blessed One.

'Is it true, O Bhikkhus, that the Bhikkhus knowingly confer the upasampadâ ordination on persons under twenty years of age?'

'It is true, Lord.'

Then the Blessed One rebuked those Bhikkhus: 'How can those foolish persons, O Bhikkhus, knowingly confer the upasampadâ ordination on persons under twenty years of age?

6. 'A person under twenty years, O Bhikkhus, cannot endure coldness and heat, hunger and thirst, vexation by gadflies and gnats, by storms and sunheat, and by reptiles; (he cannot endure) abusive, offensive language; he is not able to bear bodily pains which are severe, sharp, grievous, disagreeable, unpleasant, and destructive to life; whilst a person that has twenty years of age, O Bhikkhus, can endure coldness, &c. This will not do, O Bhikkhus, for converting the unconverted and for augmenting the number of the converted.'

Having rebuked those Bhikkhus and delivered a religious discourse, he thus addressed the Bhikkhus: 'Let no one, O Bhikkhus, knowingly confer the upasampadâ ordination on a person under twenty years of age. He who does, is to be treated according to the law[1].'

---

[1] The law alluded to is the 65th pâkittiya rule. Generally in the Khandhakas, which presuppose, as we have stated in our preface, the existence of the Pâtimokkha, direct repetition of the rules laid down there has been avoided. If, nevertheless, in the Khandhakas a transgression alluded to in the Pâtimokkha had to be mentioned again, then in most cases the Khandhakas, instead of directly indicating the penance incurred thereby, use of the guilty Bhikkhu the expression, 'yathâdhammo kâretabbo,' i.e. 'he is to be treated according to the law.' See H. O.'s Introduction to his edition of the Mahâvagga, p. xx note.

50.

At that time a certain family had died of pestilence[1]; only a father and his son were left; they received the pabbaggâ ordination with the Bhikkhus and went together on their rounds for alms. Now that boy, when food was given to his father, ran up to him and said: 'Give some to me too, father; give some to me too, father.'

People were annoyed, &c.: 'These Sakyaputtiya Samanas live an impure life; this boy is a Bhikkhunî's son.

Some Bhikkhus heard, &c.

They told this thing to the Blessed One, &c.

'Let no one, O Bhikkhus, confer the pabbaggâ ordination on a boy under fifteen years of age. He who does, is guilty of a dukkata offence.'

51.

At that time a believing, pious family, who devoted themselves to the (especial) service of the venerable Ânanda, had died of pestilence. Only two boys were left; these, when seeing Bhikkhus, ran up to them according to their old custom, but the Bhikkhus turned them away. When they were turned away by the Bhikkhus, they cried. Now the venerable Ânanda thought: 'The Blessed One has forbidden us to confer the pabbaggâ ordination

[1] Buddhaghosa explains ahivâtakaroga by mâribyâdhi, and says: 'When this plague befalls a house, men and beasts in that house die; but he who breaks through wall or roof, or is "rogâ mâdigato (?)," may be saved.'

on a boy under fifteen years of age, and these boys are under fifteen years of age. What can be done in order that these boys may not perish?' And the venerable Ânanda told this thing to the Blessed One.

'Are these boys able, Ânanda, to scare crows?'

'They are, Lord.'

In consequence of that and on this occasion the Blessed One, after having delivered a religious discourse, thus addressed the Bhikkhus: 'I allow you, O Bhikkhus, to confer the pabba*gg*â ordination on crow-keeper boys even under fifteen years of age.'

52.

At that time the venerable Upananda, of the Sakya tribe, had two novices, Ka*nd*aka and Mahaka; these committed sodomy with each other. The Bhikkhus were annoyed, &c.: 'How can novices abandon themselves to such bad conduct?'

They told this thing to the Blessed One, &c.

'Let no one, O Bhikkhus, ordain two novices. He who does, is guilty of a dukka*t*a offence[1].'

53.

1. At that time the Blessed One dwelt at Râ*g*agaha during the rainy season, and remained at the same place during winter and summer. The people were annoyed, &c.: 'The (four) regions are[2] .... and

[1] This seems very unpractical: and the rule is accordingly practically abrogated again by chapter 55.

[2] We must leave 'âhundarikâ' untranslated; Buddhaghosa says nothing about this obscure word.

covered by darkness to the Sakyaputtiya Sama*n*as; they cannot discern the (four) regions.' Some Bhikkhus heard, &c.

2. Then the Blessed One said to the venerable Ânanda: 'Go, Ânanda, take a key and tell the Bhikkhus in every cell: "Friends, the Blessed One wishes to go forth to Dakkhi*n*âgiri. Let any one of the venerable brethren who thinks fit, come to him."'

The venerable Ânanda accepted this order of the Blessed One (by saying), 'Yes, Lord,' took a key, and said to the Bhikkhus in every cell: 'Friends, the Blessed One,' &c.

3. The Bhikkhus replied: 'Friend Ânanda, the Blessed One has prescribed[1] that Bhikkhus are to live (the first) ten years in dependence (on their â*k*ariyas and upa*ggh*âyas), and that he who has completed his tenth year, may give a nissaya himself. Now if we go there, we shall be obliged to take a nissaya there; then we shall stay there for a short time, then we must go back again and take a new nissaya. If our â*k*ariyas and upa*ggh*âyas go, we will go also; if our â*k*ariyas and upa*ggh*âyas do not go, we will not go either. Otherwise our light-mindedness, friend Ânanda, will become manifest.'

4. Thus the Blessed One went forth to Dakkhi*n*âgiri followed only by a few Bhikkhus. And the Blessed One, after having dwelt at Dakkhi*n*âgiri as long as he thought fit, went back to Râ*g*agaha again.

Then the Blessed One said to the venerable Ânanda: 'How is it, Ânanda, that the perfect

---

[1] See chap. 32. 1.

One has gone forth to Dakkhi*n*âgiri with so few Bhikkhus?'

Then the venerable Ânanda told the thing to the Blessed One.

In consequence of that and on this occasion the Blessed One, after having delivered a religious discourse, thus addressed the Bhikkhus: 'I prescribe, O Bhikkhus, that a learned, competent Bhikkhu lives five years in dependence (on his â*k*ariya and upa*g*-*gh*âya), an unlearned one all his life.

5. 'In five cases, O Bhikkhus, a Bhikkhu should not live without a nissaya (i.e. independent of â*k*ariya and upa*ggh*âya): when he does not possess full perfection in what belongs to moral practices (&c., as in chap. 36. 2). In these five cases, O Bhikkhus, a Bhikkhu should not live without a nissaya.

'In five cases, O Bhikkhus, a Bhikkhu may live without a nissaya: when he possesses full perfection in what belongs to moral practices (&c., as in chap. 36. 3). In these five cases, O Bhikkhus, a Bhikkhu may live without a nissaya.

6–13. 'And also in other five cases, &c.[1]'

End of the eighth Bhâ*n*avâra, which is called the Abhayûvara Bhâ*n*avâra[2].

54.

1. Then the Blessed One, after having resided at Râ*g*agaha as long as he thought fit, went forth to

[1] Supply these pentads and hexads, respectively, from chaps. 36. 6, 7; 8, 9; 14, 15; 16, 17; 37. 1, 2; 5, 6; 7, 8; 13, 14.

[2] Abhayûvara means, 'secure from anything.' This refers to the expression used in chap. 42, § 2.

Kapilavatthu. Wandering from place to place he came to Kapilavatthu. There the Blessed One dwelt in the Sakka country, near Kapilavatthu, in the Nigrodhârâma (Banyan Grove).

And in the forenoon the Blessed One, having put on his under-robes, took his alms-bowl and with his *k*îvara on went to the residence of the Sakka Suddhodana (his father). Having gone there, he sat down on a seat laid out for him.

Then the princess, who was the mother of Râhula[1], said to young Râhula: 'This is your father, Râhula; go and ask him for your inheritance.'

2. Then young Râhula went to the place where the Blessed One was; having approached him, he stationed himself before the Blessed One (and said): 'Your shadow, Sama*n*a, is a place of bliss.'

Then the Blessed One rose from his seat and went away, and young Râhula followed the Blessed One from behind and said: 'Give me my inheritance, Sama*n*a; give me my inheritance, Sama*n*a.'

Then the Blessed One said to the venerable Sâriputta: 'Well, Sâriputta, confer the pabba*gg*â ordination on young Râhula.'

(Sâriputta replied): 'How shall I confer, Lord, the pabba*gg*â ordination on young Râhula?'

3. In consequence of that and on this occasion the Blessed One, after having delivered a religious discourse, thus addressed the Bhikkhus: 'I prescribe,

[1] The Buddha's former wife. This is, as far as we know, the only passage in the Pâli Pi*t*akas which mentions this lady, and it deserves notice that her name is not mentioned. Probably this name was unknown to the Buddhists in early times, and thus we may best account for the difference of the simply invented names given to this lady by later writers. Compare Rh. D., Buddhism, p. 50 seq.

O Bhikkhus, the pabba*gg*â ordination of novices by the threefold declaration of taking refuge.

'And you ought, O Bhikkhus, to confer the pabba*gg*â ordination (on a novice) in this way: Let him first have his hair and beard cut off; let him put on yellow robes, adjust his upper robe so as to cover one shoulder, salute the feet of the Bhikkhus (with his head), and sit down squatting; then let him raise his joined hands and tell him to say: "I take my refuge in the Buddha, I take my refuge in the Dhamma, I take my refuge in the Sa*m*gha. And for the second time, &c. And for the third time, &c."

'I prescribe, O Bhikkhus, the pabba*gg*â ordination of novices by this threefold declaration of taking refuge.'

Thus the venerable Sâriputta conferred the pabba*gg*â ordination on young Râhula.

4. Then the Sakka Suddhodana went to the place where the Blessed One was; having approached him and having respectfully saluted the Blessed One, he sat down near him. Sitting near him the Sakka Suddhodana said to the Blessed One: 'Lord, I ask one boon of the Blessed One.' (The Buddha replied): 'The perfect Ones, Gotama, are above granting boons (before they know what they are[1]).' (Suddhodana said): 'Lord, it is a proper and unobjectionable demand.' 'Speak, Gotama.'

5. 'Lord, when the Blessed One gave up the

[1] Granting a boon (vara) is a constant phrase used of princes when making an open promise to give to any one whatever they should ask. See, for instance, the *G*âtaka Story, No. 9, where the person to whom the boon was given laid it by for a convenient season; and then asked the king to make her son heir-apparent, in violation of all ancient law and custom.

world, it was a great pain to me; so it was when Nanda[1] did the same; my pain was excessive when Râhula too did so. The love for a son, Lord, cuts into the skin; having cut into the skin, it cuts into the hide; having cut into the hide, it cuts into the flesh, ... the ligaments, ... the bones; having cut into the bones, it reaches the marrow and dwells in the marrow. Pray, Lord, let their reverences not confer the pabba*gg*â ordination on a son without his father's and mother's permission.'

Then the Blessed One taught the Sakka Suddhodana (&c., see chap. 39. 7).

'Let no son, O Bhikkhus, receive the pabba*gg*â ordination without his father's and mother's permission. He who confers the pabba*gg*â ordination (on a son without that permission), is guilty of a dukka*t*a offence.'

55.

Then the Blessed One, after having resided at Kapilavatthu as long as he thought fit, went forth to Sâvatthi. Wandering from place to place he came to Sâvatthi. There the Blessed One dwelt at Sâvatthi, in the *G*etavana, the Ârâma of Anâthapi*nd*ika.

At that time a family who devoted themselves to the (especial) service of the venerable Sâriputta sent a boy to the venerable Sâriputta (with this message):

[1] Nanda was a son of Mahâpa*g*âpatî, a half-brother of the Buddha. See the story of his conversion in Rh. D.'s Buddhist Birth Stories, p. 128 (later and fuller accounts can be seen in Hardy, Manual, p. 204 seq.; Beal, Romantic Legend, p. 369 seq.)

'Might the Thera confer the pabba*gg*â ordination on this boy.' Now the venerable Sâriputta thought: 'The Blessed One has established the rule[1] that no one may ordain two novices, and I have already one novice, Râhula. Now what am I to do?'

He told the thing to the Blessed One.

'I allow, O Bhikkhus, a learned, competent Bhikkhu to ordain two novices, or to ordain as many novices as he is able to administer exhortation and instruction to.'

56.

Now the novices thought: 'How many precepts[2] are there for us, and in what (precepts) are we to exercise ourselves?'

They told this thing to the Blessed One.

'I prescribe, O Bhikkhus, ten precepts for the novices, and the exercise of the novices in these (ten precepts), viz. abstinence from destroying life; abstinence from stealing; abstinence from impurity; abstinence from lying; abstinence from arrack and strong drink and intoxicating liquors, which cause indifference (to religion); abstinence from eating at forbidden times; abstinence from dancing, singing, music, and seeing spectacles; abstinence from garlands, scents, unguents, ornaments, and finery; abstinence from (the use of) high or broad beds; abstinence from accepting gold or silver. I pre-

---

[1] See chap. 52.

[2] Sikkhâpadâni, literally, 'Paths of Training.' Compare chap. 60.

scribe, O Bhikkhus, these ten precepts for the novices, and the exercise of the novices in these (ten precepts).'

57.

1. At that time novices did not show reverence and confidence towards the Bhikkhus, and did not live in harmony with them. The Bhikkhus were annoyed, murmured, and became angry: 'How can the novices not show reverence and confidence towards the Bhikkhus, and not live in harmony with them?'

They told this thing to the Blessed One.

'I prescribe, O Bhikkhus, that you inflict punishment upon a novice in five cases: When he is intent on the Bhikkhus' receiving no alms; when he is intent on the Bhikkhus' meeting with misfortune; when he is intent on the Bhikkhus' finding no residence; when he abuses and reviles the Bhikkhus; when he causes divisions between Bhikkhus and Bhikkhus. I prescribe, O Bhikkhus, that in these five cases you inflict punishment upon a novice.'

2. Now the Bhikkhus thought: 'What punishment are we to inflict?'

They told this thing to the Blessed One.

'I prescribe, O Bhikkhus, that you forbid them (certain places, for instance, their own residences).'

At that time Bhikkhus forbad novices the whole Sa*m*ghârâma. The novices, who were not admitted to the Sa*m*ghârâma, went away, or returned to the world, or went over to Titthiya schools.

They told this thing to the Blessed One.

'Let them not, O Bhikkhus, forbid (novices) the whole Samghârâma. He who does so, commits a dukkata offence. I prescribe, O Bhikkhus, that (the Bhikkhus) forbid (a novice) the place where he lives or which he uses to frequent.'

3. At that time Bhikkhus forbad the novices the use of (certain kinds of) food that is taken with the mouth. People, when they prepared rice-milk to drink or meals for the Samgha, said to the novices: 'Come, reverend Sirs, drink rice-milk; come, reverend Sirs, take food.' The novices replied: 'It is impossible, friends; the Bhikkhus have issued a forewarning (against us).' The people were annoyed, murmured, and became angry, thinking: 'How can their reverences forbid novices the use of all food that is taken with the mouth?'

They told this thing to the Blessed One.

'Let them not, O Bhikkhus, forbid (novices) food that is taken with the mouth. He who does so, commits a dukkata offence.'

End of the section about punishment (of novices).

58.

At that time the *Kh*abbaggiya[1] Bhikkhus laid a ban upon novices without the consent of the upa*ggh*âyas (of those novices). The upa*ggh*âyas

---

[1] Here first appear the *Kh*abbaggiya Bhikkhus (the company of the 'six Bhikkhus', with their attendants), the constant and indefatigable evil-doers throughout the whole Vinaya-Pi*t*aka. Buddhaghosa (on *K*ullavagga I, 1) says that Pa*nd*uka and Lohitaka belonged to this company, and also Assa*g*i and Punabbasu are mentioned as *Kh*abbaggiyas (see Childers s. v. *kh*abbaggiyo).

searched after them, thinking: 'How is it that our novices have disappeared?' The Bhikkhus said: 'The *Kh*abbaggiya Bhikkhus, friends, have laid a ban upon them.' The upa*ggh*âyas were annoyed, &c.: 'How can the *Kh*abbaggiya Bhikkhus lay a ban upon our novices without having obtained our consent?'

They told this thing to the Blessed One.

'Let no one, O Bhikkhus, lay a ban (upon novices) without consent of the upa*ggh*âyas. He who does, commits a dukka*t*a offence.'

59.

At that time the *Kh*abbaggiya Bhikkhus drew the novices of senior Bhikkhus over (to themselves). The Theras, who were obliged to get themselves teeth-cleansers and water to rinse their mouths with, became tired.

They told this thing to the Blessed One.

'Let no one, O Bhikkhus, draw the followers of another Bhikkhu over to himself. He who does, commits a dukka*t*a offence.'

60.

At that time a novice, Ka*nd*aka by name, who was a follower of the venerable Upananda Sakyaputta, had sexual intercourse with a Bhikkhunî, Ka*nd*akâ by name. The Bhikkhus were annoyed, &c.: 'How can a novice abandon himself to such conduct?'

They told this thing to the Blessed One.

'I prescribe, O Bhikkhus, that you expel a novice (from the fraternity) in the following ten cases: When he destroys life; when he commits theft; when he commits impurity; when he is a liar; when he drinks strong drinks; when he speaks against the Buddha; when he speaks against the Dhamma; when he speaks against the Sa*m*gha; when he holds false doctrines; when he has sexual intercourse with Bhikkhunîs[1]. In these ten cases I prescribe, O Bhikkhus, that you expel the novice (from the fraternity).'

61.

At that time, &c.[2]

'Let a eunuch, O Bhikkhus, who has not received the upasampadâ ordination, not receive it; if he has received it, let him be expelled (from the fraternity).'

---

[1] The case of the novice's committing sexual intercourse with a Bhikkhunî can have found its place here only by a negligence of the redactor, as it is comprised already in the third of the ten cases (the novice's committing impurity). Buddhaghosa (who of course never admits anything like an inadvertence of the holy Theras by whom the Vinaya is compiled) says that the third case and the tenth are distinguished here, because a person that has simply committed an impurity may receive the ordination, if he is willing to refrain himself in future; whilst a bhikkhunîdûsaka cannot be ordained in any case (see chap. 67).

[2] Tena kho pana samayena a*ññ*ataro pa*nd*ako bhikkhûsu pabba*g*ito hoti, so dahare dahare bhikkhû upasa*m*kamitvâ eva*m* vadeti: etha ma*m* âyasmanto dûsethâ 'ti. Bhikkhû apasâdenti: nassa pa*nd*aka, vinassa pa*nd*aka, ko tayâ attho 'ti. So bhikkhûhi apasâdito mahante mahante moligalle (Buddhaghosa: thûlasarîre) sâma*n*ere upasa*m*kamitvâ eva*m* vadeti: etha ma*m* âvuso dûsethâ

62.

1. At that time there was a certain person of an old family, whose kinsmen had died away; he was delicately nurtured. Now this person of an old family, whose kinsmen had died away, thought: 'I am delicately nurtured; I am not able to acquire new riches or to augment the riches which I possess. What shall I do in order that I may live a life of ease and without pain?'

Then this person of an old family, whose kinsmen had died away, gave himself the following answer: 'There are the Sakyaputtiya Sama*n*as, who keep commodious precepts and live a commodious life; they have good meals and lie down on beds protected from wind. What if I were to procure myself an alms-bowl and robes on my own account, and were to have my hair and beard cut off, to put on yellow robes, to go to the Ârâma, and to live there with the Bhikkhus.'

2. Then that person of an old family, whose kinsmen had died away, procured himself an alms-bowl and robes on his own account, had his hair and beard cut off, put on yellow robes, went to the Ârâma, and respectfully saluted the Bhikkhus. The

---

'ti. Sâma*n*erâ apasâdenti: nassa pa*nd*aka, vinassa pa*nd*aka, ko tayâ attho 'ti. So sâma*n*erehi apasâdito hatthibha*nd*e assabha*nd*e upasa*m*kamitvâ eva*m* vadeti: etha ma*m* âvuso dûsethâ 'ti. Hatthibha*nd*â assabha*nd*â dûsesu*m*. Te u*ggh*âyanti khîyanti vipâ*k*enti: pa*nd*akâ ime sama*n*â Sakyaputtiyâ, ye pi imesa*m* na pa*nd*akâ te pi pa*nd*ake dûsenti, eva*m* ime sabbeva abrahma*k*ârino 'ti. Assosu*m* kho bhikkhû hatthibha*nd*âna*m* assabha*nd*âna*m* u*ggh*âyantâna*m* khîyantâna*m* vipâ*k*entâna*m*. Atha kho te bhikkhû bhagavato etam attha*m* âro*k*esu*m*.

Bhikkhus said to him: 'How many years, friend, have elapsed since your upasampadâ?'

'What does that mean, friends, "years elapsed since the upasampadâ?"'

'And who is your upagghâya, friend?'

'What does that word upagghâya mean, friends?'

The Bhikkhus said to the venerable Upâli: 'Pray, friend Upâli, examine this ascetic.'

3. Then that person of an old family, whose kinsmen had died away, when being examined by the venerable Upâli, told him the whole matter. The venerable Upâli told this thing to the Bhikkhus; the Bhikkhus told this thing to the Blessed One.

'Let a person, O Bhikkhus, who has furtively attached himself to the Saṃgha, if he has not received the upasampadâ ordination, not receive it; if he has received it, let him be expelled (from the fraternity).

'Let a person, O Bhikkhus, who has gone over to the Titthiyas' (&c., as in chap. 61).

63.

1. At that time there was a serpent who was aggrieved at, ashamed of, and conceived aversion for his having been born as a serpent. Now this serpent thought: 'What am I to do in order to become released from being a serpent, and quickly to obtain human nature?' Then this serpent gave himself the following answer: 'These Sakyaputtiya Samaṇas lead indeed a virtuous, tranquil, holy life; they speak the truth; they keep the precepts of morality, and are endowed with all virtues. If

I could obtain pabba*gg*â with the Sakyaputtiya Sama*n*as, I should be released from being a serpent and quickly obtain human nature.'

2. Then that serpent, in the shape of a youth, went to the Bhikkhus, and asked them for the pabba*gg*â ordination; the Bhikkhus conferred on him the pabba*gg*â and upasampadâ ordinations.

At that time that serpent dwelt together with a certain Bhikkhu in the last Vihâra (near the boundary wall of the *G*etavana). Now that Bhikkhu, having arisen in the night, at dawn, was walking up and down in the open air. When that Bhikkhu had left (the Vihâra), that serpent, who thought himself safe (from discovery), fell asleep (in his natural shape). The whole Vihâra was filled with the snake's body; his windings jutted out of the window.

3. Then that Bhikkhu thought: 'I will go back to the Vihâra,' opened the door, and saw the whole Vihâra filled with the snake's body, the windings jutting out of the window. Seeing that he was terrified and cried out. The Bhikkhus ran up, and said to that Bhikkhu: 'Why did you cry out, friend?' 'This whole Vihâra, friends, is filled with a snake's body; the windings jut out of the window.'

Then that serpent awoke from that noise and sat down on his seat. The Bhikkhus said to him: 'Who are you, friend?' 'I am a serpent, reverend Sirs.' 'And why have you done such a thing, friend?' Then that Nâga told the whole matter to the Bhikkhus; the Bhikkhus told it to the Blessed One.

4. In consequence of that and on this occasion the Blessed One, having ordered the fraternity of

Bhikkhus to assemble, said to that serpent: 'You serpents are not capable of (spiritual) growth in this doctrine and discipline. However, serpent, go and observe fast on the fourteenth, fifteenth, and eighth day of each half month; thus will you be released from being a serpent and quickly obtain human nature.'

Then that serpent, who thought, 'I am not capable of (spiritual) growth in this doctrine and discipline,' became sad and sorrowful, shed tears, made an outcry, and went away.

5. Then the Blessed One said to the Bhikkhus: 'There are two occasions, O Bhikkhus, on which a serpent (who has assumed human shape) manifests his true nature: when he has sexual intercourse with a female of his species, and if he thinks himself safe (from discovery) and falls asleep. These, O Bhikkhus, are the two occasions on which a serpent manifests his true nature.

'Let an animal, O Bhikkhus, that has not received the upasampadâ ordination, not receive it; if it has received it, let it be expelled (from the fraternity).'

64.

1. At that time a certain young man deprived his mother of life. He was grieved, ashamed, and loathed this sinful deed. Now this young man thought: 'What am I to do to get rid of my sinful deed?' Then this young man gave himself this answer: 'These Sakyaputtiya Sama*n*as lead indeed a virtuous, tranquil, holy life, &c. If I could obtain

pabbaggâ with the Sakyaputtiya Samanas, I might get rid of my sinful deed.'

2. Then that young man went to the Bhikkhus and asked them for the pabbaggâ ordination. The Bhikkhus said to the venerable Upâli: 'Formerly, friend Upâli, a serpent in the shape of a youth received the pabbaggâ ordination with the Bhikkhus; pray, friend Upâli, examine this young man.' Then that young man, when examined by the venerable Upâli, told him the whole matter. The venerable Upâli told it to the Bhikkhus; the Bhikkhus told it to the Blessed One.

'Let a person, O Bhikkhus, that is guilty of matricide, if he has not received the upasampadâ ordination, not receive it; if he has received it, let him be expelled (from the fraternity).'

65.

At that time a certain young man deprived his father of life (&c., as in chap. 64).

'Let a person, O Bhikkhus, that is guilty of parricide, &c.'

66.

1. At that time a number of Bhikkhus were travelling on the road from Sâketa to Sâvatthi. On the road robbers broke forth, robbed some of the Bhikkhus, and killed some of them. Then royal soldiers came from Sâvatthi and caught some of the robbers; others of them escaped. Those who had escaped, received pabbaggâ with the Bhikkhus; those who had been caught, were led to death.

2. Then those who had been ordained, saw those robbers who were being led to death; seeing them they said: 'It is well that we have escaped; had we been caught, we should also be killed thus.' The Bhikkhus said to them: 'Why, what have you done, friends?' Then those (robbers) who had been ordained, told the whole matter to the Bhikkhus. The Bhikkhus told this thing to the Blessed One.

'Those Bhikkhus, O Bhikkhus, were Arahats. Let a person, O Bhikkhus, that has murdered an Arahat, if this person has not received the upasampadâ ordination, not receive it; if he has received it, let him be expelled (from the fraternity).'

67.

At that time a number of Bhikkhunîs were travelling on the road from Sâketa to Sâvatthi. On the road robbers broke forth, robbed some of the Bhikkhunîs, and violated some of them. Then royal soldiers (&c., as in chap. 66).

The Bhikkhus told this thing to the Blessed One.

'Let a person, O Bhikkhus, that has violated a Bhikkhunî (or, that has had sexual intercourse with a Bhikkhunî), (&c., as in chap. 66).

'Let a person, O Bhikkhus, that has caused a schism among the Sa*m*gha, &c.

'Let a person, O Bhikkhus, that has shed (a Buddha's) blood,' &c.

68.

At that time a certain hermaphrodite had received pabba*gg*â with the Bhikkhus; so karoti pi kârâpeti pi.

They told this thing to the Blessed One.

'Let a hermaphrodite, O Bhikkhus,' &c.

69.

1. At that time the Bhikkhus conferred the upasampadâ ordination on a person that had no upa*ggh*âya.

They told this thing to the Blessed One.

'Let no one, O Bhikkhus, who has no upa*ggh*âya, receive the upasampadâ ordination. He who confers the upasampadâ ordination (on such a person), commits a dukka*t*a offence.'

2. At that time the Bhikkhus conferred the upasampadâ ordination with the Sa*m*gha as upa*ggh*âya.

They told this thing to the Blessed One.

'Let no one receive the upasampadâ ordination with the Sa*m*gha as upa*ggh*âya. He who confers the upasampadâ ordination (in such a way), commits a dukka*t*a offence.'

3. At that time the Bhikkhus conferred the upasampadâ ordination with a number of Bhikkhus[1] as upa*ggh*âya (&c., as before).

4. At that time the Bhikkhus conferred the upa-

[1] I.e. not with the whole fraternity residing at that place, but with a part of it.

sampadâ ordination with a eunuch as upa*ggh*âya, &c.; with a person that had furtively attached himself (to the Sa*m*gha) as upa*ggh*âya; with a person that was gone over to the Titthiyas as upa*ggh*âya; with an animal as upa*ggh*âya; with a person that was guilty of matricide as upa*ggh*âya; with a person that was guilty of parricide as upa*ggh*âya; with a person that had murdered an Arahat as upa*ggh*âya; with a person that had violated a Bhikkhunî as upa*ggh*âya; with a person that had caused a schism among the Sa*m*gha as upa*ggh*âya; with a person that had shed (a Buddha's) blood as upa*ggh*âya; with a hermaphrodite as upa*ggh*âya.

They told this thing to the Blessed One.

'Let no one,' &c. (as in the first clause).

70.

1. At that time the Bhikkhus conferred the upasampadâ ordination on persons that had no alms-bowl. They received alms with their hands. People were annoyed, murmured, and became angry, saying, 'Like the Titthiyas.'

They told this thing to the Blessed One.

'Let no one, O Bhikkhus, receive the upasampadâ ordination without having an alms-bowl. He who confers the upasampadâ ordination (on a person that has not), commits a dukka*t*a offence.'

2. At that time the Bhikkhus conferred the upasampadâ ordination on persons that had no robes. They went out for alms naked. People were annoyed (&c., as in § 1).

3. At that time the Bhikkhus conferred the upa-

sampadâ ordination on persons that had neither alms-bowl nor robes. They went out for alms naked and (received alms) with their hands. People were annoyed (&c., as in § 1).

4. At that time the Bhikkhus conferred the upasampadâ ordination on persons that had borrowed alms-bowls. After the ordination (the owners) took their alms-bowls back; (the Bhikkhus) received alms with their hands. People were annoyed (&c. . . . . down to): 'Like the Titthiyas.'

They told this thing to the Blessed One.

'Let no one, O Bhikkhus, receive the upasampadâ ordination who has borrowed the alms-bowl. He who confers,' &c. (as in the first clause).

5. At that time the Bhikkhus conferred the upasampadâ ordination on persons that had borrowed robes. After the ordination (the owners) took their robes back; (the Bhikkhus) went out for alms naked. People were annoyed (&c., as in § 1 to the end).

6. At that time the Bhikkhus conferred the upasampadâ ordination on persons that had borrowed alms-bowls and robes, &c.

Here end the twenty cases in which upasampadâ is forbidden.

71.

1. At that time the Bhikkhus conferred the pabbaggâ ordination on a person whose hands were cut off, on a person whose feet were cut off, whose hands and feet were cut off, whose ears were cut off, whose nose was cut off, whose ears and nose were cut off, whose fingers were cut off, whose

thumbs were cut off, whose tendons (of the feet) were cut, who had hands like a snake's hood[1], who was a hump-back, or a dwarf, or a person that had a goître, that had been branded, that had been scourged, on a proclaimed robber, on a person that had elephantiasis, that was afflicted with bad illness, that gave offence (by any deformity) to those who saw him, on a one-eyed person, on a person with a crooked limb, on a lame person, on a person that was paralysed on one side, on a cripple[2], on a person weak from age, on a blind man, on a dumb man, on a deaf man, on a blind and dumb man, on a blind and deaf man, on a deaf and dumb man, on a blind, deaf and dumb man.

They told this thing to the Blessed One.

'Let no person, O Bhikkhus, whose hands are cut off, receive the pabba*gg*â ordination. Let no person whose feet are cut off, receive the pabba*gg*â ordination, &c. (each of the above cases being here repeated). He who confers the pabba*gg*â ordination (on such persons), is guilty of a dukka*t*a offence.'

Here end the thirty-two cases in which pabba*gg*â is forbidden.

End of the ninth Bhâ*n*avâra.

---

[1] 'Whose fingers are grown together, like bats' wings' (Buddhaghosa).

[2] Buddhaghosa (Berlin MS.) explains '*kh*inniriyâpatha' by 'pidhasappi.' We ought to read, no doubt, pî*th*asappî, which is Sanskrit pî*th*asarpin, a cripple that is moved on in a rolling chair.

72.

1. At that time the *Kh*abbaggiya Bhikkhus gave a nissaya to shameless Bhikkhus.

They told this thing to the Blessed One.

'Let no one, O Bhikkhus, give a nissaya to shameless Bhikkhus. He who does, is guilty of a dukka*t*a offence.'

At that time some Bhikkhus lived in dependence on shameless Bhikkhus (i. e. they received a nissaya from them, they chose them for their upa*g*-*gh*âyas or â*k*ariyas); ere long they became also shameless, bad Bhikkhus.

They told this thing to the Blessed One.

'Let no one, O Bhikkhus, live in dependence on shameless Bhikkhus. He who does, is guilty of a dukka*t*a offence.'

2. Now the Bhikkhus thought: 'The Blessed One has prescribed that we shall not give a nissaya to shameless Bhikkhus, nor live in dependence on shameless Bhikkhus. Now how are we to discern modest and shameless persons?'

They told this thing to the Blessed One.

'I prescribe, O Bhikkhus, that you wait first four or five days until you have seen how a Bhikkhu behaves to the other Bhikkhus.'

73.

1. At that time a certain Bhikkhu was travelling on the road in the Kosala country. Now this Bhikkhu thought: 'The Blessed One has prescribed that we shall not live without a nissaya (of an â*k*ariya and

an upa*ggh*âya); now I want a nissaya, but I am travelling. What am I to do?'

They told this thing to the Blessed One.

'I allow, O Bhikkhus, a travelling Bhikkhu who can get no nissaya, to live without a nissaya.'

2. At that time two Bhikkhus were travelling on the road in the Kosala country. They came to a certain residence; there one of the two Bhikkhus was taken ill. Now that sick Bhikkhu thought: 'The Blessed One has prescribed that we shall not live without a nissaya; now I want a nissaya, but I am sick. What am I to do?'

They told this thing to the Blessed One.

'I allow, O Bhikkhus, a sick Bhikkhu who can get no nissaya, to live without a nissaya.'

3. Now the other Bhikkhu, who nursed that sick Bhikkhu, thought: 'The Blessed One has prescribed, &c.; now I want a nissaya, but this Bhikkhu is sick. What am I to do?'

They told this thing to the Blessed One.

'I allow, O Bhikkhus, a Bhikkhu who is nursing a sick Bhikkhu, if he can get no nissaya and the sick asks him (to remain with him), to live without a nissaya.'

4. At that time a certain Bhikkhu lived in the forest; he had a dwelling-place where he lived pleasantly. Now this Bhikkhu thought: 'The Blessed One has prescribed, &c.; now I want a nissaya, but I live in the forest and have a dwelling-place where I live pleasantly. What am I to do?'

They told this thing to the Blessed One.

'I allow, O Bhikkhus, a Bhikkhu living in the forest who finds a place where he may live pleasantly, and who can get (there) no nissaya, to live without a nissaya (saying to himself): "If a proper person to give me nissaya comes hither, I will take nissaya of that person."'

74.

1. At that time there was a person that desired to receive the upasampadâ ordination from the venerable Mahâkassapa. Then the venerable Mahâkassapa sent a messenger to the venerable Ânanda: 'Come, Ânanda, and recite the upasampadâ proclamation for this person.' The venerable Ânanda said: 'I cannot pronounce the Thera's (i. e. Mahâkassapa's) name; the Thera is too venerable compared with me.'

They told this thing to the Blessed One.

'I allow you, O Bhikkhus, to use also the family name (of the upa*ggh*âya, instead of his proper name) in the proclamation.'

2. At that time there were two persons that desired to receive the upasampadâ ordination from the venerable Mahâkassapa. They quarrelled with each other. (One said): 'I will receive the upasampadâ ordination first.' (The other said): 'Nay, I will receive it first.'

They told this thing to the Blessed One.

'I allow you, O Bhikkhus, to ordain two persons by one proclamation.'

3. At that time there were persons who desired to receive the upasampadâ ordination from different Theras. They quarrelled with each other. (One said): 'I will receive the upasampadâ ordina-

tion first.' (The other said): 'Nay, I will receive it first.' The Theras said: 'Well, friends, let us ordain them altogether by one proclamation.'

They told this thing to the Blessed One.

'I allow you, O Bhikkhus, to ordain two or three persons by one proclamation, provided they have the same upa*ggh*âya, but not if they have different upa*ggh*âyas.'

75.

At that time the venerable Kumârakassapa had received the upasampadâ ordination when he had completed the twentieth year from his conception (but not from his birth). Now the venerable Kumârakassapa thought: 'The Blessed One has forbidden us to confer the upasampadâ ordination on persons under twenty years of age[1], and I have completed my twentieth year (only) from my conception. Have I, therefore, received the upasampadâ ordination, or have I not received it?'

They told this thing to the Blessed One.

'When, O Bhikkhus, in the womb the first thought rises up (in the nascent being), the first consciousness manifests itself, according to this the (true) birth should be reckoned. I allow you, O Bhikkhus, to confer the upasampadâ ordination on persons that have completed the twentieth year from their conception (only).'

---

[1] See chap. 49. 6.

76.

1. At that time ordained Bhikkhus were seen who were afflicted with leprosy, boils, dry leprosy, consumption, and fits.

They told this thing to the Blessed One.

'I prescribe, O Bhikkhus, that he who confers the upasampadâ ordination, ask (the person to be ordained) about the Disqualifications (for receiving the ordination). And let him ask, O Bhikkhus, in this way:

'Are you afflicted with the following diseases, leprosy, boils, dry leprosy, consumption, and fits?

'Are you a man?

'Are you a male?

'Are you a freeman?

'Have you no debts?

'Are you not in the royal service?

'Have your father and mother given their consent?

'Are you full twenty years old?

'Are your alms-bowl and your robes in due state?

'What is your name?

'What is your upa*ggh*âya's name?'

2. At that time the Bhikkhus asked the persons who desired to receive the upasampadâ ordination about the Disqualifications, without having them instructed beforehand (how to answer). The persons that desired to be ordained, became disconcerted, perplexed, and could not answer.

They told this thing to the Blessed One.

'I prescribe, O Bhikkhus, that you first instruct (the persons desirous of being ordained), and then ask them about the Disqualifications.'

3. Then they instructed (the candidates) in the midst of the assembly; the persons desirous of being ordained became disconcerted, perplexed, and could not answer nevertheless.

They told this thing to the Blessed One.

'I prescribe, O Bhikkhus, that you instruct them aside, and ask them about the Disqualifications before the assembly. And you ought, O Bhikkhus, to instruct them in this way: You ought first to cause them to choose an upa*ggh*âya; when they have chosen an upa*ggh*âya, their alms-bowl and robes must be shown to them, "This is your alms-bowl, this is your sa*m*ghâ*t*i, this is your upper robe, this is your under garment; come and place yourself here."'

4. Ignorant, unlearned Bhikkhus instructed them; the persons desirous of being ordained, though they had been instructed, became disconcerted, perplexed, and could not answer.

They told this thing to the Blessed One.

'Let no ignorant, unlearned Bhikkhus, O Bhikkhus, instruct them. If they do, they commit a dukka*t*a offence. I prescribe, O Bhikkhus, that a learned, competent Bhikkhu instruct them.'

5. At that time persons instructed them who were not appointed thereto.

They told this thing to the Blessed One.

'Let no one, O Bhikkhus, instruct them without being appointed thereto. He who so instructs, commits a dukka*t*a offence. I prescribe, O Bhikkhus, that an appointed Bhikkhu is to instruct them. And (this Bhikkhu), O Bhikkhus, is to be appointed in this way: One may either appoint himself, or one may appoint another person. And how is (a Bhikkhu) to appoint himself? Let a learned, competent Bhikkhu proclaim the following *ñ*atti before the Sa*m*gha: "Let the Sa*m*gha, reverend Sirs, hear me. N.N. desires to receive the upasampadâ ordination from the venerable N.N. If the Sa*m*gha is ready, I will instruct N.N." Thus one may appoint himself.

6. 'And how is (a Bhikkhu) to appoint another person? Let a learned, competent Bhikkhu proclaim the following *ñ*atti before the Sa*m*gha: "Let the Sa*m*gha, &c. N.N. desires to receive the upasampadâ ordination from the venerable N.N. If the Sa*m*gha is ready, let N.N. instruct N.N." Thus one may appoint another person.

7. 'Then let that appointed Bhikkhu go to the person who desires to be ordained, and thus address him: "Do you hear, N.N.? This is the time for you to speak the truth, and to say that which is. When I ask you before the assembly about that which is, you ought, if it is so, to answer: 'It is;' if it is not so, you ought to answer: 'It is not.' Be not disconcerted, be not perplexed. I shall ask you thus: 'Are you afflicted with the following diseases, &c?'"'

8. (After the instruction, the instructor and the candidate) appeared together before the assembly.

'Let them not appear together. Let the instructor come first and proclaim the following *ñ*atti before the Sa*m*gha: "Let the Sa*m*gha, reverend Sirs, hear me. N.N. desires to receive the upasampadâ ordination from the venerable N.N.; he has been instructed by me. If the Sa*m*gha is ready, let N.N. come." Then let him be told: "Come on." Let him be told to adjust his upper robe (&c., see chap. 29. 2), to raise his joined hands, and to ask (the Sa*m*gha) for the upasampadâ ordination (by saying), "I ask the Sa*m*gha, reverend Sirs, for the upasampadâ ordination; might the Sa*m*gha, reverend Sirs, draw me out (of the sinful world) out of compassion towards me. And for the second time, reverend Sirs, I ask, &c. And for the third time, reverend Sirs, I ask, &c."

9. 'Then let a learned, competent Bhikkhu proclaim the following *ñ*atti before the Sa*m*gha: "Let the Sa*m*gha, reverend Sirs, hear me. This person N. N. desires to receive the upasampadâ ordination from the venerable N. N. If the Sa*m*gha is ready, let me ask N. N. about the Disqualifications.

'"Do you hear, N. N.? This is the time for you (&c., see § 7, down to:) you ought to answer: 'It is not.'"

'"Are you afflicted with the following diseases, &c.?"

10. 'Then let a learned, competent Bhikkhu proclaim the following *ñ*atti before the Sa*m*gha: "Let the Sa*m*gha, reverend Sirs, hear me. This person N. N. desires to receive the upasampadâ ordination from the venerable N. N.; he is free from the Disqualifications; his alms-bowl and robes are in due state. N. N. asks the Sa*m*gha for the upasampadâ ordination with N. N. as upa*ggh*âya. If the Sa*m*gha is ready, &c.[1]"'

End of the regulations for the upasampadâ ordination[2].

---

[1] Here follows the usual complete formula of a *ñ*atti*k*atuttha kamma; see chaps. 28. 4–6; 29. 3, &c.

[2] With these sections compare the previous chapters 12, 28 and following, 36 and following. The *ñ*attis prescribed in this chapter, together with the Three Refuges Formula prescribed in chap. 12, § 4, the whole of chap. 77, and the Four Interdictions form together

77.

'Then let them measure the shadow, tell (the newly-ordained Bhikkhu) what season and what date it is, tell him what part of the day it is, tell him the whole formula[1], and tell him the four Resources: "The religious life has the morsels of food given in alms for its resource (&c., as in chap. 30. 4)."'

End of the four Resources.

78.

1. At that time the Bhikkhus, after having conferred the upasampadâ ordination on a certain Bhikkhu, left him alone and went away. Afterwards, as he went alone (to the Ârâma), he met on the way his former wife. She said to him: 'Have you now embraced the religious life?' (He replied): 'Yes, I have embraced the religious life.' 'It is difficult to persons who have embraced religious life, to obtain sexual intercourse; come, let us have intercourse.' He practised intercourse with her, and, in consequence, came late (to the Ârâma). The Bhikkhus said: 'How is it, friend, that you are so late?'

2. Then that Bhikkhu told the whole matter to the Bhikkhus. The Bhikkhus told it to the Blessed One.

the current ceremony of ordination (the upasampadâ-kammavâkâ) as now still in use in the Order. See the Journal of the Royal Asiatic Society, New Series, VII, p. 1.

[1] I. e., according to Buddhaghosa, repeat to him all the data specified before together, in order that he might be able to give a correct answer when asked about his spiritual age.

'I prescribe, O Bhikkhus, that you give a companion to a newly-ordained Bhikkhu, and that you tell him the four Interdictions:

'"A Bhikkhu who has received the upasampadâ ordination, ought to abstain from all sexual intercourse even with an animal. A Bhikkhu who practises sexual intercourse is no Samana and no follower of the Sakyaputta. As a man whose head is cut off, cannot live any longer with his trunk alone, thus a Bhikkhu who practises sexual intercourse is no Samana and no follower of the Sakyaputta. Abstain from doing so as long as your life lasts.

3. '"A Bhikkhu who has received the upasampadâ ordination, ought to abstain from taking what is not given to him, and from theft, even of a blade of grass. A Bhikkhu who takes what is not given to him, or steals it, if it is a pâda (i. e. a quarter of a kârshâpana), or of the value of a pâda, or worth more than a pâda, is no Samana and no follower of the Sakyaputta. As a sear leaf loosed from its stalk cannot become green again, thus a Bhikkhu who takes, &c. Abstain from doing so as long as your life lasts.

4. '"A Bhikkhu who has received the upasampadâ ordination, ought not intentionally to destroy the life of any being down to a worm or an ant. A Bhikkhu who intentionally kills a human being, down to procuring abortion, is no Samana and no follower of the Sakyaputta. As a great stone which is broken in two, cannot be reunited, thus a Bhikkhu who intentionally, &c. Abstain from doing so as long as your life lasts.

5. '"A Bhikkhu who has received the upasampadâ ordination, ought not to attribute to

himself any superhuman condition, and not to say even: 'I find delight in sojourning in an empty place.' A Bhikkhu who with bad intention and out of covetousness attributes to himself a superhuman condition, which he has not, and which he is not possessed of, a state of *gh*âna (mystic meditation), or one of the vimokkhas[1], or one of the samâdhis (states of self-concentration), or one of the samâpattis (the attainment of the four *gh*ânas and four of the eight vimokkhas), or one of the Paths (of sanctification), or one of the Fruits thereof, is no Sama*n*a and no follower of the Sakyaputta. As a palm tree of which the top sprout has been cut off, cannot grow again, thus a Bhikkhu who with bad intention, &c. Abstain from doing so as long as your life lasts."'

End of the four Interdicts.

79.

1. At that time a certain Bhikkhu against whom expulsion[2] had been pronounced for his refusal to see an offence (committed by himself), returned to

[1] The vimokkhas (literally, deliverances) are eight stages of meditation different from the four *gh*ânas. The characteristics of the different vimokkhas are specified by Childers s. v.

[2] This temporary expulsion (ukkhepaniyakamma), which is pronounced against Bhikkhus who refuse to see an offence committed by themselves (âpattiyâ adassane), or to atone for such an offence (âpattiyâ appa*t*ikamme), or to renounce a false doctrine (pâpikâya di*tth*iyâ appa*t*inissagge), must be distinguished from the definitive and permanent expulsion (nâsanâ) which is pronounced against Bhikkhus who have committed a pârâ*g*ika offence, or in cases like those treated of in chapters 61 seq.

the world. Afterwards he came back to the Bhikkhus and asked them for the upasampadâ ordination.

They told this thing to the Blessed One.

'In case, O Bhikkhus, that a Bhikkhu against whom expulsion has been pronounced for his refusal to see an offence (committed by himself), returns to the world, and afterwards comes back to the Bhikkhus and asks them for the upasampadâ ordination, let them say to him: "Will you see that offence?" If he replies: "I will see it," let him be admitted to the pabba*gg*â ordination; if he replies: "I will not see it," let him not be admitted to the pabba*gg*â ordination.

2. 'When he has received the pabba*gg*â ordination let them say to him: "Will you see that offence?" If he says: "I will see it," let him be admitted to the upasampadâ ordination; if he says: "I will not see it," let him not be admitted to the upasampadâ ordination.

'When he has received the upasampadâ ordination (&c., as before). If he says: "I will see it," let him be restored[1]; if he says: "I will not see it," let him not be restored.

'When he has been restored, let them say to him: "Do you see that offence?" If he sees it, well and good; if he does not see it, let them expel him again, if it is possible to bring about unanimity (of the fraternity for the sentence of expulsion); if that is impossible, it is no offence to live and to dwell together (with such a Bhikkhu).

3. 'In case, O Bhikkhus, that a Bhikkhu against whom expulsion has been pronounced for his refusal

[1] I. e. the sentence of expulsion is abolished; compare the Samanta Pâsâdikâ, ap. Minayeff, Prâtimoksha, p. 92.

to atone for an offence (committed by himself), &c.[1] When he has been restored, let them say to him: "Atone now for that offence." If he atones for it, well and good, &c.

4. 'In case, O Bhikkhus, that a Bhikkhu against whom expulsion has been pronounced for his refusal to renounce a false doctrine, &c.[2] When he has been restored, let them say to him: "Renounce now that false doctrine." If he renounces it, well and good, &c.'

End of the first Khandhaka, which is called the Great Khandhaka[3].

---

[1] As in §§ 1, 2. Instead of 'Will you see that offence?' and, 'I will see it,' read here: 'Will you atone for that offence?' and, 'I will atone for it.'

[2] As above. Read here: 'Will you renounce that false doctrine?' and, 'I will renounce it.'

[3] Here follow some *S*lokas, probably written in Ceylon, and an elaborate Table of Contents, both of which we leave untranslated. The *S*lokas are introductory to the Table of Contents (uddâna) and belong to it. A similar Table of Contents is found in the MSS. nearly after all the other Khandhakas.

SECOND KHANDHAKA.

(THE UPOSATHA CEREMONY, AND THE PÂTIMOKKHA.)

1.

1. At that time the blessed Buddha dwelt near Râ*g*agaha, on the Gi*ggh*akû*t*a mountain ('the Vulture's Peak'). At that time the Paribbâ*g*akas belonging to Titthiya schools assembled on the fourteenth, fifteenth, and eighth day of each half month[1] and recited their Dhamma. The people went to them in order to hear the Dhamma. They were filled with favour towards, and were filled with faith in, the Paribbâ*g*akas belonging to Titthiya schools; the Paribbâ*g*akas belonging to Titthiya schools gained adherents.

2. Now when the Mâgadha king Seniya Bimbisâra was alone, and had retired into solitude, the following consideration presented itself to his mind: 'The Paribbâ*g*akas belonging to Titthiya schools assemble now on the fourteenth, fifteenth, and eighth day of each half month and recite their Dhamma. The people go to them in order to hear the Dhamma. They are filled with favour towards, and are filled with faith in, the Paribbâ*g*akas who belong to Titthiya

[1] One should be inclined to understand that the Paribbâ*g*akas assembled twice each half month, on the eighth day of the pakkha and on the fourteenth or fifteenth day, according to the different length of the pakkha. However, chap. 4 makes it probable that not two days in each pakkha are to be understood, but three. Compare, however, the remark of Buddhaghosa, quoted in the note on chap. 34. 1.

schools; the Paribbâgakas who belong to Titthiya schools gain adherents. What if the reverend ones (the Buddhist Bhikkhus) were to assemble also on the fourteenth, fifteenth, and eighth day of each half month.'

3. Then the Mâgadha king Seniya Bimbisâra went to the place where the Blessed One was; having approached him and having respectfully saluted the Blessed One, he sat down near him. Sitting near him the Mâgadha king Seniya Bimbisâra said to the Blessed One: 'Lord, when I was alone and had retired into solitude, the following consideration presented itself to my mind: "The Paribbâgakas, &c.; what if the reverend ones were to assemble also on the fourteenth, fifteenth, and eighth day of each half month." Well, Lord, let the reverend ones assemble also on the fourteenth, fifteenth, and eighth day of each half month.'

4. Then the Blessed One taught, incited, animated, and gladdened the Mâgadha king Seniya Bimbisâra by religious discourse; and the Mâgadha king Seniya Bimbisâra, having been taught . . . . and gladdened by the Blessed One by religious discourse, rose from his seat, respectfully saluted the Blessed One, passed round him with his right side towards him, and went away.

In consequence of that and on this occasion the Blessed One, after having delivered a religious discourse, thus addressed the Bhikkhus: 'I prescribe, O Bhikkhus, that you assemble on the fourteenth, fifteenth, and eighth day of each month.'

2.

At that time the Bhikkhus, considering that the Blessed One had ordered them to assemble on the fourteenth &c. day of each half month, assembled on the fourteenth &c. day of each half month and sat there silent. The people went to them in order to hear the Dhamma. They were annoyed, murmured, and became angry: 'How can the Sakyaputtiya Samanas, when they have assembled on the fourteenth &c. day of each half month, sit there silent, like the dumb, or like hogs? Ought they not to recite the Dhamma, when they have assembled?' Some Bhikkhus heard those people that were annoyed, murmured, and had become angry; these Bhikkhus told this thing to the Blessed One. In consequence of that and on this occasion the Blessed One, after having delivered a religious discourse, thus addressed the Bhikkhus: 'I prescribe, O Bhikkhus, that you recite the Dhamma, when you have assembled on the fourteenth &c. day of each half month.'

3.

1. Now when the Blessed One was alone and had retired into solitude, the following consideration presented itself to his mind: 'What if I were to prescribe that the Bhikkhus recite as the Pâtimokkha[1] the precepts which I have promulgated to

[1] On the origin and the meaning of the title 'Pâtimokkha,' see our Introduction, p. xxvii.

them; this will be their Uposatha service (service of the fast-day).'

2. And the Blessed One, having left the solitude in the evening, in consequence of that and on this occasion, after having delivered a religious discourse, thus addressed the Bhikkhus: 'When I was alone, O Bhikkhus, and had retired into solitude, the following consideration, &c., this will be their Uposatha service. I prescribe you, O Bhikkhus, to recite the Pâtimokkha.

3. 'And you ought, O Bhikkhus, to recite it in this way: Let a learned, competent Bhikkhu proclaim the following *ñ*atti before the Sa*m*gha: "Let the Sa*m*gha, reverend Sirs, hear me. To-day it is Uposatha, the fifteenth (of the half month). If the Sa*m*gha is ready, let the Sa*m*gha hold the Uposatha service and recite the Pâtimokkha. What ought to be first done by the Sa*m*gha? Proclaim the pârisuddhi[1], Sirs. I will recite the Pâtimokkha."

'"We hear it well and fix well the mind on it all of us[2]."

'"He who has committed an offence, may confess it; if there is no offence, you should remain silent; from your being silent I shall understand that the reverend brethen are pure (from offences). As a single person that has been asked a question, answers it, the same is the matter if before an

---

[1] See chap. 22. If a Bhikkhu is prevented by disease from assisting to the Pâtimokkha ceremony, he is to charge another Bhikkhu with his pârisuddhi, i. e. with the solemn declaration that he is pure from the offences specified in the Pâtimokkha.

[2] These words are evidently the answer of the Bhikkhus then present to the proclamation of the pâtimokkhuddesaka.

assembly like this a question has been solemnly proclaimed three times: if a Bhikkhu, after a threefold proclamation, does not confess an existing offence which he remembers, he commits an intentional falsehood. Now, reverend brethren, an intentional falsehood has been declared an impediment[1] by the Blessed One. Therefore, by a Bhikkhu who has committed (an offence), and remembers it, and desires to become pure, an existing offence should be confessed; for if it has been confessed, it is treated duly."'

4.[2] 'Pâtimokkha*m*:' it is the beginning, it is the face (mukha*m*), it is the principal (pamukha*m*) of good qualities; therefore it is called 'pâtimokkha*m*[3].'

'Âyasmanto:' this word 'âyasmanto' is an expression of friendliness, an expression of respect, an appellation that infers respectfulness and reverence.

'Uddisissâmi:' I will pronounce, I will show, I will proclaim, I will establish, I will unveil, I will distinguish, I will make evident, I will declare.

'Ta*m*' (it): this refers to the Pâtimokkha.

'Sabbe va santâ' (all of us): as many as are present in that assembly, aged, young, and middle-aged (Bhikkhus), are denoted by 'sabbe va santâ[4].'

'Sâdhuka*m* su*n*oma' (we hear it well): admit-

---

[1] See § 7.

[2] §§ 4–8 contain an explanation, word by word, of the formula given in § 3. This explanation is a portion of the ancient commentary on the Pâtimokkha which at the time of the redaction of the Vinaya Pi*t*aka has been admitted into it in its full extent (see the Introduction, p. xv seq.).

[3] See p. 241, note 1.

[4] See p. 1, note 5.

ting its authority, fixing our minds on it, we repeat the whole of it in our thoughts.

'Manasikaroma' (we fix our minds on it): we listen to it with concentrated, not perplexed, not confused thoughts.

5. 'Yassa siyâ âpatti' (he who has committed an offence): he who, whether an aged or young or middle-aged Bhikkhu, has committed some offence belonging to the five classes of offences or to the seven classes of offences[1].

'So âvikareyya:' he may show it, unveil it, make it evident, declare it before the Sa*m*gha (the full chapter of Bhikkhus), or before a small number, or before one person.

'Asantî âpatti' (a non-existing offence): an offence which has not been committed, or which has been committed and atoned for.

'Tu*n*hî bhavitabba*m*' (he ought to remain silent): he ought to accept (the recitation of the Pâtimokkha without any answer), he ought not to utter anything.

'Parisuddhâ 'ti vedissâmi' (I shall understand that they are pure): I shall infer, I shall know.

6. 'Yathâ kho pana pa*kk*ekaputthassa veyyâkara*n*a*m* hoti' (as a single person that has been asked a question answers it): as a single person that has been asked a question by another one, would answer it, thus (those who are present) in that assembly ought to understand: 'He asks me.'

---

[1] The five classes of offences are, the pârâ*g*ika, sa*m*ghâdisesa, pâ*k*ittiya, pâ*t*idesaniya, dukka*t*a offences; the seven classes, the pârâ*g*ika, sa*m*ghâdisesa, thulla*kk*aya, pâ*k*ittiya, pâ*t*idesaniya, dukka*t*a, dubbhâsita offences. See, for instance, *K*ullavagga IX, 3, 3.

'Evarûpâ parisâ' (an assembly like this): this refers to the assembly of Bhikkhus.

'Yâvatatiya*m* anussâvita*m* hoti' (it has been solemnly proclaimed three times): it has been solemnly proclaimed once, and the second time, and the third time.

'Saramâno' (remembering it): knowing it, being conscious of it.

'Santî âpatti' (an existing offence): an offence which has been committed, or which has been committed and not been atoned for.

'Nâvikareyya:' he does not show it, he does not unveil it, he does not make it evident, he does not declare it before the Sa*m*gha, or before a small chapter, or before one person.

7. 'Sampa*g*ânamusâvâd' assa hoti' (he commits an intentional falsehood): what is intentional falsehood? It is a sin[1].

'Antarâyiko dhammo vutto bhagavatâ' (it has been declared an impediment by the Blessed One): an impediment to what? An impediment to the attainment of the first *Gh*âna, an impediment to the attainment of the second . . . third . . . fourth *Gh*âna, an impediment to the attainment of the *Gh*ânas, Vimokkhas[2], Samâdhis (states of self-concentration), Samâpattis (the eight attainments of the four *Gh*ânas and four of the eight Vimokkhas),

---

[1] The Pâli text has 'dukka*t*a.' We cannot interpret here dukka*t*a in the technical sense of a dukka*t*a offence (see the Introduction, p. xxiv), for intentional falsehood belongs to the class of the pâ*k*ittiya offences, among which it occupies the first place.

[2] See the note on I, 78, 5.

the states of renunciation, of escape (from the world), of seclusion, of (all) good qualities.

'Tasmâ:' for that reason.

'Saramânena' (by him who remembers it): by him who knows it and is conscious of it.

'Visuddhâpekkhena' (by him who desires to become pure): by him who wishes to atone for it and to make himself pure of it.

8. 'Santî âpatti'... (see § 6).

'Âvikâtabbâ' (it is to be confessed): it is to be confessed before the Sa*m*gha, or before a small chapter, or before one person.'

'Âvikatâ hi 'ssa phâsu hoti' (for if it has been confessed, it is treated duly): duly for what purpose? In the due way for the attainment of the first *Gh*âna (and so on, as in § 7, down to:) of (all) good qualities.

4.

1. At that time the Bhikkhus, considering that the Pâtimokkha recitation had been instituted by the Blessed One, recited the Pâtimokkha every day.

They told this thing to the Blessed One.

'The Pâtimokkha, O Bhikkhus, is not to be recited every day. He who recites it (every day), commits a dukka*t*a offence. I ordain, O Bhikkhus, to recite the Pâtimokkha on the Uposatha day.'

2. At that time the Bhikkhus, considering that it had been prescribed by the Blessed One to recite the Pâtimokkha on the Uposatha day, recited the Pâtimokkha three times each half month, on the fourteenth, fifteenth, and eighth day of each half month.

They told this thing to the Blessed One.

'The Pâtimokkha, O Bhikkhus, is not to be recited three times each half month. He who recites it (three times), commits a dukka*t*a offence. I prescribe, O Bhikkhus, that you recite the Pâtimokkha once each half month, on the fourteenth or on the fifteenth day.'

5.

1. At that time the *Kh*abbaggiya Bhikkhus recited the Pâtimokkha according as they lived together, every one before his own companions.

They told this thing to the Blessed One.

'The Pâtimokkha, O Bhikkhus, is not to be recited according as (the Bhikkhus) live together, by every one before his own companions. He who recites it (in that way), commits a dukka*t*a offence. I prescribe, O Bhikkhus, that the Uposatha service is to be held by the complete fraternity.'

2. Now the Bhikkhus thought: 'The Blessed One has prescribed that the Uposatha service is to be held by the complete fraternity. How far does completeness extend, as far as one residence (or one district), or all over the earth?'

They told this thing to the Blessed One.

'I prescribe, O Bhikkhus, that completeness is to extend as far as one residence.'

3. At that time the reverend Mahâ Kappina dwelt near Râ*g*agaha, in the deer park of Maddaku*kkh*i. Now (one day) when the reverend Mahâ Kappina was alone and had retired into solitude, the following consideration presented itself to his mind: 'Shall I go to the Uposatha service or shall I not go? Shall I go to the functions of the Order

or shall I not go? Indeed I have become pure by the highest purity (i. e. I have reached Arahatship or Nirvâ*n*a).'

4. Then the Blessed One, understanding by the power of his mind the reflection which had arisen in Mahâ Kappina's mind, disappeared from the Gi*ggh*a-kû*t*a mountain and appeared in the deer park of Maddaku*kkh*i, before the reverend Mahâ Kappina (as quickly) as a strong man might stretch his bent arm out, or draw his outstretched arm back. The Blessed One sat down on a seat laid out for him, and the reverend Mahâ Kappina, after having respectfully saluted the Blessed One, sat down also near him.

5. When the reverend Mahâ Kappina was seated near him, the Blessed One said to him: 'When you were alone, Kappina, and had retired into solitude, has not the following consideration presented itself to your mind: "Shall I go (&c., as in § 3 down to:) by the highest purity?"'

'Even so, Lord.'

'If you Brâhma*n*as do not honour, do not regard, do not revere, do not pay reverence to the Uposatha, who will then honour, regard, revere, pay reverence to the Uposatha? Go to the Uposatha, O Brâhma*n*a, do not neglect to go; go to the functions of the Order, do not neglect to go.' The reverend Mahâ Kappina promised the Blessed One to do so (by saying), 'Even so, Lord.'

6. Then, having taught, incited, animated, and gladdened the reverend Mahâ Kappina by a religious discourse, the Blessed One disappeared from the deer park of Maddaku*kkh*i, from the presence of the reverend Mahâ Kappina, and appeared on the

Gi*ggh*akû*t*a mountain (as quickly) as a strong man might stretch his bent arm out, or draw his outstretched arm back.

6.

Now the Bhikkhus thought: 'The Blessed One has prescribed that completeness (of the assembled fraternity) is to extend as far as one residence[1]. Now how far does one residence extend?'

They told this thing to the Blessed One.

'I prescribe, O Bhikkhus, that you determine a boundary. And it ought to be determined, O Bhikkhus, in this way: First the landmarks are to be proclaimed: a landmark consisting in a mountain, in a rock, in a wood, in a tree, in a path, in an ant-hill, in a river, in a piece of water. The landmarks having been proclaimed, let a learned, competent Bhikkhu proclaim the following *ñ*atti before the Samgha: "Let the Sa*m*gha, reverend Sirs, hear me. If the Sa*m*gha is ready, let the Sa*m*gha, as the landmarks have been proclaimed all around, by these landmarks determine the boundary for common residence and communion of Uposatha. This is the *ñ*atti. Let the Sa*m*gha, reverend Sirs, hear me. The Sa*m*gha determines the boundary (&c., as above). Thus I understand."'

7.

1. At that time the *Kh*abbaggiya Bhikkhus, considering that fixing of boundaries had been

---

[1] See chap. 5. 2.

prescribed by the Blessed One, fixed boundaries of excessive extension, of four yo*g*anas, five yo*g*anas, six yo*g*anas. The Bhikkhus who came to the Uposatha, arrived when the Pâtimokkha was being recited, or when it had just been recited, or they were obliged to stay the night on the way.

They told this thing to the Blessed One.

'Let no one, O Bhikkhus, determine a boundary of excessive extension, of four, five, or six yo*g*anas. He who determines (such a boundary), commits a dukka*t*a offence. I prescribe, O Bhikkhus, that you determine boundaries of three yo*g*anas' extent at most.'

2. At that time the *Kh*abbaggiya Bhikkhus determined a boundary which extended to the opposite side of a river. The Bhikkhus who came to the Uposatha, were carried down (by the river), and their alms-bowls and robes were carried away.

They told this thing to the Blessed One.

'Let no one, O Bhikkhus, determine a boundary which extends to the opposite side of a river. He who determines (such a boundary), commits a dukka*t*a offence. I allow you, O Bhikkhus, if there is a regular communication by a ferry boat or a dike, at such places to determine a boundary which extends also to the opposite side of the river.'

8.

1. At that time the Bhikkhus recited the Pâtimokkha in their successive cells without appointing (a certain place for doing so). The Bhikkhus who

arrived (from distant places), did not know where the Uposatha was to be held that day.

They told this thing to the Blessed One.

'Let no one, O Bhikkhus, recite the Pâtimokkha in the successive cells without appointing a certain place for it. He who recites it (in this way), commits a dukka*t*a offence. I prescribe, O Bhikkhus, the holding of Uposatha after having fixed upon an Uposatha hall, wherever the Sa*m*gha likes, a Vihâra, or an A*ddh*ayoga, or a storied building, or a house, or a cave[1]. And you ought to appoint it in this way:

2. 'Let a learned, competent Bhikkhu proclaim the following *ñ*atti before the Sa*m*gha: "Let the Sa*m*gha, reverend Sirs, hear me. If the Sa*m*gha is ready, let the Sa*m*gha appoint the Vihâra called N. N. to be our Uposatha hall. This is the *ñ*atti. Let the Sa*m*gha, reverend Sirs, hear me. The Sa*m*gha appoints, &c. Thus I understand."'

3. At that time there were in a certain residence (or district) two Uposatha halls fixed upon. The Bhikkhus assembled in both places, because (some of them) thought, 'The Uposatha will be held here;' (and some), 'It will be held there.'

They told this thing to the Blessed One.

'Let no one, O Bhikkhus, fix upon two Uposatha halls in one district. He who does so, commits a dukka*t*a offence. I ordain, O Bhikkhus, the abolishing of one of them[2], and the holding of Uposatha (only) in one place.

4. 'And you ought to abolish it, O Bhikkhus, in this way: Let a learned, competent Bhikkhu pro-

[1] See the note on I, 30, 4.

[2] I. e. to abolish the character of uposathâgâra, conferred on the Vihâra &c. by the act of sammuti.

claim the following *ñatti* before the Sa*m*gha: "Let the Sa*m*gha, reverend Sirs, hear me. If the Sa*m*gha is ready, the Sa*m*gha may abolish the Uposatha hall called N.N. This is the *ñatti*. Let the Sa*m*gha, &c. Thus I understand."'

9.

1. At that time in a certain district too small an Uposatha hall had been appointed. On the day of Uposatha a great assembly of Bhikkhus met together. The Bhikkhus heard the Pâtimokkha sitting outside the site fixed upon. Now those Bhikkhus thought: 'The Blessed One has promulgated the precept that Uposatha is to be held after an Uposatha hall has been fixed upon, and we have heard the Pâtimokkha sitting outside the site fixed upon. Have we therefore (duly) held Uposatha or have we not held it?'

They told this thing to the Blessed One.

'Whether (a Bhikkhu) be seated inside or outside the site fixed upon, provided he hears the Pâtimokkha, Uposatha has been duly held by him.

2. 'Therefore, O Bhikkhus, let the Sa*m*gha determine as large an uposatha-pamukha[1] as it desires. And it ought to be determined, O Bhikkhus, in this way: First the landmarks are to be proclaimed. The landmarks having been proclaimed, let a learned, competent Bhikkhu proclaim the following *ñatti*

[1] Uposatha-pamukha (literally, that which has the Uposatha at its head, or, that which is situated in front of the Uposatha) evidently means the place around the uposathâgâra, in which the Pâtimokkha recitation may be heard as well as in the uposathâgâra itself.

before the Sa*m*gha: "Let the Sa*m*gha, reverend Sirs, hear me. If the Sa*m*gha is ready, let the Sa*m*gha, as the landmarks have been proclaimed all around, determine an uposathapamukha by these landmarks. This is the *ñ*atti. Let the Sa*m*gha, &c. Thus I understand."'

10.

At that time in a certain district on the day of Uposatha the young Bhikkhus, who had assembled first, thought: 'The Theras do not come yet,' and went away. The Uposatha service was held after the right time.

They told this thing to the Blessed One.

'I prescribe, O Bhikkhus, that on the Uposatha day the Theras ought to assemble first.'

11.

At that time there were at Râ*g*agaha several residences (of Bhikkhus) within the same boundary. Now the Bhikkhus quarrelled: (some of them said), 'The Uposatha shall be held in our residence;' (others said), 'It shall be held in our residence.'

They told this thing to the Blessed One.

'There are, O Bhikkhus, several (Bhikkhu) residences within the same boundary; now the Bhikkhus quarrel: (some of them say), "The Uposatha shall be held in our residence;" (others say), "It shall be held in our residence." Let those Bhikkhus, O Bhikkhus, assemble in one place all of them and hold Uposatha there, or let them assemble where the senior Bhikkhu dwells and hold Uposatha there. But in no case is Uposatha to be held by an incomplete congregation. He who holds it (in that way), commits a dukka*t*a offence.'

12.

1. At that time the reverend Mahâ Kassapa, when going to the Uposatha from Andhakavinda to Râ*g*agaha, and crossing a river on his way, was nearly[1] being carried away (by the river)[2]; and his robes got wet. The Bhikkhus said to the reverend Mahâ Kassapa: 'How have your robes got wet, friend?' (He replied): 'As I was going, friends, to the Uposatha from Andhakavinda to Râ*g*agaha, and crossing a river on my way, I was nearly being carried away (by the river); thus my robes have become wet.'

They told this thing to the Blessed One.

'Let the Sa*m*gha, O Bhikkhus, confer on the boundary which it has determined for common

[1] 'Mana*m* vu*lh*o ahosi.' Buddhaghosa: 'îsaka*m* appattavu*lh*abhâvo ahosi.' Mana*m* is evidently the equivalent of Sanskrit manâk.

[2] Buddhaghosa's note on this passage contains some details regarding the way which Mahâ Kassapa went. Andhakavinda is three gâvuta distant from Râ*g*agaha. There were eighteen (? the MS. reads: a*tth*âra mahâvihârâ) great Vihâras around Râ*g*agaha included by the same boundary which Buddha himself had consecrated. The Uposatha service for this whole district was performed in the Ve*l*uvana monastery. The river which Mahâ Kassapa crossed on his way to the Ve*l*uvana was the Sappinî, which rises in the Gi*ggh*akû*t*a mountain.

residence and for communion of Uposatha, the character of ti*k*îvarena avippavâsa[1].

2. 'And you ought, O Bhikkhus, to confer on it this character in this way: Let a learned, competent Bhikkhu proclaim the following *ñ*atti before the Sa*m*gha: "Let the Sa*m*gha, reverend Sirs, hear me. If the Sa*m*gha is ready, let the Sa*m*gha confer on the boundary which the Sa*m*gha has determined for common residence and for communion of Uposatha, the character of ti*k*îvarena avippavâsa. This is the *ñ*atti. Let the Sa*m*gha (&c., as above). Thus I understand."'

3. At that time the Bhikkhus, considering that the Blessed One had ordained the conferring of the character of ti*k*îvarena avippavâsa (on the boundaries), deposited their robes in a house. Those robes were lost, burnt, or eaten by rats; the Bhikkhus were badly dressed and had coarse robes. (Other) Bhikkhus said: 'How comes it that you are badly dressed, friends, and that you have coarse robes?' (They replied): 'Considering, friends, that the Blessed One had ordained the conferring (on the boundaries) of the character of ti*k*îvarena avippavâsa, we deposited our robes in a house; the robes have been lost, burnt, or eaten by rats;

[1] Ti*k*îvarena avippavâsa means not parting with the three robes which belong to the usual 'parikkhârâ' (requisites) of a Bhikkhu. Bhikkhus were not allowed to part with their *k*îvaras, excepting under special circumstances and for a limited time (see the Pâtimokkha, 29th nissaggiya dhamma). Conferring the character of ti*k*îvarena avippavâsa on a boundary means, we believe, to determine that it should be free to Bhikkhus residing within this boundary, to keep a set of robes wherever they liked within the same boundary (excepting in a village, § 3), and that such an act should not be considered as parting with the robes.

therefore we are badly dressed and have coarse robes.'

They told this thing to the Blessed One.

'Let[1] the Sa*m*gha, O Bhikkhus, confer on the boundary which it has determined for common residence and for communion of Uposatha, the character of ti*k*îvarena avippavâsa, excepting villages and the neighbourhood of villages[2].

4. 'And you ought, O Bhikkhus, to confer on it this character in this way, &c.[3]

5. 'Let him who determines a boundary, O Bhikkhus, first determine the boundary for common residence and for communion of Uposatha, and afterwards decree about the ti*k*îvarena avippavâsa. Let him who abolishes a boundary, O Bhikkhus, first abolish the decree about the ti*k*îvarena avippavâsa, and afterwards abolish the boundary for common residence and for communion of Uposatha.

'And you ought, O Bhikkhus, to abolish the

---

[1] Buddhaghosa observes that this rule applies to Bhikkhus only, and not to Bhikkhunîs. For Bhikkhunîs reside only in villages; there would be no *k*îvaraparihâra at all for Bhikkhunîs, if they were to use the kammavâ*k*â given in § 4. Buddhaghosa also observes at this occasion that the boundaries of the Bhikkhusa*m*gha and of the Bhikkhunîsa*m*gha are quite independent from each other, and that the rules given in chap. 13 do not refer to boundaries the one of which belongs to the Bhikkhusa*m*gha, the other to the Bhikkhunîsa*m*gha.

[2] As to the extent attributed to the 'gâmûpa*k*âra' (neighbourhood of the village), see the Vibhaṅga, quoted by Minayeff, Prâtim. p. 66, l. 1.

[3] This formula is identical with that given in § 2. The only difference is that after the words 'the character of ti*k*îvarena avippavâsa,' the words 'excepting villages and the neighbourhood of villages' are inserted.

tik*î*varena avippavâsa in this way: Let a learned, competent Bhikkhu proclaim the following *ñ*atti before the Samgha: "Let the Sa*m*gha, reverend Sirs, hear me. If the Sa*m*gha is ready, let the Sa*m*gha abolish the ti*k*îvarena avippavâsa, which the Sa*m*gha has decreed. This is the *ñ*atti. Let the Sa*m*gha, &c."

6. 'And you ought, O Bhikkhus, to abolish the boundary in this way: Let a learned, competent Bhikkhu proclaim the following *ñ*atti before the Sa*m*gha: "Let the Sa*m*gha, reverend Sirs, hear me. If the Sa*m*gha is ready, let the Sa*m*gha abolish the boundary for common residence and for communion of Uposatha which it has determined. This is the *ñ*atti. Let the Sa*m*gha, &c."

7. 'If there is no boundary determined nor fixed, O Bhikkhus, the village boundary of that village. or the nigama boundary of that nigama (market town) near which village or nigama (a Bhikkhu) dwells, is to be considered as boundary for common residence and for the communion of Uposatha. If (he lives), O Bhikkhus, in a forest where no villages are, community of residence and Uposatha extends to a distance of seven abbhantaras[1] all around. A river, O Bhikkhus, cannot be a boundary, a sea cannot be a boundary, a natural lake cannot be a boundary. In a river, O Bhikkhus, or in a sea, or in a natural lake, community of residence and Uposatha extends as far as an average man can spirt water all around.'

[1] 1 abbhantara = 28 hattha (Buddhaghosa and Abhidhânappadîpikâ, v. 197). See Rh. D., 'Coins and Measures,' &c., p. 15.

13.

1. At that time the *Kh*abbaggiya Bhikkhus made one boundary overlap another one (which had been determined before by other Bhikkhus).

They told this thing to the Blessed One.

'The act of those who have determined their boundary first is lawful, unobjectionable, and valid. The act of those who have determined their boundary afterwards is unlawful, objectionable, and invalid. Let no one, O Bhikkhus, make one boundary overlap another one. He who does, commits a dukka*t*a offence.'

2. At that time the *Kh*abbaggiya Bhikkhus made one boundary encompass another one (which had been determined before by other Bhikkhus).

They told this thing to the Blessed One.

'The act of those, &c. (see § 1). Let no one, O Bhikkhus, make one boundary encompass another one. He who does, commits a dukka*t*a offence. I prescribe, O Bhikkhus, that he who determines a boundary, is to determine it so as to leave an interstice[1] between the boundaries.'

14.

1. Now the Bhikkhus thought: 'How many Uposatha (days) are there?'

They told this thing to the Blessed One.

---

[1] Buddhaghosa prescribes to leave an interstice of one hattha, and he adds that the ancient Sinhalese commentaries differ as to the measure required for this interstice: the Kurundî requires one vidatthi, the Mahâpa*kk*arî four aṅgula.

'There are the following two Uposatha (days), O Bhikkhus, the fourteenth and the fifteenth (of the half month); these are the two Uposatha (days), O Bhikkhus.'

2. Now the Bhikkhus thought: 'How many Uposatha services are there?'

They told this thing to the Blessed One.

'There are the following four Uposatha services, O Bhikkhus: the Uposatha service which is held unlawfully (by an) incomplete (congregation)[1], the Uposatha service which is held unlawfully (by a) complete (congregation), the Uposatha service which is held lawfully (by an) incomplete (congregation), the Uposatha service which is held lawfully (by a) complete (congregation).

3. 'Now, O Bhikkhus, the Uposatha service which is held unlawfully (by an) incomplete (congregation), such an Uposatha service, O Bhikkhus, ought not to be held, nor is such an Uposatha service allowed by me. Now, O Bhikkhus, the Uposatha service which is held unlawfully (by a) complete (congregation), such an Uposatha service, O Bhikkhus, ought not to be held, nor is such an Uposatha service allowed by me. Now, O Bhikkhus, the Uposatha service which is held lawfully (by an) incomplete (congregation), such an Uposatha service, O Bhikkhus, ought not to be held, nor is such an Uposatha service allowed by me. Now, O Bhikkhus, the Uposatha service which is held lawfully (by a) complete (congregation), such an Uposatha service, O Bhikkhus, ought to be held, and such an Upo-

[1] For a definition of lawfulness and unlawfulness of the official functions of the Order as well as of completeness and incompleteness of the congregation by which such acts are performed, see IX, 3.

satha service is allowed by me. Therefore, O Bhikkhus, you ought to train yourselves thus: "The Uposatha service which is held lawfully (by a) complete (congregation), such an Uposatha service will we hold."'

15.

1. Now the Bhikkhus thought: 'How many ways are there of reciting the Pâtimokkha?'

They told this thing to the Blessed One.

'There are the following five ways of reciting the Pâtimokkha: The introduction[1] having been recited, as to the rest, it may be proclaimed: "Such and such rules are known (to the fraternity[2])." This is the first way of reciting the Pâtimokkha. The introduction having been recited, the four pârâ*g*ikâ dhammâ having been recited, as to the rest, it may be proclaimed: "Such and such rules are known (to the fraternity)." This is the second way of reciting the Pâtimokkha. The introduction having been recited, the four pârâ*g*ikâ dhammâ having been recited, the thirteen sa*m*ghâdisesâ dhammâ having been recited, . . . the introduction having been recited, the four pârâ*g*ikâ dhammâ having been recited, the thirteen sa*m*ghâdisesâ dhammâ having been recited, the two aniyatâ dhammâ having been recited, as to the rest, it may be pro-

[1] The introduction (nidâna) of the Pâtimokkha is the formula given above, chap. 3. 3.

[2] 'Avasesa*m* sutena sâvetabba*m*,' i.e. it is to be proclaimed: 'The four pârâ*g*ikâ dhammâ, &c., are known to the reverend brethren (literally, have been heard by the reverend brethren).'

claimed: "Such and such rules are known (to the fraternity)." This is the fourth way of reciting the Pâtimokkha. The fifth way is (to recite it) in its full extent. These, O Bhikkhus, are the five ways of reciting the Pâtimokkha.'

2. At that time the Bhikkhus, considering that the Blessed One had allowed to recite the Pâtimokkha abridged, always recited the Pâtimokkha abridged.

They told this thing to the Blessed One.

'You ought not, O Bhikkhus, to recite the Pâtimokkha abridged. He who does, commits a dukka*t*a offence.'

3. At that time a certain residence (of Bhikkhus) in the Kosala country was menaced on the day of Uposatha by savage people. The Bhikkhus were not able to recite the Pâtimokkha in its full extent.

They told this thing to the Blessed One.

'I allow you, O Bhikkhus, in the case of danger to recite the Pâtimokkha abridged.'

4. At that time the *Kh*abbaggiya Bhikkhus recited the Pâtimokkha abridged also when there was no danger.

They told this thing to the Blessed One.

'You ought not to recite the Pâtimokkha abridged, O Bhikkhus, if there is no danger. He who does, commits a dukka*t*a offence. I allow you, O Bhikkhus, in the case of danger only to recite the Pâtimokkha abridged. The cases of danger are the following: danger from kings, from robbers, from fire, from water, from human beings, from non-human beings, from beasts of prey, from creeping things, danger of life, danger against chastity. I ordain, O Bhikkhus, the recitation in such cases of danger of the Pâtimokkha abridged; if there is no danger, in its full extent.'

5. At that time the *Kh*abbaggiya Bhikkhus preached the Dhamma before the Sa*m*gha without being called upon (by the Thera).

They told this thing to the Blessed One.

'Let no one, O Bhikkhus, preach the Dhamma before the Sa*m*gha without being called upon. He who does, commits a dukka*t*a offence. I prescribe, O Bhikkhus, that the Thera is either to preach the Dhamma himself or to call upon another (Bhikkhu to do so).'

6. At that time the *Kh*abbaggiya Bhikkhus put questions about the Vinaya before the Sa*m*gha without being appointed thereto.

They told this thing to the Blessed One.

'Let no one, O Bhikkhus, put questions about the Vinaya before the Sa*m*gha without being appointed thereto. He who so questions, commits a dukka*t*a offence. I prescribe, O Bhikkhus, that an appointed (Bhikkhu) is to put questions about the Vinaya before the Sa*m*gha. And (this Bhikkhu) is to be appointed, O Bhikkhus, in this way: One may either appoint himself, or one may appoint another person.

7. 'And how is (a Bhikkhu) to appoint himself? Let a learned, competent Bhikkhu proclaim the following *ñ*atti before the Sa*m*gha: "Let the Sa*m*gha, reverend Sirs, hear me. If the Sa*m*gha is ready, I will question N. N. about the Vinaya." Thus one may appoint himself. And how is (a Bhikkhu) to appoint another person? Let a learned, competent Bhikkhu proclaim the following *ñ*atti before the Sa*m*gha: "Let the Sa*m*gha, &c. If the Sa*m*gha is

ready, let N. N. question N. N. about the Vinaya." Thus one may appoint another person.'

8. At that time appointed, clever Bhikkhus put questions about the Vinaya before the Sa*m*gha. The *Kh*abbaggiya Bhikkhus conceived anger (towards those Bhikkhus), conceived discontent, and threatened them with blows.

They told this thing to the Blessed One.

'I prescribe you, O Bhikkhus, that even he who has been appointed shall (not) put questions about the Vinaya before the Sa*m*gha (without) having looked at the assembly and weighed (with the mind each) person (present).'

9, 10. At that time the *Kh*abbaggiya Bhikkhus answered questions about the Vinaya before the Sa*m*gha without being appointed thereto.

They told this thing to the Blessed One.

'Let no one, O Bhikkhus, answer questions about the Vinaya before the Sa*m*gha without being appointed thereto. He who does, commits a dukka*t*a offence. I prescribe, O Bhikkhus, that questions about the Vinaya are to be answered before the Sa*m*gha (only) by an appointed (Bhikkhu). And (this Bhikkhu) is to be appointed[1], &c.'

11. At that time appointed, clever Bhikkhus answered questions about the Vinaya before the Sa*m*gha. The *Kh*abbaggiya Bhikkhus[2], &c.

---

[1] See §§ 6, 7. Read: '. . . I will answer the questions of N. N. about the Vinaya.' And, '. . . let N. N. answer the questions of N. N. about the Vinaya.'

[2] See § 8. Read: '. . . shall (not) answer questions about the Vinaya . . .'

16.

1. At that time the *Kh*abbaggiya Bhikkhus reproved for an offence a Bhikkhu who had not given them leave.

They told this thing to the Blessed One.

'No Bhikkhu, O Bhikkhus, who has not given leave, may be reproved for an offence. He who reproves (such a Bhikkhu), commits a dukka*t*a offence. I prescribe, O Bhikkhus, that you reprove (Bhikkhus) for an offence (only) after having asked for leave (by saying), "Give me leave, reverend brother, I wish to speak to you."'

2. At that time clever Bhikkhus reproved the *Kh*abbaggiya Bhikkhus for an offence after having asked for leave. The *Kh*abbaggiya Bhikkhus conceived anger (towards those Bhikkhus), conceived discontent, and threatened them with blows.

They told this thing to the Blessed One.

'I prescribe, O Bhikkhus, that you are (not) to reprove (a Bhikkhu) for an offence, even if he has given leave, (without) having weighed (with your mind) the person (concerned).'

3. At that time the *Kh*abbaggiya Bhikkhus, who thought: 'Otherwise clever Bhikkhus might ask us for leave (and reprove us for an offence),' themselves asked beforehand pure Bhikkhus who had committed no offence, for leave without object and reason.

They told this thing to the Blessed One.

'Let no pure Bhikkhus, O Bhikkhus, who have committed no offence, be asked for leave without object and reason. He who does, commits a dukka*t*a offence. I prescribe, O Bhikkhus, that you are (not) to ask for leave (without) having weighed (with your mind) the person (concerned).'

4. At that time the *Kh*abbaggiya Bhikkhus performed an unlawful official act before the Sa*m*gha.

They told this thing to the Blessed One.

'Let no one, O Bhikkhus, perform unlawful acts before the Sa*m*gha. He who does, commits a dukka*t*a offence.'

They performed an unlawful act nevertheless.

They told this thing to the Blessed One.

'I prescribe, O Bhikkhus, that you should protest, if an unlawful act is being performed.'

5. At that time clever Bhikkhus protested at an unlawful act being performed by the *Kh*abbaggiya Bhikkhus. The *Kh*abbaggiya Bhikkhus conceived anger, conceived discontent, and threatened (those Bhikkhus) with blows.

They told this thing to the Blessed One.

'I allow you, O Bhikkhus, to express your opinion only (instead of protesting formally).'

They expressed their opinion in the presence of the said (Bhikkhus). The *Kh*abbaggiya Bhikkhus conceived anger, conceived discontent, and threatened (them) with blows.

They told this thing to the Blessed One.

'I prescribe, O Bhikkhus, that four or five persons may protest, that two or three may express their opinion, and that one person may determine (in his mind): "I do not think this right."'

6. At that time the *Kh*abbaggiya Bhikkhus, when reciting the Pâtimokkha before the Sa*m*gha, intentionally recited it so that it could not be heard.

They told this thing to the Blessed One.

'Let not him who is to recite the Pâtimokkha,

O Bhikkhus, intentionally recite it so that it cannot be heard. He who does, commits a dukka*t*a offence.'

7. At that time the reverend Udâyi, who had a crow's voice, had the duty to recite the Pâtimokkha before the Sa*m*gha. Now the reverend Udâyi thought: 'It has been prescribed by the Blessed One that he who is to recite the Pâtimokkha, ought to recite it so that it may be heard; but I have a crow's voice. Well, how am I to act?'

They told this thing to the Blessed One.

'I prescribe, O Bhikkhus, that he who is to recite the Pâtimokkha may endeavour to make it audible. If he endeavours (to do so), he is free from offence.'

8. At that time Devadatta recited the Pâtimokkha before an assembly in which laymen were present.

They told this thing to the Blessed One.

'Let no one, O Bhikkhus, recite the Pâtimokkha before an assembly in which laymen are present. He who does, commits a dukka*t*a offence.'

9. At that time the *Kh*abbaggiya Bhikkhus recited the Pâtimokkha before the Sa*m*gha without being called upon (by the Thera).

They told this thing to the Blessed One.

'Let no one, O Bhikkhus, recite the Pâtimokkha before the Sa*m*gha without being called upon. He who does, commits a dukka*t*a offence. I prescribe, O Bhikkhus, that the Thera is master of the Pâtimokkha[1].'

End of the Bhâ*n*avâra of the A*ññ*atitthiyas[2].

[1] I. e. of reciting the Pâtimokkha himself or causing another Bhikkhu to do so.

[2] I. e. Sama*n*as belonging to other schools. See chap. 1.

17.

1. Then the Blessed One, after having dwelt near Râ*g*agaha as long as he thought fit, went forth on his pilgrimage to *K*odanâvatthu. Going from place to place on his pilgrimage, he came to *K*odanâvatthu. At that time there dwelt in a certain residence many Bhikkhus, the eldest of whom was an ignorant, unlearned person: he neither knew Uposatha, nor the Uposatha service, nor the Pâtimokkha, nor the recital of the Pâtimokkha.

2. Now those Bhikkhus thought: 'It has been prescribed by the Blessed One that the eldest Bhikkhu is master of the Pâtimokkha, and here the eldest of us is an ignorant, unlearned person: he neither knows Uposatha . . . nor the recital of the Pâtimokkha. Well, how are we to act?'

They told this thing to the Blessed One.

'I prescribe, O Bhikkhus, that (in such a case) that Bhikkhu who is (most) learned and competent, is to be made master of the Pâtimokkha.'

3. At that time there dwelt in a certain residence on the day of Uposatha many ignorant, unlearned Bhikkhus: they neither knew Uposatha . . . nor the recital of the Pâtimokkha. They called upon the Thera: 'May it please the Thera, reverend Sir, to recite the Pâtimokkha.' He replied: 'I am not competent to do so.' They called upon the next eldest, &c. He also replied, &c. They called upon the third eldest, &c. In this manner they called upon (all Bhikkhus) down to the youngest one: 'May it please the reverend brother to recite the Pâtimokkha.' He also replied: 'I am not competent, venerable Sirs, to do so.'

They told this thing to the Blessed One.

4, 5. 'When, O Bhikkhus, in a certain residence, &c.[1]; in that case, O Bhikkhus, these Bhikkhus are instantly to send one Bhikkhu to the neighbouring residence (of Bhikkhus): "Go, friend, and come back when you have learnt the Pâtimokkha abridged or in its full extent."'

6. Now the Bhikkhus thought: 'By whom is (this Bhikkhu) to be sent?'

They told this thing to the Blessed One.

'I prescribe, O Bhikkhus, that the Thera is to give order to a young Bhikkhu.'

The young Bhikkhus, having received that order from the Thera, did not go.

They told this thing to the Blessed One.

'Let no one who has been ordered by the Thera forbear to go, unless he be sick. He who does not go, commits a dukka*t*a offence.'

18.

1. Then the Blessed One, after having dwelt at *K*odanâvatthu as long as he thought fit, went back again to Râ*g*agaha. At that time the people asked the Bhikkhus who went about for alms: 'What day of the half month is this, reverend Sirs?' The Bhikkhus replied: 'We do not know, friends.' The people were annoyed, murmured, and became angry: 'Those Sakyaputtiya Sama*n*as do not even know how to count (the days of) the half month; what good things else will they know?'

[1] Here follows an exact repetition of the story told in § 3, which is given here, of course, in the present tense.

They told this thing to the Blessed One.

'I prescribe, O Bhikkhus, that you learn how to count (the days of) the half month.'

2. Now the Bhikkhus thought: 'Who ought to learn to count (the days of) the half month?'

They told this thing to the Blessed One.

'I prescribe, O Bhikkhus, that you learn all of you to count (the days of) the half month.'

3. At that time the people asked the Bhikkhus who went about for alms: 'How many Bhikkhus are there, reverend Sirs?' The Bhikkhus replied: 'We do not know, friends.' The people were annoyed, murmured, and became angry: 'Those Sakyaputtiya Sama*n*as do not even know each other; what good things else will they know?'

They told this thing to the Blessed One.

'I prescribe, O Bhikkhus, that you count the Bhikkhus.'

4. Now the Bhikkhus thought: 'At what time ought we to count the Bhikkhus?'

They told this thing to the Blessed One.

'I prescribe, O Bhikkhus, that you count (the Bhikkhus) on the day of Uposatha, either by way of (counting the single) troops (of which the assembly is composed)[1], or that you take (each of you) a ticket (and count those tickets).'

19.

At that time Bhikkhus who did not know that it was Uposatha day, went for alms to a distant village.

[1] This appears to be the meaning of ga*n*amaggena ga*n*etu*m*; Buddhaghosa has no note on this passage.

They came back when the Pâtimokkha was being recited, or when it just had been recited.

They told this thing to the Blessed One.

'I prescribe, O Bhikkhus, that you proclaim: "To-day is Uposatha."'

Now the Bhikkhus thought: 'Who is to proclaim so?'

They told this thing to the Blessed One.

'I prescribe, O Bhikkhus, that the Thera is to proclaim (the day of Uposatha) in due time.'

At that time a certain Thera did not think of it in due time.

They told this thing to the Blessed One.

'I allow you, O Bhikkhus, to proclaim it also at meal time.'

(The Thera) did not think of it at meal time either.

They told this thing to the Blessed One.

'I allow, O Bhikkhus, to proclaim it whenever (the Thera) thinks of it.'

20.

1. At that time the Uposatha hall in a certain residence was full of sweepings. The Bhikkhus who arrived there were annoyed, murmured, and became angry: 'How can the Bhikkhus neglect to sweep the Uposatha hall?'

They told this thing to the Blessed One.

'I prescribe, O Bhikkhus, that you sweep the Uposatha hall.'

2. Now the Bhikkhus thought: 'Well, who is to sweep the Uposatha hall?'

They told this thing to the Blessed One.

'I prescribe, O Bhikkhus, that the Thera is to order a young Bhikkhu (to sweep the Uposatha hall).'

The young Bhikkhus, having received that order from the Thera, did not sweep it.

They told this thing to the Blessed One.

'He who has been ordered by the Thera, ought not to forbear to sweep it, unless he be sick. He who does not sweep it, commits a dukka*t*a offence.'

3. At that time there were no seats prepared in the Uposatha hall. The Bhikkhus sat down on the ground. Their bodies and their robes became full of dust.

They told this thing to the Blessed One.

'I prescribe, O Bhikkhus, that you prepare seats in the Uposatha hall.'

Now the Bhikkhus thought, &c. (see § 2).

'He who does not prepare (seats), commits a dukka*t*a offence.'

4. At that time there was no lamp in the Uposatha hall. The Bhikkhus in the darkness trod upon (each other's) bodies and robes.

They told this thing to the Blessed One.

'I prescribe, O Bhikkhus, that you light a lamp in the Uposatha hall.'

Now the Bhikkhus thought, &c. (see § 2).

'He who does not light (the lamp), commits a dukka*t*a offence.'

5. At that time the resident Bhikkhus in a certair residence did not provide drink (i.e. water), nor did they provide food. The incoming Bhikkhus were annoyed, murmured, and became angry: 'How can the resident Bhikkhus neglect to provide for drink and to provide for food?'

They told this thing to the Blessed One.

'I prescribe, O Bhikkhus, that you provide drink and food.'

Now the Bhikkhus thought, &c. (see § 2).

'He who does not provide for it, commits a dukka*t*a offence.'

21.

1. At that time many ignorant, unlearned Bhikkhus who travelled to the (four) quarters (of the world) did not ask leave of their â*k*ariyas and upa*ggh*âyas (when going away).

They told this thing to the Blessed One.

'In case, O Bhikkhus, there are many ignorant, unlearned Bhikkhus who travel to the (four) quarters without asking leave of their â*k*ariyas and upa*gg*-*h*âyas; such Bhikkhus ought to be asked by their â*k*ariyas and upa*ggh*âyas: "Where will you go? with whom will you go?" If those ignorant, unlearned Bhikkhus name other ignorant, unlearned Bhikkhus, their â*k*ariyas and upa*ggh*âyas ought not to allow them (to go); if they allow them, they commit a dukka*t*a offence. If those ignorant, unlearned Bhikkhus go without the permission of their â*k*ariyas and upa*ggh*âyas, they commit a dukka*t*a offence.

2. 'In case, O Bhikkhus, there dwell in a certain residence many ignorant, unlearned Bhikkhus who neither know Uposatha, nor the Uposatha service, nor the Pâtimokkha, nor the recital of the Pâtimokkha: now there arrives (at that place) another Bhikkhu who is erudite, who has studied the âgamas (i. e. the collections of Suttas), who knows

the Dhamma, the Vinaya, the mâtikâ[1], who is wise, learned, intelligent, modest, conscientious[2], anxious for training; let those Bhikkhus, O Bhikkhus, kindly receive that Bhikkhu, let them show attention to him, exchange (friendly) words with him, provide him with powder, clay[3], a tooth-cleanser, and water to rinse his mouth with. If they do not receive him kindly, or show no attention to him, or do not exchange (friendly) words with him, or do not provide him with powder, clay, a tooth-cleanser, and water to rinse his mouth with, they commit a dukka*t*a offence.

3. 'In case, O Bhikkhus, there dwell in a certain residence on the day of Uposatha many ignorant, unlearned Bhikkhus who neither know Uposatha . . . nor the recital of the Pâtimokkha; let those Bhikkhus, O Bhikkhus, instantly send one Bhikkhu to the neighbouring residence (of Bhikkhus, saying), "Go, friend, and come back when you have learnt the Pâtimokkha abridged or in its full extent." If they succeed in this way, well and good. If they do not succeed, those Bhikkhus, O Bhikkhus, ought all to go to a residence where they (the Bhikkhus there) know Uposatha or the Uposatha service or the Pâtimokkha or the recital of the Pâtimokkha.

[1] Enumerations of terms indicating the different cases that come under a Vinaya rule or a dogmatical proposition are called mâtikâ; for instance, in discussing the first pârâ*g*ika rule the Vibhaṅga gives the following mâtikâpadâni: tisso itthiyo manussitthi amanussitthi tira*kkh*ânagatitthi, tayo ubhatovya*ñg*anakâ manussubhatovya*ñg*anako amanussubh. tira*kkh*ânagatubh., &c. Most of the works belonging to the Abhidhamma Pi*t*aka are based on and opened by such mâtikâ lists.

[2] Or 'scrupulous,' in good sense.

[3] See I, 25, 12, with our note.

If they do not go, they commit a dukka*t*a offence.

4. 'In case, O Bhikkhus, many ignorant, unlearned Bhikkhus keep vassa[1] in a certain residence who neither know, &c.[2] If they succeed in this way, well and good. If they do not succeed, they ought to send away one Bhikkhu for seven days' time (saying), "Go, friend, and come back when you have learnt the Pâtimokkha abridged or in its full extent." If they succeed in this way, well and good. If they do not succeed, those Bhikkhus, O Bhikkhus, ought not to keep vassa in that residence. If they do, they commit a dukka*t*a offence.'

22.

1. Then the Blessed One thus addressed the Bhikkhus: 'Assemble, O Bhikkhus, the Sa*m*gha will hold Uposatha.' When he had spoken thus, a certain Bhikkhu said to the Blessed One: 'There is a sick Bhikkhu, Lord, who is not present.'

'I prescribe, O Bhikkhus, that a sick Bhikkhu is to declare (lit. to give) his pârisuddhi[3]. And let it be declared, O Bhikkhus, in this way: Let that sick Bhikkhu go to one Bhikkhu, adjust his upper robe so as to cover one shoulder, sit down squatting, raise his joined hands, and say: "I declare my pârisuddhi, take my pârisuddhi, proclaim my pârisuddhi (before the fraternity)." Whether he

---

[1] See III, 1 seq. [2] See § 3.

[3] Pârisuddhi, literally, means purity. He declares that he is pure from the offences specified in the Pâtimokkha, and charges another Bhikkhu with proclaiming his declaration before the assembled chapter.

express this by gesture (lit. by his body), or by word, or by gesture and word, the pârisuddhi has been declared. If he does not express this by gesture, &c., the pârisuddhi has not been declared.

2. 'If (the sick Bhikkhu) succeeds in doing so, well and good. If he does not succeed, let them take that sick Bhikkhu, O Bhikkhus, on his bed or his chair to the assembly, and (then) let them hold Uposatha. If, O Bhikkhus, the Bhikkhus who are nursing the sick, think: "If we move this sick person from his place, the sickness will increase, or he will die," let them not move the sick, O Bhikkhus, from his place; let the Sa*m*gha go there and hold there Uposatha. But in no case are they to hold Uposatha with an incomplete congregation. If (a Bhikkhu) does so, he commits a dukka*t*a offence.

3. 'If he who has been charged with the pârisuddhi, O Bhikkhus, leaves the place at once[1], after the pârisuddhi has been entrusted (to him), the pârisuddhi ought to be declared to another. If he who has been charged with the pârisuddhi, O Bhikkhus, after the pârisuddhi has been entrusted to him, returns to the world[2] at once[1]; or dies; or admits that he is a sâma*n*era; or that he has abandoned the precepts[3]; or that he has become

[1] Literally, on the spot, i. e. without setting out on his way to the assembly.

[2] We have no doubt that this is the correct translation of vibbhamati (see I, 39, 5). The difference between vibbhamati (he returns to the world) and sikkha*m* pa*kk*akkhâti (he abandons the precepts) seems to be that the former is an informal, and the latter a formal, renunciation of the Order.

[3] The precepts are abandoned (sikkhâ pa*kk*akkhâtâ hoti) by declaring that one abandons the Buddha, or the Dhamma, or the

guilty of an extreme offence[1]; or that he is mad; or that his mind is unhinged; or that he suffers (bodily) pain; or that expulsion has been pronounced against him for his refusal to see an offence (committed by himself); or to atone for such an offence; or to renounce a false doctrine; or that he is a eunuch; or that he has furtively attached himself (to the Sa*m*gha); or that he is gone over to the Titthiyas; or that he is an animal[2]; or that he is guilty of matricide; or that he is guilty of parricide; or that he has murdered an Arahat; or that he has violated a Bhikkhunî; or that he has caused a schism among the Sa*m*gha; or that he has shed (a Buddha's) blood; or that he is a hermaphrodite: (in these cases) the pârisuddhi ought to be entrusted to another one.

4. 'If he who has been charged with the pârisuddhi, O Bhikkhus, after the pârisuddhi has been entrusted to him, and whilst he is on his way (to the assembly), leaves the place, or returns to the world, or dies, or admits that he is a sâma*n*era, &c., or admits that he is a hermaphrodite, the pârisuddhi has not been conveyed (to the Sa*m*gha). If he who has been charged with the pârisuddhi, O Bhikkhus, after the pârisuddhi has been entrusted to him, having arrived with the fraternity, leaves the place, or dies, &c., the pârisuddhi has

Sa*m*gha, or the Vinaya, &c. By such a declaration a Bhikkhu who wishes to return to a layman's life, or to go over to a Titthiya sect, gives up his character as a member of the Buddhist fraternity. The rules about the sikkhâpa*kk*akkhâna are given in the Vibhaṅga, in the explanation of the first pârâ*g*ika rule (chap. 8, § 2).

[1] Most probably antimavatthu refers to the pârâ*g*ika offences which require excommunication.

[2] See the story given in I, 63.

been conveyed. If he who has been charged with the pârisuddhi, O Bhikkhus, after the pârisuddhi has been entrusted to him, though he reaches the assembly, does not proclaim (the pârisuddhi he is charged with) because he falls asleep, or by carelessness, or because he attains (meditation), the pârisuddhi has been conveyed, and there is no offence on the part of him who has been charged with the pârisuddhi. If he who has been charged, &c., intentionally omits to proclaim (the pârisuddhi), the pârisuddhi has been conveyed, but he who has been charged with the pârisuddhi is guilty of a dukka*t*a offence.'

23.

Then the Blessed One thus addressed the Bhikkhus: 'Assemble, O Bhikkhus, the Sa*m*gha will perform an (official) act.' When he had spoken thus, a certain Bhikkhu said to the Blessed One: 'There is a sick Bhikkhu, Lord, who is not present.'

'I prescribe, O Bhikkhus, that a sick Bhikkhu is to declare (lit. to give) his consent (to the act to be performed), &c.[1] I prescribe, O Bhikkhus, that on the day of Uposatha he who declares his pârisuddhi is to declare his consent (to official acts to be performed eventually) also, for (both declarations) are required for the Sa*m*gha (and for the validity of its acts).

[1] The rules given here regarding the *kh*anda (declaration of consent of an absentee) that is required for the performance of official acts are word for word the same as those set out in chap. 22. 1–4, regarding the pârisuddhi required at the Uposatha service.

24.

1. At that time relations of a certain Bhikkhu seized him on the day of Uposatha.

They told this thing to the Blessed One.

'In case, O Bhikkhus, a certain Bhikkhu is seized on the day of Uposatha by relations of his, let the Bhikkhus say to those relations: "Pray, friends, let this Bhikkhu free for a moment until this Bhikkhu has held Uposatha."

2. 'If they succeed in this way, well and good. If they do not succeed, let the Bhikkhus say to those relations: "Pray, friends, stand apart for a moment, until this Bhikkhu has declared his pârisuddhi." If they succeed, well and good. If they do not succeed, let the Bhikkhus say to those relations: "Pray, friends, take this Bhikkhu for a moment outside the boundary, until the Samgha has held Uposatha." If they succeed, well and good. If they do not succeed, in no case is Uposatha to be held by an assembly that is incomplete. Should it be so held, (each Bhikkhu in the assembly) is guilty of a dukkata offence.

3. 'In case, O Bhikkhus, a certain Bhikkhu is seized on the day of Uposatha by kings, by robbers, by rascals, by hostile Bhikkhus, &c.[1]'

25.

1. Then the Blessed One thus addressed the Bhikkhus: 'Assemble, O Bhikkhus, the Samgha

[1] See §§ 1, 2.

has duties (official acts) to perform.' When he had spoken thus, a certain Bhikkhu said to the Blessed One: 'There is a mad Bhikkhu, Lord, called Gagga, who is not present.' 'There are, O Bhikkhus, two sorts of madmen: There is one mad Bhikkhu who now remembers the Uposatha, now does not remember it, who now remembers official acts (of the Order), now does not remember them, (and) there is (another mad Bhikkhu) who does not remember them; one who now goes to Uposatha, now does not go, who now goes to official acts, now does not go, (and another) who does not go.

2. 'Now, O Bhikkhus, that madman that now remembers, &c., that now goes to, &c., to such a madman I prescribe that you grant ummattakasammuti (i. e. the madman's leave).

3. 'And you ought, O Bhikkhus, to grant it in this way: Let a learned, competent Bhikkhu proclaim the following *ñatti* before the Sa*m*gha: "Let the Sa*m*gha, reverend Sirs, hear me. Gagga, a mad Bhikkhu, now remembers the Uposatha, now does not remember, &c., now goes to, &c.; if the Sa*m*gha is ready, let the Sa*m*gha grant ummattakasammuti to the mad Bhikkhu Gagga: let the Bhikkhu Gagga remember or not remember Uposatha, remember or not remember official acts (of the Order), let him go to Uposatha or not go, let him go to official acts or not go: (in every case) it may be free to the Sa*m*gha to hold Uposatha and to perform official acts with Gagga as well as without Gagga. This is the *ñatti*.

4. '"Let the Sa*m*gha, &c. Gagga, a mad Bhikkhu, &c.; the Sa*m*gha grants, &c. Thus I understand."'

26.

1. At that time four Bhikkhus dwelt in a certain residence (of Bhikkhus) on the day of Uposatha. Now these Bhikkhus thought: 'The Blessed One has prescribed the holding of Uposatha, and we are (only) four persons[1]. Well, how are we to hold Uposatha?'.

They told this thing to the Blessed One.

'I prescribe, O Bhikkhus, that four (Bhikkhus) may recite the Pâtimokkha.'

2. At that time three Bhikkhus dwelt in a certain residence (of Bhikkhus) at the day of Uposatha. Now these Bhikkhus thought: 'The Blessed One has prescribed to four (Bhikkhus) the reciting of the Pâtimokkha, and we are (only) three persons,' &c.

'I prescribe, O Bhikkhus, that three Bhikkhus may hold pârisuddhi-uposatha[2].

3. 'And it ought to be held in this way: Let a learned, competent Bhikkhu proclaim the following ñatti before those Bhikkhus: "Let the reverend brethren hear me. To-day is Uposatha, the fifteenth (day of the half month). If the reverend brethren are ready, let us hold pârisuddhi-uposatha with each other." Let the senior Bhikkhu adjust his upper robe so as to cover one shoulder, sit down squatting, raise his joined hands, and say to those Bhikkhus: "I am pure, friends, understand that I am pure, &c.[3]"

4. 'Let (each) younger Bhikkhu (in his turn) adjust

[1] The quorum for several official acts of the Order was five or more Bhikkhus; see IX, 4.

[2] Uposatha by mutual declaration of purity from the offences specified in the Pâtimokkha; see § 3 seq.

[3] The same phrase is repeated twice more.

his upper robe so as to cover one shoulder, sit down squatting, raise his joined hands, and say to those Bhikkhus: "I am pure, reverend Sirs, &c."'

5. At that time two Bhikkhus dwelt in a certain residence on the day of Uposatha. Now these Bhikkhus thought: 'The Blessed One has prescribed to four (Bhikkhus) the reciting of the Pâtimokkha, to three (Bhikkhus) the holding of pârisuddhi-uposatha, and we are (only) two persons,' &c.

'I prescribe, O Bhikkhus, that two persons may hold pârisuddhi-uposatha.'

6, 7. 'And it ought to be held in this way: Let the senior Bhikkhu, &c.[1]'

8. At that time there dwelt a single Bhikkhu in a certain residence on the day of Uposatha. Now this Bhikkhu thought, &c.

9. 'In case there dwell, O Bhikkhus, in a certain residence on the day of Uposatha a single Bhikkhu; let that Bhikkhu, O Bhikkhus, sweep the place which the Bhikkhus used to frequent, the refectory, or hall, or place at the foot of a tree; let him (then) provide water and food, prepare seats, put a lamp there, and sit down. If other Bhikkhus come, let him hold Uposatha with them; if they do not come, let him fix his mind upon the thought: "To-day is my Uposatha." If he does not fix his mind upon this thought, he commits a dukka*t*a offence.

10. 'Now, O Bhikkhus, where four Bhikkhus dwell (together), they must not convey the pârisuddhi[2] of one (to their assembly), and recite the

---

[1] See §§ 3, 4. The *ñ*atti prescribed in the preceding case does not apply to this case.

[2] See chap. 22.

Pâtimokkha by three. If they do, they commit a dukka*t*a offence.

'Now, O Bhikkhus, where three Bhikkhus dwell (together), they must not convey the pârisuddhi of one (to their assembly), and hold pârisuddhi-uposatha by two. If they do, they commit a dukka*t*a offence.

'Now, O Bhikkhus, where two Bhikkhus dwell, one of them must not convey the pârisuddhi of the other one, and fix (only) his thoughts (upon the Uposatha). If he does, he commits a dukka*t*a offence.'

27.

1. At that time a certain Bhikkhu was guilty of an offence on the day of Uposatha. Now this Bhikkhu thought: 'The Blessed One has prescribed: "Uposatha is not to be held by a Bhikkhu who is guilty of an offence[1]." Now I am guilty of an offence. What am I to do?'

They told this thing to the Blessed One.

'In case, O Bhikkhus, a certain Bhikkhu be guilty of an offence on the day of Uposatha; let that Bhikkhu, O Bhikkhus, go to one Bhikkhu, adjust his upper robe so as to cover one shoulder, sit down squatting, raise his joined hands, and say: "I have committed, friend, such and such an offence; I confess that offence." Let the other say: "Do you see it?" "Yes, I see it." "Refrain from it in future."

2. 'In case, O Bhikkhus, there be a Bhikkhu on the day of Uposatha who feels doubt with regard

[1] See *K*ullavagga IX, 2.

to an offence; let this Bhikkhu, O Bhikkhus, go to one Bhikkhu, &c. (§ 1), and say: "I feel doubt, friend, with regard to such and such an offence. When I shall feel no doubt, then I will atone for that offence." Having spoken thus, let him hold Uposatha and hear the Pâtimokkha. But in no case must there be any hindrance to holding Uposatha from such a cause.'

3. At that time the *Kh*abbaggiya Bhikkhus confessed in common an offence (shared by them all).

They told this thing to the Blessed One.

'You ought not, O Bhikkhus, to confess an offence in common. He who does so, commits a dukka*t*a offence.'

At that time the *Kh*abbaggiya Bhikkhus accepted the common confession of an offence (shared by several Bhikkhus).

They told this thing to the Blessed One.

'You ought not, O Bhikkhus, to accept the common confession of an offence. He who does so, commits a dukka*t*a offence.'

4. At that time a certain Bhikkhu remembered an offence, while Pâtimokkha was being recited. Now this Bhikkhu thought: 'The Blessed One has prescribed: "Uposatha is not to be held by (a Bhikkhu) who is guilty of an offence." Now I am guilty of an offence. What am I to do?'

They told this thing to the Blessed One.

'In case, O Bhikkhus, there be a Bhikkhu who remembers an offence, while Pâtimokkha is being recited; let this Bhikkhu, O Bhikkhus, say to his neighbour Bhikkhu: "I have committed such and such an offence, friend; when I have arisen from this (assembly), I will atone for that offence." Having spoken thus, &c. (§ 2).

5. 'In case, O Bhikkhus, there be a Bhikkhu who feels doubt with regard to an offence, while Pâtimokkha is being recited, &c. (§§ 2, 4).'

6. At that time the whole Sa*m*gha in a certain residence was guilty of a common offence on the day of Uposatha. Now these Bhikkhus thought: 'The Blessed One has prescribed that offences (shared by many Bhikkhus) are not to be confessed in common, and that the common confession of such offences is not to be accepted. Now this whole Sa*m*gha is guilty of a common offence. What are we to do?'

They told this thing to the Blessed One.

'In case, O Bhikkhus, the whole Sa*m*gha in a certain residence is guilty of a common offence on the day of Uposatha; let those Bhikkhus, O Bhikkhus, send instantly one Bhikkhu to the neighbouring residence of Bhikkhus (saying), "Go, friend, and come back when you have atoned for that offence (for yourself); we will (then) atone for the offence before you."

7. 'If they succeed in this way, well and good. If they do not succeed, let a learned, competent Bhikkhu proclaim the following *ñ*atti before the Sa*m*gha: "Let the Sa*m*gha, reverend Sirs, hear me. This whole Sa*m*gha is guilty of a common offence. When it shall see another pure, guiltless Bhikkhu, it will atone for the offence before him." (One of the Bhikkhus) having spoken thus, let them hold Uposatha and recite the Pâtimokkha. But in no case must there be any hindrance to holding Uposatha from such a cause.

8. 'In case, O Bhikkhus, the whole Sa*m*gha in a certain residence feels doubt with regard to a

common offence on the day of Uposatha; (in this case) let a learned, competent Bhikkhu proclaim the following *ñatti* before the Sa*m*gha: "Let the Sa*m*gha, reverend Sirs, hear me. This whole Sa*m*gha feels doubt with regard to a common offence. When it will feel no doubt, it will atone for that offence." (One of the Bhikkhus) having spoken thus, &c.

9. 'In case, O Bhikkhus, in a certain residence the Sa*m*gha that has entered (there) upon *vassa* is guilty of a common offence. Those Bhikkhus, O Bhikkhus, are instantly, &c. (§§ 6, 7). If they do not succeed, let them send away one Bhikkhu for seven days' time: "Go, friend, and come back when you have atoned for that offence (for yourself); we will (then) atone for the offence before you."'

10. At that time the whole Sa*m*gha in a certain residence was guilty of a common offence, and did not know the name nor the class to which that offence belonged. Now there arrived (at that place) another Bhikkhu, &c. (see chap. 21. 2), anxious for training. To that Bhikkhu one of the Bhikkhus went, and having gone to him, he said to him: 'He who does such and such a thing, friend, what sort of offence does he commit?'

11. He replied: 'He who does such and such a thing, friend, commits such and such an offence. If you have committed such an offence, friend, atone for that offence.' The other replied: 'Not I myself alone, friend, am guilty of that offence; this whole Sa*m*gha is guilty of that offence.' He said: 'What is it to you, friend, whether another is guilty or guiltless? Come, friend, atone for your own offence.'

12. Now this Bhikkhu, after having atoned for

that offence by the advice of that Bhikkhu, went to those Bhikkhus (to his brethren who shared in the same offence); having gone to them, he said to those Bhikkhus: 'He who does such and such a thing, friends, commits such and such an offence. As you have committed such an offence, friends, atone for that offence.' Now those Bhikkhus refused to atone for that offence by that Bhikkhu's advice.

They told this thing to the Blessed One.

13, 14. 'In case, O Bhikkhus, the whole Sa*m*gha in a certain residence is guilty of a common offence, &c. (§§ 10, 11)—

15. 'If this Bhikkhu, O Bhikkhus, after having atoned for that offence by the advice of that Bhikkhu, goes to those Bhikkhus, and having gone to them, says to those Bhikkhus: "He who does, &c.," and if those Bhikkhus, O Bhikkhus, atone for that offence by that Bhikkhu's advice, well and good; if they do not atone for it, that Bhikkhu, O Bhikkhus, need not say anything (further) to those Bhikkhus, if he does not like.'

End of the Bhâ*n*avâra on *K*odanâvatthu.

28.

1. At that time there assembled in a certain residence (of Bhikkhus) at the day of Uposatha a number of resident Bhikkhus, four or more. They did not know that there were other resident Bhikkhus absent. Intending to act according to Dhamma and Vinaya, thinking themselves to be complete while (really) incomplete, they held Uposatha and

recited the Pâtimokkha. While they were reciting the Pâtimokkha, other resident Bhikkhus, a greater number (than the first ones), arrived.

They told this thing to the Blessed One.

2. 'In case, O Bhikkhus, there assemble in a certain residence at the day of Uposatha, &c. (§ 1); while they are reciting the Pâtimokkha, other resident Bhikkhus, a greater number, arrive; let those Bhikkhus, O Bhikkhus, recite the Pâtimokkha again; they who have recited it, are free from guilt.

3. 'In case, O Bhikkhus, there assemble, &c.; while they are reciting the Pâtimokkha, other resident Bhikkhus, exactly the same number (as the first ones), arrive; in that case (the part of the Pâtimokkha) that has been recited, has been correctly recited; let those (who have arrived late), hear the rest; they who have recited it, are free from guilt.

'In case, O Bhikkhus, there assemble, &c.; while they are reciting the Pâtimokkha, other resident Bhikkhus, a smaller number, arrive, &c.[1]

4. 'In case, O Bhikkhus, there assemble, &c.; when they have just finished the recital of the Pâtimokkha, other resident Bhikkhus, &c.[2]

---

[1] The decision given for the case of a smaller number of Bhikkhus arriving late, is here, and invariably throughout the following exposition, identical with the decision of the case of the number of Bhikkhus being equal on the two sides.

[2] The same three cases are distinguished here as in §§ 2, 3, according as the number of Bhikkhus who are late, is greater, the same, or smaller than that of the other Bhikkhus. The first case is decided by Buddha as above; in the decision of the second and third cases, instead of 'let those (who have arrived late) hear the rest,' read: 'let those (who have arrived late) proclaim their pârisuddhi in the presence (of the other brethren).'

5. 'In case, O Bhikkhus, there assemble, &c.; when they have just finished the recital of the Pâtimokkha, and the assembly has not yet risen, other resident Bhikkhus, &c.[1]

6. 'In case, O Bhikkhus, there assemble, &c.; when they have just finished the recital of the Pâtimokkha, and a part of the assembly has risen, &c.[1]

7. 'In case, O Bhikkhus, there assemble, &c.; when they have just finished the recital of the Pâtimokkha, and the whole assembly has risen, &c.[1]'

End of the fifteen cases in which there is no offence.

29.

'In case, O Bhikkhus, there assemble in a certain residence on the day of Uposatha a number of resident Bhikkhus, four or more; they know that there are other resident Bhikkhus absent; intending to act according to Dhamma and Vinaya, incomplete, conscious of their incompleteness, they hold Uposatha and recite the Pâtimokkha; &c.[2]'

End of the fifteen cases of the incompletely assembled Bhikkhus who are conscious of their incompleteness.

[1] The three triads of §§ 5, 6, 7 agree exactly with the triad of § 4.

[2] Here follow fifteen cases which are arranged exactly as in chap. 28. Instead of 'they who have recited it, are free from guilt,' read: 'they who have recited it, have committed a dukka*t*a offence.'

30.

'In case, O Bhikkhus, there assemble, &c.; they know that there are other resident Bhikkhus absent. Feeling doubt as to whether they are competent to hold Uposatha or not competent, they hold Uposatha and recite the Pâtimokkha, &c.[1]'

End of the fifteen cases of the Bhikkhus who feel doubt.

31.

'In case, O Bhikkhus, there assemble, &c.; they know that there are other resident Bhikkhus absent. (Thinking): "We are competent to hold Uposatha, we are not incompetent," they abandon themselves to misbehaviour, hold Uposatha, and recite the Pâtimokkha, &c.[1]'

End of the fifteen cases of the Bhikkhus abandoning themselves to misbehaviour.

32.

'In case, O Bhikkhus, there assemble, &c.; they know that there are other resident Bhikkhus absent. They perish and become ruined[2], saying, "What are those people to us?" and risking a schism

[1] The decision of these fifteen cases is the same as in chap. 29.
[2] I. e. they destroy their own welfare by their wickedness.

(among the fraternity), they hold Uposatha and recite the Pâtimokkha, &c.[1]'

End of the fifteen cases of the Bhikkhus risking a schism.

End of the seventy-five[2] cases.

33.

'In case, O Bhikkhus, there assemble in a certain residence on the day of Uposatha a number of resident Bhikkhus, four or more; they know that other resident Bhikkhus are about to enter the boundary. They know that other resident Bhikkhus have entered within the boundary. They see other resident Bhikkhus who are about to enter, &c., who have entered within the boundary. They hear that other resident Bhikkhus are about to enter, &c., have entered within the boundary.'

Thus[3] a hundred and seventy-five systems of triads are produced which refer to resident and resident

[1] The decisions as in chap. 29; only read instead of 'dukka*t*a offence,' 'thulla*kk*aya offence' (grave sin).

[2] Five times fifteen cases, in chaps. 28–32.

[3] Remarks like this, which indicate the rules for supplying abbreviated passages, do not belong, strictly speaking, to the text of the Vinaya itself, but form a posterior addition, as is shown also by grammatical peculiarities. In chaps. 28–32 we have seventy-five cases, or twenty-five triads; all of these triads contain the words: 'They know that there are other resident Bhikkhus absent.' By successively varying these words six times, as is indicated in chap. 33, we obtain a hundred and seventy-five triads.

Bhikkhus[1]. (Then follow the same cases with regard to) resident and incoming Bhikkhus, incoming and resident Bhikkhus, incoming and incoming Bhikkhus. By putting these words (successively) into the peyyâla[2], seven hundred triads are produced.

34.

1. 'In case, O Bhikkhus, the resident Bhikkhus count the day as the fourteenth (of the pakkha), the incoming Bhikkhus as the fifteenth[3]; if the number of the resident Bhikkhus is greater, the incoming Bhikkhus ought to accommodate themselves to the resident Bhikkhus. If their number is equal, the incoming Bhikkhus ought to accommodate themselves to the resident Bhikkhus. If the number of the incoming Bhikkhus is greater, the resident Bhikkhus ought to accommodate themselves to the incoming Bhikkhus.

2. 'In case, O Bhikkhus, the resident Bhikkhus count the day as the fifteenth, the incoming Bhikkhus as the fourteenth; if, &c. (§ 1).

---

[1] I. e. the assembled Bhikkhus as well as the incoming reside in the same âvâsa.

[2] 'Peyyâla' is identical in meaning and, we believe, etymologically with 'pariyâya.' See Childers s. v.; H. O.'s remarks in Kuhn's Zeitschrift für vergleichende Sprachforschung, vol. xxv, 324; Trenckner, Pali Miscellany, p. 66.

[3] Buddhaghosa: 'They who count the day as the fifteenth, arrive from a distant kingdom, or they have held the preceding Uposatha on the fourteenth.' It seems to follow from this remark of Buddhaghosa that after an Uposatha on the fourteenth invariably an Uposatha on the fifteenth must follow, i. e. the Uposatha may not be held on the fourteenth ad libitum, but only in the second pakkha of the short months. Compare chap. 4 and the note on chap. 1. 1.

3. 'In case, O Bhikkhus, the resident Bhikkhus count the day as the first (of the pakkha), the incoming Bhikkhus as the fifteenth (of the preceding pakkha); if the number of the resident Bhikkhus is greater, the resident Bhikkhus need not, if they do not like, admit the incoming ones to their communion; let the incoming Bhikkhus go outside the boundary and hold (there) Uposatha. If their number is equal, &c. (as in the preceding case). If the number of the incoming Bhikkhus is greater, let the resident Bhikkhus either admit the incoming ones to their communion or go outside the boundary.

4. 'In case, O Bhikkhus, the resident Bhikkhus count the day as the fifteenth, the incoming Bhikkhus as the first (of the following pakkha); if the number of the resident Bhikkhus is greater, let the incoming Bhikkhus either admit the resident Bhikkhus to their communion or go outside the boundary. If their number is equal, &c. (as in the preceding case). If the number of the incoming Bhikkhus is greater, the incoming Bhikkhus need not, if they do not like, admit the resident Bhikkhus to their communion; let the resident Bhikkhus go outside the boundary and hold Uposatha (there).

5. 'In case, O Bhikkhus, the incoming Bhikkhus see the signs, the tokens, the marks, the characteristics of (the presence of) resident Bhikkhus, well prepared beds and chairs and mats and pillows, food and water well provided for, well swept cells; seeing this, they begin to doubt: "Are there here any resident Bhikkhus or are there not?"—

6. 'Being doubtful they do not search, having not searched they hold Uposatha: this is a dukkata offence. Being doubtful they search, searching they

do not see them, not seeing them they hold Uposatha: (in this case) they are free from offence. Being doubtful they search, searching they see them, seeing them they hold Uposatha together: (in this case) they are free from offence. Being doubtful they search, searching they see them, seeing them they hold Uposatha apart: this is a dukka*t*a offence. Being doubtful they search, searching they see them, seeing them they perish and become ruined[1], saying, "What are those people to us?" and risking a schism, they hold Uposatha: this is a thulla*kk*aya (grave) offence.

7. 'In case, O Bhikkhus, the incoming Bhikkhus hear the signs &c. of (the presence of) resident Bhikkhus, the sound of their footsteps when they are walking, the sound of their rehearsal (of the Dhamma), of their clearing the throat and sneezing; hearing this they begin to doubt, &c. (§§ 5, 6).

8. 'In case, O Bhikkhus, the resident Bhikkhus see the signs &c. of (the presence of) incoming Bhikkhus, unknown bowls, unknown robes, unknown seats, (the traces of) foot-washing, water sprinkled about; seeing this they begin to doubt, &c.

9. 'In case, O Bhikkhus, the resident Bhikkhus hear the signs &c. of (the presence of) incoming Bhikkhus, the sound of their footsteps when they are arriving, the sound of their shaking out their shoes, clearing the throat, and sneezing; hearing this, &c.

10. 'In case, O Bhikkhus, the incoming Bhikkhus see resident Bhikkhus belonging to a different district; they take them as belonging to the same district; taking them as belonging to the same district

[1] See chap. 32.

they do not ask; having not asked, they hold Uposatha together: (in this case) they are free from offence. They ask; having asked, they do not go through the matter; having not gone through the matter, they hold Uposatha together: this is a dukka*t*a offence. They ask, &c. (as in the last case), they hold Uposatha apart: (in this case) they are free from offence.

11. 'In case, O Bhikkhus, the incoming Bhikkhus see resident Bhikkhus belonging to the same district. They take them as belonging to a different district; taking them, &c. they do not ask; having not asked, they hold Uposatha together: this is a dukka*t*a offence. They ask; having asked, they go through the matter; having gone through the matter, they hold Uposatha apart: this is a dukka*t*a offence. They ask, &c. (as in the last case), they hold Uposatha together: (in this case) they are free from offence.

12. 'In case, O Bhikkhus, the resident Bhikkhus see incoming Bhikkhus belonging to a different district, &c. (see § 10).

13. 'In case, O Bhikkhus, the resident Bhikkhus see incoming Bhikkhus belonging to the same district, &c. (see § 11).'

35.

1. 'You ought not, O Bhikkhus, to go on the day of Uposatha from a residence in which Bhikkhus are, to a residence in which no Bhikkhus are, except with a Sa*m*gha[1] or in a case of danger[2]. You ought not,

[1] I.e. with a number of Bhikkhus sufficient for holding Uposatha.
[2] See chap. 15. 4.

O Bhikkhus, to go on the day of Uposatha from a residence in which Bhikkhus are, to a non-residence in which no Bhikkhus are, except, &c. You ought not, O Bhikkhus, to go on the day of Uposatha from a residence in which Bhikkhus are, to a residence or non-residence[1] in which no Bhikkhus are, except, &c.

2. 'You ought not, O Bhikkhus, to go on the day of Uposatha from a non-residence in which Bhikkhus are, to a residence, &c., to a non-residence, &c., to a residence or non-residence in which no Bhikkhus are, except, &c.

3. 'You ought not, O Bhikkhus, to go on the day of Uposatha from a residence or non-residence in which Bhikkhus are, to a residence, &c., to a non-residence, &c., to a residence or non-residence in which no Bhikkhus are, except, &c.

4. 'You ought not, O Bhikkhus, to go on the day of Uposatha from a residence in which Bhikkhus are, to a residence in which Bhikkhus are, if these Bhikkhus belong to a different district, except, &c.[2]

5. 'You may go, O Bhikkhus, on the day of Uposatha from a residence in which Bhikkhus are, to a residence in which Bhikkhus are, if these Bhikkhus belong to the same district, and if you know: "I can attain that place to-day." You may, &c.[2]'

36.

1. 'Let no one, O Bhikkhus, recite the Pâtimokkha in a seated assembly (of Bhikkhus) before a Bhikkhunî. He who does, commits a dukka*t*a

[1] Probably this means a place the quality of which, whether residence or non-residence, is doubtful.

[2] Nine cases are distinguished here quite as in §§ 1–3.

offence. Let no one, O Bhikkhus, recite the Pâtimokkha in a seated assembly (of Bhikkhus) before a sikkhamânâ[1], a sâma*n*era, a sâma*n*erî, one who has abandoned the precepts[2], one who is guilty of an extreme offence[2]. He who does, commits a dukka*t*a offence.

2. 'Let no one, O Bhikkhus, recite the Pâtimokkha in a seated assembly (of Bhikkhus) before a (Bhikkhu) against whom expulsion has been pronounced for his refusal to see an offence (committed by himself), before a (Bhikkhu) against whom expulsion has been pronounced for his refusal to atone for such an offence, or for his refusal to renounce a false doctrine. He who does, is to be treated according to the law[3].

3. 'Let no one, O Bhikkhus, recite the Pâtimokkha in a seated assembly (of Bhikkhus) before a eunuch, before one who has furtively attached himself (to the Sa*m*gha), &c. (see chap. 22. 3), before a hermaphrodite. He who does, commits a dukka*t*a offence.

---

[1] In the Bhikkhunîkhandhaka (*K*ullav. X, 1, 4) we are told that Buddha, when admitting women to the Order of mendicants, prescribed for them a probationary course of instruction, which should last two years, after which time they were to ask for the upasampadâ ordination. During these two years the candidates were called sikkhamâ*n*âs. Childers (Dict. s.v. sikkhati) has misunderstood the Mahâva*m*sa (p. 37), when he states that in the case of Asoka's daughter Sa*m*ghamittâ the training prescribed for the sikkhamânâs was absolved in a single day.

[2] See the note on chap. 22. 3.

[3] The law alluded to most probably is the 69th Pâ*k*ittiya rule, which expressly treats only of the conduct towards Bhikkhus refusing to renounce false doctrines, but it may be extended by analogy also to the two other categories of Bhikkhus mentioned in our passage.

4. 'Let no one, O Bhikkhus, hold Uposatha by (accepting) the pârisuddhi declaration[1] of a pârivâsika[2], except if the assembly has not yet risen (at the time when the pârisuddhi is declared). And let no one, O Bhikkhus, hold Uposatha on another day than the Uposatha day, except for the sake of (declaring the re-establishment of) concord among the Sa*m*gha[3].'

End of the third Bhâ*n*avâra in the Uposatha-khandhaka.

---

[1] See chap. 22.

[2] I. e. a Bhikkhu subject to the penal discipline of parivâsa, the rules of which are discussed at length in the second and third books of the *K*ullavagga.

[3] If a schism among the fraternity has been composed, the reconciled parties hold Uposatha together (X, 5, 14).

THIRD KHANDHAKA.

(RESIDENCE DURING THE RAINY SEASON, VASSA.)

1.

1. At that time the Blessed One dwelt at Râ*g*agaha, in the Ve*l*uvana, in the Kalandakanivâpa[1]. At that time the retreat during the rainy season had not yet been instituted by the Blessed One for the Bhikkhus. Thus the Bhikkhus went on their travels alike during winter, summer, and the rainy season.

2. People were annoyed, murmured, and became angry, saying, 'How can the Sakyaputtiya Sama*n*as go on their travels alike during winter, summer, and the rainy season? They crush the green herbs, they hurt vegetable life[2], they destroy the life of many small living things. Shall the ascetics who belong to Titthiya schools, whose doctrine is ill preached, retire during the rainy season and arrange places for themselves to live in[3]? shall the birds make their nests on the summits of the trees, and retire during

---

[1] See the note on I, 22, 17. About the name of Kalandakanivâpa (seeds of Kalandaka? feeding ground for squirrels?), see the story related in Beal, Romantic Legend, &c., p. 315, where this place is said to be the gift of a merchant named Kalandaka. A different account is given by Spence Hardy, Manual, p. 194.

[2] Literally, living creatures which have but one organ of sense; that is, which have only the organ of feeling, viz. the outward form (kâya).

[3] Sa*m*kâpayissanti = sa*m*kappayissanti? Buddhaghosa: appossukka-nibaddha-vâsa*m* vasissanti.

the rainy season, and arrange themselves places to live in; and yet the Sakyaputtiya Samaṇas go on their travels alike during winter, summer, and the rainy season, crushing the green herbs, hurting vegetable life, and destroying the life of many small things?'

3. Now some Bhikkhus heard those people that were annoyed, murmured, and had become angry.

These Bhikkhus told this thing to the Blessed One.

In consequence of that and on this occasion the Blessed One, after having delivered a religious discourse, thus addressed the Bhikkhus:

'I prescribe, O Bhikkhus, that you enter upon Vassa[1].'

2.

1. Now the Bhikkhus thought: 'When are we to enter upon Vassa?'

They told this thing to the Blessed One.

'I prescribe, O Bhikkhus, that you enter upon Vassa in the rainy season.'

2. Then the Bhikkhus thought: 'How many periods are there for entering upon Vassa?'

They told this thing to the Blessed One.

'There are two periods, O Bhikkhus, for entering upon Vassa, the earlier and the later. The earlier time for entering (upon Vassa) is the day after the

---

[1] I. e. enter upon the retreat prescribed for the rainy season. Buddhaghosa: 'They are to look after their Vihâra (if it is in a proper state), to provide food and water for themselves, to fulfil all due ceremonies, such as paying reverence to sacred shrines, &c., and to say loudly once, or twice, or thrice: 'I enter upon Vassa in this Vihâra for these three months." Thus they are to enter upon Vassa.'

full moon of Âsâ*lh*a (June–July); the later, a month after the full moon of Âsâ*lh*a[1]. These, O Bhikkhus, are the two periods for entering upon Vassa.'

3.

1. At that time the *Kh*abbaggiya Bhikkhus, having entered upon Vassa, went on their travels during the period of Vassa. People were annoyed, murmured, and became angry (saying), 'How can the Sakyaputtiya Sama*n*as go on their travels alike during winter, summer, and the rainy season, ... (&c., as in chap. 1. 2, down to:) and destroy the life of many small living things?'

2. Now some Bhikkhus heard those people that were annoyed, murmured, and had become angry. The moderate Bhikkhus were annoyed, murmured, and became angry (saying), 'How can the *Kh*abbaggiya Bhikkhus, having entered upon Vassa, go on their travels during the period of Vassa?'

These Bhikkhus told this thing to the Blessed One.

---

[1] Very probably this double period stands in connection with the double period prescribed in the Brâhma*n*as and Sûtras for most of the Vedic festivals. Thus the sacrifice of the varu*n*apraghâsâs, with which the Brahmans began the rainy season, was to be held either on the full moon day of Âshâ*dh*a or on the full moon day of the following month, *S*râva*n*a, quite in accordance with the Buddhistical rules about the vassupanâyikâ. The Brâhma*n*a texts begin the year with the full moon day of the (uttarâ) Phâlgunî; the Sûtras mention, besides the Phâlgunî, another new-year's day, the *K*aitrî paur*n*amâsî, which falls one month later. It was in connection with this dislocation of the beginning of the year that the annual festivals could be postponed accordingly. See Weber, Die vedischen Nachrichten von den Naxatra, II, p. 329 seq.

In consequence of that and on this occasion the Blessed One, after having delivered a religious discourse, thus addressed the Bhikkhus:

'Let no one, O Bhikkhus, who has entered upon Vassa, go on his travels before he has kept Vassa during the earlier or during the later three months. He who does so, commits a dukka*t*a offence.'

4.

1. At that time the *Kh*abbaggiya Bhikkhus were not willing to enter upon Vassa.

They told this thing to the Blessed One.

'Let no one, O Bhikkhus, forbear to enter upon Vassa. He who does not enter upon Vassa, commits a dukka*t*a offence.'

2. At that time the *Kh*abbaggiya Bhikkhus, who were not willing to enter upon Vassa on the prescribed day, purposely left the district (where they were living).

They told this thing to the Blessed One.

'Let no one, O Bhikkhus, purposely leave the district (where he is living), because he is not willing to enter upon Vassa on the prescribed day. He who does, commits a dukka*t*a offence.'

3. At that time the Magadha king Seniya Bimbisâra, who wished that the Vassa period might be postponed, sent a messenger to the Bhikkhus: 'What if their reverences were to enter upon Vassa on the next full moon day?'

They told this thing to the Blessed One.

'I prescribe, O Bhikkhus, that you obey kings.'

5.

1. And the Blessed One, after having resided at Râgagaha as long as he thought fit, went forth to Sâvatthi. Wandering from place to place he came to Sâvatthi. There, at Sâvatthi, the Blessed One dwelt in the *G*etavana, the garden of Anâthapi*nd*ika.

At that time an upâsaka (lay devotee) named Udena, in the Kosala country, had a Vihâra built for the Sa*m*gha. He sent a messenger to the Bhikkhus (saying), 'Might their reverences come hither; I desire to bestow gifts (on the Sa*m*gha) and to hear the Dhamma and to see the Bhikkhus.'

2. The Bhikkhus replied: 'The Blessed One has prescribed, friend, that no one who has entered upon Vassa, may go on a journey before he has kept Vassa during the earlier or during the later three months. Let the upâsaka Udena wait so long as the Bhikkhus keep their Vassa residence; when they have finished Vassa, they will go. But if there is any urgent necessity, let him dedicate the Vihâra in presence of the Bhikkhus who reside there.'

3. The upâsaka Udena was annoyed, murmured, and became angry (saying), 'How can their reverences, when I send for them, refuse to come? I am a giver and a doer (of good works), and do service to the fraternity.' Some Bhikkhus heard the upâsaka Udena, who was annoyed, &c.

These Bhikkhus told the thing to the Blessed One.

4. In consequence of that the Blessed One, after having delivered a religious discourse, thus addressed the Bhikkhus:

'I allow you, O Bhikkhus, to go (even during

the rainy season), if the affair for which you go can be accomplished in seven days, and if you are sent for, but not if you are not sent for, by a person of one of the following seven classes: Bhikkhus, Bhikkhunîs, sikkhamânâs[1], sâma*n*eras, sâma*n*erîs, lay devotees, female lay devotees. I allow you, O Bhikkhus, to go, if the thing (you go for) can be accomplished in seven days, and if you are sent for, but not if you are not sent for, by a person of one of these seven classes. Within seven days you ought to return.

5. 'In case, O Bhikkhus, an upâsaka has built a Vihâra for the Sa*m*gha. If he sends a messenger to the Bhikkhus (saying), "Might their reverences come hither; I desire to bestow gifts (on them) and to hear the Dhamma and to see the Bhikkhus," you ought to go, O Bhikkhus, if the affair for which you go can be accomplished in seven days, and if he sends for you, but not if he does not send for you. Within seven days you ought to return.

6. 'In case, O Bhikkhus, an upâsaka has built for the Sa*m*gha an a*ddh*ayoga[2], has built a storied house, has built an attic, has constructed a cave, a cell, a store-room, a refectory, a fire-room, a warehouse[3], a privy, a place to walk in, a house to walk in, a well, a well house, a *g*antâghara[4], a *g*antâghara room[5], a lotus-pond, a pavilion, a park; or

[1] See the note on II, 36, 1.

[2] See the note on I, 30, 4.

[3] This translation of kappiyaku*t*î is merely conjectural; comp. kappiyabhûmî VI, 33.

[4] See the note on I, 25, 12.

[5] See *K*ullavagga V, 16, 1.

has prepared the site for a park. If he sends a messenger to the Bhikkhus, ... (&c., as in § 5, down to the end of the section).

7. 'In case, O Bhikkhus, an upâsaka has built for a number of Bhikkhus an a*ddh*ayoga . . . . (&c., as in § 6 to the end of the section), ... for one Bhikkhu a Vihâra, an a*ddh*ayoga, a storied house . . . . (&c., as in § 6 to the end).

8. 'In case, O Bhikkhus, an upâsaka has built for the sisterhood of Bhikkhunîs, &c., for a number of Bhikkhunîs, for one Bhikkhunî, for a number of sikkhamânâs, for one sikkhamânâ, for a number of sâma*n*eras, for one sâma*n*era, for a number of sâma*n*erîs, for one sâma*n*erî a Vihâra, &c.[1] If he sends a messenger to the Bhikkhus, &c.

9. 'In case, O Bhikkhus, an upâsaka has built for his own use a residence, a sleeping room, a stable[2], a tower, a one-peaked building[3], a shop, a boutique, a storied house, an attic, a cave, a cell, a store-room, a refectory, a fire-room, a kitchen, a privy, a place to walk in, a house to walk in, a well, a well house, a *g*antâghara, a *g*antâghara room, a lotus-pond, a pavilion, a park, or has prepared the site for a park; or that his son is to choose a consort; or that his daughter is to choose a consort; or that he is sick; or that he knows how

[1] The enumeration of edifices is identical with that given in § 6, but in the cases beginning with that of the sisterhood of Bhikkhunîs (according to Buddhaghosa; we believe that the two cases referring to sâma*n*eras ought to be excepted) three of the edifices are left out, viz. the privy, the *g*antâghara, and the *g*antâghara room, the use of which is forbidden to nuns; see *K*ullavagga X, 27, 3, 4.

[2] See Abhidhânapp. v. 213, and compare assabha*nd*a, hatthibha*nd*a (Mahâvagga I, 61, 1).

[3] See Abhidhânapp. v. 209.

to recite a celebrated suttanta. If he sends a messenger to the Bhikkhus (saying), "Might their reverences come and learn this suttanta; otherwise this suttanta will fall into oblivion;"—or if he has any other business or any work to be done; and if he sends a messenger to the Bhikkhus (saying), "Might their reverences come hither" (&c.) . . . . then you ought to go (&c., as in § 5, down to :) . . . . you ought to return.

10–12. 'In case, O Bhikkhus, an upâsikâ has built a Vihâra for the Sa*m*gha (&c., as in §§ 5–9[1]).

13. 'In case, O Bhikkhus, a Bhikkhu has built, &c., a Bhikkhunî, a sikkhamânâ, a sâma*n*era, a sâma*n*erî has built for the Sa*m*gha, for a number of Bhikkhus, for one Bhikkhu, for the sisterhood of Bhikkhunîs, ... for one sâma*n*erî, for his own use, a Vihâra (&c., as in § 8).'

6.

1. At that time a certain Bhikkhu was sick. He sent a messenger to the Bhikkhus (saying), 'I am sick; might the Bhikkhus come to me; I long for the Bhikkhus' coming.'

They told this thing to the Blessed One.

'I allow you, O Bhikkhus, to go (even during the rainy season), if the affair for which you go can be accomplished in seven days, even if you are not sent for, and much more if you are sent for, by a

[1] Only it is said here of the Bhikkhus, ayyâ, 'the noble ones,' instead of bhaddantâ, 'their reverences.'

person of one of the following five classes: Bhikkhus, Bhikkhunîs, sikkhamânâs, sâmaneras, and sâmanerîs. I allow you, O Bhikkhus, to go, if the affair for which you go can be accomplished in seven days, even if you are not sent for, and much more if you are sent for, by a person of one of these five classes. Within seven days you ought to return.

2. 'In case, O Bhikkhus, a Bhikkhu is sick. If he sends a messenger to the Bhikkhus (saying), "I am sick; might the Bhikkhus come to me; I long for the Bhikkhus' coming," you ought to go, O Bhikkhus, if the thing can be accomplished in seven days, even if he had not sent for you, much more when he has sent (saying to yourselves): "I will try to get food for the sick, or food for the tender of the sick, or medicine for the sick, or I will ask him (questions referring to the Dhamma), or nurse him." Within seven days you ought to return.

3. 'In case, O Bhikkhus, inward struggles have befallen a Bhikkhu. If he sends a messenger to the Bhikkhus: "Inward struggles have befallen me; might the Bhikkhus come to me; I long for the Bhikkhus' coming," you ought to go . . . . (&c., as in § 2, down to): (saying to yourselves): "I will try to appease those struggles, or cause them to be appeased (by another), or compose him by religious conversation." Within seven days you ought to return.

4. 'In case, O Bhikkhus, a Bhikkhu in whose mind doubts of conscience have arisen sends . . . . (&c., as in § 3, down to): (saying to yourselves): "I will try to dispel those doubts, or cause

them to be dispelled, or compose him by religious conversation." Within seven days you ought to return.

5. 'In case, O Bhikkhus, a Bhikkhu takes to a false doctrine. If he sends . . . . (&c., down to): (saying to yourselves): "I will discuss that false doctrine, or cause another to discuss it, or compose (that Bhikkhu) by religious conversation." Within seven days you ought to return.

6. 'In case, O Bhikkhus, a Bhikkhu is guilty of a grave offence and ought to be sentenced to parivâsa discipline. If he sends . . . . (&c., down to): (saying to yourselves): "I will take care that he may be sentenced to parivâsa discipline, or I will propose the resolution (to the assembly), or I will help to complete the quorum (required for passing the sentence of parivâsa)." Within seven days you ought to return.

7. 'In case, O Bhikkhus, a Bhikkhu ought to be sentenced to recommence penal discipline. If he sends . . . . (&c., as in § 6, down to the end of the section).

8. 'In case, O Bhikkhus, a Bhikkhu ought to have the mânatta discipline imposed upon him. If he sends . . . . (&c., as in § 6, down to the end of the section).

9. 'In case, O Bhikkhus, a Bhikkhu (having duly undergone penal discipline) ought to be rehabilitated. If he sends . . . . (&c., as in § 6).

10. 'In case, O Bhikkhus, the Sa*m*gha is going to proceed against a Bhikkhu by the ta*gg*aniyakamma, or the nissaya, or the pabbâ*g*aniyakamma, or the pa*t*isâra*n*iyakamma, or the ukkhepaniyakamma. If that Bhikkhu sends a messenger to the Bhikkhus (saying), "The Sa*m*gha

is going to proceed against me; might the Bhikkhus come to me; I long for the Bhikkhus' coming," you ought to go . . . . (&c., as in § 2, down to): (saying to yourselves): "What can be done in order that the Sa*m*gha may not proceed (against that Bhikkhu) or may mitigate the proceeding?" Within seven days you ought to return.

11. 'Or the Sa*m*gha has instituted a proceeding against him, the ta*gg*aniyakamma . . . . (&c., down to): . . . . or the ukkhepaniyakamma; if he sends a messenger to the Bhikkhus: "The Sa*m*gha has instituted a proceeding against me; might the Bhikkhus come to me; I long for the Bhikkhus' coming," you ought to go . . . . (&c., as in § 3, down to): (saying to yourselves): "What can be done in order that this Bhikkhu may behave himself properly, live modestly, and aspire to get clear of his penance, and that the Sa*m*gha may revoke its sentence?" Within seven days you ought to return.

12–15. 'In case, O Bhikkhus, a Bhikkhunî is sick, &c.[1]

16. 'In case, O Bhikkhus, a Bhikkhunî is guilty of a grave offence and ought to be sentenced to mânatta discipline[2]. If she sends . . . . (as in § 3, down to): . . . . (saying to yourselves): "I will take care that she may be sentenced to mânatta discipline[3]." Within seven days you ought to return.

[1] See §§ 2–5. Read here and in all cases where the messenger is sent by a woman: 'Might the noble ones (ayyâ) come to me; I long for the noble ones' coming.'

[2] There is no parivâsa discipline for the Bhikkhunîs. When a Bhikkhunî has committed a Sa*m*ghâdisesa offence, no matter whether she has concealed it or not, she is sentenced to mânatta discipline for a fortnight. See *K*ullavagga X, 1, 4; 25, 3.

[3] The phrases, 'Or I will propose the resolution to the assembly,

17. 'In case, O Bhikkhus, a Bhikkhunî ought to be sentenced to recommence penal discipline . . . . (&c., as in § 7).

18. 'In case, O Bhikkhus, a Bhikkhunî who is to be rehabilitated . . . . (&c., as in § 9).

19. 'In case, O Bhikkhus, the Sa*m*gha is going to proceed against a Bhikkhunî by the ta*gg*aniyakamma . . . . (&c., as in § 10).

20. 'Or the Sa*m*gha has instituted a proceeding against her . . . . (&c., as in § 11).

21, 22. 'In case, O Bhikkhus, a sikkhamânâ is sick (&c., see §§ 2–5).

'In case, O Bhikkhus, a sikkhamânâ has violated[1] the precepts (in which she is trained). If she sends . . . . (&c., as in § 3, down to): (saying to yourselves): "I will take care that she may take upon herself the precepts (again)." Within seven days you ought to return.

23. 'In case, O Bhikkhus, a sikkhamânâ desires to receive the upasampadâ ordination. If she sends, &c., ... you ought to go (saying to yourselves): "I will take care that she may receive the upasampadâ ordination, or I will proclaim the formula (of ordination before the assembly), or I will help to complete the quorum." Within seven days you ought to return.

24, 25. 'In case, O Bhikkhus, a sâma*n*era is sick (&c., as in §§ 2–5) . . . . , a sâma*n*era desires

---

or I will help to complete the quorum' (see § 6 seq.), of course are omitted here, because, if the proceeding is directed against a Bhikkhunî, this is to be done by a Bhikkhunî and not by a Bhikkhu. See *K*ullavagga X, 6, 3.

[1] This translation of sikkhâ kupitâ hoti is merely conjectural; Buddhaghosa has no note here. Comp. kuppa and akuppa.

to ask concerning Vassa[1]. If he sends .... (saying to yourselves): "I will ask him or I will tell it to him." Within seven days you ought to return.

26. 'In case, O Bhikkhus, a sâmanera who desires to receive the upasampadâ ordination (&c., see § 23).

27, 28. 'In case, O Bhikkhus, a sâmanerî is sick (&c., see §§ 24–25).

29. 'In case, O Bhikkhus, a sâmanerî desires to take upon herself the precepts. If she sends .... &c., you should go (saying to yourselves): "I will take care that she may take upon herself the precepts." Within seven days you ought to return.'

7.

1. At that time the mother of a Bhikkhu was sick. She sent a messenger to her son (saying), 'I am sick; might my son come to me; I long for my son's coming.' Now that Bhikkhu thought: 'The Blessed One has allowed (a Bhikkhu) to go, if the affair for which he goes can be accomplished within seven days, and if he is sent for, but not if he is not sent for, by a person of any one of the seven classes; (and he has also allowed to go), if the thing he goes for can be accomplished within seven days, even if he is not sent for, and much more if he is sent for, by a person of any one of the five classes. Now my mother is sick; she is not a lay-devotee (upasikâ). What am I, therefore, to do?'

---

[1] The technical meaning of vassam pukkhitum (to ask after Vassa?) is unknown to us.

They told this thing to the Blessed One.

2. 'I allow you, O Bhikkhus, to go (even during the rainy season), if the thing you go for can be accomplished within seven days, even if you are not sent for, and much more if you are sent for, by a person of any one of the following seven classes: Bhikkhus, Bhikkhunîs, sikkhamânâs, sâmaneras, sâmanerîs, the mother, and the father. I allow you, O Bhikkhus, to go, if the thing you go for can be accomplished within seven days, even if you are not sent for, and much more if you are sent for, by a person of any one of these seven classes. Within seven days you ought to return.

3. 'In case, O Bhikkhus, a Bhikkhu's mother is sick. If she sends a messenger to her son (saying), "I am sick; might my son come to me; I long for my son's coming (&c., see chap. 6. 2)."

4. 'In case, O Bhikkhus, a Bhikkhu's father is sick . . . . (&c., as in § 3).

5. 'In case, O Bhikkhus, a Bhikkhu's brother is sick. If he sends a messenger to his brother (saying), "I am sick; might my brother come to me; I long for my brother's coming," he ought to go, O Bhikkhus, if the affair can be accomplished within seven days, and if he sends for him, but not if he does not send for him. Within seven days he ought to return.

6. 'In case, O Bhikkhus, a Bhikkhu's sister is sick . . . . (&c., see § 5).

7. 'In case, O Bhikkhus, a relation of a Bhikkhu is sick. If he sends a messenger to that Bhikkhu (saying), "I am sick; might his reverence come to me" . . . . (&c., as in § 5).

8. 'In case, O Bhikkhus, a person that used to

live with the Bhikkhus[1] is sick. If he sends a messenger to the Bhikkhus (saying), "I am sick; might the Bhikkhus come to me" . . . . (&c., as in § 5).'

8.

At that time a Vihâra belonging to the Samgha went to ruin. A certain upâsaka had a quantity of wood cut in the forest. He sent a messenger to the Bhikkhus (saying), 'If their reverences will fetch that wood, I will give it to them.'

They told this thing to the Blessed One.

'I allow you, O Bhikkhus, to go out on the Samgha's business. Within seven days you ought to return.'

End of the first Bhânavâra about the Vassa residence.

9.

1. At that time the Bhikkhus of a certain district in the Kosala country who had entered upon Vassa, were troubled[2] by beasts of prey; the beasts carried them off and killed them.

They told this thing to the Blessed One.

'In case, O Bhikkhus, the Bhikkhus who have entered upon Vassa, are troubled by beasts of prey, and the beasts carry them off and kill them: this is

[1] Buddhaghosa: bhikkhugatika is a person that dwells in the same Vihâra with the Bhikkhus.

[2] Compare Gâtaka I, 300.

to be considered as a case of danger, and they ought to leave that residence. They are not guilty of interruption of Vassa.

'In case, O Bhikkhus, the Bhikkhus who have entered upon Vassa, are infested by snakes; they bite them and kill them. This is to be considered as a case of danger, ... (&c., as in § 1 down to) . . . . Vassa.

2. 'In case, O Bhikkhus, the Bhikkhus who have entered upon Vassa, are troubled by robbers; the robbers plunder them and beat them. This is to be considered . . . . (&c., as in § 1) . . . . Vassa.

'In case, O Bhikkhus, the Bhikkhus who have entered upon Vassa, are troubled by demons; the demons enter into them and take their power from them. This is to be considered . . . . (&c., as in § 1) . . . . Vassa.

3. 'In case, O Bhikkhus, the village near which the Bhikkhus have entered upon Vassa, is destroyed by fire; the Bhikkhus suffer from want of food. This is to be considered . . . . (&c., as in § 1) . . . . Vassa.

'In case, O Bhikkhus, the places of rest of the Bhikkhus who have entered upon Vassa, are destroyed by fire; the Bhikkhus suffer from having no place of rest. This is to be considered . . . . (&c., as in § 1) . . . . Vassa.

4. 'In case, O Bhikkhus, the village near which the Bhikkhus have entered upon Vassa, is destroyed by water; the Bhikkhus suffer from want of food, ... (&c., as in § 1) . . . . Vassa.

'In case, O Bhikkhus, the places of rest of the Bhikkhus who have entered upon Vassa, are destroyed by water; the Bhikkhus suffer from having no place of rest, ... (&c., as in § 1) . . . . Vassa.'

10.

At that time the village near which the Bhikkhus of a certain district had entered upon Vassa, was transferred to another place through (fear of) robbers.

They told this thing to the Blessed One.

'I prescribe, O Bhikkhus, that you go where the village is.'

The village (people) divided themselves in two parts.

They told this thing to the Blessed One.

'I prescribe, O Bhikkhus, that you go where the greater part is.'

The greater part were unbelieving, unconverted people.

They told this thing to the Blessed One.

'I prescribe, O Bhikkhus, that you go where the believing, converted people are.'

11.

1. At that time the Bhikkhus of a certain district in the Kosala country who had entered upon Vassa, could get (there) neither coarse nor fine food sufficiently as required.

They told this thing to the Blessed One.

'In case, O Bhikkhus, the Bhikkhus who have entered upon Vassa, can get neither coarse nor fine food sufficiently as required. This is to be considered as a case of danger, and they ought to leave that residence. They are not guilty of interruption of Vassa.

'In case, O Bhikkhus, the Bhikkhus who have entered upon Vassa, get food coarse or fine sufficiently as required, but they cannot get sustaining food. This is to be considered . . . . (&c., as in § 1) . . . . Vassa.

2. 'In case, O Bhikkhus, the Bhikkhus who have entered upon Vassa, get food coarse or fine sufficiently as required, they get sustaining food, but they cannot get proper medicine. This is to be considered . . . . (&c., as in § 1) . . . . Vassa.

'In case, O Bhikkhus, the Bhikkhus . . . . (&c., as § 1, down to) . . . . sustaining food, and they can get profitable medicine, but they cannot find suitable laymen to do service to them. This is to be considered . . . . (&c., as in § 1) . . . . Vassa.

3. 'In case, O Bhikkhus, to a Bhikkhu who has entered upon Vassa, a woman makes an offer (in these words): "Come, venerable Sir, I give you gold, or I give you bullion[1], or I give you a field, or I give you a site (for a house or a garden), or I give you an ox, or I give you a cow, or I give you a slave, or I give you a female slave, or I give you my daughter as your wife, or I will be your wife, or I get another wife for you." In that case, if the Bhikkhu thinks: "The Blessed One has said that the mind of men is easily changeable; danger might arise to the purity of my life," he ought to go away from that place. He is not guilty of interruption of Vassa.

4. 'In case, O Bhikkhus, to a Bhikkhu who has entered upon Vassa, a harlot makes an offer, &c., an adult girl makes an offer, &c., a eunuch makes an offer, &c., relations make an offer, &c., kings make

[1] See Rh. D.'s 'Ancient Coins and Measures of Ceylon,' p. 5 ('Numismata Orientalia,' vol. i).

an offer, &c., robbers make an offer, &c., rascals make an offer (in these words): "Come, venerable Sir, we give you gold, ... (&c., down to) . . . . or we give you our daughter as your wife, or we get another wife for you." In that case, ... (&c., as in § 3) . . . . Vassa.

'In case, O Bhikkhus, a Bhikkhu who has entered upon Vassa, finds an ownerless treasure. In that case, ... (&c., as in § 3, down to) . . . . Vassa.

5. 'In case, O Bhikkhus, a Bhikkhu who has entered upon Vassa, sees a number of Bhikkhus who strive to cause divisions in the Sa*m*gha. In that case, if that Bhikkhu thinks: "The Blessed One has said that it is a grievous sin to cause divisions in the Sa*m*gha; may no division arise in the Sa*m*gha in my presence," let him go away. He is not guilty of interruption of Vassa.

'In case, O Bhikkhus, a Bhikkhu who has entered upon Vassa, hears: "A number of Bhikkhus are striving to cause divisions in the Sa*m*gha." In that case, ... (&c., as in § 5, down to) . . . . Vassa.

6. 'In case, O Bhikkhus, a Bhikkhu who has entered upon Vassa, hears: "In such and such a district a number of Bhikkhus are striving to cause divisions in the Sa*m*gha." If that Bhikkhu thinks: "Those Bhikkhus are friends of mine; I will say to them: 'The Blessed One, my friends, has said that it is a grievous sin to cause divisions in the Sa*m*gha; let not divisions in the Sa*m*gha please you, Sirs;' then they will do what I say, they will obey me and give ear," in that case let him go (to that place). He is not guilty of interruption of Vassa.

7. 'In case, O Bhikkhus, a Bhikkhu who has entered upon Vassa, hears: "In such and such a

district a number of Bhikkhus are striving to cause divisions in the Sa*m*gha." If that Bhikkhu thinks: "Those Bhikkhus are not friends of mine, but their friends are friends of mine; to these I will say, and they will say to their friends: 'The Blessed One, ... (&c.,' as in § 6, down to) ..... Vassa.

8. 'In case, O Bhikkhus, a Bhikkhu who has entered upon Vassa, hears: "In such and such a district divisions in the Sa*m*gha have been caused by a number of Bhikkhus." If that Bhikkhu .... (&c., as in § 6, down to) .... Vassa.

9. 'In case, O Bhikkhus, a Bhikkhu who has entered upon Vassa, hears: "In such and such a district divisions in the Sa*m*gha have been caused by a number of Bhikkhus." If that Bhikkhu .... (&c., as in § 7) .... Vassa.

10–13. 'In case, O Bhikkhus, a Bhikkhu who has entered upon Vassa, hears: "In such and such a district a number of Bhikkhunîs strive to cause divisions in the Sa*m*gha .... (&c.[1])"'

12.

1. At that time a Bhikkhu desired to enter upon Vassa in a cattle-pen.

They told this thing to the Blessed One.

'I allow you, O Bhikkhus, to enter upon Vassa in a cattle-pen.'

The cattle-pen was moved from its place.

[1] See §§ 6–9. Instead of 'A number of Bhikkhus' in these paragraphs, the subject is 'A number of Bhikkhunîs.' Instead of 'Friends' or 'Sirs,' the address is 'Sisters.' In §§ 11, 13 read: 'Those Bhikkhunîs are not friends of mine, but their (female) friends are friends of mine, &c.'

They told this thing to the Blessed One.

'I allow you, O Bhikkhus, to go with the cattle-pen.'

2. At that time a Bhikkhu, when the time for entering upon Vassa approached, desired to go on a journey with a caravan.

They told this thing to the Blessed One.

'I allow you, O Bhikkhus, to enter upon Vassa in a caravan.'

At that time a Bhikkhu, when the time for entering upon Vassa approached, desired to go on a journey in a ship.

They told this thing to the Blessed One.

'I allow you, O Bhikkhus, to enter upon Vassa in a ship.'

3. At that time some Bhikkhus entered upon Vassa in a hollow tree. People were annoyed, murmured, and became angry: '(These Bhikkhus behave) like goblins[1].'

They told this thing to the Blessed One.

'Let no one, O Bhikkhus, enter upon Vassa in a hollow tree. He who does, commits a dukka*t*a offence.'

4. At that time some Bhikkhus entered upon Vassa on a branch of a tree. People were annoyed, &c.: '(These Bhikkhus behave) like huntsmen.'

They told this thing to the Blessed One.

'Let no one, O Bhikkhus, enter upon Vassa on a branch of a tree. He who does, commits a dukka*t*a offence.'

5. At that time some Bhikkhus entered upon Vassa in the open air. When it began to rain,

[1] This must be about the sense of pisâ*k*illika (comp. *K*ullavagga V, 10, 2; 27, 5), although we are not sure how -illika ought to be explained.

they ran up to the foot of a tree, or to the hollow of a Nimba tree.

They told this thing to the Blessed One.

'Let no one, O Bhikkhus, enter upon Vassa in the open air. He who does, commits a dukka*t*a offence.'

6. At that time some Bhikkhus entered upon Vassa without having a place of rest. They suffered from coldness and heat.

They told this thing to the Blessed One.

'Let no one, O Bhikkhus, enter upon Vassa without having a place of rest. He who does, commits a dukka*t*a offence.'

7. At that time some Bhikkhus entered upon Vassa in a house for keeping dead bodies in. People were annoyed, &c.: '(These Bhikkhus are) like those who burn corpses.'

They told this thing to the Blessed One.

'Let no one, O Bhikkhus, enter upon Vassa in a house for keeping dead bodies. He who does, commits a dukka*t*a offence.'

8. At that time some Bhikkhus entered upon Vassa under a sun-shade. People were annoyed, &c.: 'Like cowherds.'

They told this thing to the Blessed One.

'Let no one, O Bhikkhus, enter upon Vassa under a sun-shade. He who does, commits a dukka*t*a offence.'

9. At that time some Bhikkhus entered upon Vassa under an earthenware vessel. People were annoyed, &c.: 'Like Titthiyas.'

They told this thing to the Blessed One.

'Let no one, O Bhikkhus, enter upon Vassa under an earthenware vessel. He who does, commits a dukka*t*a offence.'

13.

1. At that time the Sa*m*gha at Sâvatthi had made an agreement that nobody should receive the pabba*gg*â ordination during the rainy season. A grandson of Visâkhâ Migâramâtâ[1] went to the Bhikkhus and asked them for the pabba*gg*â ordination. The Bhikkhus said to him: 'The Sa*m*gha, friend, has made an agreement that nobody shall receive the pabba*gg*â ordination during the rainy season. Wait, friend, as long as the Bhikkhus keep Vassa; when they have concluded the Vassa residence, they will confer on you the pabba*gg*â ordination.'

When those Bhikkhus had concluded the Vassa residence, they said to the grandson of Visâkhâ Migâramâtâ: 'Come now, friend, you may receive the pabba*gg*â ordination.' He replied: 'If I had received the pabba*gg*â ordination before, reverend Sirs, I should remain (in the religious life), but now, reverend Sirs, I will not receive the pabba*gg*â ordination.'

2. Visâkhâ Migâramâtâ was annoyed, murmured, and became angry (saying), 'How can the noble ones make such an agreement that nobody shall receive the pabba*gg*â ordination during the rainy season? At what time ought the duties of the Dhamma not to be performed?'

Some Bhikkhus heard Visâkhâ Migâramâtâ, who was annoyed, murmured, and had become angry.

[1] Visâkhâ was the most distinguished among the upâsikâs, and occupied a place among them similar to that which Anâthapi*nd*ika, with whom she is frequently mentioned together, did among the upâsakas. See Dhammapada A*tth*ak. p. 78, &c.

Those Bhikkhus told the thing to the Blessed One. 'Such an agreement, O Bhikkhus, ought not to be made—that nobody shall receive the pabba*gg*â ordination during the rainy season. He who makes (an agreement like this), commits a dukka*t*a offence.'

14.

1. At that time the venerable Upananda Sakyaputta had promised to king Pasenadi of Kosala to take up his Vassa residence (with him) at the earlier period[1]. When he was going to the district (where he had consented to go to), he saw on his way two districts in which there were plenty of robes, and he thought: 'What if I were to keep Vassa in these two districts; thus shall I obtain many robes.' And he kept Vassa in those two districts.

King Pasenadi of Kosala was annoyed, murmured, and became angry (saying), 'How can the noble Upananda Sakyaputta, after he has promised us to take up his Vassa residence (with us), break his word? Has not falsehood been reproved, and abstinence from falsehood been praised by the Blessed One in many ways?'

2. Some Bhikkhus heard king Pasenadi of Kosala, who was annoyed, &c. The moderate Bhikkhus were annoyed, murmured, and became angry (saying), 'How can the venerable Upananda Sakyaputta, after he has promised to king Pasenadi of Kosala, &c.? Has not falsehood .... (&c., as in § 1)?'

3. Those Bhikkhus told the thing to the Blessed One.

[1] See chap. 2, § 2.

In consequence of that, the Blessed One, after having ordered the fraternity of Bhikkhus to assemble, ásked the venerable Upananda Sakyaputta: 'Is it true, Upananda, that you have broken your word, having promised to king Pasenadi of Kosala to take up your Vassa residence (with him)?'

'It is true, Lord?'

Then the blessed Buddha rebuked him: 'How can you, O foolish one, break your word, having promised, &c.? Has not falsehood, O foolish one, been reproved, and abstinence from falsehood been praised by me in many ways? This will not do, O foolish one, for converting the unconverted, and for augmenting the number of the converted, but it will result, O foolish one, in the unconverted being repulsed (from the faith) and many of the converted being estranged.'

Having reproved him and delivered a religious discourse, he thus addressed the Bhikkhus:

4. 'In case, O Bhikkhus, a Bhikkhu has promised (to a lay-devotee) to take up his Vassa residence (with him) at the earlier period, and when he goes to that district, he sees on his way two districts in which there are plenty of robes, and he thinks: "What if I were to keep Vassa in these two districts; thus shall I obtain many robes;" and he keeps Vassa in those two districts. This Bhikkhu's (entering upon Vassa), O Bhikkhus, (at the) earlier period is not valid, and as to his promise he has committed a dukka*t*a offence.

5. 'In case, O Bhikkhus, a Bhikkhu has promised (to a lay-devotee) to take up his Vassa residence (with him) at the earlier period, and when going to that district, he holds Uposatha outside (on the last

day of the half month), and on the first day (of the next half month) he goes to the Vihâra, prepares himself a place of rest, gets (water to) drink and food, sweeps the cell, and goes away that same day without having any business. This Bhikkhu's (entering upon Vassa) . . . . (&c., as in § 4, down to) . . . . offence.

'In case, O Bhikkhus, a Bhikkhu has promised (&c., as in the preceding case, down to:) and goes away that same day having business. This Bhikkhu's (entering upon Vassa) . . . . (&c., as in § 4, down to) . . . . offence.

6. 'In case, O Bhikkhus, a Bhikkhu has promised, &c., and having resided there two or three days, he goes away without having any business, &c.; he goes away having business. This Bhikkhu's (entering upon Vassa) . . . . (&c., as in § 4, down to) . . . . offence.

'In case, O Bhikkhus, a Bhikkhu has promised, &c., and having resided there two or three days, he goes away having a business which can be accomplished within seven days[1]; he is absent above those seven days. This Bhikkhu's (entering upon Vassa).... (&c., as in § 4, down to) . . . . offence.

'In case, O Bhikkhus, &c., he returns within those seven days. This Bhikkhu's (entering upon Vassa), O Bhikkhus, (at the) earlier period is valid, and as to his promise he has committed no offence.

7. 'In case, O Bhikkhus, a Bhikkhu has promised, &c., and goes away seven days before the Pavâra*n*â[2] having business. No matter, O Bhikkhus, whether that Bhikkhu comes back to that district or

[1] See chap. 5 seq.

[2] I. e. before the concluding ceremony of Vassa; see IV, 1, 13.

does not come back, this Bhikkhu's entering, &c., is valid, and as to his promise he has committed no offence.

8–10. 'In case, O Bhikkhus, a Bhikkhu has promised, &c., and having gone to that district, he holds Uposatha there (on the last day of the half month), and on the first day (of the next half month) he goes to the Vihâra, &c.[1]

11. 'In case, O Bhikkhus, a Bhikkhu has promised (to a lay-devotee) to take up his Vassa residence (with him) at the later period, and when going to that district, he holds Uposatha outside, &c.[2]'

End of the third Khandhaka, which treats of entering upon Vassa.

[1] Here follows an exact repetition of all the cases given in §§ 5–7; the only difference is, that in the former cases it was said: 'When going to that district, he holds Uposatha outside,' instead of which it is said now: 'Having gone to that district, he holds Uposatha there.'

[2] The cases given in §§ 5–10 are repeated here; instead of 'Earlier period,' it is said here 'Later period;' instead of 'Before the Pavâra*n*â' (§ 7), 'Before the komudî *k*âtumâsinî.' The komudî *k*âtumâsinî is the full moon day in the month Kattika, which is frequently called Kaumuda in the Epic literature; the epithet *k*âtumâsinî refers to the Vedic *K*âturmâsya festival, which falls upon that day (Kâtyâyana, *S*rautasûtra V, 6, 1). For those who entered upon Vassa at the later period (in the *S*râva*n*a month), the end of Vassa fell on the Komudî day.

FOURTH KHANDHAKA.

(THE PAVÂRA*N*Â CEREMONY AT THE END OF THE RAINY SEASON, VASSA).

1.

1. At that time the blessed Buddha dwelt at Sâvatthi, in the *G*etavana, the garden of Anâthapi*nd*ika. At that time a number of Bhikkhus, companions and friends of each other, entered upon Vassa in a certain district of the Kosala country. Now those Bhikkhus thought: 'What shall we do in order that we may keep Vassa well, in unity, and in concord, and without quarrel, and that we may not suffer from want of food?'

2. Then those Bhikkhus thought: 'If we do not speak to or converse with each other, if he who comes back first from the village, from his alms-pilgrimage, prepares seats, gets water for washing the feet, a foot-stool, and a towel[1], cleans the slop-basin and gets it ready, and puts there (water to) drink and food,—

3. 'And if he who comes back last from the village, from his alms-pilgrimage, eats, if there is any food left (from the dinner of the other Bhikkhus) and if he desires to do so; and if he does not desire (to eat), throws it away at a place free from grass, or pours it away into water in which no living things are; puts away the water for washing the feet, the foot-stool, and the towel[1]; cleans the slop-basin and

[1] See the note on I, 6, 11.

puts it away, puts the water and the food away, and sweeps the dining-room,—

4. 'And if he who sees a water-pot, or a bowl for food, or a vessel for evacuations, empty and void, puts it (into its proper place), and if he is not able to do so single-handed, calls some one else and puts it away with their united effort[1] without uttering a word on that account,—thus shall we keep Vassa well, in unity, and in concord, and without quarrel, and not suffer from want of food[2].'

5–7. And those Bhikkhus did not speak to or converse with each other. He who came back from the village from his alms-pilgrimage first, prepared seats (&c., as above, § 4, down to) . . . . without uttering a word on that account.

8. Now it is the custom of the Bhikkhus who have finished their Vassa residence, to go to see the Blessed One. Thus those Bhikkhus, when they had finished their Vassa residence, and when the three months (of Vassa) had elapsed, set their places of rest in order, took their alms-bowls and robes, and went on their way to Sâvatthi. Wandering from place to place, they came to Sâvatthi, to the *G*etavana, the garden of Anâthapi*nd*ika, to the Blessed One; having approached the Blessed One and respectfully saluted him, they sat down near him.

9. Now it is the custom of the blessed Buddhas

[1] We are not quite sure of the meaning of the compounds hattha-vikârena and hattha-vilaṅghakena. Buddhaghosa says merely hatthavilaṅghakenâ 'ti hatthukkhepakena.

[2] For this whole passage, compare *K*ullavagga VIII, 5, 3. The single actions which these Bhikkhus do, are quite correct, except that they keep silence during the whole time of Vassa, and especially at the end of it, for which time Buddha, on this occasion, prescribes the Pavâra*n*â ceremony.

to exchange greeting with incoming Bhikkhus. And the Blessed One said to those Bhikkhus: 'Do things go well with you, O Bhikkhus? Do you get enough to support yourselves with? Have you kept Vassa well, in unity, and in concord, and without quarrel? and have you not suffered from want of food?'

'Things go tolerably well with us, Lord; we get enough, Lord, wherewith to support ourselves; we have kept Vassa well, in unity, in concord, and without quarrel; and have not suffered from want of food.'

10. The Tathâgatas sometimes ask about what they know; sometimes they do not ask about what they know. They understand the right time when to ask, and they understand the right time when not to ask. The Tathâgatas put questions full of sense, not void of sense; to what is void of sense the bridge is pulled down for the Tathâgatas. For two purposes the blessed Buddhas put questions to the Bhikkhus, when they intend to preach the doctrine, or when they intend to institute a rule of conduct to their disciples.

11. And the Blessed One said to those Bhikkhus: 'In what way, O Bhikkhus, have you kept Vassa well, in unity, and in concord, and without quarrel, and not suffered from want of food?'

'We have entered upon Vassa, Lord, a number of Bhikkhus, companions and friends of each other, in a certain district of the Kosala country. Now, Lord, we thought: "What shall we do (&c., as in § 1)?" Then we thought, Lord: "If we do not speak (&c., as in §§ 2–4)." Thus, Lord, we did not speak to or converse with each other (&c., down to:) without uttering a word on that account. In that way, Lord, we have kept Vassa well, in unity, and in concord, and without quarrel; and have not suffered from want of food.'

12. Then the Blessed One thus addressed the Bhikkhus: 'Indeed, O Bhikkhus, these foolish men who profess to have kept Vassa well, have kept it badly; indeed, O Bhikkhus, these foolish men who profess to have kept Vassa well, have kept it like a herd of cattle; indeed . . . . have kept it like a herd of rams; indeed . . . . have kept it like a company of indolent people. How can these foolish persons, O Bhikkhus, take upon themselves the vow of silence, as the Titthiyas do?

13. 'This will not do, O Bhikkhus, for converting the unconverted (&c., as in Book III, chapter 14, § 3).'

And when he had rebuked them and delivered a religious discourse, he thus addressed the Bhikkhus:

'Let no one, O Bhikkhus, take upon himself the vow of silence, as the Titthiyas do. He who does, commits a dukkaṭa offence.

'I prescribe, O Bhikkhus, that the Bhikkhus, when they have finished their Vassa residence, hold Pavâraṇâ with each other[1] in these three ways: by what has been seen, or by what has been heard, or by what is suspected. Hence it will result that you live in accord with each other, that you atone for the offences (you have committed), and that you keep the rules of discipline before your eyes.

14. 'And you ought, O Bhikkhus, to hold Pavâraṇâ in this way:

[1] Literally, invite each other; i. e. every Bhikkhu present invites his companions to tell him if they believe him guilty of an offence, having seen that offence, or having heard of it, or suspecting it.

'Let a learned, competent Bhikkhu proclaim the following *ñ*atti before the Sa*m*gha: "Let the Sa*m*gha, reverend Sirs, hear me. To-day is the Pavâra*n*â day. If the Sa*m*gha is ready, let the Sa*m*gha hold Pavâra*n*â."

'Then let the senior Bhikkhu adjust his upper robe so as to cover one shoulder, sit down squatting, raise his joined hands, and say: "I pronounce my Pavâra*n*â, friends, before the Sa*m*gha, by what has been seen, or by what has been heard, or by what is suspected[1]; may you speak to me, Sirs, out of compassion towards me; if I see (an offence), I will atone for it. And for the second time, &c. And for the third time I pronounce my Pavâra*n*â.... (&c., down to) .... if I see (an offence), I will atone for it."

'Then let (each) younger Bhikkhu adjust his upper robe .... (&c.)[2]'

2.

1. At that time the *Kh*abbaggiya Bhikkhus, while the senior Bhikkhus were crouching down and were performing their Pavâra*n*â, remained on their seats. The moderate Bhikkhus were annoyed, murmured, and became angry: 'How can the *Kh*abbaggiya Bhikkhus remain on their seats, while the senior

---

[1] I. e. I invite the Sa*m*gha to charge me with any offence they think me guilty of, which they have seen, or heard of, or which they suspect.

[2] As in the preceding sentence, except that the younger Bhikkhus do not address the Sa*m*gha, 'Friends,' but, 'Reverend Sirs.'

Bhikkhus crouch down, and perform their Pavâranâ?'

Those Bhikkhus told the thing to the Blessed One.

'Is it true, O Bhikkhus, that the *Kh*abbaggiya Bhikkhus, &c.?'

'It is true, O Lord.'

Then the blessed Buddha rebuked them: 'How can these foolish men, O Bhikkhus, remain on their seats (&c., as above)? This will not do, O Bhikkhus, for converting the unconverted (&c., as in chap. 1, § 13).'

Having rebuked them and delivered a religious discourse, he thus addressed the Bhikkhus: 'Let no one, O Bhikkhus, remain on his seat, while the senior Bhikkhus crouch down, and perform their Pavâranâ. He who does, commits a dukkata offence. I prescribe, O Bhikkhus, that all of you crouch down while Pavâranâ is being performed.'

2. At that time a certain Bhikkhu weak from age, who waited crouching till all had finished their Pavâranâ, fell down fainting.

They told this thing to the Blessed One.

'I prescribe, O Bhikkhus, that (every Bhikkhu) crouches down the whole while till he has performed his Pavâranâ, and sits down on his seat when he has performed it.'

3.

1. Now the Bhikkhus thought: 'How many Pavâranâ (days) are there?'

They told this thing to the Blessed One.

'There are the two following Pavâranâ (days),

O Bhikkhus: the fourteenth and the fifteenth (of the half month)[1]; these are the two Pavâranâ (days), O Bhikkhus.'

2. Now the Bhikkhus thought: 'How many Pavâranâ services are there?'

They told this thing to the Blessed One.

'There are the four following Pavâranâ services, O Bhikkhus, &c.[2]'

3. Then the Blessed One thus addressed the Bhikkhus: 'Assemble, O Bhikkhus, the Samgha will hold Pavâranâ.' When he had spoken thus, a certain Bhikkhu said to the Blessed One: 'There is a sick Bhikkhu, Lord, who is not present.'

'I prescribe, O Bhikkhus, that a sick Bhikkhu shall declare (lit. give) his Pavâranâ. And let him declare it, O Bhikkhus, in this way: Let that sick Bhikkhu go to some Bhikkhu, adjust his upper robe so as to cover one shoulder, sit down squatting, raise his joined hands, and say: "I declare my Pavâranâ, take my Pavâranâ, perform the Pavâranâ for me." If he expresses this by gesture, or by word, or by gesture and word, the Pavâranâ has been declared. If he does not express this by gesture, &c., the Pavâranâ has not been declared.

4–5. 'If (the sick Bhikkhu) succeeds in doing so, well and good. If he does not succeed, let them take that sick Bhikkhu, O Bhikkhus, on his bed or his chair to the assembly, &c.[3]

---

[1] Comp. II, 14, 1, and the note on II, 34, 1.

[2] This passage is exactly identical with II, 14, 2. 3, replacing 'Uposatha service' by 'Pavâranâ service.'

[3] This passage is a repetition of II, 22, 2–4, the words, 'Hold Uposatha,' 'Declare the Pârisuddhi,' &c., being replaced respectively by 'Hold Pavâranâ,' 'Declare the Pavâranâ,' &c.

'I prescribe, O Bhikkhus, that on the day of Pavâra*n*â he who declares his Pavâra*n*â, is to declare also his consent[1] (to acts to be performed eventually by the Order), for (both declarations) are required for the Sa*m*gha (and for the validity of its acts)[2].'

4.

At that time relations of a certain Bhikkhu kept him back on the day of Pavâra*n*â, &c.[3]

5.

1. At that time five Bhikkhus dwelt in a certain district (or, in a certain residence of Bhikkhus) on the day of Pavâra*n*â.

Now these Bhikkhus thought: 'The Blessed One has prescribed the holding of Pavâra*n*â by the Sa*m*gha, and we are (only) five persons[4]. Well, how are we to hold Pavâra*n*â?'

They told this thing to the Blessed One.

'I prescribe, O Bhikkhus, that five Bhikkhus should hold Pavâra*n*â in a (regular) chapter[5].'

2. At that time four Bhikkhus dwelt in a certain

---

[1] See II, 23.

[2] Comp. the finishing clause of II, 23.

[3] This is a repetition of II, 24, but instead of 'Uposatha' and 'Pârisuddhi' read 'Pavâra*n*â.'

[4] As a general rule five Bhikkhus were sufficient to form the quorum; but for the performance of several among the official acts of the Order the presence of more than five members was required; see IX, 4, 1 seq.

[5] See IX, 4, 1.

district on the day of Pavâranâ. Now these Bhikkhus thought: 'The Blessed One has prescribed that five Bhikkhus shall hold Pavâranâ in a (regular) chapter, and we are (only) four persons. Well, how are we to hold Pavâranâ?'

They told this thing to the Blessed One.

'I prescribe, O Bhikkhus, that four Bhikkhus should hold Pavâranâ with each other.

3. 'And let them hold Pavâranâ, O Bhikkhus, in this way: Let a learned, competent Bhikkhu proclaim the following *ñatti* before those Bhikkhus: "Hear me, Sirs. To-day is Pavâranâ day. If you are ready, Sirs, let us hold Pavâranâ with each other."

'Then let the senior Bhikkhu adjust his upper robe, &c., and say to those Bhikkhus: "I pronounce my Pavâranâ, friends, before you, by what has been seen, or by what has been heard, or by what is suspected; may you speak to me, Sirs, out of compassion towards me; if I see (an offence), I will atone for it. And for the second time, &c.; and for the third time, &c."

'Then let each younger Bhikkhu, &c.'

4. At that time three Bhikkhus dwelt in a certain district on the day of Pavâranâ. Now these Bhikkhus thought: 'The Blessed One has prescribed that five Bhikkhus shall hold Pavâranâ in a (regular) chapter, that four Bhikkhus shall hold Pavâranâ with each other, and we are (only) three persons. Well, how are we to hold Pavâranâ?'

'I prescribe, O Bhikkhus, that three Bhikkhus should hold Pavâranâ with each other. And let them hold Pavâranâ (&c., see § 3).'

5. At that time two Bhikkhus dwelt in a certain

district on the day of Pavâranâ. Now these Bhikkhus thought: 'The Blessed One has prescribed that five Bhikkhus, &c., that four Bhikkhus, &c., that three Bhikkhus, &c., and we are (only) two persons. Well, how are we to hold Pavâranâ?'

'I prescribe, O Bhikkhus, that two Bhikkhus should hold Pavâranâ with each other.

6. 'And let them hold Pavâranâ, O Bhikkhus, in this way: Let the senior Bhikkhu adjust his upper robe, &c., and say to the junior Bhikkhu: "I pronounce my Pavâranâ, friend, &c."

'Then let the junior Bhikkhu, &c.'

7. At that time there dwelt a single Bhikkhu in a certain district on the day of Pavâranâ. Now this Bhikkhu thought: 'The Blessed One has prescribed that five Bhikkhus, &c., &c., and I am only one person. Well, how am I to hold Pavâranâ?'

8. 'In case there dwell, O Bhikkhus, in a certain district on the day of Pavâranâ, a single Bhikkhu: Let that Bhikkhu, O Bhikkhus, sweep the place which the Bhikkhus use to frequent,—the refectory, or hall, or place at the foot of a tree; let him (then) provide water and food, prepare seats, put a lamp there, and sit down. If other Bhikkhus come, let him hold Pavâranâ with them; if they do not come, let him fix his mind upon the thought: "To-day is my Pavâranâ." If he does not fix his mind upon this thought, he commits a dukkata offence.

9. 'Now, O Bhikkhus, where five Bhikkhus dwell (together), they must not convey the Pavâranâ[1] of one (to their assembly) and hold Pavâranâ by

[1] See chap. 3, § 3. Compare II, chap. 22, and chap. 26, § 10.

four (as) in a (regular) chapter. If they do, they commit a dukka*t*a offence.

'Now, O Bhikkhus, where four Bhikkhus dwell (together), they must not convey the Pavâra*n*â of one (to their assembly) and hold Pavâra*n*â with each other by three. If they do, they commit a dukka*t*a offence.

'Now, O Bhikkhus, where three Bhikkhus (&c., as in the last clause).

'Now, O Bhikkhus, where two Bhikkhus dwell, one of them must not convey the Pavâra*n*â of the other one, and fix (only) his thoughts (upon the Pavâra*n*â). If he does, he commits a dukka*t*a offence.'

6.

1. At that time a certain Bhikkhu was guilty of an offence on the day of Pavâra*n*â. Now this Bhikkhu thought: 'The Blessed One has prescribed: "Pavâra*n*â is not to be held by a Bhikkhu who is guilty of an offence[1]." Now I am guilty of an offence. What am I to do?'

They told this thing to the Blessed One.

'In case, O Bhikkhus, a certain Bhikkhu be guilty of an offence on the day of Pavâra*n*â (&c., as in II, 27. 1, 2, down to:) "When I shall feel no doubt, then I will atone for that offence." Having spoken thus, let him hold Pavâra*n*â. But in no case must there any hindrance arise to holding Pavâra*n*â from such a cause.'

2–3. At that time a certain Bhikkhu remembered

[1] See chap. 16, § 1.

an offence, while Pavâra*n*â was being held (&c., see II, 27. 4–8).

End of the first Bhâ*n*avâra.

7–13.

7. 1. At that time there assembled in a certain residence (or district) on the day of Pavâra*n*â a number of resident Bhikkhus, five or more. They did not know that there were other resident Bhikkhus absent. Intending to act according to Dhamma and Vinaya, thinking themselves to be complete while (really) incomplete, they held Pavâra*n*â. While they were holding Pavâra*n*â, other resident Bhikkhus, a greater number (than the first ones), arrived.

They told this thing to the Blessed One.

2. 'In case there assemble, O Bhikkhus, in a certain residence on the day of Pavâra*n*â (&c., as in § 1, down to) . . . . they hold Pavâra*n*â. While they are holding Pavâra*n*â, other resident Bhikkhus, a greater number, arrive. Let (all) those Bhikkhus, O Bhikkhus, hold Pavâra*n*â again; they who have held Pavâra*n*â, are free from guilt.

3. 'In case there assemble, &c. . . . . While they are holding Pavâra*n*â, other resident Bhikkhus, exactly the same number (as the first ones), arrive. Those who have held Pavâra*n*â, have held it correctly; let the other ones hold Pavâra*n*â; they who have held Pavâra*n*â, are free from guilt.'

. . . .

. . . .

. . . .[1]

[1] The following paragraphs and chapters exactly follow the course indicated by II, 28–35. The alterations to be made are

14.

1–3. 'Let no one, O Bhikkhus, hold Pavâra*n*â in a seated assembly (of Bhikkhus) before a Bhikkhunî, ... (&c.[1])

4. 'Let no one, O Bhikkhus, hold Pavâra*n*â by (accepting) the Pavâra*n*â declaration of a pârivâsika[2], except if the assembly has not yet risen (at the time when the Pavâra*n*â is declared). And let no one, O Bhikkhus, hold Pavâra*n*â on another day than the Pavâra*n*â day, except for the sake of (preserving) concord among the Sa*m*gha[3].'

15.

1. At that time a certain residence (of Bhikkhus) in the Kosala country was menaced on the day of Pavâra*n*â by savage people. The Bhikkhus were not able to perform Pavâra*n*â with the threefold formula.

They told this thing to the Blessed One.

---

obvious and sufficiently indicated by §§ 1–3; instead of, 'Let them proclaim their Pârisuddhi' (II, 28, 4, &c.), read here, 'Let them pronounce their Pavâra*n*â.'

[1] See II, 36, 1–3.

[2] Comp. II, 36, 4, with the note.

[3] See, for instance, the cases in chap. 17. Buddhaghosa's explanation is different; he says: 'Concord among the Sa*m*gha is to be understood of such cases as that of Kosambî.' It is said in the account of the schism of Kosambî that, if concord has been re-established, the reconciled parties hold Uposatha together (X, 5, 14; comp. II, 36, 4); Buddhaghosa apparently extends this to holding Pavâra*n*â also.

'I allow you, O Bhikkhus, to perform Pavâranâ with the twofold formula[1].'

The danger from savage people became still more urgent. The Bhikkhus were not able to perform Pavâranâ with the twofold formula.

They told this thing to the Blessed One.

'I allow you, O Bhikkhus, to perform Pavâranâ with the onefold formula[1].'

The danger from savage people became still more urgent. The Bhikkhus were not able to perform Pavâranâ with the onefold formula.

They told this thing to the Blessed One.

'I allow, O Bhikkhus, that all the Bhikkhus who have kept Vassa together, perform Pavâranâ (by one common declaration).'

2. At that time in a certain district on the day of Pavâranâ the greater part of the night had passed away while (lay-)people were offering gifts (to the Bhikkhus). Now the Bhikkhus thought: 'The greater part of the night has passed away while the people were offering gifts. If the Samgha performs Pavâranâ with the threefold formula, it will not have finished the Pavâranâ when day breaks. Well, what are we to do?'

They told this thing to the Blessed One.

3. 'In case, O Bhikkhus, in a certain district on the day of Pavâranâ the greater part of the night has passed away while people were offering gifts (to the Bhikkhus). Now if those Bhikkhus think: "The greater part (&c., down to:) when day breaks,"

[1] This means apparently that the Bhikkhus were not obliged to pronounce the formula of Pavâranâ (chap. 1, 14) thrice, but twice or once respectively.

let a learned, competent Bhikkhu proclaim the following *ñ*atti before the Samgha: "Let the Sa*m*gha, reverend Sirs, hear me. While people were offering gifts, the greater part of the night has passed away. If the Sa*m*gha performs Pavâra*n*â with the threefold formula, it will not have finished the Pavâra*n*â when day breaks. If the Sa*m*gha is ready, let the Sa*m*gha hold Pavâra*n*â with the twofold formula, or with the onefold formula, or by common declaration of all the Bhikkhus who have kept Vassa together."

4. 'In case, O Bhikkhus, in a certain district on the day of Pavâra*n*â the greater part of the night has passed away while the Bhikkhus were in confusion: the Bhikkhus were reciting the Dhamma, those versed in the Suttantas were propounding the Suttantas, those versed in the Vinaya were discussing the Vinaya, the Dhamma preachers were talking about the Dhamma. Now if those Bhikkhus think: "The greater part of the night has passed away while the Bhikkhus were in confusion. If the Sa*m*gha performs Pavâra*n*â with the threefold formula, it will not have finished the Pavâra*n*â when day breaks," let a learned, competent Bhikkhu proclaim the following *ñ*atti before the Sa*m*gha: "Let the Sa*m*gha, &c. The greater part of the night has passed away while the Bhikkhus were in confusion. If the Sa*m*gha performs Pavâra*n*â (&c. as in § 3)."'

5. At that time in a certain district in the Kosala country a great assembly of Bhikkhus had come together on the day of Pavâra*n*â, and there was but a small place protected from rain, and a great cloud was in the sky. Now the Bhikkhus thought: 'A great assembly of Bhikkhus has come together

here, and there is but a small place protected from rain, and a great cloud is in the sky. If the Sa*m*gha performs Pavâra*n*â with the threefold formula, it will not have finished the Pavâra*n*â when this cloud will begin to rain. Well, what are we to do?'

They told this thing to the Blessed One.

6. 'In case, O Bhikkhus, in a certain district a great assembly of Bhikkhus has come together on the day of Pavâra*n*â, and there is but a small place protected from rain, and a great cloud is in the sky. Now if those Bhikkhus think . . . . (&c., as in § 3 to the end).

7. 'In case, O Bhikkhus, in a certain district on the day of Pavâra*n*â danger arises from kings, danger from robbers, danger from fire, danger from water, danger from human beings, danger from non-human beings, danger from beasts of prey, danger from creeping things, danger of life, danger against chastity. Now if those Bhikkhus think: "Here is danger for our chastity. If the Sa*m*gha performs Pavâra*n*â with the threefold formula, it will not have finished the Pavâra*n*â when this danger for chastity will arise," let a learned, competent Bhikkhu . . . .' (&c., as in § 3 to the end).

16.

1. At that time the *Kh*abbaggiya Bhikkhus held Pavâra*n*â being guilty of an offence.

They told this thing to the Blessed One.

'Let no one, O Bhikkhus, hold Pavâra*n*â who is guilty of an offence. He who does, commits a dukka*t*a offence. I prescribe, O Bhikkhus, that you ask a Bhikkhu who holds Pavâra*n*â being guilty of an offence, for his leave[1] and reprove him for that offence.'

2. At that time the *Kh*abbaggiya Bhikkhus, when asked for leave, were not willing to give leave (to Bhikkhus who were going to reprove them for an offence).

They told this thing to the Blessed One.

'I prescribe, O Bhikkhus, that you inhibit the Pavâra*n*â of a Bhikkhu who does not give leave. And you ought to inhibit it, O Bhikkhus, in this way: Let (a Bhikkhu) say on the day of Pavâra*n*â, on the fourteenth or on the fifteenth day (of the half month), in presence of that person, before the assembled Samgha: "Let the Sa*m*gha, reverend Sirs, hear me. Such and such a person is guilty of an offence; I inhibit his Pavâra*n*â; Pavâra*n*â must not be held in his presence." Thus his Pavâra*n*â is inhibited.'

3. At that time the *Kh*abbaggiya Bhikkhus, who thought: 'Otherwise good Bhikkhus might inhibit our Pavâra*n*â,' themselves inhibited beforehand, without object and reason, the Pavâra*n*â of pure Bhikkhus who had committed no offence, and they also inhibited the Pavâra*n*â of Bhikkhus who had already performed their Pavâra*n*â.

They told this thing to the Blessed One.

'Let no one, O Bhikkhus, inhibit, without object and reason, the Pavâra*n*â of pure Bhikkhus who have committed no offence. He who does, commits a dukka*t*a offence. And further, O Bhikkhus, let no

[1] Comp. II, 16, 1.

one inhibit the Pavâranâ of Bhikkhus who have already performed their Pavâranâ. He who does, commits a dukkata offence.

4. 'And thus, O Bhikkhus, (you may discern whether) the Pavâranâ is (duly) inhibited or not inhibited.

'In what cases is the Pavâranâ, O Bhikkhus, not inhibited? When Pavâranâ, O Bhikkhus, is pronounced, declared, and finished with the threefold formula, and if (a Bhikkhu then) inhibits the Pavâranâ (of another Bhikkhu), the Pavâranâ is not inhibited. When Pavâranâ, O Bhikkhus, is pronounced, declared, and finished with the twofold formula, with the onefold formula, by common declaration of all Bhikkhus who have kept Vassa together, and if (a Bhikkhu then) inhibits, ... (&c., as before). In these cases, O Bhikkhus, the Pavâranâ is not inhibited.

5. 'And in what cases, O Bhikkhus, is the Pavâranâ inhibited? When Pavâranâ, O Bhikkhus, is pronounced, declared, but not finished[1] with the threefold formula, and if (a Bhikkhu then) inhibits the Pavâranâ (of another Bhikkhu), the Pavâranâ is inhibited, ... (&c.[2]). In these cases, O Bhikkhus, the Pavâranâ is inhibited.

6. 'In case, O Bhikkhus, one Bhikkhu, on the day of Pavâranâ, inhibits the Pavâranâ of another Bhikkhu: then if the other Bhikkhus know with regard to that (inhibiting) Bhikkhu: "This vene-

---

[1] Correct in the Pâli text pariyositâya into apariyositâya.

[2] The paragraph is repeated with the phrases, 'With the twofold formula,' 'with the onefold formula,' and 'by common declaration of all the Bhikkhus who have kept Vassa together,' respectively, instead of 'with the threefold formula.'

rable brother is not of a pure conduct in his deeds, nor in his words, nor as regards his means of livelihood, he is ignorant, unlearned, unable to give explanation when he is questioned," (let them say to him): "Nay, friend, let not quarrel arise, nor strife, nor discord, nor dispute," and having thus put him to silence, let the Sa*m*gha hold Pavâra*n*â.

7–9. 'In case, O Bhikkhus, &c.[1]

10. 'In case, O Bhikkhus, one Bhikkhu on the day of Pavâra*n*â inhibits the Pavâra*n*â of another Bhikkhu: then if the other Bhikkhus know with regard to that (inhibiting) Bhikkhu: "This venerable brother is of a pure conduct in his deeds and in his words and with regard to his means of livelihood, he is clever, learned, and able to give explanation when he is questioned," let them say to him: "If you inhibit, friend, the Pavâra*n*â of this Bhikkhu, on what account do you inhibit it, on account of a moral transgression, or on account of a transgression against the rules of conduct, or on account of heresy?"

11. 'If he replies: "I inhibit it on account of a moral transgression, I inhibit it on account of a transgression against the rules of conduct, I inhibit it on account of heresy," let them say to him: "Well, do you know, Sir, what a moral transgression is, what a transgression against the rules of conduct is, what heresy is?" If he replies, "I

[1] As in § 6. But instead of 'Not of a pure conduct in his deeds, nor in his words, nor as regards his means of livelihood,' read respectively, 'Of a pure conduct in his deeds, but not in his words, nor as regards his means of livelihood' (§ 7); 'Of a pure conduct in his deeds and in his words, but not with regard to his means of livelihood' (§ 8); 'Of a pure conduct in his deeds and in his words and with regard to his means of livelihood' (§ 9).

know, friends, what a moral transgression is, &c.," let them say to him: "And what is, friend, a moral transgression, &c.?"

12. 'If he replies: "The four pârâgika offences and the thirteen samghâdisesa offences are the moral transgressions; thullakkaya offences, pâkittiya offences, pâtidesanîya offences, dukkata offences, and wicked language are the transgressions against the rules of conduct; false doctrine and . . . . doctrine[1] are heresy," let them say to him: "If you inhibit, friend, the Pavâranâ of this Bhikkhu, do you inhibit it on account of what you have seen, or of what you have heard, or of what you suspect?"

13. 'If he replies: "I inhibit it on account of what I have seen, or on account of what I have heard, or on account of what I suspect," let them say to him: "If you inhibit, friend, the Pavâranâ of this Bhikkhu on account of what you have seen, what have you seen? What is it that you have seen? When have you seen it? Where have you seen it? Have you seen him committing a pârâgika offence? Have you seen him committing a samghâdisesa offence? Have you seen him committing a thullakkaya offence, a pâkittiya offence, a pâtidesanîya offence, a dukkata offence, or making himself guilty of wicked language? And where were you? And where was this Bhikkhu? And what did you do? And what did this Bhikkhu do?"

[1] The meaning of antaggâhikâ ditthi (Sanskrit ântargrahikâ drishti? ântagrahikâ drishti?) is unknown to us; Buddhaghosa gives no explanation. Perhaps it may mean doctrine partly false and partly correct (eclectic).

14. 'If he then replies: "I do not inhibit, friends, the Pavâranâ of this Bhikkhu on account of what I have seen, but I inhibit it on account of what I have heard," let them say to him: "If you inhibit, friend, the Pavâranâ of this Bhikkhu on account of what you have heard, what have you heard? What is it that you have heard? When have you heard it? Where have you heard it? Have you heard that he has committed a pârâgika offence, ... (&c., down to) .... or that he has made himself guilty of wicked language? Have you heard it from a Bhikkhu? Have you heard it from a Bhikkhunî? Have you heard it from a sikkhamânâ, from a sâmanera, from a sâmanerî, from an upâsaka, from an upâsikâ, from kings, from royal officers, from Titthiyas, from Titthiya disciples?"

15. 'If he then replies: "I do not inhibit, friends, the Pavâranâ of this Bhikkhu on account of what I have heard, but I inhibit it on account of what I suspect," let them say to him: "If you inhibit, friend, the Pavâranâ of this Bhikkhu on account of what you suspect, what do you suspect? What is it that you suspect? When do you suspect it? Where do you suspect it? Do you suspect that he has committed a pârâgika offence, ... (&c., down to) .... wicked language? Does your suspicion come from what you have heard from a Bhikkhu, ... (&c., down to) .... from Titthiya disciples?"

16. 'If he then replies: "I do not inhibit, friends, the Pavâranâ of this Bhikkhu on account of what I suspect; I do not know the reason why I inhibit the Pavâranâ of this Bhikkhu," and if that Bhikkhu, O Bhikkhus, who reproves (the other one), being questioned by intelligent fellow Bhikkhus, is not able

to convince their minds, you are right in saying that in such case the Bhikkhu who has been reproved is blameless. But if that Bhikkhu, O Bhikkhus, who reproves (the other one), being questioned by intelligent fellow Bhikkhus, is able to convince their minds, you are right in saying that in such case the Bhikkhu who has been reproved is blamable.

17. 'If that Bhikkhu, O Bhikkhus, who reproves (another one), admits that he has charged him unfoundedly with a pârâgika offence, let the Samgha enter upon the samghâdisesa proceedings[1] (against the accuser) and then hold Pavâranâ.

'If that Bhikkhu, O Bhikkhus, who reproves (another one), admits that he has charged him unfoundedly with a samghâdisesa offence, let the Samgha treat (the accuser) according to the law[2] and then hold Pavâranâ.

'If that Bhikkhu, O Bhikkhus, who reproves (another one), admits that he has charged him unfoundedly with a thullakkaya offence, or with a pâkittiya offence, or with a pâtidesanîya offence, or with a dukkata offence, or with having used wicked language, let the Samgha treat (the accuser) according to the law[3] and then hold Pavâranâ.

18. 'If that Bhikkhu, O Bhikkhus, who has been reproved, admits that he has committed a pârâgika offence, let the Samgha expel him and then hold Pavâranâ.

'If that Bhikkhu, &c., admits that he has com-

[1] See the 8th Samghâdisesa rule.

[2] See the 76th Pâkittiya rule.

[3] According to Buddhaghosa, the Bhikkhu who brings such an unfounded charge against a fellow Bhikkhu, is guilty of a dukkata offence.

mitted a samghâdisesa offence, let the Samgha enter upon the samghâdisesa proceedings (against him) and then hold Pavâranâ.

'If that Bhikkhu, &c., admits that he has committed a thullakkaya offence, or a pâkittiya offence, ... (&c., down to) . . . . wicked language, let the Samgha treat him according to the law and then hold Pavâranâ.

19. 'In case, O Bhikkhus, a Bhikkhu on the day of Pavâranâ is guilty of a thullakkaya offence. Some Bhikkhus believe that it is a thullakkaya offence, other Bhikkhus believe that it is a samghâdisesa offence. In that case, O Bhikkhus, let those Bhikkhus who take it for a thullakkaya offence, take that Bhikkhu, O Bhikkhus, aside, treat him according to the law, go back to the Samgha, and say: "The offence, friends, which this Bhikkhu has committed, he has atoned for according to the law. If the Samgha is ready, let the Samgha hold Pavâranâ."

20. 'In case, O Bhikkhus, a Bhikkhu on the day of Pavâranâ is guilty of a thullakkaya offence. Some Bhikkhus believe that it is a thullakkaya offence, other Bhikkhus believe that it is a pâkittiya offence. Some Bhikkhus believe that it is a thullakkaya offence, other Bhikkhus believe that it is a pâtidesanîya offence; a thullakkaya offence; a dukkata offence; a thullakkaya offence, an offence by wicked language. In that case (&c., as in § 19, down to the end).

21, 22. 'In case, O Bhikkhus, a Bhikkhu on the day of Pavâranâ is guilty of a pâkittiya offence, of a pâtidesanîya offence, of a dukkata offence, of an offence by wicked language. Some Bhikkhus believe that it is an offence by wicked language, other Bhikkhus believe that it is a saṁghâdisesa offence, &c. Some Bhikkhus believe that it is an offence by wicked language, other Bhikkhus believe that it is a dukkaṭa offence. In that case, O Bhikkhus, let those Bhikkhus who take it for an offence by wicked language, take that Bhikkhu, O Bhikkhus, aside (&c., see § 19).

23. 'If, O Bhikkhus, a Bhikkhu speaks thus before the assembly on the day of Pavâraṇâ: "Let the Saṁgha, reverend Sirs, hear me. Here this deed is known (to me), but not the (guilty) person. If the Saṁgha is ready, let the Saṁgha hold Pavâraṇâ excluding this deed," (the Bhikkhus) ought to reply: "The Blessed One, friend, has prescribed that they who hold Pavâraṇâ, ought to be pure. If a deed is known, but not the (guilty) person, report it (to us) now."

24. 'If, O Bhikkhus, a Bhikkhu speaks thus before the assembly on the day of Pavâraṇâ: "Let the Saṁgha, reverend Sirs, hear me. Here a person is known (to me as guilty), but not his deed. If the Saṁgha is ready, let the Saṁgha hold Pavâraṇâ excluding this person," (the Bhikkhus) ought to reply: "The Blessed One, friend, has prescribed that they who hold Pavâraṇâ, ought to be complete. If a person is known to you (as guilty), but not his deed, report it (to us) now."

25. 'If, O Bhikkhus, a Bhikkhu speaks thus before the assembly on the day of Pavâraṇâ: "Let the Saṁgha, reverend Sirs, hear me. Here a deed is known (to me) as well as the (guilty) person. If the Saṁgha is ready, let the Saṁgha hold Pavâraṇâ excluding this deed and this person," (the

Bhikkhus) ought to reply: "The Blessed One, friend, has prescribed that they who hold Pavâranâ, ought to be pure as well as complete. If the deed and the (guilty) person are known to you, report it (to us) now."

26. 'If, O Bhikkhus, a deed becomes known before the Pavâranâ, and the (guilty) person afterwards (i. e. after the Pavâranâ), it is right to bring it forward (then)[1].

'If, O Bhikkhus, the (guilty) person becomes known before the Pavâranâ, and his deed afterwards, it is right to bring it forward (then).

'If, O Bhikkhus, the deed as well as the (guilty) person becomes known before the Pavâranâ, and if (a Bhikkhu) raises up that matter again after the Pavâranâ, he makes himself guilty of a pâkittiya offence for raising up (a matter that has been settled)[2].'

17.

1. At that time a number of Bhikkhus, companions and friends of each other, entered upon Vassa in a certain district of the Kosala country. In their neighbourhood other Bhikkhus, litigious, contentious, quarrelsome, disputatious persons, who used to raise questions before the Samgha, entered upon Vassa with the intention of inhibiting, on the Pavâranâ day, the Pavâranâ of those Bhikkhus when

[1] 'Because it had not been possible to decide the matter at the Pavâranâ' (Buddhaghosa).

[2] See the 63rd Pâkittiya rule.

they should have finished their Vassa residence. Now those Bhikkhus heard: 'In our neighbourhood other Bhikkhus, &c. Well, what are we to do?'

They told this thing to the Blessed One.

2. 'In case, O Bhikkhus, a number of Bhikkhus, companions and friends of each other, enter upon Vassa in a certain district. In their neighbourhood other Bhikkhus, ... (&c., § 1). I prescribe, O Bhikkhus, that those Bhikkhus hold Uposatha twice or thrice on the fourteenth day (of the half-month)[1] in order that they may be able to hold Pavâranâ before those (other) Bhikkhus. If those litigious, contentious, ... (&c., § 1) Bhikkhus approach that district, let the resident Bhikkhus, O Bhikkhus, quickly assemble and hold Pavâranâ; having held Pavâranâ, let them say to them: "We have held our Pavâranâ, friends; do you do, Sirs, as you think fit."

3. 'If those litigious, ... (&c., § 1) Bhikkhus come to that residence unexpectedly, let the resident Bhikkhus, O Bhikkhus, prepare seats (for them), get water for the washing of their feet, foot-stools, and towels[2], then let them go to meet them, take their bowls and their robes, and offer them (water) to drink; having thus looked after those Bhikkhus, let them go outside the boundary and hold Pavâranâ; having held Pavâranâ, let

[1] In this way, when the inimical Bhikkhus are arriving about the time of Pavâranâ, the resident Bhikkhus count the day which is the thirteenth or fourteenth to the other Bhikkhus, as the fifteenth, and thus they are enabled to finish their Pavâranâ before they can be prevented.

[2] See I, 6, 11.

them say: "We have held our Pavâra*n*â, friends, do you do, Sirs, as you think fit."

4. 'If they succeed in this way, well and good; if they do not succeed, let a learned, competent, resident Bhikkhu proclaim the following *ñ*atti before the resident Bhikkhus: "Let the resident Bhikkhus hear me, Sirs. If you are ready, Sirs, let us now hold Uposatha and recite the Pâtimokkha, and let us hold Pavâra*n*â on the next new-moon day." If, O Bhikkhus, the litigious, ... (&c., § 1) Bhikkhus say to those Bhikkhus: "Well, friends, hold Pavâra*n*â with us now," let them reply: "You are not masters, friends, of our Pavâra*n*â; we will not hold Pavâra*n*â now."

5. 'If, O Bhikkhus, those litigious, ... (&c., § 1) Bhikkhus stay there till that new-moon day, let a learned, competent, resident Bhikkhu, ...[1]

6. 'If, O Bhikkhus, those litigious, ... (&c., § 1) Bhikkhus stay there still till that full-moon day, those Bhikkhus, O Bhikkhus, ought to hold Pavâra*n*â all of them, no matter whether they like it or not, on the next full-moon day, on the day of the komudî *k*âtumâsinî[2].

7. 'If those Bhikkhus, O Bhikkhus, hold Pavâra*n*â, and a sick Bhikkhu inhibits the Pavâra*n*â of a healthy Bhikkhu, let them say (to the inhibiting Bhikkhu): "You are sick, Sir, and the Blessed One has said that a sick person cannot endure being questioned. Wait, friend, until you have recovered;

---

[1] As in § 4, down to the end of the paragraph; instead of, 'On the next new-moon day,' it is to be read here, 'On the next full-moon day.'

[2] See the note on III, 14, 11.

having recovered, you may reprove him, if you like." If they speak to him thus, and he reproves (that Bhikkhu) notwithstanding, he makes himself guilty of the pâkittiya offence of disregard[1].

8. 'If those Bhikkhus, O Bhikkhus, hold Pavâranâ, and a healthy Bhikkhu inhibits the Pavâranâ of a sick Bhikkhu, let them say (to the inhibiting Bhikkhu): "This Bhikkhu is sick, friend, and the Blessed One has said that a sick person cannot endure being questioned. Wait, friend, until this Bhikkhu has recovered; when he has recovered you may reprove him, if you like." If they speak to him thus, ... (&c., as in § 7).

9. 'If those Bhikkhus, O Bhikkhus, hold Pavâranâ, and a sick Bhikkhu inhibits the Pavâranâ of another sick Bhikkhu, let them say (to the inhibiting Bhikkhu): "You are sick, Sirs, and the Blessed One has said that a sick person cannot endure being questioned. Wait, friend, until you have recovered; when he has recovered[2] you may reprove him, if you like." If they speak to him thus, ... (&c., as in § 7).

10. 'If those Bhikkhus, O Bhikkhus, hold Pavâranâ, and a healthy Bhikkhu inhibits the Pavâranâ of another healthy Bhikkhu, let the Samgha question and examine them both and treat them according to the law, and then hold Pavâranâ.'

---

[1] See the 54th Pâkittiya rule.

[2] Probably we should read in the Pâli text, 'ârogo ârogam âkankhamâno kodessasîti.' Then the translation would be: 'When you have recovered and he has recovered, &c.'

18.

1. At that time a number of Bhikkhus, companions and friends of each other, entered upon Vassa in a certain district of the Kosala country. These Bhikkhus, living in unity, and concord, and without quarrel, had found a comfortable place to dwell in. Now those Bhikkhus thought: 'Living in unity, &c., we have found a comfortable place to dwell in. If we hold Pavâra*n*â now, (other Bhikkhus) might come on a journey, having held their Pavâra*n*â, (and might occupy this place); thus we should lose this place which is comfortable to dwell in. Well, what are we to do?'

They told this thing to the Blessed One.

2. 'In case, O Bhikkhus, a number of Bhikkhus, companions and friends of each other, have entered upon Vassa in a certain district. These Bhikkhus, ... (&c., § 1).

'If these Bhikkhus think: "Living in unity, ... (&c., § 1, down to:) thus we should lose this place which is comfortable to dwell in," I allow, O Bhikkhus, these Bhikkhus to agree upon pavâra*n*â-sa*m*gaha[1].

3. 'And you ought, O Bhikkhus, to agree upon it in this way: Let them all assemble together. When

[1] Literally this word means, we believe, 'Keeping back one's own Pavâra*n*â.' Buddhaghosa says: 'When the decree of pavâra*n*âsa*m*gaha has been issued, the Bhikkhus (who have issued it) ought to live as in the rainy season. Incoming Bhikkhus are not allowed to take possession of their places of rest. On the other side, they ought not to interrupt their Vassa residence.'

they have assembled, let a learned, competent Bhikkhu proclaim the following ñatti before the Samgha: "Let the Samgha, reverend Sirs, hear me. Living in unity, ... (&c., § 1, down to:) thus we should lose this place which is comfortable to dwell in. If the Samgha is ready, let the Samgha agree upon pavâranâsamgaha; let it now hold Uposatha and recite the Pâtimokkha, and let the Samgha hold Pavâranâ on the next komudî kâtumâsinî day. This is the ñatti."

4. '"Let the Samgha, &c.[1]"

5. 'If, O Bhikkhus, after those Bhikkhus have agreed upon pavâranâsamgaha, a Bhikkhu should say: "I wish, friends, to go on my travels through the country; I have a business in the country," let them reply to him: "Good, friend, hold Pavâranâ and go." If that Bhikkhu, O Bhikkhus, when holding Pavâranâ inhibits the Pavâranâ of another Bhikkhu, let (that other Bhikkhu) say to him: "You are not master of my Pavâranâ, friend; I will not hold Pavâranâ now."

'If, O Bhikkhus, when that Bhikkhu holds Pavâranâ, another Bhikkhu inhibits his Pavâranâ, let the Samgha question and examine them both and treat them according to the law.

6. 'If that Bhikkhu, O Bhikkhus, has finished that business in the country and comes back to that district before the day of komudî kâtumâsinî, and if a Bhikkhu, O Bhikkhus, when the Bhikkhus hold Pavâranâ, inhibits the Pavâranâ of that Bhikkhu (who has been absent), let him say (to the

[1] Here follows the usual formula of a ñattidutiya kamma as in Book II, chap. 6. Comp. the note on Book I, chap. 28, § 3.

inhibiting Bhikkhu): "You are not master of my Pavâra*n*â, friend; I have held my Pavâra*n*â."

'If, O Bhikkhus, when the Bhikkhus hold Pavâra*n*â, this Bhikkhu inhibits the Pavâra*n*â of another Bhikkhu, let the Sa*m*gha question and examine them both and treat them according to the law, and then hold Pavâra*n*â.'

End of the Pavâra*n*â-Khandhaka.

TRANSLITERATION OF ORIENTAL ALPHABETS ADOPTED FOR THE TRANSLATIONS OF THE SACRED BOOKS OF THE EAST.

CONSONANTS.	MISSIONARY ALPHABET.			Sanskrit.	Zend.	Pehlevi.	Persian.	Arabic.	Hebrew.	Chinese.
	I Class.	II Class.	III Class.							
Gutturales.										
1 Tenuis	k	...	...	क	𐬐	[illegible]	ك	ك	כּ	k
2 „ aspirata	kh	...	...	ख	𐬑	[illegible]	...	...	כ	kh
3 Media	g	...	...	ग	𐬔	[illegible]	گ	...	גּ	...
4 „ aspirata	gh	...	...	घ	𐬖	[illegible]	...	...	ג	...
5 Gutturo-labialis	q	...	...	...	...	...	ق	ق	ק	...
6 Nasalis	ṅ (ng)	...	...	ङ	{ 𐬢 (ng) / 𐬣 (N) }	...	...	...	...	...
7 Spiritus asper	h	...	...	ह	𐬵 (𐬓 *hv*)	[illegible]	ه	ه	ה	h, hs
8 „ lenis	’	...	...	...	...	...	ا	ا	א	...
9 „ asper faucalis	‘h	...	...	...	...	...	ح	ح	ח	...
10 „ lenis faucalis	’h	...	...	...	...	...	ع	ع	ע	...
11 „ asper fricatus	...	‘*h*	...	...	...	...	خ	خ	ח	...
12 „ lenis fricatus	...	’*h*	...	...	...	...	...	...	...	...
Gutturales modificatae (palatales, &c.)										
13 Tenuis	...	*k*	...	च	𐬗	[illegible]	چ	...	...	*k*
14 „ aspirata	...	*kh*	...	छ	...	...	...	...	...	*kh*
15 Media	...	*g*	...	ज	𐬘	[illegible]	ج	ج	...	...
16 „ aspirata	...	*gh*	...	झ	...	...	غ	غ	...	...
17 „ Nasalis	...	*ñ*	...	ञ	...	...	...	...	...	...

CONSONANTS (*continued*).	MISSIONARY ALPHABET. I Class.	II Class.	III Class.	Sanskrit.	Zend.	Pehlevi.	Persian.	Arabic.	Hebrew.	Chinese.
18 Semivocalis	y	...	...	य	𐬌𐬌, 𐬫 [illegible] (init.)	[illegible]	ي	ي	י	y
19 Spiritus asper	...	(ẏ)	...	...	...	...	...	...	...	...
20 " lenis	...	(ẏ)	...	...	...	...	...	...	...	...
21 " asper assibilatus	...	*s*	...	श	𐬱	[illegible]	ش	ش	...	...
22 " lenis assibilatus	...	*z*	...	...	𐬲	[illegible]	ژ	...	...	*z*
Dentales.										
23 Tenuis	t	...	...	त	𐬙	[illegible]	ت	ت	תּ	t
24 " aspirata	th	...	...	थ	𐬚	...	...	...	ת	th
25 " assibilata	...	...	TH	...	...	...	ث	ث	...	...
26 Media	d	...	...	द	𐬛	[illegible]	د	د	דּ	...
27 " aspirata	dh	...	...	ध	𐬜	...	...	...	ד	...
28 " assibilata	...	...	DH	...	...	...	ذ	ذ	...	...
29 Nasalis	n	...	...	न	𐬥	[illegible]	ن	ن	נ	n
30 Semivocalis	l	...	...	ल	...	[illegible]	ل	ل	ל	l
31 " mollis 1	...	*l*	...	ळ	...	...	...	...	...	...
32 " mollis 2	...	...	L	...	...	...	...	...	...	...
33 Spiritus asper 1	s	...	...	स	𐬯	[illegible]	س (ث)	س	שׂ	s
34 " asper 2	...	...	s (ʃ)	...	...	...	...	...	ס	...
35 " lenis	z	...	...	...	𐬰	[illegible]	ز (ذ)	ز	ז	z
36 " asperrimus 1	...	...	z (ʒ)	...	...	...	ص	ص	צ	ʒ, ʒh
37 " asperrimus 2	...	...	ẓ (ʒ̣)	...	...	...	ض	...	...	...

	I	II	III	Sanskrit	Zend	Pehlevi	Persian	Arabic	Hebrew	Chinese
Dentales modificatae (linguales, &c.)										
38 Tenuis	...	*t*	....	ट	....	...	ط	ط	ט	...
39 „ aspirata	...	*th*	....	ठ	....	...	ظ	ظ	...	...
40 Media	...	*d*	....	ड	[illegible]	[illegible]	...	...	...	...
41 „ aspirata	...	*dh*	....	ढ	....	...	...	ض	...	...
42 Nasalis	...	*n*	....	ण	[illegible]	...	...	...	...	...
43 Semivocalis	r	...	....	र	[illegible]	[illegible]	ر	ر	ר	...
44 „ fricata	...	*r*	....	....	....	...	...	...	...	*r*
45 „ diacritica	...	...	R	....	....	...	...	...	...	...
46 Spiritus asper	sh	...	....	ष	[illegible]	[illegible]	...	...	...	sh
47 „ lenis	zh	...	....	....	....	...	...	...	...	...
Labiales.										
48 Tenuis	p	...	....	प	[illegible]	[illegible]	پ	...	פּ	p
49 „ aspirata	ph	...	....	फ	....	...	...	...	פ	ph
50 Media	b	...	....	ब	[illegible]	[illegible]	ب	ب	בּ	...
51 „ aspirata	bh	...	....	भ	....	...	...	...	ב	...
52 Tenuissima	...	*p*	....	....	....	...	...	...	...	...
53 Nasalis	m	...	....	म	[illegible]	[illegible]	م	م	מ	m
54 Semivocalis	w	...	....	....	[illegible]	...	...	...	...	w
55 „ aspirata	hw	...	....	....	....	...	...	...	...	...
56 Spiritus asper	f	...	....	....	[illegible]	[illegible]	ف	ف	...	f
57 „ lenis	v	...	....	व	[illegible]	[illegible]	و	و	ו	...
58 Anusvâra	...	*m*	....	ं	[illegible] ã	...	...	...	...	...
59 Visarga	...	*h*	....	ः	....	...	...	...	...	...

VOWELS.	MISSIONARY ALPHABET. I Class.	II Class.	III Class.	Sanskrit.	Zend.	Pehlevi.	Persian.	Arabic.	Hebrew.	Chinese.
1 Neutralis	0	...	....	...	....	...	...	...	ְ	ă
2 Laryngo-palatalis	ĕ	...	....	...	....	...	...	...	...	...
3 „ labialis	ŏ	...	....	...	....	𐭠 fin.	...	...	...	...
4 Gutturalis brevis	a	...	....	अ	𐬀	𐭠 init.	َ	َ	ַ	a
5 „ longa	â	(a)	....	आ	𐬁	𐭠	َا	َا	ָ	â
6 Palatalis brevis	i	...	....	इ	𐬌	...	ِ	ِ	ִ	i
7 „ longa	î	(i)	....	ई	𐬍	𐭩	ِي	ِي	ִי	î
8 Dentalis brevis	*li*	...	....	ऌ	....	...	...	...	...	...
9 „ longa	*lî*	...	....	ॡ	....	...	...	...	...	...
10 Lingualis brevis	*ri*	...	....	ऋ	....	...	...	...	...	...
11 „ longa	*rî*	...	....	ॠ	....	...	...	...	...	...
12 Labialis brevis	u	...	....	उ	𐬎	...	ُ	ُ	ֻ	u
13 „ longa	û	(u)	....	ऊ	𐬏	𐭥	ُو	ُو	וּ	û
14 Gutturo-palatalis brevis	e	...	....	...	𐬈(e) 𐬉(e)	...	...	...	ֶ	e
15 „ longa	ê (ai)	(e)	....	ए	𐬆, 𐬇	𐭩	...	...	ֵ	ê
16 Diphthongus gutturo-palatalis	âi	(ai)	....	ऐ	....	...	َيْ	َيْ	...	âi
17 „ „	ei (ĕi)	...	....	...	....	...	...	...	...	ei, êi
18 „ „	oi (ŏu)	...	....	...	....	...	...	...	...	...
19 Gutturo-labialis brevis	o	...	....	...	𐬊	...	...	...	ָ	o
20 „ longa	ô (au)	(o)	....	ओ	𐬋	𐭥	...	...	וֹ	...
21 Diphthongus gutturo-labialis	âu	(au)	....	औ	𐬁𐬎 (âu)	...	َوْ	َوْ	...	âu
22 „ „	eu (ĕu)	...	....	...	....	...	...	...	...	...
23 „ „	ou (ŏu)	...	....	...	....	...	...	...	...	...
24 Gutturalis fracta	ä	...	....	...	....	...	...	...	...	...
25 Palatalis fracta	ï	...	....	...	....	...	...	...	...	...
26 Labialis fracta	ü	...	....	...	....	...	...	...	...	ü
27 Gutturo-labialis fracta	ö	...	....	...	....	...	...	...	...	...